The Law Commission
Consultation Paper No 185

REFORMING BRIBERY

A Consultation Paper

The Law Commission was set up by section 1 of the Law Commissions Act 1965 for the purpose of promoting the reform of the law.

The Law Commissioners are:

The Honourable Mr Justice Etherton, *Chairman*
Mr Stuart Bridge
Mr David Hertzell
Professor Jeremy Horder
Kenneth Parker QC

Professor Martin Partington CBE is Special Consultant to the Law Commission responsible for housing law reform.

The Chief Executive of the Law Commission is Steve Humphreys and its offices are at Conquest House, 37-38 John Street, Theobalds Road, London WC1N 2BQ.

This consultation paper, completed on 31 October 2007, is circulated for comment and criticism only. It does not represent the final views of the Law Commission.

The Law Commission would be grateful for comments on its proposals before 20 March 2008. Comments may be sent either –

By post to:

David Hughes
Law Commission
Conquest House
37-38 John Street
Theobalds Road
London
WC1N 2BQ

Tel: 020-7453-1212
Fax: 020-7453-1297

By email to:

criminal@lawcommission.gsi.gov.uk

It would be helpful if, where possible, comments sent by post could also be sent on disk, or by email to the above address, in any commonly used format.

We will treat all responses as public documents in accordance with the Freedom of Information Act and we may attribute comments and include a list of all respondents' names in any final report we publish. Those who wish to submit a confidential response should contact the Commission before sending the response. We will disregard automatic confidentiality disclaimers generated by an IT system.

This consultation paper is available free of charge on our website at:
http://www.lawcom.gov.uk/bribery.htm

THE LAW COMMISSION

REFORMING BRIBERY – A CONSULTATION PAPER

CONTENTS

PART 1
REFORMING BRIBERY

INTRODUCTION

1.1 This consultation paper ('CP') is intended to build on a previous Law Commission report on bribery and corruption ('our previous report').[1] We now have Parliamentary[2] and Government[3] reactions to that report and its appended draft Bill. We have been asked by the Home Office[4] to consider what changes to our previous recommendations would be desirable. Therefore, in this CP we will examine the criticisms made of our earlier report and evaluate how best they can be accommodated. Further, since the publication of our previous report, the United Kingdom ('the UK') has signed a series of international Conventions relating to bribery and corruption. It will therefore be of equal importance to ensure our proposals are consistent with the UK's international obligations.

OBJECTIVE

1.2 Our previous report examined the law of corruption with a view to its reform and codification, taking account of the recommendations made by the Salmon Commission[5] and the Nolan Committee.[6] In broad terms this is still our intention. However, we are now addressing a slightly different question.

1.3 The focus of this project is on corruption in the narrow sense of offences relating to bribery: the broader meaning of 'corruption', including insider dealing and certain offences against competition law, is outside the scope of our project.[7] For this reason, the project is entitled 'bribery' rather than 'corruption'.

TERMS OF REFERENCE

1.4 Our terms of reference are:

(1) To review the various elements of the law on bribery with a view to modernisation, consolidation and reform; and to produce a draft Bill. The review will consider the full range of structural options including a single general offence covering both public and private sectors, separate offences for the public and private sectors, and an offence dealing separately with bribery of foreign public officials. The review will make recommendations that:

---

[1] Legislating the Criminal Code: Corruption (1998) Law Com No 248.

[2] Joint Committee on the Draft Corruption Bill, Session 2002-2003, HL Paper 157, HC 705 (2003).

[3] The Government Reply to the Report from the Joint Committee on the Draft Corruption Bill, Session 2002-2003, HL Paper 157, HC 705 (2003) Cm 6086.

[4] This was before the creation of the Ministry of Justice.

[5] Royal Commission on Standards in Public Life (1976) Cmnd 6524.

[6] Committee on Standards in Public Life, Standards in Public Life (1995) Cm 2850 ('the Nolan Report').

[7] See Appendix D below.

(a)   provide coherent and clear offences which protect individuals and society and provide clarity for investigators and prosecutors;

(b)   enable those convicted to be appropriately punished;

(c)   are fair and non-discriminatory in accordance with the European Convention on Human Rights and the Human Rights Act 1998; and

(d)   continue to ensure consistency with the UK's international obligations.

(2)   The process used will be open, inclusive and evidence-based and will involve:

(a)   a review structure that will look to include key stakeholders;

(b)   consultation with the public, criminal justice practitioners, academics, parliamentarians, and non-governmental organisations;

(c)   consideration of the previous attempts at reform (including the recent Home Office consultation) and the experiences of law enforcement and prosecutors in using the current law; and

(d)   comparing, in so far as is possible, the experience in England and Wales with that in other countries: this will include making international comparisons, in particular looking at relevant international Conventions and the body of experience around their implementation.

(3)   The review will also look at the wider context of corrupt practices to see how the various provisions complement the law of bribery. This will provide the wider context in which the specific reform of bribery law can be considered. This part of the review will comprise a summary of provisions, not recommendations for reform.

THE PROBLEMS WITH THE CURRENT LAW[8]

1.5 The criminal law of bribery presently consists of one general common law offence[9] and also various statutory offences. The most important statutes are the Public Bodies Corrupt Practices Act 1889 ('the 1889 Act'), the Prevention of Corruption Act 1906 ('the 1906 Act') and the Prevention of Corruption Act 1916 ('the 1916 Act') They are collectively referred to as the Prevention of Corruption Acts.[10] In addition, there are a number of specific statutory offences, for example, the Honours (Prevention of Abuses) Act 1925.[11]

1.6 It is almost universally believed that the current law is in need of rationalisation and simplification. As observed in a recent Government consultation paper:

> ... the present law is fragmented and out of date and needs to be reformed.[12]

1.7 The Organisation of Economic and Cultural Development ('the OECD') has been highly critical of our present law observing that:

> ... it is widely recognised that the current substantive law governing bribery in the UK is characterised by complexity and uncertainty.[13]

The OECD has also commented about what it perceives as:

> ... a lack of clarity among the different legislative and regulatory instruments in place[14]

Specific problems

The distinction between public sector and private sector bribery

1.8 Under the current law, an imperfect distinction is made between bribery in the public sector and bribery in the private sector. The 1889 Act is confined to bribery of members, officers and servants of public bodies. By contrast, the 1906 Act extends to bribery of 'agents' irrespective of whether the agent is employed or serving in the public or the private sector.

---

[8] In Part 2 below, we provide a brief outline of the current law.

[9] In addition there are several specific common law offences, including embracery (bribing of jurors), attempting to bribe a privy councillor, attempting to bribe a police constable and the taking of a bribe by a coroner not to hold an inquest.

[10] Prevention of Corruption Act 1916, s 4.

[11] In fact, in our previous consultation paper Legislating the Criminal Code: Corruption (1997) Consultation Paper No 145, para 1.2 we noted that corruption and bribery offences could be found in at least 11 different statutes. For analysis of many of these, see Nicholls, Daniel, Polaine and Hatchard, *Corruption and misuse of public office* (2006) paras 2.92 to 2.110.

[12] Bribery: Reform of the Prevention of Corruption Acts and SFO Powers in Cases of Bribery of Foreign Officials: a Consultation Paper (Dec 2005) p 3.

[13] OECD Phase 2 Report on the Application of the Convention on combating bribery of foreign public officials in international business transactions, para 194.

[14] Above, para 15.

1.9 Given that there are two different statutes, it might be thought that the substantive law governing bribery in the public sector would be markedly different from the substantive law governing bribery in the private sector but this is not so. The distinction has no direct bearing on the question of which conduct is corrupt because the meaning of 'corruptly' under the 1889 Act and the 1906 Act is the same.

1.10 Rather, the distinction only affects the ease of proving corruption. This is because there is a presumption of corruption in cases where the person given an advantage is an employee of the Crown, a Government Department or a public body and the person giving the advantage is someone who holds or is seeking a contract with such a body.[15] Whether, such a presumption is necessary or desirable is questionable.

SHOULD THE LAW CONTINUE TO DRAW A DISTINCTION BETWEEN BRIBERY IN THE PUBLIC SECTOR AND BRIBERY IN THE PRIVATE SECTOR?

1.11 We think that it would be helpful to deal with this issue at the outset. In our previous consultation paper and in our previous report, we considered why there should be a separate offence confined to those who were members, officers or servants of public bodies. We recommended that the distinction should be abandoned and that the new law that we were recommending should not include a presumption comparable to that under the current law.[16]

1.12 However, the issue was raised again in a consultation paper issued by the Home Office in 2005.[17] Consultees were asked whether offences applicable in the public sector should be separate from those in the private sector. It was acknowledged that this would be a radical alternative to the Commission's earlier recommendation. The majority of consultees opposed such a separation.

Principal arguments for and against retaining a distinction between the public and private sector

1.13 Some maintain that higher standards of conduct should be required of those working in the public sector and that there should be a separate offence to reflect those higher standards. Indeed the Home Office has stated that:

> There is a recognisable difference between the standards that we expect as regards giving gifts from those who clearly exercise essential public functions, as compared with those clearly in the private sector.[18]

---

[15] Prevention of Corruption Act 1916, s 2. The presumption applies to employees of public bodies but not to agents of public bodies who are not employees.

[16] Legislating the Criminal Code: Corruption (1998) Law Com No 248, Part IX para 2.

[17] Bribery: Reform of the Prevention of Corruption Acts and SFO powers in Cases of Bribery of Foreign Officials: a Consultation Paper (Dec 2005).

[18] Above, para 46.

1.14 However, in our view, the main objection to having separate offences is that it is very difficult to define with sufficient clarity the distinction between public sector and private sector functions. Increasingly, what were formerly public sector functions are sub-contracted out to private companies while public bodies now frequently form joint ventures with private companies. Indeed, it has been observed that the stance adopted in our previous report:

> … was especially welcome in that it recognises that in the modern world of privatisation many functions formerly carried out by public bodies are now carried out by private contractors subject to regulation.[19]

Conclusion

1.15 In the reply to the responses that it received to its consultation paper, the Home Office acknowledged the force of the argument against retaining a distinction. However, they questioned whether this parity, which is desirable in principle, is actually achievable in practice[20] in the light of the fact that it is generally held that a stricter standard should apply to the public sector.

1.16 We believe that there is a preferable way to deal with the issue of stricter standards. There may be instances where public officials should be held to a higher standard of conduct. However, as the state ultimately has control over such individuals, internal compliance measures - including the severe sanction of dismissal - can be imposed in such instances. A criminal offence of bribery should be founded on a clear and consistent threshold criterion. As will become apparent, we are recommending that the threshold should be breach of a legal or equitable duty that involves a betrayal of a relation of trust or a breach of a duty to act impartially or in the best interests of another.[21] Where a person breaches such a duty in return for the conferral or promise of an advantage from another, both should be guilty of bribery irrespective of whether the recipient is a public official. A person who does not breach such a duty should not be guilty of a criminal offence, even if a public official. Other kind of misconduct should be dealt with under the relevant disciplinary regime.

Provisional proposal

1.17 **We provisionally propose that in the domestic context the law of bribery should not draw a distinction between bribery in the public sector and bribery in the private sector.**

1.18 However, we recognise that, whilst an offence of bribery based on breach of a legal or equitable duty is practical and appropriate in cases of domestic bribery of public officials, cases involving bribery of foreign public officials pose their own particular problems. In Part 7, we explain why we believe that there should be a discrete offence of bribery of a foreign public official.

---

[19] Nicholls, Daniel, Polaine and Hatchard, *Corruption and Misuse of Public Office* (2006) para 5.83

[20] Consultation on Bribery: Reform of the Prevention of Corruption Acts and SFO Powers in Cases of Bribery of Foreign Officials: Summary of responses and next steps (2007) para 46.

Further problems caused by the co-existence of the 1889 Act and the 1906 Act

CHARGING UNDER THE WRONG STATUTE

1.19   Although the 1889 Act is restricted to public sector bribery, it does not cover all cases of bribery of those working in the public sector. In *Natji*,[22] P was charged with and convicted of bribing an official who worked in the Immigration and Nationality Department of the Home Office. He was convicted under the 1889 Act. On appeal his conviction was quashed because, although employed in the public sector, the 1889 Act did not encompass bribery of those employed by the Crown or by a government department.

THE SCOPE OF THE RESPECTIVE STATUTES

1.20   Under the 1889 Act, the recipient ('R') does not have to be the public official whose conduct the payer ('P') is seeking to influence. Accordingly, it is an offence under the 1889 Act for P to give money to R's wife in exchange for R, a local authority employee, allocating P a tenancy of a local authority property in breach of the council's criteria for granting tenancies. By contrast, under the 1906 Act, R has to be the agent whose conduct P is seeking to influence.

NO CONSISTENT TERMINOLOGY

1.21   The 1889 Act and the 1906 Act employ different terminology to describe the form the bribe must take.[23]

The meaning of 'agent'

1.22   The 1906 Act defines 'agent' as meaning any person "employed by or acting for another" including any person serving under the Crown or any public body. There has been criticism concerning the uncertainty of the meaning of the word "agent".[24]

The meaning of 'corruptly'

1.23   Under both the 1889 Act and the 1906 Act, for P or R to be convicted of an offence, he or she must have conferred or received an advantage 'corruptly'. Neither Act contains a definition of the word and the case law has left its meaning unclear. Professor Lanham has described the authorities as being in "impressive disarray".[25]

---

[21]   See Part 5 and para 5.50 below.

[22]   [2002] EWCA Crim 271, [2002] 1 WLR 2337.

[23]   See Part 2, para 2.17 below.

[24]   See Part 2, paras 2.14 to 2.16 below.

[25]   D Lanham, "Bribery and Corruption", *Essays in Honour of J C Smith* (1987) 92, 104

Bribery committed outside England and Wales

1.24   Until 2001, it was not an offence known to English law for a British national or a company incorporated under the law of England and Wales to commit an act abroad which, if committed in England and Wales, would constitute an offence under either the 1889 or the 1906 Act. This has now changed by virtue of section 109 of the Anti-Terrorism, Crime and Security Act 2001. It remains the case, however, that foreign nationals outside England and Wales who commit an act which, if done in England and Wales would constitute an offence under either the 1889 or the 1906 Act, commit no offence known to English law. This is so even if they are domiciled or habitually resident in England and Wales. The same is true of companies incorporated under a law other than that of England and Wales even if their headquarters are in England and Wales.

GENERAL CONSIDERATIONS

1.25   In our previous report, we recommended rationalisation of, and some extensions to, the current law. It is universally agreed that this is the right course. However, as we will explain, we no longer believe that our previous recommendations represent the most desirable option for reform.

1.26   In shaping our provisional proposals we have been guided amongst other things by five general considerations that seem to us to be of special relevance, given the nature of this particular project.[26]

1.27   First, bribery laws should, so far as possible, observe principles of equal treatment. As we have explained, it is sometimes suggested that public officials should be held to a stricter standard of conduct (in relation to the acceptance of gifts in the course of their employment) than those employed in the private sector. However, we do not regard it as a proper function of the criminal law of bribery to secure adherence by public officials to a higher standard of probity in that respect. It is a matter for internal disciplinary codes and the sanctions threatened for breach of those codes.[27] Workers, whether in the public or the private sector, should face conviction for bribery on the same basis. To give another example, we are proposing that foreign nationals who are resident in England and Wales should be liable to conviction for bribery in the courts in the same way as British nationals currently are.[28]

---

[26]   These principles are, of course, not the only principles of relevance to criminal law reform. They are not set out here in order of importance.

[27]   Disciplinary action sanctioned under a contract of employment may, of course, include demotion or dismissal, actions that may be feared by some employees even more than a criminal conviction. The existence of codes of conduct to deter the acceptance of gifts or other advantages also means that reliance can be placed on training given in relation to a code of conduct in advance of any offence being committed. This may be more likely to prevent problems arising than a criminal penalty imposed after the fact.

[28]   See Part 11 below.

1.28   Secondly, at the very least, any new criminal law of bribery must comply with the obligations to combat bribery which are contained in international Conventions to which the UK is a signatory. Such obligations include the obligation to ensure that the law adequately covers the bribery of foreign public officials.[29] They also include the obligation to ensure, whilst avoiding the danger of over-regulation, that the law covers conduct amounting to bribery when that conduct is engaged in by a company.[30]

1.29   Thirdly, a new offence of bribery must be expressed as simply and clearly as possible so that it can readily be understood by people (and by their legal advisers) concerned about whether their conduct is lawful. However, simplicity must not be pursued to the point where the price to be paid is vagueness and uncertainty. For example, it may seem tempting to rely on a law which says simply that someone should not agree to act 'corruptly', or should not offer someone an advantage to act 'corruptly', and simply leave the tribunal of fact to decide whether the action in question was 'corrupt'.[31] Although clear and straightforward enough in one way, our view is that such a law would be gravely deficient. It would give no indication of the kinds of conduct that are prohibited by the law of bribery. Irrelevant factors such as a jury's mere moral disapproval of the conduct in question would not be excluded in the way that they should be. Further, similar cases could be decided in very different ways, simply because they are decided by different tribunals of fact, even when the proceedings arise out of the same incident.

1.30   Fourthly, the right relationship between a reformed law of bribery and other related criminal offences must be created or maintained. To give one example, the reformed law must not distort the operation of well-established competition law offences.[32] It should not normally be possible to secure a conviction for bribery in circumstances where the conduct in question – although perhaps involving sharp practice – was intentionally excluded from the scope of the criminal law by the competition law regime.

1.31   However, where the existing criminal law already covers certain kinds of conduct, it may not be wrong to extend the law of bribery to cover that conduct as well. An example is provided by the extensions made to the reach of the criminal law by the Fraud Act 2006. That Act now brings within the potential scope of fraud some instances in which an agent selling financial products recommends the purchase of a product by a customer as in the customer's 'best interests' when the agent realises that the purchase may not be in the customer's best interests. When, in such a case, the main reason the agent has for selling the product is the commission he or she will receive from the provider, rather than what is in the customer's best interests, the agent may also be guilty of bribery. We see nothing wrong with, and indeed there may be some virtue in, such overlapping of offences.[33]

---

[29]   See Part 7 below.

[30]   See Part 9 below.

[31]   See Part 5 below.

[32]   See Appendix D below.

[33]   See Appendix E below for a comparison between bribery and fraud.

1.32 Fifthly and finally, in this area of the law (as in others) it is not right to criminalise and punish conduct simply because it is immoral. In this context this means that conduct should not be subject to criminal sanctions unless, in a broad sense, it threatens to corrupt decision-making that should be guided by duty.[34] For example, some forms of 'corporate hospitality' may involve immorality, such as the provision of entertainment with an improper sexual element. The basis for making the provision or acceptance of such hospitality a criminal offence must be the potential it has to corrupt what should be duty-guided decision-making. It should not be the mere fact that many would disapprove, however strongly, of the provision of such hospitality.

SUMMARY OF MAIN PROPOSALS

1.33 We are provisionally proposing that:

(1) in the domestic context the law of bribery should not draw a distinction between bribery in the public sector and bribery in the private sector;[35]

(2) the existing statutory and common law offences should be repealed or abolished;[36]

(3) there should be a comprehensive bribery offence setting out the potential liability of the payer of the bribe (P) and the recipient (R);

(4) the conduct element of the offence in relation to P is that P should confer an advantage on R or another person;[37]

(5) the conduct element of the offence in relation to R is that R should receive or solicit an advantage for him or herself or any other person[38] and:

> (i) do an improper act or make an improper omission;
>
> (ii) represent a willingness to do an improper act or make an improper omission;
>
> (iii) uses his or her influence to induce a third party to do an improper act or make an improper omission; or
>
> (iv) represents a willingness to induce a third party to do an improper act or make an improper omission;

(6) an improper act or omission is one that constitutes a breach of a legal or equitable duty that involves a betrayal of a relation of trust or a breach of a duty to act impartially or in the best interests of another;[39]

---

[34] Even this is a necessary rather than a sufficient condition. Not all conduct of this kind should automatically fall within the scope of a bribery offence.

[35] See paras 1.11 to 1.17 above.

[36] See Part 8 below.

[37] 'Conferral' includes agreeing to confer and promising to confer. See further Part 5 below.

(7)   the basic fault element of the offence in relation to P is that P should:

   (a)   intend that the advantage should be the primary reason for R doing an improper act; or

   (b)   foresee that there is a serious risk that the advantage would create the primary reason for R to do an improper act;[40]

(8)   the basic fault element of the offence in relation to R is that the advantage conferred must be the primary reason for doing the improper act;[41]

(9)   there should be a discrete offence of bribery of a foreign public official;[42]

(10)   P should have a defence if it was reasonable to confer an advantage in order to avert what P reasonably believed to be an imminent danger of physical harm to himself or another;[43]

(11)   P should have a defence if he or she conferred an advantage in the reasonable belief that to do so was legally required;[44]

(12)   the consent of the Director of Public Prosecutions (or the Director of the Serious Fraud Office as appropriate) should be required for any prosecution for the general offence of bribery or for an inchoate offence relating to that bribery offence;[45]

(13)   if an offence of bribery involves an extra-territorial element, the consent of the Attorney General should be required for any prosecution;[46]

(14)   a new offence of inadequately supervising foreign subsidiary companies should not be created;[47]

---

[38] "Receive" includes agreeing to receive and representing a willingness to receive. See further Part 5 below.

[39] See Part 5 below for an examination of what is meant by "legal or equitable duty".

[40] See Part 6 below for a detailed account of the fault element required of P.

[41] See Part 6 below for a detailed account of the fault element required of R.

[42] See Part 7 below for the details of this offence

[43] See Part 8 below.

[44] See Part 8 below.

[45] See Part 8 below

[46] See Part 8 below.

[47] See Part 9 below.

(15)   an act, which if done in England and Wales would constitute a bribery offence, should constitute a bribery offence if done outside the United Kingdom if done by a British national, a body incorporated under the law of England and Wales or a foreign national who is resident in the United Kingdom.[48]

SUMMARY OF THE PAPER

1.34   In Part 2 we provide a brief outline of the current law.

1.35   In Part 3 we set out the previous attempts to reform the law of bribery.

1.36   In Part 4 we explain the various models that can inform how offences of bribery are defined. We explain why our preference is for an offence of bribery based on the breach of duty model.

1.37   In Part 5 we set out our provisional proposals relating to the conduct element of a new bribery offence.

1.38   In Part 6 we set out our provisional proposals relating to the fault element of a new bribery offence.

1.39   In Part 7 we explain our provisional proposals for a new discrete bribery offence to deal with the bribery of foreign public officials.

1.40   In Part 8 we set out our provisional proposals for defences to bribery, the requirement of consent to prosecution and a few ancillary matters.

1.41   In Part 9 we consider corporate liability for bribery.

1.42   In Part 10 we consider criminal liability for assisting and encouraging bribery.

1.43   In Part 11 we consider criminal liability for bribery committed, or assisted or encouraged, outside England and Wales.

1.44   Part 12 contains a list all of the provisional proposals and questions.

1.45   In Appendix A we set out in detail the various international Conventions and other materials on bribery that are currently binding on the UK.

1.46   In Appendix B we examine current bribery legislation in other jurisdictions.

1.47   Appendix C is an account by Professor Stuart Green of the law of bribery in the United States of America ('the USA').

1.48   In Appendix D is a brief discussion of competition law offences, where we explain why we believe that the law of bribery should focus on betrayal by individuals rather than harm caused to the markets.

1.49   In Appendix E we set out how the new offence of bribery would relate to existing fraud offences.

---

[48] See Part 11 below.

1.50   In Appendix F we consider how our proposals would apply to facilitation payments, commission payments and instances of corporate hospitality.

1.51   In Appendix G we explain how our proposals would meet the United Kingdom's international obligations.

PART 2
THE CURRENT LAW

2.1　In this Part we set out a brief exposition of the existing law of bribery. We outline the common law offence of bribery before turning to the Prevention of Corruption Acts 1889 to 1916. We also explain the extraterritorial jurisdiction that domestic courts have in respect of acts of bribery as a result of the enactment of the Anti-terrorism, Crime and Security Act 2001.

THE COMMON LAW

2.2　Bribery at common law has evolved over time. Opinions vary as to whether it is to be regarded as a general offence or made up of a number of individual offences distinguished by the office or function involved.[1] *Russell on Crime* provides the following general statement of the offence:

> Bribery is the receiving or offering [of] any undue reward by or to any person whatsoever, in a public office, in order to influence his behaviour in office, and incline him to act contrary to the known rules of honesty and integrity.[2]

The bribe: "any undue reward"

2.3　The bribe must amount to an undue reward. A reward that is so small as not to be considered a reward at all will not suffice.[3] David Lanham also draws a distinction between bribes and treats,[4] citing the South African case *S v Deal Enterprises (Pty) Ltd*:

> The difference between legitimate entertainment and bribery lies in the intention with which the entertainment is provided, and that is something to be inferred from all the circumstances, including the relationship between giver and recipient, their respective financial and social positions and the nature and value of the entertainment.[5]

---

[1]　For example, bribery of a privy councillor (*Vaughan* (1769) 4 Burr 2494; 98 ER 308) and bribery of a coroner (*Harrison* (1800) 1 East PC 382). See Archbold, *Criminal Pleading, Evidence and Practice* (2007) para 31–129.

[2]　*Russell on Crime* (12th ed 1964) p 381.

[3]　In the *Bodmin Case* (1869) 1 O'M & H 121 Willes J mentioned how he had been required to swear that he would not take any gift from a man who had a plea pending unless it was "meat or drink, and that of small value".

[4]　D Lanham, *Criminal Fraud* (1987) p 204.

[5]　1978 (3) SA 302, 311, by Nicholas J.

A "public officer"

2.4 The most widely cited definition concerning who is to be regarded as a public officer for the purposes of common law bribery is from the Court of Appeal decision in *Whitaker*.[6] It was argued that the law of bribery applied only to judicial and ministerial officers and that the defendant army officer belonged to neither category. The Court of Appeal disagreed, holding that every officer who was not a judicial officer was a ministerial officer. A public officer was hence defined as

> an officer who discharges any duty in the discharge of which the public are interested, more clearly so if he is paid out of a fund provided by the public.[7]

2.5 This includes persons discharging *ad hoc* public duties, such as electors at a parliamentary[8] or local government election,[9] who are thus "public officers" capable of being bribed for the purpose of the common law offence. Embracery (bribery of jurors) is also an offence at common law, though now considered obsolete.[10]

The mental element

2.6 The payer must intend to influence the behaviour of the public officer and incline him to act "contrary to the known rules of honesty and integrity". Although this includes giving a bribe to induce the recipient to act in breach of their duties of office, this does not seem to be a necessary feature. In *Gurney*[11] it was held sufficient that the defendant, charged with attempting to bribe a justice of the peace, had intended to produce any effect at all on the justice's decision.

THE 1889 ACT

2.7 The 1889 Act was introduced following revelations of malpractice within the Metropolitan Board of Works, the body exercising the powers of local government in London at that time.[12] Section 1 provides:

> (1) Every person who shall by himself or by or in conjunction with any other person, corruptly solicit or receive, or agree to receive, for himself, or for any other person, any gift, loan, fee, reward, or advantage whatever as an inducement to, or reward for, or otherwise on account of any member, officer, or servant of a public body as in this Act defined, doing or forbearing to do anything in respect of any matter or transaction whatsoever, actual or proposed, in which the said public body is concerned, shall be guilty of an offence.

[6]   [1914] 3 KB 1283.

[7]   Above, 1296, by Lawrence J.

[8]   *Pitt and Mead* (1762) 3 Burr 1335, 97 ER 861.

[9]   *Worrall* (1890) 16 Cox CC 737.

[10]   *Owen* [1976] 1 WLR 840.

[11]   (1867) 10 Cox CC 550.

[12]   P Fennell and P A Thomas, "Corruption in England and Wales: An Historical Analysis" (1983) 11 *International Journal of Sociology and Law* 167, 172.

(2) Every person who shall by himself or by or in conjunction with any other person corruptly give, promise, or offer any gift, loan, fee, reward, or advantage whatsoever to any person, whether for the benefit of that person or of another person, as an inducement to or reward for or otherwise on account of any member, officer, or servant of any public body as in this Act defined, doing or forbearing to do anything in respect of any matter or transaction whatsoever, actual or proposed, in which such public body as aforesaid is concerned, shall be guilty of an offence.

The bribe: "gift, loan, fee, reward, or advantage"

2.8 The terms "gift", "loan", "fee" and "reward" are not defined. "Advantage" includes

> any office or dignity, and any forbearance to demand any money or money's worth or valuable thing, and includes any aid, vote, consent, or influence, or pretended aid, vote, consent, or influence, and also includes any promise or procurement of or agreement or endeavour to procure, or the holding out of any expectation of any gift, loan, fee, reward, or advantage, as before defined.[13]

2.9 The bribe must act as an inducement to, a reward for, or otherwise on account of any public officer doing or forbearing to do anything in respect of a matter concerning their office.

A "public body"

2.10 As originally enacted, the 1889 Act was concerned only with local public bodies in the UK, meaning

> any council of a county or county of a city or town, any council of a municipal borough, also any board, commissioners, select vestry, or other body which has power to act under and for the purposes of any Act relating to local government, or the public health, or to poor law or otherwise to administer money raised by rates in pursuance of any public general Act ... .[14]

2.11 Section 4(2) of the 1916 Act extends this definition to encompass "local and public authorities of all descriptions". However, this does not include the Crown or a government department, which are distinguished in section 2 of the 1916 Act.[15] Part 12 of the Anti-terrorism, Crime and Security Act 2001 extends the definition further to include public bodies existing outside the UK.[16] Part 5 of the Local Government and Housing Act 1989 makes provision for including companies "under the control of one or more local authorities", but this is not yet in force.[17]

---

[13] 1889 Act, s 7.

[14] Above.

[15] *Natji* [2002] EWCA Crim 271, [2002] 1 WLR 2337.

[16] See paras 2.26 to 2.29 below.

[17] Local Government and Housing Act 1989, sch 11, para 3.

THE 1906 ACT

2.12 A report published in 1898 by the Secret Commissions Committee of the London Chamber of Commerce called for the law of corruption to be extended into the private sector.[18] Section 1(1) of the 1906 Act provides:

> If any agent corruptly accepts or obtains, or agrees to accept or attempts to obtain, from any person, for himself or for any other person, any gift or consideration as an inducement or reward for doing or forbearing to do, or for having after the passing of this Act done or forborne to do, any act in relation to his principal's affairs or business, or for showing or forbearing to show favour or disfavour to any person in relation to his principal's affairs or business; or

> If any person corruptly gives or agrees to give or offers any gift or consideration to any agent as an inducement or reward for doing or forbearing to do, or for having after the passing of this Act done or forborne to do, any act in relation to his principal's affairs or business, or for showing or forbearing to show favour or disfavour to any person in relation to his principal's affairs or business

> … he shall be guilty [of an offence].

The bribe: "any gift or consideration"

2.13 The expression "consideration" is defined as including "valuable consideration of any kind".[19] "Gift" is not defined.

An "agent"

2.14 "Agent" is defined as meaning "any person employed by or acting for another",[20] including a person serving under the Crown or any local or public authority.[21] Serving under the Crown does not require employment by the Crown.[22]

2.15 It is unclear whether police officers, judicial officers and local councillors can be classified as "agents" for the purposes of the 1906 Act,[23] though in such cases there may be recourse to the common law or the 1889 Act.

2.16 It is doubtful whether a person can be guilty under the Act when only purporting to be an agent.[24]

---

[18] P Fennell and P A Thomas, "Corruption in England and Wales; An Historical Analysis" (1983) 11 *International Journal of Sociology and Law* 167, 174.

[19] Prevention of Crime Act 1906 Act, s 1(2).

[20] Above.

[21] Above, s 1(3), as amended by the 1916 Act, s 4(2) and (3).

[22] In *Barrett* [1976] 1 WLR 946, a superintendent registrar of births, deaths and marriages was serving under the Crown despite not being appointed, paid or liable to dismissal by it.

[23] In the English civil case of *Fisher v Oldham Corporation* [1930] 2 KB 364, a police officer was held to be a servant of the State; but in the Scottish case of *Graham v Hart* [1908] SC (J) 26, a police officer was held to be an agent of the Chief Constable.

[24] A T H Smith, *Property Offences* (1994) pp 792 to 793, para 25–04.

Differences in scope between the 1889 and 1906 Acts

2.17 As can now be seen, the 1889 and 1906 Acts vary in application. The bribe takes different forms ("gift, loan, fee, reward or advantage" in contrast with "gift or consideration"); the persons covered are different (officers of public bodies in contrast with "agents", whether public or private). There are further inconsistencies.

2.18 Under the 1889 Act the bribe must be connected to a particular "matter or transaction".[25] Under the 1906 Act it can be a "sweetener" designed to secure more favourable treatment generally.

2.19 Under the 1889 Act, the recipient of the bribe does not have to be the public officer whose conduct is to be influenced. The language of the 1906 Act, however, requires both roles to be played by the same person.

2.20 The 1889 Act can apply to circumstances where the public officer is no longer or yet to be in office at the time of the bribe. Conversely, the 1906 Act appears to require the agent to receive, or agree to receive, the bribe during the currency of his or her agency.

2.21 Importantly, the presumption of corruption only applies in cases concerning public bodies.[26]

The meaning of "corruptly"

2.22 Both the 1889 and 1906 Acts require the defendant to have acted "corruptly", but neither provides a definition. The result has been differing judicial interpretations and hence lack of certainty. In the House of Lords decision in *Cooper v Slade*,[27] the majority took the view that "corruptly" did not mean "dishonestly" but rather "doing an act which the law forbids as tending to corrupt". This was not followed in *Lindley*[28] and *Calland*,[29] which suggest that dishonesty must be proved. However, *Smith*[30] and most recent appellate authority[31] have favoured the earlier view of requiring proof of intent to corrupt without needing dishonesty.

---

[25] See para 2.7 above.

[26] See paras 2.24 to 2.25 below.

[27] (1858) 6 HL Cas 746; 10 ER 1488.

[28] [1957] *Criminal Law Review* 321.

[29] [1967] *Criminal Law Review* 236.

[30] [1960] 2 QB 423.

[31] *Wellburn* (1979) 69 Cr App R 254; *Harvey* [1999] *Criminal Law Review* 70; *Godden-Wood* [2001] EWCA Crim 1586; [2001] *Criminal Law Review* 810.

THE 1916 ACT

2.23 The 1916 Act was passed as an emergency measure, prompted by wartime scandals involving contracts with the War Office.[32] It broadened the definition of "public body"[33] and increased the maximum sentence for bribery in relation to contracts with the Government or public bodies.[34] It also introduced the presumption of corruption.

The presumption of corruption

2.24 Section 2 of the 1916 Act provides:

> Where in any proceedings against a person for an offence under the Prevention of Corruption Act 1906, or the Public Bodies Corrupt Practices Act 1889, it is proved that any money, gift, or other consideration has been paid or given to or received by a person in the employment of [Her] Majesty or any Government Department or a public body by or from a person, or agent of a person, holding or seeking to obtain a contract from [Her] Majesty or any Government Department or public body, the money, gift, or consideration shall be deemed to have been paid or given and received corruptly as such inducement or reward as is mentioned in such Act unless the contrary is proved.

2.25 The presumption shifts the burden of proof so that it is for the defence to prove (on a balance of probabilities)[35] that a given payment was not corrupt. It applies only to payments made to employees of public bodies, and only to cases involving contracts.[36] It does not, therefore, apply to cases against agents who cannot be classified as employees of the Crown, Government departments or public bodies.[37]

EXTRATERRITORIAL JURISDICTION

2.26 Part 12 of the Anti-terrorism, Crime and Security Act 2001 came into force on 14 February 2002. Its effect is to extend the jurisdiction of domestic courts in relation to offences of bribery.

---

[32] P Fennell and P A Thomas, "Corruption in England and Wales; An Historical Analysis" (1983) 11 *International Journal of Sociology and Law* 167, 174 and 186 to 186.

[33] See para 2.11 above.

[34] From 2 years' hard labour to 7 years in cases to which the 1916 Act applied. The disparity in sentencing between the 1889 and 1906 Acts was removed by the Criminal Justice Act 1988, s 47.

[35] *Carr-Briant* [1943] KB 607.

[36] *Asseling*, *The Times* 10 September 1916. Low J had considered it impossible to prosecute a civil servant found in possession of banknotes that had been traced to a contractor with whom he had had official dealings, because the prosecution was unable to prove why the money was paid. This case helped to prompt the passing of the 1916 Act and explains the restricted application of the presumption of corruption.

[37] Such as employees of private companies engaged in contracted-out work or private sector secondees to Government departments.

2.27 References to public bodies in the 1889 and 1916 Acts now include "any body which exists in a country or territory outside the United Kingdom".[38] It is also immaterial if the functions of the recipient, or the affairs of the recipient agent's principal, have no connection with the UK and are carried out in another country.[39]

2.28 Further, domestic courts now have jurisdiction over anything done abroad by a UK national, or a body incorporated under UK law, that would constitute an offence (at common law or under the Prevention of Corruption Acts 1889 to 1916) if done within the UK.[40]

2.29 The presumption of corruption does not apply to anything that would not have been an offence prior to Part 12 of the Anti-terrorism, Crime and Security Act 2001.[41]

PROSECUTION AND CONVICTION STATISTICS

2.30 Below are two tables showing the number of defendants proceeded against and convicted under the 1889 and 1906 Acts, in all courts in England and Wales from 2001 to 2005. Where the "found guilty" column exceeds the "proceeded against" column, it may be that the defendant was convicted in the Crown Court the year after proceedings were issued in the magistrates' court; or that the defendant was originally charged with a different offence.[42]

	Giving and receiving a bribe; Public Bodies Corrupt Practices Act 1889				
	2001	2002	2003	2004	2005
Proceeded against	1	1	4	1	-
Found guilty	2	-	1	-	-

	Corrupt transactions with agents; Prevention of Corruption Act 1906				
	2001	2002	2003	2004	2005
Proceeded against	9	8	12	3	1
Found guilty	12	20	6	4	1

No comparable statistics exist for the common law offence of bribery.

---

[38] 1889 Act, s 7.

[39] Anti-terrorism, Crime and Security Act 2001, s 108.

[40] Above, s 109.

[41] Above, s 110.

[42] Source: Office for Criminal Justice Reform, Ministry of Justice. Every effort has been made to ensure the accuracy of the data, which have been extracted from large administrative data systems generated by the courts and police forces. The inevitable limitations should be taken into account.

PART 3
PREVIOUS ATTEMPTS TO REFORM THE LAW OF BRIBERY

INTRODUCTION

3.1   In this section we set out the background to this project. We begin by considering our previous work on corruption. We then consider the Government's response to our previous report and draft Bill. We explain how the Government's draft Bill, based on our draft Bill, encountered Parliamentary criticism which led to the Government unsuccessfully trying to forge a consensus on the best way forward.

OUR PREVIOUS PROJECT ON CORRUPTION

3.2   The starting point for our original project on corruption was the Nolan Report in 1995.[1] The Commission published a consultation paper[2] in 1997 ('our previous CP') and a final report[3] with an appended draft Bill in 1998.

3.3   In summary, our previous report recommended that:

(1)   corruption should be codified within a single Bill;

(2)   the single Bill should remove the distinction between public and non-public bodies, and in particular should abolish the presumption of corruption established by the 1916 Act for "public" cases;[4]

(3)   in order to extend the present law, it should be an offence to act corruptly in the "hope" or "expectation" of a bribe, even when no such bribe had been agreed;[5]

(4)   bribery should be split into five offences. The first two would cover persons who either corruptly conferred an advantage or corruptly offered to confer an advantage. The second two would cover persons who either corruptly obtained an advantage or corruptly solicited or agreed to obtain an advantage. The final offence would cover persons who performed their functions as agents corruptly;

(5)   the Bill should list relevant fiduciary relationships, that is relationships in which one person is an agent and the other is his or her principal;[6]

---

[1]   The Nolan Committee, now the Committee on Standards in Public Life, was set up in response to concerns about unethical conduct of those in public office. See www.parliament.uk/works/standards.cfm

[2]   Legislating the Criminal Code: Corruption (1997) Law Commission Consultation Paper No 145.

[3]   Legislating the Criminal Code: Corruption (1998) Law Com No 248.

[4]   Above, Part IV.

[5]   Above, para 5.58.

[6]   Above, para 5.36.

(6)   acting corruptly should be defined as acting "primarily in return for the conferring of an advantage".[7] This would be subject to a number of defences including acting in return for remuneration from the principal (employer) and acting with the principal's consent;[8]

(7)   there should be no extension of the investigative powers of the police. This was decided because of human rights considerations and in order to maintain a level of consistency with other offences;[9]

(8)   the offence created by the Bill should be added to the list of Group A offences in Part 1 of the Criminal Justice Act 1993 ('the 1993 Act').[10] The effect of doing so would be that certain acts of bribery which occur outside England and Wales would for jurisdictional purposes be deemed to have occurred in England and Wales; and

(9)   procurement of a breach of duty through threats or deception should not be included in the law of corruption.[11]

The Government's response to our previous report[12]

3.4   The Government welcomed the report and stated their intention to present a Bill to Parliament, modelled on the Commission's draft, as soon as possible. They also moved to set up an interdepartmental working group to consider the draft Bill.

3.5   The Government stated that the Commission's draft Bill met all the international obligations on corruption which the Government was party to, including those ratified after our previous report was published.[13]

Approval of our previous report

3.6   The Government stated that it accepted:

(1)   the definition of corruption and the use of express exceptions to this rule;

(2)   the abolition of the public/non-public distinction as well as the presumption of corruption in public cases;

(3)   the definition of the relevant fiduciary relationships;

(4)   the extension of jurisdiction to cover persons abroad; and

(5)   the proposal that the corruption offences should be triable either way.

---

[7]   Above, para 5.99.

[8]   Above. The latter defence (consent) would only have applied to private bodies.

[9]   Above, para 6.29.

[10]   Above, para 7.15. The relevant provisions of the 1993 Act came into force 1 June 1999.

[11]   Above, para 8.20.

[12]   "Raising Standards and Upholding Integrity: the Prevention of Corruption" (2000) (Cm 4759).

[13]   Above, para 4.1.

Proposals contrary to, or in extension of, our previous report

3.7 However, the Government questioned some of the recommendations. It suggested some modifications, including:

(1) contrary to the Law Commission's recommendation, the consent of a Law Officer should still be required prior to every prosecution for corruption;

(2) corruption should be extended to cover third parties corruptly trading their influence over an agent, in conformity with the, then unratified, Council of Europe Criminal Law Convention of Corruption;[14]

(3) jurisdiction should be further extended so as to cover UK nationals committing acts of corruption in other jurisdictions; and

(4) corruption should be extended, in line with the report of the Joint Committee on Parliamentary Privilege, to cover MPs.

THE JOINT COMMITTEE ON THE DRAFT CORRUPTION BILL[15]

3.8 The Joint Committee did not challenge the need for the Government's draft Bill, but highlighted what they considered to be several problems with it:

(1) a failure to cover some corrupt conduct, for example: when heads of firms bribe each other;[16] or when an agent unreasonably believes that his or her principal has consented to the advantage/bribe;[17]

(2) a failure to state the general law of corruption with sufficient clarity;

(3) a failure to give an adequate definition of corruption. The Committee said that the language used was too vague and unhelpful for businesses attempting to understand the law. Beyond this, the Committee stated that the definition could be interpreted in a manner that was inconsistent with the UK's international obligations;[18]

(4) the focus upon the agent/principal relationship was too restrictive and the offence should thus be widened;[19] and

(5) the waiver of Parliamentary privilege in corruption cases should be narrowed.

The Committee concluded that the agent/principal focus, which formed the heart of the draft Bill, should be reassessed.[20]

---

[14] Article 12 of the Council of Europe Criminal Law Convention on Corruption.

[15] Joint Committee on the Draft Corruption Bill, Session 2002-2003, HL Paper 157, HC 705 (2003).

[16] Above, para 87.

[17] Above, paras 30 to 31.

[18] Above, para 26. The Joint Committee advanced alternative definitions at para 92.

[19] Above, para 81.

The Government's response to the Joint Committee[21]

3.9 The Government supported some of the amendments to the draft Bill that the Committee had suggested. It accepted that:

(1) Parliamentary privilege should not be narrowed as much as was initially recommended;

(2) the Director of Public Prosecutions or one nominated Deputy should be able to give consent for prosecutions; and

(3) the exemption given to the intelligence services should be reviewed.

3.10 However, the Government did not accept all of the recommendations of the Committee. It said that:

(1) the core concept of agent and principal should be retained.[22] The Government contended that bribes between principals were already covered by other legislation[23] and that to abandon this structure would "cast the criminal net unacceptably wide";[24] and

(2) the proposed rule that the advantage offered had to be a 'primary' motivator would prevent small gratuities from being caught by the offence.[25]

THE MOST RECENT GOVERNMENT CONSULTATION

3.11 Despite the Government's indication that they were minded to take forward the Law Commission's draft Bill, its momentum was effectively undermined by the criticisms of the Joint Committee.

3.12 In an effort to find a way forward, the Home Office published a consultation paper in December 2005.[26] The response to that consultation was published in March 2007. At the same time, the Government announced that it had asked the Law Commission to re-examine the law of bribery.

---

[20] Above, para 89.

[21] The Government reply to the report from the Joint Committee on the draft Corruption Bill session 2002-2003 HL Paper 157, HC 705 (2003) Cm 6086.

[22] Above, paras 12 to 16.

[23] Above, para 14. An example cited is the cartel offence in the Enterprise Act 2002. See Appendix D below.

[24] Above, paras 14 to 15.

[25] Above, para 9.

[26] Bribery: Reform of the Prevention of Corruption Acts and SFO Powers in Cases of Bribery of Foreign Officials: Summary of responses and next steps (2007).

The Government's response to consultation

3.13   The Government considered that the Commission's focus in this project should be on the narrow category of offences similar to bribery and that this should be the name of any new offence. However, they found no strong views on whether the title of any Bill should refer to "bribery", "corruption" or simply "criminal justice".

3.14   On the definition of the mental element, the Government preferred "corruptly" to "improper" or other epithets. They also preferred a more detailed definition rather than simply leaving the issue to be determined by the jury, as happens with "dishonestly" in the Theft Act 1968. However, they were not satisfied with any of the suggested definitions that they had received as each one was insufficiently comprehensive. As they had no definition of their own, this is one of the main issues that they wish the Law Commission to address in this project.

3.15   The Government did not express a strongly decided view on whether there should be a single bribery offence or one each for the private and public sectors. However, they appeared marginally to prefer the former. They acknowledged the force of the argument that the rules for the public sector should be stricter but suggested that this could be achieved by having some exemptions applicable only to the private sector.

3.16   In private sector cases, the Government were of the view that there could possibly be additional defences:

    (1)   the principal's consent: the Government acknowledged that this would exempt cases of "principal to principal bribery" but stated that they believed that such cases should properly fall within the field of competition law rather than that of bribery;

    (2)   corporate hospitality: this defence might be acceptable provided that it was of a kind and degree acceptable both by the standards of ordinary people and by the prevailing practice of the industry;

    (3)   normal practice: this might be a defence but would not operate in the sphere of corporate hospitality.

3.17   As explained, the Government favoured the principal and agent model that was central to our previous report and appended draft Bill. However, extensive criticism, from both the Joint Committee and during the consultation process, has been sufficient to persuade the Government that the draft Bill is not suitable for presentation to Parliament.

3.18   The Government's response does not express a decided view on whether to retain the test that the decision should be "primarily" motivated by the bribe. One possibility would be to make this test refer to "substantially". However, they agreed that the "primarily" test would be useful as a way of excluding normal corporate hospitality from the ambit of the offence.

3.19   The Government agreed that there is no need for a reverse burden of proof of corrupt intention in public sector cases.

3.20   They also agreed with the suggestion that in cases involving the bribery of foreign officials, but only in such cases, the Serious Fraud Office ('SFO') should have the same powers of investigation as it does in fraud cases. These powers are conferred by section 2 of the Criminal Justice Act 1987. They permit the SFO, at the vetting stage of an investigation, to compel the production of documents and require explanations for them. However, the Government did not think that bribery of foreign officials should be a separate offence.

3.21   The Government agreed with the suggestion in the Joint Committee report that the requirement that the Attorney General consent to any prosecution should be replaced by a requirement for the consent of the Director of Public Prosecutions or a nominated deputy. They did not consider that there should be a special obligation of disclosure by Her Majesty's Revenue and Customs to support prosecutions, beyond the voluntary procedure already provided by the Anti-terrorism, Crime and Security Act 2001.

3.22   The Government did not accept the suggestion that UK companies should be subject to criminal liability for the acts of subsidiaries operating abroad, unless the parent companies have themselves done something to authorise those acts. In addition, they did not accept that there should be a specific provision for corporate liability for bribery offences in advance of the Law Commission's review of corporate criminal liability generally.

3.23   The Government also stated that they did not see a need for a separate offence of bribing sportsmen, as this was already covered by the Prevention of Corruption Acts. The Government also did not wish to pursue the suggestions that there should be separate offences of bid-rigging and trading in influence, and stated they believed that the codification of the offence of misuse of public office should be left for another time. Other topics, which could be worthy of review in themselves but which it was felt should be left for separate review, included Parliamentary privilege and donations to political parties.

CONCLUSION

3.24   The above discussion demonstrates that, although the debate in several areas is at an advanced stage, there is still little consensus as to the best way forward. What the discussion does provide, however, is a useful evaluation of the various options. This enables us to move forward with this project on a firmer foundation.

PART 4
A MODEL FOR BRIBERY

THE ISSUES

4.1 The most important issue, and the first step towards the reform of bribery, is the identification of the nature of the wrong. Why is it that bribery should be criminal and what kind of wrongdoing can unify it as a distinct offence? There are several possible answers to this question, each of which leads to a different definition of the offence.

4.2 A preliminary question is: who is in a position to be bribed? Historically speaking, the answer to this comprises three concentric circles:

   (1)   the classic case of the corrupt judge;

   (2)   by extension, any case where a person has a public duty to make a decision, political or administrative: for example, to consider an application for a permit;

   (3)   by a further extension, the case where the duty to decide is derived from a private law relationship, such as employment or trusteeship.

4.3 In any case of bribery there must be an advantage conferred, agreed or sought; an action or omission which the payer hopes to obtain; and a nexus between the two. Two questions arise:

   (1)   One question is, in which of these lies the evil that turns the transaction into a case of bribery: that is to say, at what point in the overall transaction does the breach of duty occur? Is the core evil that the recipient is being bribed to do something wrong, or that he or she is doing wrong by receiving a bribe?

   (2)   The other question is, of what must that wrongdoing consist and, in particular, who or what is being wronged?

4.4 Addressing the first question, definitions of bribery fall into three main groups: the improper payment model, the improper influence model and the improper conduct model.

   (1)   On the improper payment model, the essence of bribery is the receipt of an undue payment by a person whose official or contractual position makes that payment improper. In the pure form of this model, it is irrelevant whether the recipient was in fact, or was even intended to be, influenced by that payment. Some countries, such as Germany and Italy, have an offence of this form affecting public officials, but the offence is not generally characterised as bribery in the full sense.

   (2)   On the improper influence model, the payment may or may not be described as "undue", but the central requirement is that the recipient was (or was intended to be) influenced by it in the exercise of his or her official or contractual duties. This does not mean that he or she was

influenced to do something improper, but that the influence itself is improper. The French Criminal Code follows this model, as do many of the international Conventions.[1] A variant of this model, used in the USA and many Commonwealth countries, requires not an objective link between the payment and the act of the recipient, but a corrupt intention in the defendant.

(3)   The improper conduct model requires that a person receive a payment (whether "undue" or not) in return for contravening a duty. In other words, it is not the bribe or the influence, but the thing one is bribed to do, that must be "improper". To avoid circularity, the impropriety cannot consist simply of the fact that something was done in return for a bribe. Germany, Italy and South Africa all have offences drafted on these lines.

4.5   There are two other models that we will be considering. The first of these, the "principal and agent model", cuts across the distinctions between the three main models, but is of special relevance to the meaning of impropriety under the improper conduct model:

(4)   The principal and agent model. The principal and agent model regards the impropriety in bribery (connected to an advantage conferred or to be conferred on the agent) as the breach of a duty of loyalty owed by an agent to his or her principal. Thus, under this model, it is by no means every breach of duty (induced by promise of, or rewarded by, an advantage) that falls within the scope of bribery.[2]

4.6   Finally, there is the "market model":

(5)   The market model regards the wrongdoing in bribery as a distortion of an existing market, or the creation of a market that should not exist, rather than as a breach of a duty by a named person or as an injury to a named principal.[3]

4.7   In summary, we need to choose among the following models:

(1)   the principal and agent model;

(2)   the improper payment model;

(3)   the improper influence model;

(4)   the improper conduct model;

(5)   the market model.

---

[1]   See Appendices A and B below.

[2]   The principal and agent model may be sub-divided into improper payment, improper influence and improper conduct versions, depending on which stage of the transaction constitutes the wrong done to the principal, thus bringing the theoretical number of models to seven. However, they may not all need separate discussion. If we conclude that the principal and agent approach is mistaken in itself, there will be no need to distinguish between its three sub-forms.

[3]   For further discussion, see Appendix D below.

THE HISTORY

4.8   Our previous project did not discuss either the improper payment model or the market model.

4.9   The remaining models can be subdivided according to how they answer two questions.

    (1)   Need the favour conferred by the recipient be misconduct, in the sense of an actual breach of some duty owed by him or her, or can it be any act or omission in relation to that duty, provided that it is influenced by the bribe? ("Conduct" versus "influence".)

    (2)   Need the duty be owed to a named principal, or can it be any duty recognised by law? ("Personal" versus "impersonal".)

4.10   These two questions are independent of each other, and thus yield four permutations: personal/conduct, personal/influence, impersonal/conduct and impersonal/influence. The two "personal" models are forms of the principal and agent model, while the other two are what this paper respectively refers to as the improper conduct model and the improper influence model.

4.11   Our previous CP opted for the principal and agent model, but in its discussion of the definition of "corruptly" eventually concluded that this should consist of a breach of duty (personal/conduct). Many of the responses to the CP criticised this on the ground that the definition would then exclude many instances where a person was "bribed to do the right thing".

4.12   Accordingly our previous report, which also opted for the principal and agent model, recommended an influence test as a way of defining "corruptly" (personal/influence). This too was subsequently criticised, partly for being too abstract and partly for being over-inclusive.

4.13   The arguments, both in the two previous documents (CP and report) and in the responses to them, are all formulated within the context of the principal and agent model. If we reject that model, there will still be the choice between the impersonal/duty and the impersonal/influence models, and much of the discussion in our previous report will remain relevant in this new context. These arguments will therefore be set out in some detail when we come to those models.

THE PRINCIPAL AND AGENT MODEL

4.14   According to the principal and agent model, the essential evil of bribery is betrayal of trust. That is, a person owes a duty of loyalty to another and should act in that other's best interests. By accepting the bribe, the recipient is acting in his or her own interests, or those of the payer, and betraying the trust of the person to whom loyalty is owed. The most obvious example is when the recipient is an employee or other agent, and betrays the trust of the employer or principal. In what follows, we argue that the term "principal" is misleading, both because the person to whom loyalty is owed need not be a principal in any normally accepted sense and because the loyalty may not be owed to a person at all.

4.15   The definition of bribery in the 1906 Act explicitly adopts the relationship of principal and agent as its basis. This covers both private sector cases and those public sector cases in which an agency relationship exists. However, it does not purport to provide a template for all cases of bribery: most public sector bribery cases continue to be covered by the common law offence or the offence under the 1889 Act, which do not depend on a principal and agent model. By contrast, the scheme set out in our previous report applies a principal and agent model to all bribery offences. By this scheme, where the recipient is a public officer, he or she is regarded as an "agent" of the public; but, by way of contrast with the case where the principal is an individual, there is no defence of principal's consent.

4.16   In the 1906 Act, and still more in our previous report, it is made clear that "principal" and "agent" are terms of art, with a far wider meaning than they bear in general law. First, there is the fact that every public officer is an "agent" even though there is no identifiable principal. Secondly, "agent" includes trustees, directors, partners, professional persons, employees and, generally, anyone performing a function under an agreement, as well as agents in the normal sense.

4.17   In this wide sense, "agent" appears to mean simply "functionary", that is to say any person on whom a duty is imposed. The choice of term is immaterial as a matter of language. The important question is whether it is necessary to retain the role of the "principal".

4.18   There are two arguments against this. One relates to the case where there is a personal victim but "principal" is not an appropriate description for that person. The other relates to the case where there is no personal principal or victim at all.

Cases where "principal" points to the wrong person

4.19   We have already identified the "agent" as meaning simply a person in a position of owing a duty. The "principal", then, means the person to whom that duty is owed and whose trust is betrayed by the acceptance of the bribe. This may be quite different from the person normally described as the recipient's principal.

4.20   Where the relationship in question is bilateral, for example that of trustee and beneficiary, the point is simply one of language: "principal" would be defined in an extended sense in the same way as "agent". Such a scheme could work as a matter of drafting, though from the point of view of public accessibility it is desirable to avoid artificial definitions which take words too far away from their normal use.

4.21   The more important objection is that some cases may be trilateral, and there may be a real identifiable principal who is different from the person to whom the duty is owed.

Example 4A
An employee of a bank or trust company accepts a bribe to invest trust money in a particular fund.

This will almost certainly be a breach of the terms of employment (except in the unlikely event that the employer is complicit in the transaction), but it would be artificial to make this the incriminating factor. The actual trust betrayed is that of the beneficiaries, rather than of the employer, but it would be a very strange use of language to describe a beneficiary as the employee's principal.

4.22 This is not just a problem of definitions, to be solved by interpreting "principal" and "agent" in a wider sense. In the case described, it is not certain that there is any direct legal relationship between the employee and the beneficiary (except that following the receipt of the bribe there may be a constructive trust of the money received). Even if the relationship of principal and agent were redefined to include beneficiary and trustee, the employee would still not be an agent for the beneficiary because he or she is not the trustee.

4.23 This brings us to the main practical reason against the principal and agent approach, which has been put forward by the Serious Fraud Office as well as by Transparency International. In Example 4A, a principal and agent approach would require us first to ascertain the position of the employee's employer.

  (1) If the employer is not complicit, the basis of the employee's guilt is betrayal of the trust of the employer: on a principal and agent approach, there is no nexus between the employee and the beneficiary.

  (2) If the employer is complicit, then the trust betrayed is that which the employer owes to the beneficiary: as the employee owes no such trust, he is not in a position to commit the offence, except as an accessory to a crime of the employer. On the other hand, it is the employee, and not the employer, who has committed all the physical acts constituting that betrayal. This is confusing and unsatisfactory.

  (3) In many cases, for example where the employer lives abroad, it is impossible to prove anything about the employer's state of mind one way or the other. It is therefore impossible to know which basis should be used for prosecuting the employee.

4.24 This is unnecessarily complicated, and may lead to many prosecutions being dropped because of the impossibility of determining the exact role of the employer. That is, the employee may adduce some evidence of complicity on the part of the employer, sufficient to prevent conviction for betraying the trust of the employer, but not enough to prove the case as against the employer (and thus against the employee as an accessory). It would be preferable to say that, regardless of the part played by the employer (or even of whether there is an employer), the person receiving the bribe has clearly betrayed the trust placed in him or her and that the beneficiary is the sole or main victim of the offence.

4.25 It would be possible to circumvent this problem by extending the relationship of principal and agent beyond cases where there is a direct legal nexus between the parties, to include persons linked through a chain of intermediaries. In this case the employee owes a duty to the company, which owes a duty to the beneficiaries, so the beneficiaries and the employee will be in a relationship of "principal and agent" (extended sense).

4.26 This solution is technically possible, but seems needlessly complicated. For simplicity's sake, it should not be adopted unless it can be shown that the definition of bribery is not coherent in the absence of an identified principal. It would be far simpler to identify the "agent" as a person under a duty, never mind to whom, and to define bribery as a betrayal of that duty. This takes us outside the principal and agent model and into the improper payment, improper influence or improper conduct model.

Cases where there is no principal

4.27 The argument is stronger in relation to public sector bribery. Whether or not a public sector worker has a personal principal (and this is often debatable), the worker's primary loyalty is to the public. In one sense, this means the public interest as an abstraction, or some aspect of it: for example, the rule of law. In another, it means whichever members of the public are affected by a particular decision.

4.28 In this case, as well as in the private sector case, the intellectually economical solution is to define bribery as involving breach of a legal duty, whether or not it is possible to say with certainty that the duty was owed to a "principal" (defined either as a person or as an abstraction).

Why do we need a principal anyway?

4.29 One function of the "principal" in the 1906 Act and our previous report was simply as correlative to the "agent", so as to provide a means of identifying the people in a position to be bribed. All this does is to identify the recipient as a person with duties to perform. For this purpose, there is no need for a personal principal and, as argued in relation to the public sector cases, there may well not be one: it is sufficient for the recipient to be a functionary of some kind. There may be a need to circumscribe the kind of duties required, for example that they must be legal or equitable and not merely moral. This will be discussed further when we consider the "improper conduct" model.[4]

4.30 The second function of the "principal" is as the victim of the offence, in other words the person whose trust is betrayed. As argued above, this need not be the same person as the agent's own principal, in the sense required for the first function, or indeed a person at all.

4.31 The main relevance of the existence of a personal victim is to the defence of consent. We discuss in a later section whether there should be a defence of consent at all, and if so whether it should be explicitly stated or left, as at present, as an inference from general principles of criminal law. Briefly, the point is that such a defence is only conceivable where the only interest betrayed by the bribe is that of particular persons and they all agree to the transaction in advance.

4.32 This is the one instance in which the existence of a personal principal makes a real difference to the offence of bribery. However, far from being an essential ingredient of the offence, it serves to differentiate offences that involve a personal principal from a wider class of offences that do not. It is therefore an argument against, rather than for, a principal and agent definition of bribery.

---

[4] See para 4.115 and following and Part 5 paras 5.29 to 5.54 below.

Principal to principal bribery

4.33 One argument that has been raised against the principal and agent model (for example by the Joint Committee) is that it fails to cover the situations known as "principal to principal bribery". This is a somewhat vague category, but could cover cases such as the following.

Example 4B

An applicant for a job or contract makes a payment to induce the potential employer to award the job or contract to him.

4.34 It is not always clear that this is bribery at all.

(1) In some cases, it could be held that this is a purely private deal between employer and employee or contractor and concerns no one else, and that there is no duty, either to the public or to the applicants, to choose the best candidate. In effect, there is simply a reduction in the eventual amount of the employee's or contractor's remuneration and the transaction should not be regarded as criminal in any way.

(2) In a few cases, there may be some kind of fraud on the public, because the real remuneration is different from the nominal remuneration. This will only be relevant where the proper remuneration is subject to some statutory requirement or code of conduct, such as a minimum wage or a fair rent. Nevertheless, the offence is not one of bribery as such.

(3) In some cases, the duties to be performed by the employee or contractor may have some impact on the public, so that the employer has a responsibility to choose the best applicant. In these cases, the transaction is bribery in the full sense.

Example 4C

There are two or more applicants for a job or a contract. One applicant pays another to withdraw his or her application.

4.35 In most cases it is not clear that this should be criminal at all. Neither of the applicants has any duty to the prospective employer to maximise the field of choice, or to allow him or her to choose the best candidate. In some cases, such as where the applicant company is in effect using its financial muscle to create a monopoly for itself or otherwise seeking to exclude an actual or potential competitor, the act would amount to an offence under competition law rather than a bribery offence.

4.36 The current competition law regime already has methods of sanctioning the company through the civil law,[5] and the company directors through the criminal law,[6] for this type of conduct. Where consent is demonstrated, it is contended

---

[5] Competition Act 1998, Part 1.

[6] The cartel offence in the Enterprise Act 2002.

that these are the appropriate legal sanctions and there is insufficient justification for extending the borders of bribery as well.

4.37 That said, we do not consider the offences of bribery and of distorting competition to be necessarily mutually exclusive: one can, for example, be bribed to perform an anti-competitive act. The relationship between bribery and competition offences is discussed in more detail in Appendix D.

4.38 A third example sometimes raised is that of a company where the directors receive a bribe.

Example 4D

Company X bribes the directors of company Y to award a contract to company X.

The directors are agents of company Y and would therefore seem to have betrayed their trust. On the other hand, they are also the directing mind of the company and can, therefore, according to this argument, (cause the company to) authorise the breach. Morally, however, the directors have clearly betrayed the trust of the shareholders and the transaction remains bribery in the true sense.

4.39 One criticism of this example is that it is questionable whether the directors have the legal authority to authorise a transaction of this kind. Another is that this is not in fact an example of "principal to principal bribery", but rather an instance of bribery of an agent with the principal's consent.

4.40 The position is a little more complicated when the bribe is not paid to the directors but goes into the company's funds. On the surface this is like the case of the bribed human principal (Example 4B); the directors are not guilty of preferring their own interests to the interests of the company, but were acting in what they thought were the interests of the company. Nevertheless, they may be betraying the trust of the shareholders in one sense, in that the shareholders are entitled to trust the directors not to involve the company in criminality. This, however, can only be relevant when the criminality in question takes some form other than bribery, as otherwise the argument is circular.

4.41 In conclusion we do not find that the examples of principal to principal bribery in themselves provide a strong argument against the principal and agent model. However, they do seem to bear out our contention that the criterion for bribery should be whether the recipient was under a duty.

Conclusion on principal/agent model

4.42 In conclusion, whether or not the recipient is described as an agent, there is no need for a principal, either to define the recipient's position or as the victim of the offence, except for the purposes of the defence of victim's consent. If acceptance of bribes is to be treated as a betrayal of trust, the essential ingredients are as follows:

(1) The recipient must be in a position defined by law where he or she owes duties, whether or not to another individual. One possibility would be to list these positions, by defining several broad categories. The position of

agent for a named principal may survive as one of these categories; public officials may be another.

(2)   The recipient must, in connection with the receipt of that benefit, betray some sort of trust or loyalty. This may or may not be the same as, or owed to the same person as, the primary duty which he or she is employed to perform, but must in some sense be a consequence of it. (For example, it could be the duty to act impartially or in good faith, as opposed to the duty to work at all).

(3)   If there is to be a defence of victim's consent, it should be available only when all persons to whom that trust or loyalty is owed are clearly identified and there is no remaining duty to other persons or to the public.

4.43   In summary, the "principal and agent model" defines bribery as the betrayal of a loyalty, that is to say a duty to an identified person. By eliminating the need for an identified person, we can reduce this to the betrayal of a duty in general. This may then take the form of either the "improper payment", the "improper conduct" or the "improper influence" model.

THE MARKET MODEL

4.44   Before attempting to choose between the "improper payment", "improper conduct" and "improper influence" models, we must mention one other explanation of the harm of bribery which has been suggested as the basis for a definition. This may be referred to as the market model: instead of identifying the harm of bribery in terms of individual harm, it is identified with the harm to the financial market. This may take two forms:

(1)   distorting the operation of an existing market;

(2)   creating a market in things which ought not to be sold.

4.45   For a full explanation and evaluation of this model, see Appendix D. Whatever its merits as an explanation in policy terms of what is wrong with bribery in general, we believe that it is less helpful in formulating a legal definition of bribery in individual cases.

4.46   Further, there are already competition offences which cover the distortion of legitimate markets. Not all instances of such offences can be described as bribery in any normal sense. Those that can be so described invariably cross the line into the second category, of trading in things that ought not to be sold.

4.47   Even if we take the second category on its own, it does not advance the discussion much further. Although the practice of bribery generally can be said to "create a market" in things that ought not to be sold, a single act of bribery does not – it is simply an instance of an act taking place within that market. This, on analysis, means no more than that there was an exchange of favours, and that one of them was of such a kind that the exchange should not have happened. As a legal definition, as opposed to an analysis of social harm, this is merely circular. At best, it leads us back to the improper payment, improper influence or improper conduct model.

IMPROPER PAYMENT MODEL

4.48 The most obvious feature of bribery is the payment itself. One approach, then, is to make bribery cover every situation in which the recipient of a payment is in a position of owing a duty, whether public, contractual or other, which make receipt of the payment improper. For example, it is obviously wrong for a judge to receive a payment from either party to litigation, without any need to go on to investigate whether the judge is in fact influenced by that payment.

4.49 While this seems reasonable in the case of a judge, it seems harsh and over-inclusive to extend it to all cases as the general definition of bribery.

Example 4E

X, the owner of a restaurant, prides himself on paying good wages and on this basis he forbids tipping. It is part of the staff contract and is clearly displayed in the restaurant. P, visiting the restaurant whilst on holiday, is so impressed with the service that, despite the signs, he slips the waiter, R, a small tip. R is reluctant to accept but, not wishing to offend P, does so.

R, by accepting the tip, has breached his contractual duty. At the same time, P, although conferring an advantage, is not expecting anything in return.

4.50 A technical fix to this problem could take either of two forms.

(1) There could be a lesser offence of accepting unethical payments, separate from whatever definition we choose for the main bribery offence.

(2) Alternatively, there could be a limited class of officials, including judges, for whom accepting payments is regarded as equal to bribery in weight. This could be recognised either by creating a separate offence or by creating a presumption that all payments to officials within this class are bribes within whatever definition is chosen for the main offence.

4.51 Both these solutions involve rejecting the improper payment model as the definition of the main bribery offence. There still remains the essential issue, which is whether bribery exists when the recipient has done nothing outside the course of duty except to receive the payment. This is one form of the question of what to do about "payment to do the right thing" (another form will be discussed under the improper influence model).

4.52 It is questionable whether the real evil of bribery exists in a case where the recipient is rewarded for doing something which he or she was obliged to do anyway. By that, we mean not a case where the recipient had a choice to make but was bribed to choose what would in any case be the right side, but a case where there was no choice at all. An example would be where an official is processing routine applications, such as for dog licences, and there is no judicial or policy decision to be made.

4.53 Payments of this kind are often called "facilitation payments", and are discussed in detail in Appendix F. Briefly, the conclusions of that discussion are as follows.

(1) There should be no criminal liability where the payment made no difference *at all* to the recipient's performance of his or her functions.

(2) There should be liability where the effect of the payment is that the payer's matter is moved up the queue, to the detriment of others dealing with the recipient.

The problem case

> **Example 4F**
>
> R is a state employee responsible for completing routine paperwork. P is a private individual who wants the paperwork relevant to him processed quickly. At 6 o'clock on Friday evening, R is about to leave the office. P phones R to ask if his paperwork has been completed. R explains that he is working his way through the list of names and that P is next so will be dealt with first thing on Monday morning. In order to persuade R to stay after hours to complete P's paperwork immediately, P offers to pay R a small sum of money. R accepts the money and completes the paperwork that Friday evening.

4.54 Before we go on to explore the three options for dealing with the problem case, it is important not to exaggerate its significance. This is because most serious cases involving a facilitation payment will involve R breaching a legal or equitable duty, including a duty to act impartially. For example, if R is paid in order to provide an export licence to P that he or she might not otherwise have got, this is likely to involve R in breaching a legal or equitable duty. Equally, if the payment induces R to advance P in the queue, it is likely that R will be breaching a duty to act impartially. There are three options for addressing the problem case.

Option 1: Include all types of 'breach of duty'

4.55 Under this option, the mere acceptance of an advantage, without more, constitutes a breach of duty, and the vast majority of facilitation payments would be included. This is because, especially in the public sector, codes of conduct incorporated in contracts of employment are very likely to include provisions that forbid officials to accept advantages without permission. Therefore, in Example 4F above, if breach of a legal or equitable duty included merely accepting an advantage that one was forbidden to accept, R would have acted improperly if he or she was forbidden to accept the money by the terms of his or her contract of employment.

4.56 Although extending the offence in this way may seem attractive in the sense that it would prevent the law being under-inclusive, there would be problems. First, as already mentioned, it affects the whole notion of what it is to bribe. There would be the potential for cases to fall within the scope of the extended offence where P is not expecting anything in return for the advantage offered.[7]

4.57 Secondly, the policy would inevitably lead to a greater reliance on internal codes of conduct and contractual terms, as this would be where the courts would have to look in order to determine whether the mere acceptance of an advantage constituted a breach of duty. This in turn may create problems where the code is ambiguous. For example, in the Civil Service Code it is stated that employees must not "accept gifts … which might reasonably be seen to compromise [one's] personal judgement or integrity".[8] It would be unfortunate if this type of provision led to extended litigation in court.

4.58 Equally, it may be questioned whether borderline cases, for example the actions of a civil servant seen as going slightly beyond what is expected, should be subject to criminal sanction and labelled as bribery.[9] Therefore, if we adopt option 1, there would almost certainly be a need further to refine the test to exclude all but *clear* breaches of duty.[10] However, it is obvious that this may lead to gaps in the law as it would apply in other situations. The alternative solution would be to rely on prosecutorial discretion. This is not something that we favour.

4.59 Thirdly, it could result in an over-inclusive offence in relation to private sector employees, as in Example 4E above. Again, it might be possible to rely on prosecutorial discretion but we do not believe that this is a satisfactory solution.

Option 2: Create a separate offence for facilitation payments

4.60 Under this option, there would be a specific offence to criminalise facilitation payments in cases where the mere acceptance of the payment constitutes a breach of duty but this would be separate from the full bribery offence. One advantage would be that the offence could be confined to cases where R is a public official.

4.61 However, it might be thought that such an offence would be undesirable in the light of our general aim to produce a consolidated and simple Bill. In addition, there are more fundamental objections. The Government has already made clear that, although committed to facilitation payments remaining criminal, it is unlikely that the making of such payments should result in prosecution. With this in mind, it is important to consider whether a separate offence for facilitation payments would be desirable. This question must be considered in the light of our opinion that the most serious facilitation payment cases would be caught by our general policy.[11] This would be so, even if both this option and option 1 were rejected.

Option 3: Exclude from the ambit of bribery those cases where the only breach of duty is the acceptance of the conferred advantage

4.62 If it is accepted that the most serious cases of facilitation payments would be captured by our general policy, we believe that there is a strong case for concluding that those whose only breach of duty lies in accepting an advantage (as in Example 4E) should not be held criminally liable. It is likely that they will be subject to internal disciplinary measures involving exposure to sanctions,

---

[7] See Example 4E above (in para 4.49).

[8] Civil Service Code (2006), para 6.

[9] One must consider whether this type of case is better dealt with through internal regulation including possibly suspension and dismissal.

[10] At least as it applies to those who have breached a duty merely by accepting the advantage.

[11] See Appendix F, paras F.29 to F.30.

including dismissal. In our view, the availability of such measures is sufficient to express disapproval of their conduct.

Provisional proposal and question for consultees

4.63 **We provisionally propose that the acceptance of an advantage in breach of a duty not to accept the advantage should not, without more, constitute a bribery offence.** (Option 3)

4.64 **We invite comment on whether there should be a separate offence of accepting an advantage in breach of a duty not to accept it.**

IMPROPER INFLUENCE MODEL

4.65 The conclusion of the above discussion is that the improper payment model is too broad unless confined to cases where the payment influenced, or was intended to influence, the recipient in the performance of his or her duty.

4.66 One argument in support of this view is that the essential evil of bribery lies, not in the payment as such or the favour sought as such, but in the nexus between the two. We normally think of this nexus as consisting of an exchange, "you'll scratch my back and I'll scratch yours". However, it would be wrong to limit this to a defined contractual arrangement. If the offence were so limited, it would be too easy to evade liability by making the arrangement loose and informal. Additionally, there is some conceptual doubt whether an arrangement to which illegality is so central can be a "contract" at all. The "influence" test preserves the importance of the nexus, but also imports the desired element of flexibility.

4.67 The main differences between the improper influence model and the improper conduct model are as follows.

(1) In the improper influence model, while the influence or the payment must be "improper" in some sense, there is no requirement that the favour for which the recipient is paid be improper in itself. In the improper conduct model there is such a requirement. So the question dividing them is whether it is bribery to pay someone for doing the right thing.

(2) Conversely, in the improper conduct model there is no requirement that the favour be influenced by the payment: the payment could be a reward given subsequently. We consider this question under the improper conduct model.

Forms of the influence model

4.68 Once influence is made the crucial factor in bribery, there is still a choice of possibilities, depending on where the element of impropriety attaches.

4.69 One definition relies on the payment itself being "undue" or improper, but adds the requirement that the recipient was influenced, without saying anything about whether the influence was proper or not. This is a cross between the improper payment and improper influence models, and is followed by the French Criminal Code[12] and some of the international Conventions.[13]

4.70 Another possibility is to require that the influence itself be improper, whether or not "undue" is retained for the payment. A variant of this appears in the OECD Convention, where the payment must be "undue" but there is also a requirement of the ulterior motive of obtaining an improper advantage.

4.71 A third possibility is to require that the recipient be influenced to *do* something improper: this approximates to the improper conduct model, to be considered later in this Part. (The difference is that the pure improper conduct model also includes cases where the bribe is a reward offered subsequently and, therefore, cannot have influenced the conduct). We shall discuss this possibility together with the improper conduct model and therefore leave it aside for now.

4.72 The fourth possibility is to have no express requirement of impropriety at all, and hold the offence proved as soon as there is a payment and the recipient is in fact influenced in the performance of his or her duties. In other words, the very fact of there being any influence is automatically improper. This however would risk extending bribery to many cases of unexceptionable business practice, for example, an employee acting under an incentive scheme. We can therefore eliminate this possibility and concentrate on the first and second possibilities.

An example of the influence model

4.73 The wider approach, as stated, is to say that bribery exists whenever a benefit is given with the purpose of influencing the recipient in the performance of a duty. An example of this approach is in the OECD Convention, where the definition of the acts to be criminalised is as follows.

> Each Party shall take such measures as may be necessary to establish that it is a criminal offence under its law for any person intentionally to offer, promise or give any undue pecuniary or other advantage, whether directly or through intermediaries, to a foreign public official, for that official or for a third party, in order that the official act or refrain from acting in relation to the performance of official duties, in order to obtain or retain business or other improper advantage in the conduct of international business.

4.74 Here the burden of impropriety is thrown onto the payment, rather than onto the favour expected in return for the payment, which may consist of any act or omission related to the recipient's duties.

4.75 One possibility is to create a new general bribery offence, based more or less closely on this definition. It would need modifying:

---

[12] See Appendix B, paras B.2 to B.13 below.

[13] For example, the United Nations Convention against Corruption. See Appendix A, paras A.69 to A.89 below.

(1)   in order to catch the receipt as well as the giving of the bribe; and

(2)   in order to catch other categories of persons owing a duty, as well as foreign officials.

4.76   If, on the other hand, it is thought preferable to use a different model, such as that in the TI Bill,[14] for the general bribery offence, there may need to be a separate offence, based on the OECD model, for the bribery of foreign public officials. This option is further discussed in Part 7.

"Payment to do the right thing"

4.77   We have already considered, under the improper payment model, the situation where a person has a fixed duty to do, does it, and receives a payment but is not influenced by it in any way. Here we are considering a case where there are two or more possible courses of action, or ways of carrying out the same course of action, the person is influenced to adopt one of them, but the decision is correct or defensible on other grounds.

4.78   One example of this is where a judge receives a payment from the litigant whom he or she in any case considers to be in the right and proceeds to decide in that litigant's favour. This is clearly bribery. The reason for this, however, is not that it is always bribery to receive a payment for doing the right thing but that the judge has a special duty of impartiality. This case is therefore bribery equally under the improper influence model and the improper conduct model.

4.79   Another example is where the recipient exercises his or her functions correctly but is rewarded for doing so more quickly. Sometimes this may be a matter of facilitation payments, as discussed in Appendix F, rather than of bribes in the strict sense. In other cases, it approaches bribery in the full sense: for example, if a person makes a present to a judge or clerk for moving a case up the list. A similar situation may arise in connection with an administrative rather than a judicial duty. In the extreme case, the system may reach the point where one must be prepared to pay in order to have one's case considered at all. That is almost as grave as bribery in return for a favourable decision: here, not making the payment will result in no decision at all, which is often tantamount to a decision against.

4.80   There may equally be examples from outside the judicial sphere, where P pays R to do something that R is already bound to do:

Example 4G

P is tendering for a contract with X Ltd. P, concerned that a rival will submit a more competitive tender, pays R (an employee of X Ltd) £10,000 to ensure that his tender is successful. R accepts the money and awards P the contract. When R agreed to receive the advantage, he already knew that P had submitted the most competitive tender and R would have had to award the contract to P even without the inducement.

---

[14]   See paras 4.118 to 4.120 below.

4.81   The tribunal of fact may, if left without further legal guidance, conclude that R was not asked to do anything 'wrong' and therefore has not acted 'corruptly' (or 'improperly').[15] However, we believe that an offence of bribery should encompass such a case. In some cases of blackmail,[16] the blackmailer is legally permitted to do what he or she is threatening to do but is nevertheless guilty of blackmail because he or she is threatening to do it for an impermissible reason. Likewise, in Example 4G, R has done something he or she is permitted or bound to do but he or she has done it for an impermissible reason. It is on this basis that a criminal conviction is justified.[17]

4.82   For these reasons, in our previous report we recast our definition of corruption's 'fundamental mischief'. Rather than the inducement of a breach of duty, we concluded that it should be sufficient for an agent to be induced in a manner that 'influences the agent's conduct as an agent'.[18] As a result, the focus shifted from the actions of R, the recipient, to R's reasoning process. Even if the act did not constitute a breach of duty, it would still be corrupt if P's inducement was the primary factor in bringing it about.[19]

4.83   On this approach, bribery exists where:

        (1)   the recipient has a choice between two or more legally possible courses of action;

        (2)   in making that choice, he or she has a responsibility (either to a named principal or to the public) to make it properly, that is, to seek the better option;

        (3)   the bribe is, or is intended to be, or is in danger of being, or may be seen to be, an improper influence on the choice to be made.

Further examples

4.84   There are two interesting but marginal situations raised in American cases, and it might be worth seeing how they would be treated by the "wrongful influence" approach.

4.85   In the case of *Singleton*[20] the prosecution made a promise of leniency in exchange for giving evidence against other defendants. This was held not to be bribery as the prosecution was not a "person" capable of committing the offence. The result may be a desirable one but the reasoning appears to rely on accidental features of the case rather than on any consistent underlying policy.

---

[15]   Although, ironically, as we pointed out in our previous report, most people would regard P's conduct as a form of bribery. Legislating the Criminal Code: Corruption (1998) Law Com No 248, para 5.8.

[16]   Theft Act 1968, s 21.

[17]   In fact, arguably, P also acts immorally in Example 4G. However, different juries may reach different conclusions.

[18]   Legislating the Criminal Code: Corruption (1998) Law Com No 248, para 5.10. The new formulation was based upon a suggestion by Professor Sir John Smith.

[19]   For a discussion of the fault element of bribery, see Part 6.

[20]   (1999) 165 F 3d 1297.

On the "wrongful influence" approach, this would not count as bribery because the choice whether or not to give evidence at all is not one concerning which the witness owes any public duty to come to the best decision.[21] On the other hand, a payment to a witness to testify to a particular account of the facts (whether true or false) would be caught: once a person is certainly going to be a witness, he does have a public duty to choose the most accurate account. Where the account is false, there are separate offences of subornation, inciting to perjury and perverting the course of justice.

4.86 The case of *Myers*[22] concerned a person who took a bribe without any intention of performing the desired favour. Whether this is better or worse than the recipient who delivers is an interesting question. We would suggest that, at the very least, the payer has committed an offence (even if only of attempt), and the recipient has assisted and encouraged him to do so.[23] The "wrongful influence" approach would suggest that the payer's offence is complete and not inchoate, as he made a payment with the intention of influencing the recipient's decision. So far, the "wrongful influence" model seems to include the right cases and for approximately the right reasons.

Definition of impropriety

4.87 The essence of bribery, on this approach, is not simply that the recipient was influenced in the performance of his or her duties, but that he or she was *improperly* influenced.[24] The definition of the offence would therefore need to be qualified in one of two ways.

(1) One would be to speak of "improper influence", or some similar qualification such as "dishonest" or "corrupt".

(2) The other is that the definition should in principle cover all forms of influence, but subject to a series of expressed exceptions designed to exclude the innocent cases. Among these exceptions would be cases of consent and cases where the payment is part of the recipient's normal remuneration. This is the approach adopted in our previous report.

The first approach: requiring impropriety as an element

4.88 The definition could simply require that the influence be "improper", either without defining it at all or by referring to the terms governing the recipient's position of duty. This may be too vague to be acceptable in the definition of a criminal offence. It also risks criminalising acts which should be treated only as a breach of professional ethics.

---

[21] It is uncertain how this argument would apply to the case of a witness bribed by a private person not to give evidence, though such a case would fall within other offences.

[22] (1982) 692 F 2d 823.

[23] On whether, under the present law, one can aid and abet an attempt, or attempt to aid and abet, see *R v Dunnington* [1984] Cr. App. Rep. 171.

[24] See para 4.72 above.

4.89 In our previous report we considered the possibility of using the qualification "corruptly" without further definition.[25] We concluded that, given the state of the authorities on the meaning of this word in the existing statutes, this would be undesirable. We see no reason to depart from that conclusion.

4.90 One other possibility is to use the word "dishonestly", which has a reasonably settled meaning in the context of the Theft Acts and therefore needs no further definition. However, it is not certain that all instances of bribery are "dishonest" in the sense required.[26]

4.91 The equivalent question arises in connection with the improper conduct model and is discussed fully there.[27] Briefly, we conclude that improper conduct should consist of the breach of any duty recognised by law, so far as that breach betrays a relation of trust or infringes an obligation to act impartially or in the best interests of another person. This definition cannot be transposed so as to describe the influence itself, as opposed to the conduct induced by it.

The second approach: relying on specific defences

DEFENCE OF PRINCIPAL'S CONSENT

4.92 One defence provided for in our previous report was that of principal's consent.[28] In the scheme envisaged by the report, if an agent were influenced to do an act by a third party, that act would not come within the scope of the offence if the agent had the consent of his or her principal. Importantly, the defence would have applied in cases where the agent honestly, but unreasonably, believed that had his or her principal been aware of the circumstances he or she would have consented.[29]

4.93 This defence has been criticised on several levels. First, there are said to be practical difficulties. As the defence would only have applied to individuals in the private sector, it would have re-introduced the public/private distinction into every case where the defence was raised.[30] Further, there may be some difficulty in proving a lack of consent, especially where the investigation is taking place in another jurisdiction.[31]

---

[25] Legislating the Criminal Code: Corruption (1998) Law Com No 248, paras 5.62 to 5.66. See also Part 5, paras 5.9 to 5.12 below.

[26] See paras 1.23 and 2.22 above.

[27] See Part 5, paras 5.9 to 5.54 below.

[28] Legislating the Criminal Code: Corruption (1998) Law Com No 248, paras 5.88 to 5.98 and 5.99(ii).

[29] Above, para 5.99(2).

[30] Joint Committee on the Draft Corruption Bill, Session 2002-2003, HL Paper 157, HC 705 (2003), para 30. Although the focus of this criticism is often upon the practical difficulty of distinguishing the public from the private sector, it can also be presented as a principled objection to the two sectors being treated differently for the purposes of bribery.

[31] It is a point recently echoed by the then Attorney General Lord Goldsmith in an interview with the Financial Times following the termination of a large part of the SFO's investigation into BAE Industries. *The Financial Times* 31 January 2007.

4.94 Secondly, the consent defence has also been criticised as a matter of principle. Certain commentators have expressed concern that otherwise corrupt behaviour should not be excused simply by proof of principal's consent. It is a concern that is made more acute in the light of the defence's formulation. When the agent receives the advantage, he or she must believe that the principal would consent if he or she was aware of all the circumstances, but this belief does not have to be *reasonably* held. The Joint Committee's report highlights concerns that the defence could be 'too broad' and thereby exclude cases that should come within the offence.[32]

Abandoning the defence

4.95 A simple response to this criticism would be to abandon the defence altogether or to reduce it to a factor to be considered as part of the issue of whether someone has acted improperly[33] rather than making it a full defence. However, dispensing with the defence would result in the offence being over-inclusive.

4.96 Without the requirement of breach of duty as a limiting factor on the scope of the offence, problems would emerge. For example:

Example 4H

R, an academic employed to do research by a University (X) is given access to a specialist database. P, another academic doing similar research offers R a small sum of money in exchange for R looking out for some other material whilst working on the database. R asks X if he is free to accept P's offer and X gives permission.

P has offered R an advantage in order to influence him to do an act which would affect his duty to X.[34] Therefore, under an influence model that does not include a defence of consent, both R and P are likely to be guilty of bribery.[35] This is clearly not appropriate.

4.97 This example demonstrates that the defence of principal's consent is an essential element of the influence model. If the influence model were to be adopted, the defence, whatever its limitations, would have to be retained.

4.98 It is worth noting that if the breach of duty model were applied to the facts of Example 4H, neither P nor R would fall within the bribery offence because R does not breach his duty to X.

---

[32] Joint Committee on the Draft Corruption Bill, Session 2002-2003, HL Paper 157, HC 705 (2003), para 31.

[33] This is how it was dealt with in our previous CP: *Legislating the Criminal Code: Corruption* (1997) Law Commission Consultation Paper No 145, para 8.20.

[34] At the moment when D makes the offer, P's acceptance of it would clearly affect his existing duty to X. P's duty is also, of course, affected even when X gives consent in the sense that it is subtly modified by that consent.

[35] Assuming P was aware of R's employment.

REMUNERATION DEFENCE

4.99   When an employer pays the wages of an employee he or she does so expecting the money to influence the employee's conduct, if only to ensure that the employee continues to work at all. To deal with this, the Commission recommended that it should be a defence if the agent's principal conferred an advantage as 'remuneration or reimbursement in respect of the performance of [his or her] functions'.[36]

4.100   This defence is of course implicit in the defence of principal's consent: if the principal conferred the advantage, it necessarily follows that the principal consented to the agent's receiving it.

4.101   One criticism would be that both defences depend on identifying a principal, and therefore make sense only within the principal and agent model. So even though this formulation made sense in the context of our previous report, it does not survive the transition from a principal and agent to a pure improper influence approach. In other words, within the fourfold classification in paragraph 4.10, the impersonal/influence permutation appears to be incoherent.

4.102   It may be possible to get round these objections. For example, the "consent" defence could be reformulated to mean the consent of members of some class of potential victims rather than of a principal. Alternatively, it could be argued that, though the definition of bribery no longer depends on a relationship of principal and agent, nevertheless there will still be a principal on the facts of some cases, and that the defences can be confined to these cases. Either way, the resulting scheme would be extremely tortuous.

OTHER CRITICISMS OF THIS APPROACH

4.103   A more general criticism is that it is wrong in principle to start by defining the scope of the offence in a very general way, thereby casting the net of the criminal law very wide, and then to rely on defences to exculpate wholly innocent persons engaged in perfectly permissible conduct. Rather, the primary definition should show clearly what is wrong with the conduct in question.

4.104   In addition, it is arguable that, even allowing for the effect of the two proposed defences, the "influence" definition still makes the scope of the offence too wide.

4.105   An example relates to 'commission payments'.[37]

Example 4J

P is an insurance provider. R is an independent broker of insurance policies who sells, amongst others, P's policies. X, a company looking for insurance, employs R to find them the best policy. However, R does not receive payment from X. Rather, R receives a commission from P every time he sells one of P's policies.

---

[36]   Legislating the Criminal Code: Corruption (1998) Law Com No 248, para 5.99. The provision of this defence is open to the criticism that it thereby makes normal and indeed desirable conduct (paying one's employees) into a defence to a crime rather than excluding such conduct from the scope of the offence in the first place.

[37]   This is discussed in greater detail in Appendix F, paras F.38 to F.58.

In this example R has done an act (selling the insurance policy) and that act may be done *primarily* in return for the commission payment. Under the influence model, R is therefore likely to fall within the bribery offence even though he is operating in a highly regulated and generally accepted environment for selling insurance policies.[38]

4.106   Such a conclusion would not inevitably follow if, in order to be criminally liable, R had to breach a duty. The relevant duty would be that imposed by X and the regulators requiring R to act impartially. The question would be whether R, although acting primarily in return for the commission payment,[39] has also *breached* the duty to act impartially. On this basis, only those brokers who have sold a policy *not* believing it is in the best interests of X would be caught by the bribery offence.

4.107   As we indicate in Appendix E, this outcome accords with the new legislation governing fraud.[40] If, in Example 4J, R offered to sell X a policy but failed to disclose to X that he or she (R) did not believe that it was in X's best interests, or represented that it was in X's best interests when R knew that it was not, other things being equal, R would be guilty of fraud.

4.108   Apart from the criticisms arising from the proposed defences, a number of criticisms were made of the influence definition itself. Although the Government expressed support for the Commission's definition and incorporated it into their draft Corruption Bill,[41] due in part to this criticism the Government eventually decided not to present their draft Bill to Parliament. Many of these criticisms can be identified in the report of the Joint Committee[42] that was set up to evaluate the draft Bill.

4.109   A general criticism voiced by those who gave evidence to the Joint Committee was that the definition of 'corruptly' had become over-complicated and unclear.[43] The OECD, for example, commented that,

> The high-level, abstract language used is difficult to translate into concrete terms. This is especially so with regard to the key definition of 'corruptly', which seeks to define the mental element of the offence by reference to exceptions which are themselves unclear.[44]

---

[38]   Concern was expressed by consultees of the latest Government consultation that the defences available under the influence model (as defined in our Report) would fail to remove this type of arrangement from the offence.

[39]   In the sense that P is unlikely to have sold any policy at all had it not been for the expectation of some future payment.

[40]   See the Fraud Act 2006.

[41]   Raising Standards and Upholding Integrity: the Prevention of Corruption (2000) (Cm 4759), paras 2.4 to 2.7.

[42]   Joint Committee on the Draft Corruption Bill, Session 2002-2003, HL Paper 157, HC 705 (2003).

[43]   Above, para 26. Quoting the OECD's evidence – Ev 165 DCB 26 2(a) line 17-19.

[44]   Above.

With this same criticism in mind, the then Attorney General advocated a return to the 'breach of duty model' (in other words, the improper conduct model) in order to provide a greater degree of legal certainty.[45]

Conclusion

4.110 When evaluating the influence model one must accept that some elements of our previous report that have attracted criticism are nevertheless essential to it as a working policy. The influence model has some merit. However, we now believe that its defects outweigh its merits. In particular, in the absence of defences (which themselves have their own particular drawbacks), it is over-inclusive, and a narrower definition would be more desirable. In its evidence to the Joint Committee, the OECD observed:

> The intention of the UK legislative drafters seems to have been to construct an offence that is as broad as possible. This approach is certainly coherent, but it does not make for legislation which is clear and readily understandable to those charged with enforcing it.[46]

4.111 The improper conduct model offers an alternative explanation which, although originally rejected in our previous report, we now believe is, subject to refinement, capable of providing a secure foundation for a new bribery offence. It is significant that Transparency International's definition of 'improperly' (also based upon breach of duty) has gained wide support, including that of the All-Party-Panel.[47]

4.112 The breach of duty formulation is also the preferred option in many of the international Conventions to which the UK is a signatory.[48] As the Government noted in their reply to the Joint Committee that considered the draft Corruption Bill,[49] the breach of duty model is the preferred version in all the international instruments that address the private sector. Beyond this, we also believe that if the improper conduct model is formulated in the way we are proposing, it will also satisfy the UK's international commitments in relation to public sector bribery.[50]

4.113 In conclusion, the simplest course is to revert to the impersonal/duty permutation, i.e. the improper conduct model. That is to say, bribery consists of a payment or other benefit calculated to induce the recipient to breach a legal or equitable duty or to reward the recipient for so doing. This definition may need refining at certain points, for example to clarify that the duty can be a secondary duty, such as a duty of impartiality in the exercise of functions, rather than the primary function which the recipient is there to perform. These refinements are minor and

---

[45] Above, para 74.

[46] Above, para 19.

[47] Consultation on Bribery: Reform of the Prevention of Corruption Acts and SFO Powers in Cases of Bribery of Foreign Officials: Summary of responses and next steps (2007), para 30.

[48] For discussion of the International Conventions, see Appendix A below.

[49] The Government Reply to the Report from the Joint Committee on the Draft Corruption Bill, Session 2002-2003, HL Paper 157, HC 705 (2003) Cm 6086, para 4.

[50] See Appendix G.

straightforward compared with those necessary to make the influence model work. They are discussed further in Parts 5 and 6.

Provisional proposal

4.114 **We provisionally propose that the making or acceptance of a payment to influence the recipient in the performance of his or her duties should not, without more, constitute a bribery offence.**

THE IMPROPER CONDUCT MODEL

4.115 The improper conduct model focuses on the conduct of the recipient. Like the improper influence model, it avoids the inherent complications of the principal and agent model. In addition, there is no need for a defence of consent. However, as in the improper influence model, the open textured nature of 'improper' means that the model risks casting the net of criminality too wide.

4.116 As explained, it differs from the improper influence model in two respects.

(1) It requires that the favour sought from the recipient be improper. It is not sufficient that the payment is one that ought not to have been made, or that the recipient is improperly influenced by that payment.

(2) In the pure form of the model, there is no requirement that the conduct of the recipient be influenced by the payment: for example, the payment could be a reward conferred afterwards. One question for consideration is whether to adopt the model in its pure form or to opt for a hybrid form in which influence as well as improper conduct plays a part.

4.117 Impropriety, in this context, may be defined as a breach of a duty owed by the recipient. There are two possible flaws in the model, though these may be reasons to refine the definition rather than to reject it altogether.

(1) In one respect, the model may be under-inclusive. There are instances, under the general heading of "payment to do the right thing", where the action of the recipient is perfectly legal but may still be regarded as corrupt when done in return for payment.

(2) Conversely, if all types of duty are included, the model may be over-inclusive. For example paying someone to commit a murder is an offence of incitement but would not normally be regarded as bribery.

We discuss both these dangers below.[51]

An example of the improper conduct model

4.118 One form of this model is that used in the Bill[52] currently before Parliament, which follows the suggestions of Transparency International ("the TI Bill").

4.119 The definitions of the main offences in the TI Bill are as follows.

---

[51] See para 4.129 and following.

[52] HL Bill 18.

1.—(1) A person commits an offence if he—

> (a) gives an advantage to or procures an advantage for any person, or

> (b) offers or agrees to give an advantage to or to procure an advantage for any person

with the intention of influencing that person or another person to exercise a function improperly or as a reward for so exercising a function.

(2) A person commits an offence if he—

> (a) obtains an advantage for himself or another person, or

> (b) solicits or agrees to obtain an advantage for himself or another person

on the basis that it will or may influence him or another person to exercise a function improperly or as a reward for so exercising a function.

4.120　In the Bill, 'improperly' is defined widely:[53]

> a breach of duty, whether express or implied, and whether private or public in nature, including any duty to act in good faith or impartially.

Our previous proposal

4.121　In our previous CP, we provisionally proposed that acting corruptly should be defined in terms of inducing another person to breach his or her duty.[54]

4.122　We first identified the central harm, or 'fundamental mischief', that corruption was trying to prevent as a breach of duty.[55] However, we concluded that this alone was not enough to justify invoking the criminal law. Criminalising every breach of duty would be unduly draconian and would not reflect society's common understanding of corruption.[56] Rather, it was the role of the third party in inducing the breach through the conferral of an advantage that distinguished corruption and justified the imposition of criminal liability.[57]

4.123　Our provisional proposal was that an advantage would be conferred or accepted 'corruptly' if:

---

[53]　TI Bill, cl 7.

[54]　Legislating the Criminal Code: Corruption (1997) Law Commission Consultation Paper No 145, para 5.17.

[55]　Above, Part V.

[56]　Above, para 5.4.

[57]　Above, para 5.17.

(1)   it was an inducement to an agent to act or refrain from acting *in breach of duty* or was a reward for an agent's so acting or refraining from so acting; or

(2)   it was an inducement to an agent to act or refrain from acting *in any way*, or a reward for an agent's so acting or refraining, *provided* that the transaction has a substantial tendency to encourage that agent, or others in comparable positions, to act in breach of duty.[58]

Criticisms of our proposal

4.124   Several criticisms of the breach of duty model emerged during the consultation process.[59] First, there were conceptual difficulties about what kinds of duty were covered. Secondly, there could be practical and evidential difficulty in determining whether a duty existed, and whether it was breached, in a particular case. The criminal courts would therefore be required to consider many questions which properly belong to civil law. These criticisms influenced the Commission to conclude that an alternative definition of 'corruptly' was more desirable.

4.125   Although the Commission acknowledged these criticisms, it was eventually convinced to abandon the breach of duty model by a more "fundamental objection".[60] This objection related to the way the model dealt with those defendants who, as in Example 4G above, were bribed to do that which they were already obliged to do. The Commission did not believe that such conduct constituted a breach of duty. Rather, it created an *incentive* to breach a duty in the future: if R is consistently given money, he or she is more likely to refuse to comply with his or her duty in the future if the money is no longer provided.[61] The second part of the Commission's provisional proposal[62] was designed to capture such cases.

4.126   The majority of consultees objected to this second limb of the breach of duty model. This was not because they viewed the conduct illustrated in Example 4G as lacking a corrupt element,[63] but rather that they felt the vague language of the test would lead to significant problems. Particularly, issue was taken with the idea of a "substantial tendency". It was a concept which may be difficult to prove but, more importantly, it may result in individuals being convicted of corruption despite neither intending nor being aware that their conduct had the 'tendency' to influence third parties.[64]

4.127   The Commission reasoned that the second part of the definition of 'corruptly' was essential to the breach of duty model. Therefore, with a rejection of the second

[58]   Above, para 8.20.

[59]   Critics included the Financial Law Panel, the Bar Council and the Criminal Bar Association, the Serious Fraud Office, the Strategic Investment Board, Professor G R Sullivan and the Metropolitan Police Company Fraud Department.

[60]   Legislating the Criminal Code: Corruption (1997) Law Commission Consultation Paper No 145, para 5.8.

[61]   Above, paras 8.12 to 8.13.

[62]   Above, para 8.20.

[63]   Legislating the Criminal Code: Corruption (1998) Law Com No 248, para 5.71.

part of the definition of 'corruptly', came the rejection of the breach of duty model altogether.

4.128　However, given the problems since identified in the improper influence model, we need to consider the breach of duty/improper conduct model once more. The question is whether that model can be refined so as to overcome the criticisms which have been made.

Under-inclusive: payment to do the right thing?

4.129　The main criticism of the improper conduct model is that in many cases the thing which the recipient is bribed to do is in itself perfectly proper, and that it is only the fact that it forms part of a corrupt bargain that makes it wrong. A model based on improper conduct, narrowly interpreted, would therefore be under-inclusive. On the other hand, if "impropriety" were defined so as to include the fact of being performed in return for payment, that would either make the definition circular or lead back to the improper payment or improper influence model.

4.130　As we have seen, however, the improper influence model has been criticised as over-inclusive, precisely because it covers instances of "payment to do the right thing" which are not necessarily corrupt.

4.131　If a model which excludes payments to do the right thing is too narrow and a model which includes them is too broad, we appear to have the makings of a deadlock. Any way out must include a test to distinguish clearly between acceptable and unacceptable instances of such payments.

4.132　One such test has been suggested above.[65] A judge who receives a payment in return for a judgment that happens to be correct is corrupt, not because payment to do the right thing is always wrong but because in this instance there is a special duty of impartiality. Considerations of this kind led the draft Bill to speak of "a breach of duty, whether express or implied, and whether private or public in nature, *including any duty to act in good faith or impartially*".

4.133　In other words, the duty in question is not confined to the primary duty which the recipient is there to perform but extends to secondary duties concerning the way in which he or she does so. To the extent that these secondary duties relate to good faith or impartiality they will usually fall within the description "equitable duties". This modification appears to meet the objection of under-inclusivity. It also avoids the need for a second branch of the definition, relating to payments having a substantial tendency to induce breaches of duty in the future.

[64]　Above, para 5.70.

[65]　See para 4.78 above.

Over-inclusive: what duties should be included?

4.134 The discussion of the principal and agent model concluded that a definition of bribery confined to the betrayal of a duty owed by an agent to a principal would be too narrow. However, it might be that expanding this to cover every duty recognised by the law would be too great a leap. For example, everyone has a duty not to commit criminal offences, and most people are from time to time subject to various tortious and contractual duties of care. Breaching these duties in return for pecuniary advantage is reprehensible but would not normally be regarded as bribery.

4.135 This question is discussed in full in Part 5 below. Briefly, we conclude that it is not every breach of a legal duty (in return for an advantage) that should engage the law of bribery. The approach in the TI Bill, taken a little further, suggests the makings of an answer. Instead of covering every duty, *including* a duty to act impartially or in good faith, it should cover every duty, *so far as* it requires one to act impartially or in good faith.

4.136 However, in Part 5 below we conclude that the reference in the TI Bill to "good faith" is vague and unsatisfactory. In the final form of the test that we are provisionally proposing, there are two requirements. First, there must be a breach of a duty recognised by law. Secondly, that breach must either betray a relation of trust or breach a duty to act impartially or in the best interests of another person.

Gifts after the event: whether to retain influence test

4.137 In paragraph 4.116, we saw that there is a choice between a hybrid model, in which the payment must influence the recipient to act improperly, and a "pure" improper conduct model in which influence is not crucial.

4.138 The difference between the two is that, on the hybrid model, a gift made after the event that is unsolicited, not promised and unexpected is not a bribe (since the gift does not influence the recipient, who has already acted improperly). It could be argued, in favour of the pure improper conduct model, that such conduct should be criminal because it sends a message to the recipient, and to others in the same position, that future decisions favourable to the payer might be rewarded with further gifts.

4.139 Another argument might be made for the sake of symmetry: where a person acts improperly in order to influence a person to make a payment or confer an advantage, this should be just as criminal as the opposite permutation. Or, if it is not, this should be because the recipient lacks the requisite mental element, rather than because there is no act of bribery on the part of the payer.[66]

4.140 In both cases, the issue often concerns a link perceived by the payer or recipient, rather than a link existing objectively. Accordingly, there may be cases where the conduct of one party amounts to bribery while the other is innocent. This issue properly belongs to consideration of the fault element of the offence and is discussed in Part 6 below.

---

[66] This question is discussed in full in Part 6, paras 6.37 to 6.47 below.

4.141   Once it is fully demonstrated that there is a link between the payment and the conduct in the mind of the defendant, the question of whether there is an objective link, or a link in the mind of the other party, is comparatively unimportant. It may be best for the conduct element of the offence to incorporate some neutral expression, such as a payment made "in connection with" the improper conduct, while providing fully for a fault element that includes the necessary mental nexus.

4.142   In conclusion, in defining the conduct element of the defence, we prefer the "pure" improper conduct model. The question of influence will reappear in the definition of the fault element.

Provisional proposal

4.143   **We provisionally propose that the conduct element of bribery should exist where an advantage is conferred, promised, received or solicited in connection with an improper act performed or promised by or solicited from the recipient.**

4.144   Part 5 will contain more detailed proposals for the conduct element of the offence or offences, including the definitions of "improper act" and "advantage". Part 6 will consider the fault element.

PART 5
THE CONDUCT ELEMENT OF THE NEW BRIBERY OFFENCE

INTRODUCTION

5.1 As we have already made clear, we are proposing that there should be two separate bribery offences. The principal offence will apply generally. We consider this offence in this Part and in Part 6. However, in addition, we are provisionally proposing to supplement the general offence by the creation of a new and separate offence to deal specifically with the bribery of a foreign public official. We consider that offence in Part 7.

The structure of Parts 5 and 6

5.2 Although there may be some overlap, we have decided to split our discussion of the general offence into two. Part 5 will deal with the conduct element of bribery: the physical actions that constitute the offence. Part 6 will deal with the fault element of bribery: the state of mind that must accompany the actions in order to bring the payer or recipient within the offence.

5.3 We also believe it would be useful to sub-divide our discussion further. Bribery is most commonly presented as a criminal arrangement or even a criminal agreement between two separate individuals. However, under the current law and under our provisional proposals it will remain possible for one party to commit the offence even though the other party does not. In order to reflect this, we intend to discuss both the conduct and the fault elements separately in relation to the recipient (R) and the payer (P).

Core concepts

5.4 In order to begin constructing an offence of bribery, it is necessary to identify what should be the core elements of the offence. Following our discussion in Part 4, in any case of bribery there must be two elements:

   (1)   an advantage conferred or promised by, or received or solicited from, P;

   (2)   an improper act or omission performed or promised by, or solicited from, R.[1]

5.5 We begin by considering the meaning of 'improper conduct'[2] and 'advantage'.[3] We then proceed to consider the position of P and R separately in relation to these elements,[4] in order to build up a definition of the conduct element of a bribery offence. The position of P and R will also need to be considered

---

[1]   As will become apparent, the order in which these two components come is interchangeable.

[2]   See para 5.6 and following.

[3]   See para 5.56 and following.

[4]   See para 5.65 and following.

separately when we come to consider the fault element in Part 6, as there will be cases where one party has a corrupt intention though the other is behaving perfectly properly.

IMPROPER CONDUCT

Introduction

5.6 A workable definition of 'improper' is essential to the reform of bribery. In some respects, the problems in defining 'improper' are equivalent to those encountered in the discussion of 'corruptly' in our previous report. Those problems mainly fell into two areas.

(1) For the overall transaction, or the defendant's part in it, to be "corrupt", to what feature of the transaction must the requirement of impropriety attach?

(2) Of what does the requirement of impropriety consist?

5.7 The first question has been discussed at length in Part 4. We raised the question whether the requirement of "impropriety" should attach to the payment, the favour or the relationship between the two, and we decided that it should attach to the favour. We therefore turn to the second question, of how to define impropriety.

5.8 In arriving at a definition, there are two fairly obvious dangers to avoid.

(1) First, the definition must not be over-inclusive. It should not be so broad as to encompass conduct that, whilst immoral, involves no harm or threat of harm worthy of criminalisation. Further, it should not extend so widely that it encompasses harms best dealt with by other criminal offences, or by means other than criminal sanction.

(2) Secondly, it must avoid being under-inclusive, failing to catch conduct that should clearly be criminalised as bribery.

Using "improperly" without defining it

5.9 One possibility is to speak of "improperly" or "improper conduct" without defining it. This is similar to the use of "corruptly" in existing law. Certain commentators still believe that 'corruptly' (or 'improperly') should be left undefined.[5]

5.10 In our previous CP and report, we criticised the lack of definition in the existing law and highlighted the "impressive disarray"[6] caused by conflicting common law interpretations.

5.11 In *Cooper v Slade*[7], a majority of the House of Lords agreed that 'corruptly' amounted to "purposely doing an act which the law forbids as tending to corrupt".

---

[5] This was noted in para 5.63 of Law Com No 248. It was also noted in the Government's response to their 2005 consultation – Consultation on bribery: Reform of the Prevention of Corruption Acts and SFO powers in Cases of Bribery of Foreign Officials: Summary of responses and next steps (2007) paras 13 to 23.

[6] D Lanham, "Bribery and Corruption" *Essays in honour of J C Smith* (1987) 92, 104.

This rather circular definition left the question still very much open. In the *Bradford Election Case (No 2)*[8] by contrast, Martin B held that 'corruptly' should be defined and he described it as akin to an 'evil mind'. More recently, Pearce J directed the jury in *Lindley*[9] that 'corruptly' required the *dishonest* transfer of loyalty from an individual's master to the defendant. However, the most recent case law has once again established that corruption is not an offence of dishonesty.[10]

5.12   Repeatedly, in the course of consultations, there has been criticism of the uncertainty associated with the meaning of the word. In our previous report, we concluded that the lack of definition was "one of the most important defects of the present law"[11] and that a definition was therefore an essential element of reform. We remain of this view.

Purely moral duties

5.13   If left undefined, 'corruptly' (or 'improperly') does not automatically require there to be anything other than a moral duty to act or refrain from acting. For example:

Example 5A

R is meant to be chaperoning his younger sister (aged 16) at a party. P, a friend of R who is already dating R's older sister, pays R to leave his younger sister alone for a time so that he (P) can attempt to persuade her to have sexual intercourse with him.

The conduct of both P and R may be morally wrong, but we believe that the criminal law would overstep its bounds if it encroached so far into an individual's freedom to act as to regard their conduct as criminal bribery.

5.14   Although most commentators accept that bribery should not be defined in such a way that it punishes immorality as such, some commentators nonetheless argue that moral considerations should affect the scope of bribery with the ability to 'trump' legal ones. For example, it has been contended that those detained in concentration camps during the Second World War would not have committed bribery when they paid their guards to free them even if their guards' conduct had amounted to the breach of a legal duty.[12] A similar contention might also extend to certain extreme groups of animal rights protesters who would surely not

---

[7]   [1857] HL Case 746; 10 ER 1488.

[8]   (1869) 19 LT 723, 728.

[9]   [1957] *Criminal Law Review* 321.

[10]   *Harvey* (1999) *Criminal Law Review* 70.

[11]   Legislating the Criminal Code: Corruption (1998) Law Com No 248, para 5.65.

[12]   Green *Lying, cheating and stealing – A moral theory of white collar crime* (2006) 206 – 207. Green contends that this example should not be seen as bribery because, although the guard has a legal duty to the Nazi officials, "one cannot be loyal in the moral sense to a thoroughly evil principal".

consider it bribery to pay a laboratory technician to let out animals from a laboratory where they are being subjected to suffering in the cause of research.

5.15 Whatever the merits of this view, its adoption would be at the expense of a great deal of legal certainty. This is most obviously so where it is suggested that an (allegedly) superior moral duty should trump a legal duty. The difficulty is that in many contexts it will be very unlikely that throughout society there will be a consensus as to whether (and when) a moral duty is superior to a legal duty.

Provisional proposal

5.16 **We provisionally propose that the scope of improper conduct:**

   (1)   should not be extended to cases of non-justiciable moral duties; and

   (2)   should not be restricted so as to exclude cases where breach of a legal duty is considered morally justifiable.

Legal and equitable duties

5.17 So far as the discussion has gone, improper conduct must be restricted to the breach of a duty recognised by the law. This should not be restricted to duties imposed by statute: duties arising from obligation-creating conduct of the parties, such as the making of binding contracts or trusts, should also be included. We also wish to avoid any confusion arising from the narrower sense of "law" as opposed to equity. Although appropriate wording is always a matter for Parliamentary Counsel, a definition in terms of breach of a legal *or* equitable duty would do something to avoid such confusion.

The duty of impartiality

5.18 The criticism that led to the Law Commission's rejection of the breach of duty model was that it failed to cover defendants bribed 'to do the right thing'.[13] As in Example 4G above, this is where an advantage is conferred but it does not change R's behaviour in relation to his or her duty. An alternative example is where R has to choose between two equally good options and is swayed to choose one of them because of a bribe. In each case, it was contended, no duty was breached because R was not induced to do something that he or she would not have done anyway.[14]

5.19 We are still of the opinion that such behaviour should be caught by a new bribery offence. However, we believe that the fuller account of breach of duty that we are proposing in this paper, based upon a breach of legal or equitable duty, will be able to deal with most of these cases. This is because, although the outcome of the decision does not indicate a breach of duty, R, by basing his or her decision on the advantage offered, is breaching a duty to act impartially. This breach of duty, as in Example 4G, would constitute improper conduct.

---

[13] See Part 4, paras 4.125 to 4.127 above.

[14] This led to the separate provision in our previous CP that addressed acts which encourage future breaches of duty. See Part 4, para 4.123 above.

5.20 It is important to understand why being induced to 'do the right thing' in breach of duty (which we believe should amount to bribery) differs from the receipt of commission payments, discussed above,[15] which we believe should not be bribery. In the case of commission payments, though the commission is the motive for the agent's *action*, it is not the motive for the agent's initial *choice*, as the agent would get commission whichever supplier was chosen. There is therefore no breach of the duty to act impartially or of the duty to act in the interests of the client. There would be a breach if the agent deliberately chose the most expensive supplier in order to maximise the commission, even if the choice of that supplier could be justified on other grounds.

5.21 We believe that the duty of impartiality in such cases is covered by the notion of legal or equitable duty. However, to make it absolutely clear, a possibility would be to use a formulation similar to that in the TI Bill,[16] where clause 7(c) provides that:

> 'Improperly' means a breach of any duty, whether express or implied, and whether of a public or a private nature, including any duty to act in good faith or impartially.

Practical difficulties

5.22 The first criticism made in response to our previous CP related to the conceptual difficulty of defining a duty. We believe that this criticism is overstated. We believe that a formulation such as a 'breach of legal or equitable duty' uses concepts with which the courts are familiar, and would enable them to meet the need for the certainty and predictability that is required in the definition of an offence such as bribery. At the same time, extending the concept of duty to encompass equitable duties, whilst retaining the virtue of a high degree of certainty in application, would enable the courts to interpret the offence in such a way that it could keep pace with developments in commercial law and practice more generally.[17]

5.23 The second criticism focused on the practical and evidential difficulties of ascertaining a breach of duty. The Strategic Investment Board, for example, pointed out that a court would have to determine first whether a duty was owed and secondly whether it was breached. Both questions, they contended, would slow down trials and would be better suited to the civil law.[18] Beyond this, the Bar Council and the Criminal Bar Association said that juries would be ill-equipped to second guess the decisions of agents (in order to identify a breach of duty) in complicated cases.

---

[15] See Part 4, paras 4.105 to 4.107 above. The receipt of a commission payment will not be a form of bribery unless R intends to sell the relevant policy to people irrespective of whether it is in their best interests to buy it. See Appendix F, paras F.38 to F.58.

[16] Corruption Bill, HL18.

[17] P J Millett, "Equity's place in the law of commerce" (1998) 114 *Law Quarterly Review* 214

[18] Legislating the Criminal Code: Corruption (1998) Law Com No 248, para 5.5.

5.24 We do not see this criticism as fatal.[19] It is already the case that juries sometimes have to decide whether a legal duty has been breached: gross negligence manslaughter is an example. It will be the role of the court through the guidance of the trial judge (assisted by expert evidence where relevant) to aid the jury in their task.

5.25 Later on in this Part we consider whether all breaches of a legal or equitable duty should be covered, and conclude that there is a need for some limitations.[20] The proposed limitations narrow the field so much that, once a case falls within them, establishing the existence of a duty, and a breach of that duty, should not normally involve questions of legal difficulty.

5.26 The meaning of legal or equitable duty, and whether a given set of facts to be ascertained by the jury falls within the description, will of course be a question of law for the judge. This will not always be true of the question of whether a duty has been breached: for example, if the duty is one of care and the question is one of fact and degree.

Recipient's belief in breach of duty

5.27 In our previous Report, the Commission mooted the idea that the offence of bribery could be extended to include cases where R did not act in breach of duty but *believed* that he or she had done so.[21] Such an extension would remove the perceived problem of juries being unable to decide whether a legal duty had been breached. This is because a jury could be invited to look at other factors (for example, whether the advantage was received covertly) in determining whether the recipient, R, believed that he or she would be acting in breach of duty. If the jury found that R had such a belief, R would be liable whether or not there was a breach of duty.

5.28 Although it is a policy that might seem attractive at first glance, we do not believe such an extension of the law of bribery is either desirable or necessary. It is not desirable because we believe that for R to be guilty of the full offence of bribery he or she should have performed or promised an objectively improper act.[22] It is not necessary because if R believes that he or she is being induced to breach a duty, even if he or she is not breaching a duty in fact, R will be guilty of attempted bribery. This will be true in the same way that an individual who believes they are handling stolen goods will be guilty of attempting to handle stolen goods, even if it turns out that the goods are not stolen. If guilty of attempted bribery, R will be

---

[19] See para 5.22 above.

[20] Specifically, that any breach must also constitute breach of a relation of trust or of a duty to act impartially or in the best interests of another – see para 5.48 below.

[21] This was in response to the criticisms of our previous CP. However, we eventually concluded that our response was insufficient due to the more serious issue of under-inclusiveness within the policy. See Legislating the Criminal Code: Corruption (1998) Law Com No 248, paras 5.7 to 5.8.

[22] Or, intending to do so, to have represented that he or she will do an improper act in the future: see paras 5.67 to 5.70 below.

potentially liable to the same punishment as if he or she had committed the full offence.[23]

What kind of duty?

5.29 The next question is whether every breach of a legal or equitable duty, if performed in return for an advantage, should qualify as bribery or whether there is a need for some further limitation. We shall consider different types of duty in turn.

Crime

5.30 One obvious category of duty is the duty not to break the criminal law.

Example 5B

P pays R, a professional 'hitman', to murder V. R does so.

P's conduct is of course criminal, as it amounts to incitement to murder. However, it would not normally be regarded as a form of bribery, even though R is being asked to breach a legal duty. Similarly R is guilty of murder, but the offence should not take on an entirely different legal character (bribery) simply because it was done for money. Contrast:

Example 5C

R is a doctor or nurse in charge of caring for V. P pays him to withdraw a life-saving treatment from V.

This clearly amounts to bribery, whatever other offences may be involved. The difference is that here R is in a position of trust and is in breach of a paramount duty (under a code of professional ethics) to protect the best interests of the patient.

5.31 It could be queried whether there is any harm in the bribery offence being extended beyond its natural boundaries, given that the area of extension is already covered by the criminal law. We believe that this would be undesirable, both because the area of extension would be enormous and because it leads to inappropriate labelling of offenders if a crime is extended too far beyond its natural meaning.

Tort

5.32 Equally, it is not clear that breaking a duty within the law of tort, such as a duty of care, in return for an advantage, should always be bribery.

---

[23] Criminal Attempts Act 1981, s 4.

> **Example 5D**
>
> R owns a field in which he keeps a bull. P, an adjoining occupier, pays R to remove or lower a fence, in order to preserve the light and prospect that P's property enjoys. P does so even though he realises that the bull might escape. The bull escapes and tramples a child.

We believe that this would not normally be regarded as bribery. R's act is reprehensible and tortious, but it should not become criminal simply because it was done for financial reward. It would have been as bad if done at P's simple request, or to preserve R's own light and prospect. Similarly, it should not be bribery to pay for the insertion of a libellous advertisement in a newspaper.

5.33 This should be contrasted with cases involving an element of trust or loyalty, such as bribing a doctor or a financial adviser. Here there is a duty of disinterestedness and the very idea of the doctor or adviser making a profit (other than the normal remuneration) out of his or her position is a kind of betrayal, which adds the extra dimension to the misconduct in question that makes it right to regard it as bribery.

5.34 It appears from these examples that the commission of a crime or a tort should only constitute "improper conduct" for the purpose of defining bribery where they involve a breach of some kind of duty of loyalty or impartiality, going beyond the normal duty not to commit crimes or torts.

5.35 The current Bill, as sponsored by TI, speaks of "any legal or equitable duty, *including* a duty to act impartially or in good faith". So far as crime and tort are concerned, it might be more accurate to speak of "any legal or equitable duty, *so far as* it includes a duty to act impartially or in good faith".

5.36 The reference to "good faith" should perhaps be treated as a placeholder, to be superseded by a more precise formulation when we have considered some more examples. Good faith has a precise meaning in insurance law (a duty of total disclosure) and another meaning in administrative law (a duty to decide properly without allowing for personal or extraneous factors), but outside these contexts it is loose and rhetorical. The flavour is one of acting disinterestedly for the sake of some person or duty, or of something being what it purports to be.

Contract

5.37 Very often, the duty betrayed in a case of bribery is one arising out of a contract, especially a contract of employment. The question arises whether, for the purposes of defining bribery, these duties need to be limited in the same way as duties under criminal or tort law. In other words, does every contractual term requiring some (in)action necessarily involve a duty of loyalty or a duty to act exclusively in someone's best interests, making an express limitation to this effect unnecessary?

5.38 There will generally be bribery where the breach of contract is also a breach of professional standards, because that will almost always involve a breach of a duty to act in the best interests of another person, such as a patient in this example:

The same will be true where an investment company secretly pays a financial adviser or trustee to invest in its funds, except in cases where the payment is a standard commission which would equally have been payable by any other investment company. In such cases, R breaches a duty to act in someone else's best interests, abusing the role they were entrusted to fulfil in that regard.

5.39 The next question is how this approach applies to other contractual situations.

5.40 Not everything an employee does must be done with only the best interests of the employer in mind. For example, it may be in the best interests of the employer for the employee to work extra hours. This does not in itself impose any obligation or expectation on the employee to do so.

5.41 Another example is where an employee or contractor is in breach of a contractual duty of care. The reasoning here is similar to that in tort cases (Example 5D): the breach does not become a betrayal of the employer or other contracting party simply because it was in return for money. On the other hand, it might become so if the duty of care is connected with an area of the employee's special responsibility towards the employer, or concerning which there is otherwise an express or implied duty to do the best for the employer:

This is bribery because, where the maintenance of confidentiality is concerned, R has a duty selflessly to look after Z Ltd's best interests. R's breach of duty therefore contains the vital element of abuse of position. Contrast:

This is not bribery because it does not involve any respect in which R is under a duty selflessly to promote Z Ltd's best interests. Although R has let Z Ltd down in breaching his contract, there is not the element of abuse of position in relation to Z Ltd's best interests that there is in Example 5F.

5.42 The common feature is that there is always bribery when the employee is betraying a trust inherent in his or her position: for example, if the employee is paid to divulge the employer's secrets. That does not mean that employees will have to be divided into "trusted" and "non-trusted" categories. Rather, one looks at the individual term breached and decides whether it amounts to an abuse of trust or position, involving a breach of duty to safeguard someone's best interests. ("Trust" here is used in a strong sense, involving loyalty and disinterestedness. We do not mean the minimal sense in which every employee is trusted to do the job at all).

5.43 There will of course be grey areas.

Example 5H

P pays R, an employee of V Ltd, to introduce a virus into V Ltd's computer system.

This is certainly bribery if R works in the IT department. It is arguably bribery if R is an authorised user, as R is trusted to use the system properly. It will also be bribery, regardless of R's area of duty, if the virus is spyware which will send confidential data to P. Contrast:

Example 5J

P pays R, an employee of V Ltd, to do private work for P involving word processing, using V Ltd's computer system, in breach of the rule that the system must be used only for V Ltd's work purposes.

This is misconduct within the terms of employment but scarcely bribery.

5.44 This does not affect the validity of the general proposition that there is bribery when there is breach of trust. The uncertainty about whether there is bribery on the facts is the same as the uncertainty about whether there is breach of trust on the facts. This supports rather than undermines the equation between the two.

5.45 In conclusion not every breach of a contractual duty or a duty under an employment contract in return for an advantage is bribery. However, the test for distinguishing relevant breaches is not exactly the same as the "impartially or in good faith" mentioned in the TI Bill, and tentatively suggested for crime and tort cases. Rather it is the breach of any duty to act disinterestedly or in the best interests of another person, or of any duty arising from a position or relation of trust.

Public office

5.46 The analogous series of questions arises where the duty is not contractual but arises out of a public office, and can be answered in much the same way.

> **Example 5K**
>
> P, a civil servant who has lost his or her own office key, pays R, a fellow civil servant, to lend P the key to the office, contrary to an office rule against lending meant to reduce numbers of lost keys, to enable P to work at the weekend.

This is not bribery, but only a breach of the office rules on R's part. As in Example 5G, although R has let his or her employer down by breaching the contract, the breach does not concern a rule requiring R selflessly to act in his or her employer's best interests. Contrast the following:

> **Example 5L**
>
> P, an investigative journalist, pays R, a civil servant, to lend P the key to the office so that P can copy confidential files.

This is clearly bribery, as it is a betrayal of a respect in which R is meant to act only in the interests of the employer, by maintaining the confidentiality of documents. It is the reason that the rule comes to be breached – abuse of position – rather than the breach of the rule in itself (prohibiting the lending of keys) that makes R's conduct "improper" and hence bribery.

Conclusion

5.47 Bribery, then, can involve the breach of (a) any duty arising from a public position (b) any duty under a contract or trust and (c) any other duty, legal or equitable (such as under the criminal law or the law of tort). Whether these should be itemised like that, or be expressed as a legal or equitable duty without particularising further, is a drafting question that can be considered at a later stage.

5.48 However, in each of these cases, the breach amounts to bribery only insofar as the breach contravenes an obligation to act impartially or in the best interests of another person, or insofar as it amounts to abuse of the trust inherent in that position of duty.

5.49 This conclusion makes some concession to the principal and agent model, by taking a middle position between "duties owed to a principal" and "all duties recognised by law". It has the advantage of incorporating that model's focus on trust or loyalty so as to coincide with the normal understanding of bribery, while avoiding the artificiality of having to identify a principal in every case.

Provisional proposal

5.50 **We provisionally propose that an improper act, for the purposes of the definition of bribery offences:**

   (1) **must be a breach of a legal or equitable duty; and**

   (2) **must involve betrayal of a relation of trust, or breach of a duty to act impartially or in the best interests of another.**

5.51 The trust/impartiality/best interests trio is there to give the flavour, rather than being a precise draft. It is possible that in any draft statute these three alternatives could be reduced to two or even to one: for example, if we are certain that every relation of trust necessarily involves the duty to act in the best interests of another.

Question for consultees

5.52 **As a way of narrowing the scope of 'improper conduct', is the limitation to cases involving a breach of a relation of trust, a breach of a duty of impartiality or a breach of a duty to act in the best interests of another the best that can be devised, or can it be simplified?**

5.53 The presence of one of these duties will normally be a question of law for the judge, even though the question of whether such a duty existed may involve the judge in the determination of some questions of fact.

5.54 As with all the other models, the question arises whether there should be a defence of consent. There may well be no "principal" in the case, as the duty of impartiality may be owed to many. For there to be a defence, there would have to be a limited number of victims, all of whom consent. In our opinion this result will in any case emerge from the general principles of criminal law and need not be stated specifically in the definition of the bribery offence. The question is dealt with in more detail in Part 8.

Practicality and the bribery of foreign public officials

5.55 For the reason set out above, we believe that the improper conduct model, based upon the breach of a legal or equitable duty, is equipped to deal with the criticisms relating to practicality. However, we are not convinced that this is so in cases involving the bribery of foreign public officials. The courts are well equipped to identify domestic legal or equitable duties, and likewise in relation to international commerce. However, we believe that having to prove the breach of a legal or equitable duty by those working in the public sector in other jurisdictions (that may well be resisting the investigation) would create an unacceptable burden. We are therefore provisionally proposing that a separate bribery offence should be created to deal with this specific issue.[24]

DEFINING AN 'ADVANTAGE'

5.56 In this section we consider whether the inducement conferred by P to R should have to take any particular form. It is a matter that was dealt with in some detail in our previous CP[25] and report.[26] It has given rise to very little controversy.

5.57 Section 1 of the 1889 Act refers to the offer or acceptance of "any gift, loan, fee, reward or advantage" whereas the 1906 Act refers to "any gift or consideration".

---

[24] For discussion of this separate offence, see Part 7.

[25] Legislating the Criminal Code: Corruption (1997) Law Commission Consultation Paper No. 145, paras 8.59 to 8.64.

[26] Legislating the Criminal Code: Corruption (1998) Law Com No. 248, paras 5.38 to 5.43.

5.58 In our previous report, we concluded that the language of the 1889 Act is slightly more expansive than that in the 1906 Act.[27] We also concluded (preferring the wider definition) that the term 'advantage' within the 1889 Act was able to do the work of the other terms. It was felt (and still is) that 'advantage' lends itself to a wide interpretation, capable of encompassing omissions as well as acts for example.

5.59 In addition, 'advantage' has been almost universally adopted in a host of Conventions that the UK has ratified. These include, for example, the OECD Convention against the Bribery of Foreign Public Officials, the United Nations Convention against Corruption and the Council of Europe's Criminal Law Convention against Corruption. This lends support to its employment in domestic legislation.

Provisional proposal[28]

5.60 **We provisionally propose that:**

    (1) **a person should be regarded as conferring an advantage if:**

        (a) **he or she does something (or omits to do something which he or she has the right to do), and**

        (b) **the act or omission is done or made in consequence of another's request (express or implied) or with the result (direct or indirect) that another benefits; and**

    (2) **a person should be regarded as obtaining an advantage if:**

        (a) **another does something (or omits to do something which he or she has the right to do), and**

        (b) **the act or omission is done or made in consequence of the first person's request (express or implied) or with the result (direct or indirect) that the first person benefits.**

5.61 Through this definition, we are able to demonstrate clearly the breadth of our interpretation. 'Advantage' should therefore be read to encompass both acts and omissions, in a situation where this is the request of P *or* is likely to benefit P.

---

[27] Above, 5.38.

[28] Our provisional proposal is quoted directly from the recommendation in our previous report. See Law Com No. 248, para 5.43.

An 'undue' advantage

5.62 Whilst adopting 'advantage', several of the international Conventions qualify it with the term 'undue'. In our previous report we did not do so and this attracted some criticism, notably from the Joint Committee.[29] However, this criticism has to be seen in the light of the offences that we were then recommending together with the defences that we were recommending in order to limit the scope of those offences. The Joint Committee highlighted the availability of 'undue advantage' (as opposed to 'advantage') as a better method of limiting the scope of the offences.

5.63 However, the Joint Committee quoted evidence received from the Confederation of British Industry that makes the point that other terms, including 'improperly', would be equally beneficial.[30] It is our view that the requirement of improper conduct, as we have defined it, can satisfy those concerns. On this basis, we believe that an additional requirement that the advantage should be 'undue' would complicate the definition by incorporating elements from the "improper payment" model.[31] This would not serve a useful purpose and may cause further problems.

Provisional proposal

5.64 **We provisionally propose that an advantage should not have to be 'undue' in order to come within the scope of the bribery offence that we are provisionally proposing.**

APPLYING THE TERMS

5.65 Having identified the core terms ("improper conduct" and "advantage") and made provisional proposals on how to define them, we are now able to start employing them to build a definition of the conduct element of bribery.

5.66 As previously mentioned, the liabilities of R and of P are entirely independent of one another. Therefore, we will assess the liability of each potential defendant separately. For convenience, we shall follow the terminology of the international conventions and speak of R's offence (receiving the advantage or engaging in the improper conduct) as passive bribery and P's offence (conferring the advantage or obtaining the improper conduct) as active bribery.

The recipient's conduct element

5.67 The central component of the conduct element in relation to the recipient (R), is the performance of an improper act, namely the breach of a legal or equitable duty, in such a way as to betray a relation of trust or infringe a duty to act impartially or in the best interests of another. In very many cases, it will therefore have to be demonstrated that R completed this act before R can satisfy the conduct element.

---

[29] Joint Committee on the Draft Corruption Bill, Session 2002-03 HL Paper 157, HC 705, paras 32 and 33.

[30] Above, para 33.

[31] See Part 4 paras 4.48 to 4.62 above.

Soliciting an advantage by representing a willingness to act improperly

5.68   However, under the current law, it is possible for R to satisfy the conduct element of bribery without having completed the principal act. In the 1889 Act, this is where R 'solicits, receives or agrees to receive' an advantage.[32] In the 1906 Act, this is where R 'accepts or obtains, or agrees to accept or attempts to obtain' an advantage.[33] In our previous CP, we concluded that the terms 'solicit' and 'agrees to obtain' were wide enough to encompass the other terms.[34] This was not challenged at consultation.[35]

5.69   We remain of the belief that an offence of bribery would be too narrowly defined if it did not encompass cases where R 'solicits' or 'agrees to obtain' an advantage from P by representing to P that he or she would be willing to act improperly. Providing that R genuinely intends to act, we do not believe that the nexus between the improper act and the conferral of the advantage will be broken.[36]

5.70   Arguably, this type of activity should be regarded as a criminal attempt. Taking this line would confine bribery to situations where R has acted improperly. However, the soliciting of an advantage will not necessarily amount to an act which is 'more than merely preparatory'[37] towards the commission of the full offence. As a result it would sit outside the scope of attempt. Admittedly, R could be liable for inciting P to commit bribery. However, we believe that in certain instances R's culpability can only be fairly reflected and labelled with a conviction for the full offence.[38] In that regard, we note that offences of fraud are now likewise defined in a partly inchoate mode.[39]

Provisional proposal

5.71   **We provisionally propose that the recipient should be regarded as satisfying the conduct element of bribery if he or she:**

   (1)   **acts improperly: in breach of a legal or equitable duty;[40] or**

   (2)   **represents a willingness to or agrees to act improperly.[41]**

---

[32]   1889 Act, s 1(1).

[33]   1906 Act, s 1(1).

[34]   Legislating the Criminal Code: Corruption (1997) Law Commission Consultation Paper No. 145, paras 8.66 and 8.67.

[35]   Legislating the Criminal Code: Corruption (1998) Law Com No. 248, para 5.52.

[36]   See our discussion of the fault element in Part 6.

[37]   Criminal Attempts Act 1981, s 1. Section 1(4)(a) also rules out the opportunity for convicting R for attempting to conspire to commit bribery.

[38]   For further discussion of this point, see Appendix E below.

[39]   Fraud Act 2006.

[40]   Subject to the limitation in para 5.48 above.

[41]   The requirement that this is done in order to solicit an advantage from P will be reflected in the fault element of the offence - see Part 6 below.

5.72   As articulated, our provisional proposal encompasses cases where, in exchange for or in anticipation of an advantage, R acts improperly or represents a willingness to do so.[42] However, there will be cases where, rather that doing or representing a willingness to do the improper act himself or herself, R seeks to influence a third party to do an improper act. In the next section we consider such cases.

Trading in influence

5.73   Trading in influence refers to cases where R in return for an advantage seeks to influence X to breach a legal or equitable duty. The question is whether such conduct on the part of R should satisfy the conduct element of the offence of bribery that we are provisionally proposing.

ILLUSTRATING THE PROBLEM

5.74   In our view, not all cases of trading in influence should constitute bribery:

Example 5M

P hates V and would like X to assault him. However, P realises that X is unlikely to accept the plan and so he pays R (X's girlfriend) to talk X into it.

If R were to encourage X to assault V, R would undoubtedly be breaching a legal duty, namely the duty not to encourage anyone to commit a criminal offence. However, the breach of duty would not involve R betraying a relationship of trust or a duty to act in the best interests of another. Accordingly, R should stand to be convicted of incitement to assault and P of inciting R to incite assault but neither R nor P should stand top be convicted of bribery. To alter the example slightly:

(1)   Suppose that X is V's personal bodyguard. Although X is in a position of trust in relation to V's security, it remains the case that R's breach of duty does not betray any relationship of trust or a duty to act in the best interests of another. Accordingly, again neither R nor P should stand to be convicted of bribery as opposed to incitement to commit assault.

(2)   Suppose instead that R is the person in a position of trust in relation to V. Here, R's act is at once a breach of duty (as it is the criminal offence of incitement) and a betrayal of her position of trust. Both P and R should stand to be convicted of bribery as well as incitement.

5.75   Another example involves a chain of bribery:

Example 5N

P is trying to set up a new business. In order to do so he needs a licence from X that he does not qualify for. P pays R for R in turn to pay X, so that X will grant the licence.

---

[42]   Provided that they satisfy the fault element – see Part 6 below.

In Example 5N, P has conferred an advantage on R in order to induce R to do the same for X (a chain of bribery). Bribery is and will remain a criminal offence. Therefore, by inducing R to commit bribery, P is inducing R to breach a legal duty. However, R is not in a position of trust so P should stand to be convicted not of bribery but of inciting R to commit bribery. By contrast, although guilty of active bribery in relation to X, R is not guilty of passive bribery in relation to P. Were R a public official in the same department as X, then all three parties would be guilty of bribery as principal offenders in their different ways.

5.76 Another example involves intermediaries:

> **Example 5P**
>
> P is trying to set up a new business. In order to do so he needs a licence from X that he does not qualify for. P pays R to find out whether X would accept a bribe and, if so, to act as a middleman for its payment.

In almost all cases like Example 5P, R will be guilty of the offence of inciting (encouraging) bribery.[43] The question is whether he or she should also be guilty of bribery as a principal offender. In our previous corruption project we had some difficulty with the question of intermediaries. In our previous CP, we concluded that R should not come within the bribery offence.[44] However, in our previous report we concluded that there were situations where he or she should.[45] If our analysis of Examples 5M and 5N is accepted, it follows that R should fall within the conduct element of bribery. As in Example 5N, R will be guilty of active bribery in relation to X, or of some inchoate offence of assisting and encouraging. R will not be guilty of passive bribery (in relation to P) unless R is also a public official.

5.77 However, in certain cases involving intermediaries, R may not be acting in exchange for payment from P. This may arise where R will benefit alongside P if the corrupt deal goes ahead. In this situation the essential nexus between the conferral of an advantage and the improper act (inciting bribery) will be broken. Therefore, R will only be guilty of inciting bribery and will not be guilty as a principal offender.

---

[43] To the extent that there is a problem under the current law, it relates to the lack of an inchoate offence alongside incitement to catch those individuals who assist (without encouraging) a criminal offence. In our Report on Inchoate Liability for Assisting and Encouraging Crime (2006) Law Com No. 300, we recommended that new inchoate offences should be created to criminalise acts of assistance. This recommendation has since been incorporated by the Government in the Serious Crime Act 2007, ss 44 to 46.

[44] Legislating the Criminal Code: Corruption (1997) Law Commission Consultation Paper No 145, paras, 8.78 and 8.79.

[45] Legislating the Criminal Code: Corruption (1998) Law Com No. 248, paras 5.48 to 5.50.

5.78   We believe that the results of our model in Examples 5M to 5P are reasonable.[46] The same cannot be said of our final example, which involves a pure trade in influence:

Example 5Q

P is trying to set up a new business. In order to do so he needs a licence from X that he does not qualify for. P pays R (X's wife) a considerable amount of money for her to convince her husband to act improperly and grant the licence.

In this example, X is not committing a criminal offence. He is breaching an equitable duty but, as he is not being induced to do so by the conferral of an advantage, he is not committing bribery, unless he has agreed to the payment being made to R in return for X granting the licence.

5.79   As X has not committed a criminal offence, R's use of influence (encouraging the breach of duty) cannot be caught either by the law of incitement or by the doctrine of complicity. Therefore, R's act (although it has been induced by the conferral of an advantage from P) does not amount to an 'improper act': it breaches neither an equitable nor a legal duty. R will therefore sit outside the conduct element of bribery that we proposed above, even apart from the fact that she is not in a position of trust and owes no duty of impartiality or duty to act in the best interests of another. Accordingly, P would also not be guilty of bribery either: crudely put, there was no one for him to bribe. Further, as X's conduct does not constitute a criminal offence, neither P nor R can be convicted of incitement.

5.80   Although the discussion of trading in influence is often clouded with reference to examples such as those in 5M to 5P, it is the scenario in Example 5Q that represents the biggest challenge to the law in this area.

Convention requirements

5.81   The issue of trading in influence is most fully articulated in the Council of Europe's Criminal Law Convention on Corruption.[47] Article 12 requires parties to create a criminal offence to catch:

> … the promising, giving or offering, directly or indirectly, of any undue advantage to anyone who asserts or confirms that he or she is able to exert an improper influence over the decision-making of any person referred to [in relation to the principal offence].

---

[46]   The result in the case in the first sentence of para 5.74(1) above (following Example 5M) may be an exception, but as P can be convicted of incitement the oddity is one of labelling rather than substance.

[47]   Trading in influence is also mentioned in the United Nations Convention (Art 18). However, it is only presented as an issue that states should consider legislating against.

5.82 Although this provision would clearly encompass our problem case (Example 5Q), and would therefore require a change in the law, it is a provision that does not bind the UK. This is because the UK has made a specific reservation[48] in relation to Article 12.

Current law and our previous recommendations

5.83 Neither the current law nor our previous recommendations contained a specific reference to trading in influence. However, as our previous recommendations defined 'corruptly' in relation to influence (and not breach of duty), the draft Bill annexed to our previous report would have had the potential to encompass certain cases of trading in influence.

5.84 However, it would only have included cases that also involved an agency relationship. Thus, if in Example 5Q R had been an adviser employed by X, then the trade in R's influence would have affected his or her duty to X and R would have committed bribery. However, if, as was the case in Example 5Q, there is not an agency relationship, the situation would fall outside the bribery offence.

Options for reform

5.85 When looking forward, two things are clear. The first is that the only problem case we need to deal with involves Example 5Q and what we describe as the pure trade in influence. The second is that, if we employ the breach of duty model, cases like Example 5Q will only be caught if they are specifically provided for.

5.86 There are two central options for reform. The first option is to allow cases like Example 5Q to remain outside the law of bribery. This appears to be the option preferred by the Government. In two recent statements, one in response to the third round of evaluation of the UK's conformity with the Council of Europe's Criminal Law Convention[49] and one in reply to the Government's most recent consultation on bribery,[50] the Government has confirmed its intention not to expand this area of the law. The Government has expressed particular concern that lobbyists might be caught by an expanded offence.

5.87 The second option is to expand bribery in order to include R where he or she does not breach a legal or equitable duty, but induces another person to do so.[51] This option would bring R (and P) in Example 5Q within the principal offence.[52] It would also allow the UK to conform to Article 12 of the Council of Europe's Criminal Law Convention.

---

[48] An option provided by Article 37 of the Convention.

[49] Greco Eval III (2006) 1E, para 9.0.

[50] Consultation on Bribery: Reform of the Prevention of Corruption Acts and SFO powers in Cases of Bribery of Foreign Officials: Summary of responses and next steps (2007) paras 108 and 109.

[51] This would, of course, be subject to a fault element. See Part 6. It would also have to be clarified that the requirement of acting in breach of trust /impartiality/best interests applies to the third party and not to R.

[52] It would also include the case in the first sentence in para 5.74(1) above.

5.88 It is arguable that such an extension of the currently proposed bribery offence would avoid most of the Government's concerns. The Government partly based their recent comments on that fact that trading in influence would be caught where an agency relationship is identified.[53] This would no longer be the case under the breach of duty model. Further, concerns expressed by the Government in relation to lobbying would also be recast. Their concerns were related to our previous recommendations which defined 'corruptly' using the influence model. Under the breach of duty model, lobbying would only be caught where the intention of the lobbyist is to influence the decision-maker to breach a legal or equitable duty. This is obviously a much narrower target.

Provisional proposal

5.89 **We provisionally propose that the recipient should be regarded as satisfying the conduct element of bribery if he or she:**

> **(1)   acts improperly: in breach of a legal or equitable duty;[54]**
>
> **(2)   represents a willingness to or agrees to act improperly;**
>
> **(3)   uses his or her influence to induce a third party to act improperly; or**
>
> **(4)   represents a willingness to or agrees to induce a third party to act improperly.[55]**

5.90 This result could be achieved either by setting out the four possibilities separately, as above, or by defining 'improper conduct' so as to include influencing a third party to act in breach of a legal or equitable duty (again, subject to the limitation concerning a relation of trust, a duty of impartiality or a duty to act in the best interests of another).

Note to reader

5.91 In order to avoid lengthy repetition, where we refer to 'improper conduct' in the rest of this CP, 'improper conduct' should be read to include the use of an influence to induce a third party to breach a legal or equitable duty that involves a betrayal of a relation of trust or a breach of a duty to act impartially or in the best interests of another.

Receipt of the advantage

DOES R, AS OPPOSED TO SOME OTHER PERSON, HAVE TO RECEIVE THE ADVANTAGE?

5.92 Two problem areas can be identified. First, where the advantage is not conferred at all. Secondly, where it is conferred on a third party.

---

[53] Consultation on bribery: Reform of the Prevention of Corruption Acts and SFO powers in Cases of Bribery of Foreign Officials: Summary of responses and next steps (2007), para 108.

[54] Subject to the limitation in para 5.48 above.

[55] This provisional proposal represents an expanded version of that in para 5.71.

Where the advantage is not conferred at all

5.93 Under our provisional proposals R can satisfy the conduct element of bribery by acting improperly, influencing another to act improperly, or soliciting an advantage from P on the basis that he or she (R) will do either of these things. As long as R satisfies the requisite fault element,[56] it should not be essential for the advantage to be conferred upon or even offered to R.

5.94 If it were essential for the advantage to have been conferred, R would avoid liability for the principal offence where he or she acts improperly in expectation of an advantage or where he or she solicits an advantage (intending to act improperly) and is turned down. We do not think this would be acceptable.[57]

Provisional proposal

5.95 **We provisionally propose that, provided that the improper conduct requirement is satisfied, the recipient should satisfy the conduct element of bribery even where the advantage has not been conferred and there has been no agreement regarding its conferral.[58]**

Where the advantage is conferred on a third party

5.96 The question here is whether R has to be shown to have received the advantage. For example:

Example 5R

In exchange for R acting improperly, P agrees to give X (R's brother) a job within his company. R acts improperly and P gives X the job.

In this example, P has done something at R's request and it is something that benefits R (albeit indirectly). As a result, P's act clearly comes within our provisionally proposed definition of 'advantage'.[59] However, the principal beneficiary is X.

5.97 The current law is inconsistent in relation to this issue, with differing requirements between the 1889 Act and the 1906 Act.[60] We recommended in our previous report that the law should be clarified by explicitly allowing for bribery where the advantage is conferred on a third party.[61] We remain of this view.

---

[56] See Part 6.

[57] As we pointed out above, there is an analogy with the way that offences are defined in the Fraud Act 2006. For example, in section 2, so long as P makes a false representation with a view to making a gain or imposing a risk of loss, P commits the offence whether or not the false representation leads to any gain or risk of loss in fact.

[58] It will still be necessary that R should act with a view to obtaining that advantage, but this belongs to the fault element: see Part 6.

[59] See para 5.60 above.

[60] Legislating the Criminal Code: Corruption (1998) Law Com No. 248, para 5.47.

[61] As long as the advantage is either requested by R or benefits R in some way.

Provisional proposal

5.98   **We provisionally propose that it should be immaterial to the recipient's liability whether the advantage is conferred on the recipient or a third party.**

DOES R HAVE TO HOLD A CERTAIN POSITION WHEN THE ADVANTAGE IS CONFERRED?

5.99   This question required a considerable amount of attention in our previous review of bribery because we structured our recommendations around the agent/principal model.[62] As a result, in order to be bribed, R had to be an agent and the act or omission that he or she was bribed to do had to relate to his or her functions as an agent.

5.100 As part of the current review, we have chosen to abandon the agent/principal model. As a result, it will no longer be essential, when establishing the liability of either P or R, to demonstrate that R was an agent. However, R's status may remain relevant when determining improper conduct, since the existence of a legal or equitable duty (involving an element of trust, impartiality or best interests) will often follow from his or her position.

Provisional proposal

5.101 **We provisionally propose that, for the purposes of establishing the liability of either the payer or the recipient, the recipient's status (for example, being an agent) should be immaterial except in so far as it is relevant to whether the recipient is acting in breach of a legal or equitable duty.**

The payer's conduct element

5.102 The central component of the conduct element in relation to the payer (P) is the conferral of an advantage. In very many cases, it will therefore have to be demonstrated that P completed this conferral before P can satisfy the conduct element.

Soliciting or inducing an improper act by representing a willingness to confer an advantage

5.103 When discussing R's conduct element we noted that R should fall within the conduct element of bribery if he or she either acted improperly or solicited an advantage by representing a willingness to act improperly. Likewise in relation to P, we believe that P's conduct element should go beyond the conferral of an advantage to include the inducing of an improper act by representing a willingness to confer an advantage.

5.104 Under the current law, P can already commit the conduct element of the offence by offering or agreeing to confer an advantage.[63] Based upon the current law, we employed this same terminology in our previous recommendations.[64]

---

[62] Legislating the Criminal Code: Corruption (1998) Law Com No. 248, paras 5.11 to 5.37.

[63] In the 1889 Act, the term 'promise' is preferred to agree.

[64] Legislating the Criminal Code: Corruption (1998) Law Com No. 248, paras 5.45 to 5.46.

5.105   In our previous report, we rejected 'promise' as an alternative to 'agree' because we concluded that 'agree' was the wider term of the two.[65] However, we now believe that a more expansive term (bringing those who represent a willingness to confer an advantage within the conduct element of the offence) would be beneficial. For example:

Example 5S

P is desperate to gain entrance to an exclusive upcoming reception being held at a restaurant, but knows he is not invited. In order to induce an employee of the restaurant (R) to let him in (breach a duty), P attends the restaurant on multiple occasions, tips the staff extravagantly and announces loudly that he always rewards those who 'look after him'. As a result, R (who overheard P's announcement) lets P into the reception. P subsequently refuses to give R any reward.

In this example, it is debatable whether or not P's conduct could be construed as an implied offer to, or agreement with, R. However, P has clearly induced R's improper act by representing a willingness to confer an advantage.

5.106   Under the current law P (in Example 5S) will have committed bribery as a secondary party, having 'aided and abetted' R as a principal offender.[66] As a secondary party, P will be labelled in the same way as R and liable to the same sanction. Therefore, our belief that P's conduct element within the principal offence should be widened will not create any dramatic changes in the law. We simply believe that P, where he or she represents a willingness to confer an advantage, should be brought explicitly within the conduct element of the offence.

Provisional proposal

5.107   **We provisionally propose that the payer should be regarded as satisfying the conduct element of bribery if he or she:**

  (1)   confers an advantage on the recipient; or

  (2)   represents a willingness to confer an advantage on the recipient.

The circumstances surrounding the conferral of the advantage

5.108   We have identified the central component of P's conduct element as the conferral of an advantage. We have also explained our belief that those who induce an improper act by representing that they are willing to confer an advantage should also satisfy the conduct element of bribery. In this section we discuss the necessary circumstances that must surround this core action.

---

[65]   Above, para 5.45.

[66]   The language of the Accessories and Abettors Act 1861, s 8, and the Magistrates Courts Act 1980, s 44.

DOES R HAVE TO RECEIVE THE ADVANTAGE 'PERSONALLY'?

5.109   When answering this question, much of our discussion above concerning R's liability will apply equally here. However, it is worth summarising the law from P's perspective.

Where the advantage is conferred on a third party in order to induce R to act improperly

5.110   We concluded above that R could come within the conduct element of bribery even if the advantage was conferred by P on a third party.[67] Thus, the advantage would still have to be requested by R or benefit R in some way, but R would not escape liability if, for example, the advantage was conferred on someone within R's family. On this basis we do not believe that P should escape liability if he or she confers the advantage on a person who is not R.[68]

Where R is an intermediary

5.111   In Examples 5M to 5P we concluded that R, despite being (in some senses) an intermediary, could still come within the conduct element of the full bribery offence. Therefore, if our reasoning is accepted, there would be little difficulty in catching P within the conduct element of the full offence where P (as in these examples) confers an advantage on R.

5.112   Example 5Q involved what we have termed as a pure trade in influence: where R does not breach a duty personally, but encourages a third party to breach an equitable duty. In this case we believed that the only way to catch R within the full offence was expressly to extend R's conduct element so that 'improper conduct' should include both acting in breach of a legal or equitable duty and inducing a third party to act in breach of a legal or equitable duty. If this provisional proposal is accepted, it is clear that P in Example 5Q will also come within the conduct element of the full offence by conferring an advantage on R.

DOES P HAVE TO CONFER THE ADVANTAGE 'PERSONALLY'?

5.113   This question also relates to intermediaries. However, here we are discussing a third party who is responsible for conferring the advantage.

5.114   In order to expose areas that may require reform, it is first important to reflect upon the law's built-in safeguards. For example, P cannot shield him or herself from liability simply by conferring the advantage through an 'innocent' third party (the doctrine of innocent agency). In the same way that P would come within the conduct element of murder if he or she gave poisoned food to X to pass to V, P would come within the conduct element of bribery if he or she gave an innocent third party an advantage to pass to R.

5.115   However, reflecting upon our provisional proposal to extend R's liability to include a pure trade in influence, we must consider whether a similar extension would be necessary in relation to P. For example:

---

[67] See paras 5.92 to 5.95 above.

[68] Provided that P satisfies the requisite fault element – see Part 6 below.

> **Example 5T**
>
> P wants R to act improperly and R has represented to P that he or she is willing to do so for £1000. P uses his influence to induce X to transfer £1000 to R, but does not tell X what the money concerns.

In this example, P has used his influence to induce X to confer an advantage to R. However, unlike where R uses his or her influence to induce a third party to act improperly, X's conduct in this example is wholly innocent. Therefore, we are able to apply the doctrine of innocent agency and P will be liable as a principal offender.

5.116 The converse example is where X realises P's intentions:

> **Example 5U**
>
> P wants R to act improperly and R has represented to P that he or she is willing to do so for £1000. P uses his influence to induce X to transfer £1000 to R, X realises why P wishes the money to be transferred.

In this example, X will clearly come within the conduct element of bribery as a payer.[69] However, because X is no longer an innocent agent, P will not be liable as a principal offender. Instead, P will be liable as a secondary party for having 'aided and abetted' X's principal offence.[70] He or she will be labelled and punished in the same way as X.

5.117 As these two examples demonstrate, the gap in the law that we exposed in relation to R's liability for the pure trade in influence is not present in relation to P. This is because where P induces a third party to confer an advantage without also informing them of the surrounding circumstances, that third party is likely to be an innocent agent, allowing liability to be traced back to P. Where R (in our previous discussion) induces a third party to act improperly under similar circumstances, that third party's breach of an equitable duty prevents the application of the doctrine of innocent agency and therefore necessitates an extension of the law.

DOES R HAVE TO HAVE PERFORMED THE IMPROPER ACT?

5.118 Just as R's conduct element does not rely on P conferring the advantage, it is equally true that P's conduct element does not rely on R's improper act. However, where the two components are not completed, the nexus between the two components is nevertheless maintained by each party's fault element.

5.119 If R's improper act were required to have been completed in order to convict P, P would avoid liability where he or she confers an advantage in expectation of an improper act and where P has represented to R that he or she will confer an advantage (in exchange for an improper act) and is turned down. We do not think this would be acceptable.

---

[69] He or she is also likely to satisfy the fault element.

Provisional proposal

5.120 **We provisionally propose that the payer should be regarded as satisfying the conduct element of bribery even where the improper act has not been completed and there has been no agreement concerning its completion.**

DOES R HAVE TO HOLD A CERTAIN POSITION WHEN THE ADVANTAGE IS CONFERRED?

5.121 As discussed above,[71] the abandonment of the agent/principal model means that it is no longer necessary for R to be defined as an agent. Hence neither P's nor R's liability will depend upon the status of R, except in so far as this status gives rise to the duty which R is alleged to have breached in acting improperly.

[70] If the offence is not completed, P will nevertheless be inchoately liable for having incited X to commit bribery.

[71] See paras 5.99 to 5.101 above.

PART 6
THE FAULT ELEMENT OF THE NEW BRIBERY OFFENCE

INTRODUCTION

6.1   For the purposes of this paper, the "fault element" is the state of mind that P and R must satisfy if each is to be convicted of the offence of bribery that we are provisionally proposing. The fault element must ensure that there is a proper nexus between the two central components of the conduct element: the conferral of the advantage and the improper act. For example:

Example 6A

P makes an anonymous charitable donation to a local care home. Some time later, P makes an inquiry with R (an employee of the care home) concerning the future care of his (P's) mother. There is a long waiting list, but R makes a mistake processing the application (breaching a duty to his employer) and grants P's mother a room immediately.

In this example, both P and R do acts that satisfy the conduct element of bribery. However, their conduct does not deserve to be labelled as bribery. P has conferred an advantage but without any intention to induce R to do an improper act. Likewise, R has accepted the advantage and has done an improper act but has done so in error and could not have even been aware of P's conferral of an advantage. Accordingly, the two components that make up the conduct element of the offence are present but the nexus between them (the fault element) is lacking.

6.2   In this Part, we consider the fault element that should be required if R and P are each to be convicted of bribery. We begin by considering the fault element in the case of R.

THE RECIPIENT'S FAULT ELEMENT

6.3   Unlike the payer, R's conduct element (an improper act or the representation of a willingness to do an improper act) already attracts some level of culpability. The question is how that culpability should be connected to the conferral of an advantage from P if R is to be held criminally liable.

6.4   We can identify three principal scenarios in which R will satisfy the conduct element of the offence of bribery that we are proposing:

        (1)   R does an improper act after P confers an advantage;

        (2)   R does an improper act before P confers an advantage;

        (3)   R represents a willingness to do an improper act.

In the following section we will explore the fault element required of R in each of these scenarios.

R does an improper act after P confers an advantage (scenario 1)

Introduction

6.5   This scenario represents the most common form of bribery: P confers an advantage on R and then R does an improper act. It is clear that R must be aware that P has conferred an advantage.[1] Further, R must knowingly accept the advantage. This is to ensure that R cannot be guilty of the offence if, for example, he or she mistakenly accepts an advantage.

6.6   However, these two requirements represent relatively low hurdles for establishing liability. Therefore, assuming R has knowingly accepted an advantage from P, we must now ask what effect, if any, this must have on R's decision to do an improper act in order to bring R within the offence.

Must the advantage have to influence R's decision to do the improper act?

THE CURRENT LAW AND OUR PREVIOUS RECOMMENDATIONS

6.7   Under the current law, the prosecution does not have to prove that R was in fact influenced to act in a certain way by P's conferral of an advantage. Rather, provided that R accepts the advantage under the guise that he or she will act in a certain way, R commits the offence.[2] Although on its own this would represent a very wide fault element, the prosecution must also prove that R acted "corruptly" (acted in a manner that tends to corrupt).[3]

6.8   In line with the current law, in our previous report we did not recommend that P's conferral of an advantage had to influence R to do an improper act. Instead, we focused on the requirement that R's act must "tend to corrupt". We did this by focusing not on how R was influenced by the advantage but on R's appreciation of P's own state of mind.

6.9   We recommended that:

(1)   A person who obtains an advantage should be regarded as obtaining it corruptly if he or she:

(a)   knows or believes that the person conferring it confers it corruptly, and

(b)   gives his or her express or implied consent to obtaining it (in a case where he or she does not request it); and

(2)   A person who agrees to obtain an advantage should be regarded as agreeing to obtain it corruptly if he or she knows or believes that the person agreeing to confer it agrees corruptly.[4]

---

[1]   If R is not aware that P has conferred an advantage, he or she may still be liable for bribery if he or she is acting in expectation of a future advantage from P. See, paras 6.37 to 6.47.

[2]   *Carr* [1957] 1 WLR 165; *Mills* (1978) 68 Cr App R 154.

[3]   *Cooper v Slade* [1857] HL Case 746; 10 ER 1488.

[4]   Legislating the Criminal Code: Corruption (1998) Law Com No 248, para 5.118.

Under this recommendation, if R realised that P was conferring the advantage believing that it would probably cause R to act in a certain way, and R consented to its receipt, R would be guilty of bribery irrespective of whether the advantage influenced R to do the improper act.

DEPARTING FROM OUR PREVIOUS RECOMMENDATION

6.10 We are no longer attracted to our previous recommendation for two principal reasons.

6.11 First, there is a need for simplicity. One of the main criticisms levelled at our previous recommendations was that they were over-complicated and difficult for non-legal specialists to understand.

6.12 Secondly, for R to be convicted of bribery as a principal offender, there must be a sufficient connection between the two components of the conduct element: the conferral of the advantage and the doing of the improper act. In our view, this means that R's decision to do the improper act must have been influenced by the advantage in doing the improper act. Unless R is found to have been influenced to do the improper act by the advantage conferred by P, there will be an insufficient nexus between the two external components.

6.13 Under our previous recommendation, R could be convicted of bribery as a principal offender even in cases where there was no nexus between P's conferral of the advantage and R's commission of the improper act because the advantage had not influenced R to do the improper act. Consider the following examples:

Example 6B

Z Ltd is tendering for a contract with X Ltd. R, an employee of X Ltd, has several family members that work for Z Ltd and would benefit from Z Ltd being awarded the contract. On this basis, and in breach of a legal duty, R ensures that Z Ltd is awarded the contract.

Example 6C

P, an employee of Z Ltd, is tendering for a contract with X Ltd. R, an employee of X Ltd, has several family members that work for Z Ltd and would benefit from Z Ltd being awarded the contract. On this basis, and in breach of duty, R ensures that Z Ltd is awarded the contract. Just prior to the announcement, P contacts R and offers him £1000 to make sure Z Ltd get the contract. Although R is unconcerned with such small sums, he nevertheless tells P that he will accept the money.

In Example 6B, it is common ground that, although R has breached a legal duty, he has not committed a criminal offence. In Example 6C, the conferral of an advantage from P has not influenced R's decision to do the improper act and yet, under the current law and under our previous recommendations, R has committed bribery as a principal offender.

6.14   In our view, in Example 6C, R ought not to be convicted of bribery as a principal offender because the decision to award the contract to Z Ltd was not influenced by the conferral of the advantage by P. Accordingly, the essential nexus between the conferral of an advantage and the doing of the improper act is lacking.

6.15   However, by informing P that he will accept the advantage, R has encouraged P to commit bribery. R should therefore be convicted as an accessory to the offence of bribery that P has committed as a principal offender.[5] Accordingly, as under the current law, R would be guilty of bribery. However, convicting R as an accessory to P's offence of bribery rather than as a principal offender more accurately reflects the nature of R's criminality.

To what extent must the advantage influence R's decision to act improperly?

6.16   We have so far concluded that, in order to maintain the proper nexus between P's conferral of the advantage and R's commission of the improper act, the conferral of the advantage must have influenced R's doing of the improper act. The question remains: to what extent must R's improper act be influenced by the advantage if he or she is to be convicted of bribery as a principal offender?

6.17   One possibility would be to require that R's improper act was 'substantially' or 'significantly' influenced by the advantage. However, in our view, a test based on 'substantiality' or 'significance' would be too broad. In particular, the courts have interpreted 'substantial' as meaning anything that is more than trivial. Accordingly, we believe that it would be better to require that the advantage be the *primary* reason for R's improper act.

6.18   In proposing that the advantage must be the primary reason for R's improper act, we are following the recommendation in our 1998 report. In that report, the view taken was that the net of criminal liability would be cast too wide if the advantage had to be merely a substantial reason for R's improper act. In criticising the view that there need only be a connection between the advantage to be conferred and R's improper act, we said:

> The difficulty is that most commercial enterprises are constantly trying to bring in business in a variety of ways all of which involve 'influencing' those agents or other firms whose job it is to decide where their firms' business should go.[6]

Provisional proposals

6.19   **We provisionally propose that for the recipient to be convicted of bribery as a principal offender, the advantage conferred must be the primary reason for the recipient doing the improper act.**

---

[5]   It is true that in Example 6C P commits bribery when he offers the money to R, at which point R has done nothing to encourage P. However, P's conduct element for bribery can be satisfied in more than one way: through a representation of a willingness to confer an advantage and through the actual conferral, P subsequently commits bribery by paying the money to R (conferring the advantage) who, having told P that he or she would accept the money, has encouraged P to commit the offence.

[6]   Legislating the Criminal Code: Corruption (1998) Law Com No 248, para 5.74.

6.20 **We provisionally propose that if the recipient knowingly accepts or states that he or she will accept an advantage from the payer:**

   (1)   realising that if the payer confers the advantage the payer will do so with the intention to influence the recipient to act improperly; but

   (2)   the advantage is not the primary reason for the recipient doing the improper act

the recipient should be guilty of bribery not as a principal offender but as an accessory to the offence of bribery committed by the payer as a principal offender.

If the primary reason for R doing the improper act is the advantage, should it make any difference that R realises that P is not conferring the advantage in order to influence R to do the improper act?

6.21   Our policy is that for R to be convicted of bribery as a principal offender, R should no longer have to realise that P's intention in conferring the advantage is to influence R to do an improper act. As a result, the possibility emerges that R could be convicted of bribery as a principal offender if the advantage was the primary reason for R doing the improper act but R knew or believed that, in conferring the advantage, it was not P's intention that R should do any improper act.

6.22   An example of this could arise in the context of commission payments. [7] R may mis-sell a policy to a consumer primarily because of the commission payment being conferred, even though P, the party conferring that payment, does not intend R to have acted improperly in this way and R knows this.

6.23   In our previous consultation paper, we drew attention to case law from South Africa that considered this question.[8] Although the case law is inconsistent, the most recent authority holds that R would be liable even if he or she realised that P was not trying to induce a particular act. However, in that paper, our proposed fault element was based upon R's foresight of P's "corrupt" intention, and so we proposed that R should not be liable in this situation.

6.24   In this paper, we are recasting the fault element required of R to focus, not on P's intention, but on the existence of a nexus (in R's mind) between the conferral of the advantage and the improper act. In the example in paragraph 6.22 above, even though P does not intend R to commit an improper act, the conferral of the advantage has had that effect. In R's mind, the nexus is complete.

---

[7]   See Appendix F, paras F.38 to F.58 below.

[8]   For example, *S v Gouws* [1975] 1 SALR 1 (A); *Geel* [1953] 2 SA 398 (AD).

6.25 We acknowledge that were R to be convicted of bribery, this would create an offence of bribery without a briber. That said, if R is prepared to do an improper act primarily in exchange for or in anticipation of an advantage, it might be thought that he or she should not escape criminal liability merely because he or she knows that P's intention in conferring the advantage is entirely innocent. Further, it is not clear why a conviction for bribery should be dependent on there being a briber. Suppose that R approaches P and says that, for a considerable sum of money, he, R, can secure a commercial benefit for P. P tells R to 'get lost' and reports R to the police. Why should R not be convicted of bribery?

6.26 However, we recognise the contrary arguments, particularly where, unlike in the example in the preceding paragraph, the conferral of the advantage is not at R's instigation. Suppose P makes a charitable donation to X Ltd, with which R is connected. R then makes decisions in P's favour, hoping that further donations will follow. P did not make the donation to influence R and R knows that. One probable consequence of convicting R of bribery would be that P would be stigmatised as having 'bribed' R although P has not done so on any ordinary use of language.

Question for consultees

6.27 **We ask consultees whether the fact that the recipient knows or believes that the payer has conferred the advantage without intending it to influence the recipient to do any improper act should preclude the recipient being convicted of bribery, even if the advantage was the primary reason for the recipient doing the improper act.**

Must R know or believe that the act is an 'improper' act?

6.28 There is always the possibility that R will be induced to do an act without realising that it constitutes a breach of a legal or equitable duty that involves betrayal of a relation of trust or breach of a duty to act impartially or in the best interests of another. In such cases, it might be thought that R ought not to be convicted of bribery. However, were R to be exonerated, this would be an exception to the general rule that a person cannot plead mistake of law in order to avoid criminal liability. For example, a person can be convicted of gross negligence manslaughter regardless of whether they recognised that their conduct would amount to a breach of a duty to take care.

6.29 As in our previous consultation paper, we believe that R is in the best position to understand the duties that he or she is under and is already expected by the civil law to avoid breaching them. If R were able to avoid liability on this ground, it would create a significant grey area. This could then be exploited in cases where R was in fact aware of the duty in question, as it would be much easier for R to claim ignorance of the fact that his or her conduct constituted a breach of duty than it would be for a prosecutor to prove that R was aware that it did.

Provisional proposal

6.30 **We provisionally propose that it should be immaterial whether or not the recipient knew or believed that his or her act constituted a breach of a legal or equitable duty involving betrayal of a relation of trust or breach of a duty to act impartially or in the best interests of another.**

The improper act done by R is different from that which was intended or agreed

6.31 In some cases, the improper act committed by R, although influenced by the conferral of the advantage, will be different from that originally intended or agreed between P and R.[9] In this section, we will consider whether this should affect R's liability.

6.32 One possibility is that R, in doing an improper act, misinterprets P's wishes. For example:

Example 6D

R is an independent agent acting for both X Ltd and Z Ltd. Both companies are tendering for a contract. P, an employee of Z Ltd, confers an advantage on R in order to induce R to do an improper act by preventing X Ltd being awarded the contract. R accepts the advantage. However, R wrongly believes that P is an embittered employee of Z Ltd and wishes him to act improperly by ensuring that the contract is awarded to X Ltd. X Ltd is awarded the contract.

In this example, as far as R is concerned, an advantage was given in exchange for R doing an improper act and he or she has completed the improper act as agreed. On this basis, the nexus between the conferral of the advantage and the improper act remains intact (in R's mind) and, in our view, there is no reason why R should not be convicted of bribery.

6.33 In Part 5, we provisionally proposed that there should be two alternative ways in which R could satisfy the conduct element of bribery as a principal offender. One was by doing an improper act by breaching a legal or equitable duty (provided it involved betraying a relation of trust or breaching an obligation to act impartially or in the best interests of another).[10] The other was by doing an improper act in using his or her influence to induce a third party to breach a legal or equitable duty (with the same limitation).[11] On this basis, if the conferral of an advantage by P influences R to act improperly in either of these ways, R would commit bribery.

6.34 The question is whether it should make any difference to R's liability that the improper act that he or she does is the alternative to that represented to or agreed with P. For example:

---

[9] If there is an agreement between the parties prior to either the improper act or the conferral of the advantage, R's fault element will be assessed under scenario 3 (on the basis of R's representation of a willingness to complete an improper act).

[10] See Part 5 above.

[11] See Part 5 above.

> **Example 6E**
>
> P needs a licence in order to set up a new business but does not qualify for one. P therefore contacts R, an employee of the licensing office, and offers him a large sum of money to grant P the licence in breach of R's duties. R does not have the power to grant the licence but, keen to receive the money, he pretends to P that he has the power and makes the deal. In fact, R is intending to use his influence over X, a senior manager at R's office, to persuade X, in breach of X's duties, to grant P the licence. X grants P the licence.

In this example, P has conferred an advantage on R in exchange for R doing an improper act by breaching a duty in issuing a licence improperly. However, this is not what R has done. Rather, R has done an improper act by using his influence to induce a third party (X) to act in breach of duty.

6.35 We believe that in this situation R should stand to be convicted of bribery regardless of the exact manner in which he or she represented to P that he or she was going to do an improper act.[12] This is because the nexus between the conferral of the advantage and the improper act is one identified in R's mind. In this example, R may not intend to do an improper act in the exact manner that he or she has represented to P but, influenced by the advantage, R is still induced to do an improper act.

Provisional proposal

6.36 **We provisionally propose that, provided the payer's conferral of the advantage is the primary reason for the recipient doing an improper act, it should be immaterial if the improper act done by the recipient differs from the improper act that was intended or agreed.**

R does an improper act before P confers an advantage (scenario 2)

Introduction

6.37 In scenario 2, R does an improper act not as a result of the conferral of an advantage from P (scenario 1) but in the expectation of one. This can come about in one of two ways. First, there may be an agreement between the parties that if R does an improper act then P will confer an advantage.[13] Secondly, where R and P have not formed an agreement, R may nevertheless do an improper act hoping or believing that P will confer an advantage as a reward for the act. Whichever of these two situations arises should not make a difference to R's potential liability. Further, if R does an improper act in expectation of P conferring an advantage, the principles that govern R's liability as a principal offender should be the same regardless of whether in the event P goes on to confer the advantage. Must the prospective advantage have to influence R's decision to do the improper act?

---

[12] It is interesting to note that if we did not include trading in influence within the law of bribery, R could only potentially be guilty as a secondary party: for encouraging P to commit bribery.

[13] In this case, R's liability will be assessed under scenario 3.

The current law and our previous recommendations

6.38 Under the current law and under our previous recommendations, there is no requirement that the prospective advantage must have influenced R's decision to do the improper act. Instead, R can be guilty of bribery within scenario 2 if he or she does an improper act intending to solicit an advantage from P[14] provided that, in addition, R has acted 'corruptly'.

6.39 Under our previous recommendations, the definition of "corruptly" again required that R foresaw P's state of mind. Clause 7 of the draft Corruption Bill[15] provided that:

(1) A person who agrees to obtain an advantage agrees to obtain it corruptly if he knows or believes that the person agreeing to confer it agrees to confer it corruptly.

(2) A person who solicits an advantage solicits it corruptly if –

(a) he intends a person to confer it or agree to confer it, and

(b) he believes that if the person did so he would probably do so corruptly.

6.40 The circumstances in which P should be considered as conferring an advantage corruptly were defined by clause 6:

(1) A person who confers an advantage, or offers or agrees to confer an advantage, does so corruptly if –

(a) he knows or believes that in performing his functions as an agent a person has done an act or made an omission,

(b) he knows or believes that the person has done the act or made the omission primarily in order to secure that a person confers an advantage (whoever obtains it), and

(c) he intends the person known or believed to have done that act or made the omission to regard the advantage (or the advantage when conferred) as conferred primarily in return for the act or omission.

6.41 Thus, in cases falling within scenario 2, for R to satisfy the fault element he or she would have to believe that, if P conferred the advantage, P would probably do so:

(1) knowing or believing that R had done the improper act primarily in expectation of the advantage, and

---

[14] It is possible to do an improper act intending to solicit an advantage without the prospective advantage influencing the decision to do the improper act – see Example 6F below.

[15] Legislating the Criminal Code: Corruption (1998) Law Com No 248, Appendix A.

(2)   intending that R should regard the advantage as conferred primarily in return for the improper act.

Departing from our previous recommendations

6.42   We no longer believe that our previous recommendation provides the most desirable option. There are two reasons.

6.43   First there is again the need for simplicity. In cases where P's conferral of an advantage precedes R's improper act (scenario 1), we highlighted the inherent deficiencies if R's fault element were dependent on awareness of P's own state of mind. In the context of scenario 2, this problem is magnified. This is because, in scenario 2, R's liability turns on R predicting P's state of mind in relation to an act, the conferral of an advantage, that P is yet to perform.

6.44   Secondly, there is the potential for R to fall within the scope of the bribery offence in a situation where R's improper act is not done in expectation of an advantage. This will arise if R believes that P will assume that he or she, R, is acting because of the advantage. For example:

Example 6F

P, an employee of Z Ltd, is tendering for a contract with X Ltd. R, an employee of X Ltd, has several family members that work for Z Ltd and would benefit from Z Ltd being awarded the contract. On this basis, and in breach of duty, R ensures that Z Ltd is awarded the contract. In doing so, he is aware that P has told acquaintances that he will give R £1000 if Z Ltd get the contract. Although R is unconcerned with such small sums, he nevertheless tells P that he will accept the money.

This example is based upon a slight variation of the facts of Example 6C. In this example, R has done an improper act and he intends P to confer the advantage. Further, he believes that if P does confer the advantage, the probability is that P will do so believing that R did the improper act primarily in expectation of the advantage and intending that R should regard the advantage as conferred primarily in return for the improper act.

6.45   Under our previous recommendations, in Example 6F, R would be guilty of bribery as a principal offender. However, no matter what P believed, it was not the £1000 that caused R to act improperly. Accordingly, R ought not to be convicted of bribery as a principal offender because, within R's mind, there is no nexus between the improper act that he has done and the advantage subsequently conferred by P. However, we believe that R should be convicted of being an accessory to the offence of bribery that P has committed as a principal offender.[16]

---

[16]   See paras 6.12 to 6.15 above.

Provisional proposals

6.46 **We provisionally propose that in cases where the improper act of the recipient precedes the conferral of the advantage by the payer, it should be a necessary and sufficient condition of liability that the primary reason for the recipient doing the improper act was that the payer should confer an advantage on the recipient or another person.**

6.47 **We provisionally propose that if the recipient does an improper act:**

    (1)   intending that the payer should confer an advantage on the recipient or another person;

    (2)   knowing or believing that, if the payer confers the advantage, the payer will do so intending it as a reward for the improper act; but

    (3)   the primary reason for the recipient doing the improper act is not that the payer should confer an advantage on the recipient or another person

the recipient should be guilty of bribery not as principal offender but as an accessory to the offence of bribery that the payer commits as a principal offender.

Ancillary matters relating to the fault element required of R

6.48 Certain aspects of R's fault element that we discussed in relation to scenario 1 will apply equally to scenario 2. Accordingly:

    (1)   provided the prospective conferral of the advantage is the primary reason for R doing an improper act, it should be immaterial if the improper act done by R differs from the improper act that was intended or agreed; [17] and

    (2)   the fact that R was unaware that his or her act constituted a breach of a legal or equitable duty or a duty to act impartially should be immaterial.[18]

R represents a willingness to do an improper act (scenario 3)

6.49 As in scenario 2 above, at the time R represents a willingness to act improperly R has not yet received an advantage from P. Therefore, in order to create a nexus between the potential improper act and the potential conferral of the advantage, the primary reason for R representing a willingness to act improperly must be the expectation of an advantage from P. However, scenario 3 differs from scenario 2 because R has not yet done an improper act.

---

[17]   See paras 6.31 to 6.36 above.

[18]   See paras 6.28 to 6.30 above.

Our previous recommendations

6.50   In our previous consultation paper and report we endorsed a South African authority in this area.[19] That case held that R can be guilty of bribery as a principal offender, even if he or she does not intend to do the improper act, provided R does intend to solicit the conferral of an advantage by P.[20]

6.51   Under our previous recommendation, for R to be liable the prosecution would have to prove that R solicited an advantage from P foreseeing that, if P conferred the advantage, P would probably do so believing that it would influence R. The prosecution would not have to prove that R intended to do the improper act.

Departing from our previous recommendations

6.52   We no longer believe that our previous recommendations represent the best option for reform in this area.

6.53   We have already encountered, in relation to scenario 2, the particular difficulties caused by requiring R to foresee P's future intentions. We concluded that it is more appropriate to focus on R's own state of mind in order to identify whether the expectation of a future advantage had been the primary reason for induced him or her to do an improper act (or in this case to represent a willingness to act improperly).

6.54   In addition to the need for simplicity, we made this policy choice because we believed that it is the only way to maintain the nexus between R's improper act and P's conferral of the advantage. We also believe that, in order to maintain this nexus, R, must intend, at the time he or she represents a willingness to do the improper act, to do the improper act if P agrees to confer the advantage.

6.55   Without this intention, we believe that the nexus will be lost. For example:

Example 6G

R is in charge of a mass tendering process. R spreads the word that he will accept bribes to award the contracts in a certain way. In response to this, P, an employee of X Ltd, pays R £10,000 to award the main contract to X Ltd. As it turns out, R was spreading lies and has no intention of being influenced by the bribes. R awards the contract to Z Ltd.

In this example R represents a willingness to act improperly and intends, by doing so, to induce P to confer an advantage and to believe that the conferral will influence his or her (R's) reasoning.

[19]   *S v Kok* [1960] 4 SALR 638.

[20]   Legislating the Criminal Code: Corruption (1997) Law Commission Consultation Paper No 145, para 8.84.

6.56   However, the advantage does not affect R's reasoning and when R made the representation he or she did not intend that his or her reasoning should be affected. We believe that R ought not to be convicted of bribery as a principal offender because there is no causal connection between the future advantage and improper act (there will not be an improper act).

6.57   However, R has encouraged P to commit bribery. Accordingly, R ought to be convicted as an accessory to the offence of bribery that P has committed as a principal offender. The doctrine of complicity ensures that R's culpable conduct can be punished whilst also ensuring that the fault element of bribery is accurately defined.

Provisional Proposal

6.58   **We provisionally propose that, in cases where the primary reason for the recipient representing a willingness to do an improper act is that the payer should confer an advantage on the recipient or another person, the recipient, if he or she is to be convicted of bribery as a principal offender, must intend to do the improper act if the payer agrees to confer the advantage.**

6.59   It should be noted that this provisional proposal, if accepted, would affect the liability of those individuals who solicit bribes in order to expose others as being willing to confer them (entrapment). In our previous report, we discussed at some length whether there should be a specific defence for those individuals that act in this manner. Alongside the vast majority of our consultees, we concluded that there should not be. We remain of this view.

6.60   Under our current provisional proposals, where R solicits an advantage in order to expose P as a person willing to confer such an advantage, R will continue to be criminally liable, not as a principal offender, but as an accessory to the offence of bribery that P commits as a principal offender.

Ancillary matters relating to R's fault element

6.61   Other requirements in relation to R's fault element that have already been fully discussed in the context of other scenarios also apply here. These include:

   (1)   provided the prospective conferral of the advantage is the primary reason for R representing a willingness to do an improper act, it should be immaterial if the improper act that R intended to do is different from the improper act that he represents a willingness to do;[21] and

   (2)   the fact that R was unaware that the act that he or she was representing a willingness to do constituted a breach of a legal or equitable duty or a duty to act impartially should be immaterial.[22]

---

[21]   See paras 6.31 to 6.36 above.

[22]   See paras 6.28 to 6.30 above.

THE PAYER'S FAULT ELEMENT

6.62   The state of mind (fault element) of the payer, unlike the recipient, can never create a perfect causal nexus between the two central components of the conduct element (the conferral of the advantage and the improper act). This is because the conferral of an advantage does not dictate the actions of R: there is always a choice for R to make. However, P does confer the advantage in order to create a reason in R's mind for doing an improper act.

6.63   R commits bribery if he or she accepts the advantage from P as the primary reason for doing an improper act. However, in relation to P, the focus should be on his or her efforts to induce R to do an improper act. If P's liability were to be conditional on the subsequent fact that R accepted the advantage as the primary reason for acting improperly, P's liability would depend on the culpability of R. We do not believe there is any difference in culpability between D1 and D2 who each offer an advantage in the hope or expectation that it will be accepted, but in the one case it is and in the other it is not.

6.64   We can identify three principal scenarios in which P will fall within the conduct element of bribery:

(1)   P confers an advantage before R does an improper act;

(2)   P confers an advantage after R does an improper act.

(3)   P represents a willingness to confer an advantage.

P confers an advantage on R before R does an improper act (scenario 1)

Introduction

6.65   In this scenario, P confers an advantage on R, and the conferral of the advantage is intended to induce R to do an improper act.

6.66   P's fault element in scenario 1 is a controversial issue. This is because it is standard practice within many areas of life and business to confer advantages to others.[23] Often, especially in the business context, individuals who receive advantages have the ability to make decisions that will either benefit or work against the giver of the advantage.[24] There is therefore a built-in temptation to abuse the legitimate conferring of advantages and to manipulate the system in order to induce the recipient to act improperly.

6.67   The formulation of P's fault element is thus required to perform a nuanced role: to catch those seeking to abuse the system but to avoid attributing liability to those who are not.

---

[23]   For detailed discussion of "corporate hospitality", see Appendix F, paras F.59 to F.113.

[24]   If this were not the case, it is unlikely that advantages would be given at all.

Legitimate and illegitimate influence

6.68 In order to formulate a test which only catches those who are trying to abuse the system, it is necessary to identify and distinguish between legitimate and illegitimate reasons for conferring an advantage.

6.69 In our previous report we explored this issue when considering "corporate hospitality". We asked why a company might want others to attend a corporate function. We then provided three possible reasons:

(1) the agent may acquire information about the host company which militates in that company's favour when the agent comes to compare it with its rivals; or

(2) the agent's existing relationships with employees of the host company may be cemented, and new ones formed, and the agent may have a natural preference for doing business with people he or she knows; or

(3) the agent may simply decide to favour the host company in return for an enjoyable occasion.[25]

6.70 We concluded that whilst (1) and (2) were legitimate reasons for providing hospitality (conferring an advantage), (3) was not legitimate. We are still of this opinion. However, we recognise that our previous recommendations may not have been entirely satisfactory for those operating in industry and business who have to make specific decisions on what level of hospitality is legitimate.

6.71 We believe that our current policy has the potential to provide a greater level of legal certainty both in the context of corporate hospitality and more generally to other areas of gift-giving (including within the public sector).[26] It distinguishes between what is legitimate, on the one hand, and what is illegitimate, on the other hand, by making criminal liability depend on whether there has been a breach, or a willingness to breach, a legal or equitable duty. If the conferral of any advantage is designed to induce a breach of duty then it is illegitimate.

6.72 It is also important to remember that legitimacy and illegitimacy are not clearly defined concepts: what appears legitimate on its face may not be so on closer inspection. For example:

Example 6H

P, the directing manager of X Ltd, is concerned that his company has begun losing out to its rivals in a very competitive industry. In order to repair and create new links with the other companies in the supply chain, P hosts an extremely lavish corporate event in which no expense is spared to ensure that every guest leaves happy and confident in the stability of X Ltd.

---

[25] Legislating the Criminal Code: Corruption (1998) Law Com No 248, para 5.78.

[26] We discuss (and eventually reject) the contention that public officials should be treated separately in this area in Appendix F, paras F.80 and F.106 to F.108 below.

In this example, P appears to be conferring an advantage, the corporate hospitality), for a legitimate reason (to reassure those around him concerning the state of his company). However, it may be that P is aware that a series of meetings are planned for the following day in which the other companies are to decide on continuing their contracts with X Ltd. Perhaps, in addition, the corporate hospitality provided is well in excess of what could usually be expected at the type of function hosted by P.

6.73 Consider this further example, this time involving a public official:

Example 6J

P is a foreign national trying to start up a new business in the UK. P finds out that he does not qualify for the licence that he requires for starting his business. However, he decides to apply for it anyway. In P's home nation it is expected that applications of this sort should include gifts for the official who considers the case. P sends both the application and the gifts.

In this example, P could again claim that he was conferring an advantage (the gifts) for a legitimate reason (conformity with normal practice). However, we may again adapt the facts. For example, P may have been perfectly aware that gift giving was not generally seen as appropriate in this context in the UK. It may also be the case that the gifts were particularly valuable and that P realised that the employee who would be considering the claim was likely to be low level and low paid.

6.74 The point is that it will be necessary to look at all the circumstances, beyond P's stated intention, before a decision can be made as to the legitimacy or otherwise of his or her behaviour.

Our previous provisional proposals

6.75 In our previous consultation paper, we provisionally proposed that P must act "corruptly". We considered whether the following should be specific defences:

(1) what was done was done openly;

(2) what was done was done with the consent of the agent's principal;

(3) the agent was under no obligation to account for the benefit in question;

(4) what was done was normal practice in the environment in question; or

(5) the benefit in question was of small value.

We provisionally concluded that none of them should be specific defences, but that each should be capable of bearing on the issue of whether P's conduct was corrupt.[27]

---

[27] Legislating the Criminal Code: Corruption (1997) Law Commission Consultation Paper No 145, para 8.58.

6.76 The advantage of this approach is its flexibility. Arguably, it ensures that all the factors that are relevant in determining whether bribery has occurred are taken into account.[28] For example, for those who emphasise the importance and relevance of cultural factors, it has the advantage that culturally accepted norms can be taken into consideration.

6.77 However, such an approach is imprecise. It would be difficult to predict what conduct would be permitted. Further, what is "normal practice in the environment in question" may be difficult to establish and may allow businesses to exploit undesirable customs.[29] In addition, it can be criticised for not expressly referring to the reason why the advantage was conferred, a matter which might be thought to be of central importance.

Our previous report

6.78 In our previous report we decided not to follow the approach set out in the consultation paper. Instead, we sought to achieve a greater level of certainty by focusing on a single factor: the foresight of P in relation to R's state of mind. The relevant question became: when conferring the advantage, did P foresee that R would probably receive it as the "primary reason" for acting in a certain way? Our recommendation was set out in clause 6 of our draft Bill:

(1)   A person who confers an advantage, or offers or agrees to confer an advantage, does so corruptly if—

(a)   he intends a person in performing his functions as an agent to do an act or make an omission, and

(b)   he believes that if the person did so it would probably be primarily in return for the conferring of the advantage (or the advantage when conferred), whoever obtains it.[30]

As long as P satisfied this test of foresight, it was deemed that he or she was attempting to create (or at least knowingly creating) the controlling reason and, therefore, he or she was within the scope of the offence.

6.79 We are still attracted to the general approach embodied in this recommendation. Focusing on P's foresight means that P will be liable if he or she foresaw that the conferral of the advantage would probably be the primary reason for R to act improperly (a case where the nexus would be completed).

---

[28] Professor G R Sullivan has expressed support for a similar approach that would "put (these factors) to the jury in the form of a *Ghosh* style test". See "Proscribing corruption – some comments on the Law Commission's Report" (1998) *Criminal Law Review*, p 553.

[29] See, for example, our discussion of facilitation payments in Appendix F, paras F.59 to F.113.

[30] Legislating the Criminal Code: Corruption (1998) Law Com No 248, Appendix A.

6.80   However, we have abandoned the language of "probability".[31] This is because we believe that it is unrealistic to expect a tribunal of fact to find beyond a reasonable doubt that someone foresaw a particular degree of likelihood that something would or would not occur. Rather, we prefer the language of "serious risk".[32]

Going beyond our previous recommendations

6.81   Our previous report concluded that a test based on foresight was sufficient for determining whether P came within the fault element of bribery. We are now of the view that this may not go far enough. For example:

Example 6K

P is about to appear in court on a charge of murder. P realises that he is certain to be convicted and so he offers the presiding judge (R) £1000 to rule in his favour. Although P's only reason for offering the advantage is to try to induce R to act improperly, P doubts his plan has any realistic chance of success.

In this example, P is conferring the advantage for an illegitimate reason. However, if the test is one of foresight alone, P may escape liability on the basis that he did not foresee that R would actually do an improper act due to the conferral. We do not believe that this would be an acceptable result.

6.82   It is our policy that P can satisfy the fault element of bribery if he or she acted for the primary reason that the advantage would encourage R to act improperly. We believe that this is consistent with our overriding rationalisation of the law in terms of the nexus between an improper act and the conferral of an advantage. This is because, although P may doubt whether R will accept the advantage as the primary reason for acting improperly, he or she does not have control over whether this comes about. Therefore, we believe that the fact that it is P's primary reason for conferring the advantage should be sufficient to bring him or her within the offence.

Provisional proposal

6.83   We provisionally propose that the payer should satisfy the fault element of bribery if, by conferring an advantage, he or she either:

> **(1)   intends that the advantage should be the primary reason for the recipient doing an improper act; or**

> **(2)   foresees a serious risk that the advantage will create the primary reason for the recipient to do an improper act.**

---

[31]   The term "probably" in our previous draft Bill was also removed by the Government from their draft Corruption Bill that was modelled on our recommendations.

[32]   For further discussion, see our report, Murder, Manslaughter and Infanticide' (2006) Law Com No 304, paras 3.36 to 3.40.

6.84 We believe that (1) will be especially useful in relation to the bribery of public officials. This is because, by way of contrast with certain areas of private business, there are relatively few legitimate reasons for conferring an advantage on a public servant. On this basis, prosecutors will only have to establish that P's primary reason for conferring the advantage was to influence R to do an improper act and not that he or she foresaw a serious risk that R would do so.

Must P know or believe that the act that he or she intends R to do is an improper act?

6.85 In discussing the fault element of R,[33] we concluded that his or her liability should not be affected by a lack of appreciation that the act performed constituted an improper act. We did so because R is best placed to know or to find out what duties R is under. The same is not true of P.

6.86 As a result, although P will satisfy the fault element of the offence, we are provisionally proposing that there should be a specific defence to excuse P's conduct where he or she could *not reasonably have been expected to know that the conferral of the advantage was not legally required*. The details of this defence are set out in Part 8.

Where P confers an advantage, but R does not complete an improper act

6.87 On the basis of the provisional proposals already set out, in order to satisfy the fault element of bribery, P's primary reason for conferring the advantage must be that it will influence R to do an improper act or, if not P's primary reason, P must foresee a serious risk that it will be a primary reason for R doing an improper act.

6.88 As soon as the advantage is conferred with that fault element, P commits bribery. The fact that R does not do the improper act should make no difference. P's culpability is unaffected.[34] The nexus is still completed within the mind of P.

P confers an advantage after R does an improper act (scenario 2)

6.89 Here, R has already acted improperly, and P is conferring an advantage as a reward for that improper conduct. P may confer the advantage for three principal reasons:

(1) in order to demonstrate to R that if he or she (R) acts improperly in a similar way in the future advantages will be conferred; or

(2) because he or she has made an agreement with R that he or she (P) would confer the benefit after the improper act was completed; or

(3) because he or she believes that R completed the improper act primarily in order to gain the advantage and so its conferral is in some way expected.

---

[33] See paras 6.28 to 6.30 above.

[34] This will include the situation where, contrary to P's belief, R does not have the power to do the improper act.

Although conferring an advantage for one or more of these reasons may amount to bribery, in this section we are only concerned with cases where P acts for the third reason. If P acts for the first reason, his or her behaviour is better characterised as an attempt to induce R to perform a future act improperly because it is only that future act that P is able to affect (it will therefore come within scenario 1). If P acts for the second reason, R's agreement will amount to a representation of a willingness to confer an advantage (coming within scenario 3). It is only if P acts for the third reason that he or she is truly conferring the advantage in order to reward R's improper act.

Our previous recommendations

6.90 In our previous report, we dealt with P's fault element in relation to rewards in a very similar way to the way we dealt with inducements to act. P would commit the offence if he or she believed that R acted primarily in order to secure the advantage and he or she (P) intended to confer the advantage on this basis.

6.91 We set out our recommendation in clause 6(2) of our draft Bill:[35]

(1) A person who confers an advantage, or offers or agrees to confer an advantage, does so corruptly if –

(a) he knows or believes that in performing his functions as an agent a person has done an act or made an omission,

(b) he knows or believes that the person has done the act or made the omission primarily in order to secure that a person confers an advantage (whoever obtains it), and

(c) he intends the person known or believed to have done the act or made the omission to regard the advantage (or the advantage when conferred) as conferred primarily in return for the act or omission.

Adapting our previous recommendations

6.92 We still believe that the general approach in the previous report was correct. However, in the light of some important policy changes, it will now have to take account of the fact that "corruptly" (now "improperly") is defined as a breach of a legal or equitable duty that involves a betrayal of a relation of trust or a breach of a duty to act impartially or in the best interests of another.

6.93 In addition, clause 6(2)(c) is unsatisfactory. It requires P to intend R to believe that P is conferring the advantage primarily in order to reward R's act. We do not believe that such a complicated requirement is necessary or desirable in order to demonstrate P's fault and complete the nexus between the improper act and the conferral of the advantage. Rather, as long as P believes R completed the improper act primarily in order to secure an advantage, and P confers the advantage intending to reward that act, the nexus will be satisfied.

---

[35] Legislating the Criminal Code: Corruption (1998) Law Com No 248, Appendix A.

Provisional proposal

6.94 **We provisionally propose that the payer should satisfy the fault element of bribery if he or she confers an advantage on the recipient:**

    (1)   knowing or believing that the primary reason for the recipient doing an improper act was to secure an advantage from the payer; and

    (2)   intending to reward that improper act.

Where P does not realise that R's act is improper

6.95 As discussed above,[36] there will be a defence available to P where he or she has reasonable grounds for thinking that the conferral of the advantage was legally required.

P represents a willingness to confer an advantage on R (scenario 3)

6.96 Scenario 3 arises whenever there is an agreement between P and R prior to both the conferral of the advantage and the completion of the improper act. By representing a willingness to confer an advantage, P satisfies the conduct element of the offence. We now consider what fault element has to be satisfied if P is to be convicted of the offence.

6.97 In discussing R's fault element where he or she represents a willingness to act improperly,[37] we provisionally proposed that R must act with the intention of inducing an advantage from P and carrying out the improper act. Only if both of these requirements were met would the nexus be complete.

6.98 Likewise, where P represents a willingness to confer an advantage, we believe that he or she should have to fulfil the same requirements as if he or she had conferred the advantage (set out in scenario 1). Thus, P should stand to be convicted of bribery only if it was his or her intention that the advantage should be the primary reason for R to do an improper act or P foresaw a serious risk that the prospective advantage will create the primary reason for R to do an improper act.

6.99 The more difficult question is whether, like R, P should only be liable if he or she intends to act upon the representation. We do not believe that it should be necessary for P to intend to confer the advantage in order to complete the nexus and justify P's liability for bribery. For example:

Example 6L

P is tendering for a contract with X Ltd. P, concerned that a rival will submit a more competitive tender, agrees to pay R (an employee of X Ltd) £10,000 to ensure that his tender is successful. R accepts the offer and awards P the contract. P refuses to pay R the money, as P always intended to do.

---

[36] See paras 6.85 to 6.86 above.

[37] See paras 6.49 to 6.58 above.

In this example P has successfully induced R to complete an improper act. In this sense, the central harm that an offence of bribery is meant to prevent has materialised.

6.100 The reason that we believe that P, where he or she represents a willingness to confer an advantage, should not have to intend to confer the advantage in order to be convicted of bribery is due to the particular role P and the advantage play. The representation that he or she is willing to confer an advantage is a tool employed by P that is designed to influence R to do an improper act. The mischief lies in P's intention to bring about an improper act by 'dangling the carrot' of a prospective advantage for R.

Provisional proposal

6.101 **We provisionally propose that the payer should satisfy the fault element of bribery if, when representing a willingness to confer an advantage, he or she either:**

(1) **intends that the prospective advantage should be the primary reason for the recipient to do an improper act; or**

(2) **foresees a serious risk that the representation will create the primary reason for the recipient to do an improper act.**

Where P does not realise that R's act is improper

6.102 As discussed above,[38] there will be a defence available to P where he or she has reasonable grounds for thinking that the conferral of the advantage was legally required.

---

[38] See paras 6.85 to 6.86 above.

PART 7
A SEPARATE OFFENCE OF BRIBING A FOREIGN PUBLIC OFFICIAL

INTRODUCTION

7.1 The OECD Convention (which the UK has ratified) requires each Party to take such measures as are necessary to establish that it is a criminal offence to bribe a foreign public official.[1] However, the Commentaries on the OECD Convention make it clear that a Party can comply with the obligation by enacting offences prohibiting the bribery of persons generally even if the offences do not specifically address bribery of foreign public officials. We have done this by proposing an offence of bribery of general application. Nonetheless, at this stage we believe that there ought to be an additional discrete offence of bribery of a foreign public official to supplement our general offence.

THE CASE FOR A DISCRETE OFFENCE OF BRIBERY OF A FOREIGN PUBLIC OFFICIAL

7.2 In cases involving bribery of domestic public officials, proscribing the actions of corrupt officials is as important as proscribing the actions of those who seek to corrupt them. This is because in the domestic context it is as easy to prosecute corrupt public officials as it is to prosecute those who bribe them. By contrast, in cases involving corrupt foreign public officials, it may be impossible or extremely difficult for the courts in the country of the payer to prosecute the foreign official. Accordingly, the current emphasis in international Conventions is on prosecuting those who seek to bribe foreign public officials rather than on prosecuting the foreign public officials for breaching the obligations that they owe to their respective governments and populaces. The current view is that the most effective method of combating bribery of foreign public officials is by focusing on the supply side.

7.3 It is true that, under our provisional proposals, breach of a legal or equitable duty includes failing to act impartially. We acknowledge that in some cases involving bribery of foreign public officials, the prosecution may be able, without undue difficulty, to prove that P intended or foresaw a serious risk that the official would not act impartially. However, we are concerned that there will be cases where the prosecution will not be able to proceed on this basis.

7.4 Accordingly, we question whether the general bribery offence that we have constructed would, on its own, be sufficient in cases of bribery of foreign public officials, even if, as will usually not be the case, the bribery occurs in England and Wales. Our provisional view is that what is required is an additional bribery offence.

---

[1] Article 1.

102

7.5 The general offence of bribery that we have provisionally proposed requires the acceptance or giving of an advantage in exchange for or in expectation of or as a reward for R acting or promising to act in breach of a legal or equitable duty. If those who bribe foreign public officials had to be prosecuted under that offence, in every case the prosecution would have to prove that the foreign public official had breached, or had represented that he or she would breach, a legal or equitable duty. The problem is that it may be very difficult for the prosecution to identify the officials' legal and equitable duties and to prove that such duties have been or would have been breached.

Provisional proposal

7.6 **We provisionally propose that there should be a discrete offence of bribery of foreign public officials.**[2]

WHY NOT A DISCRETE OFFENCE OF BRIBERY OF A FOREIGN PRIVATE PERSON?

7.7 In this section, we explain why we are not advocating a discrete offence of bribery of a foreign private person. We believe that the most serious problems that we have identified in the application of the general offence to foreign public officials will not arise, or will not arise to the same extent, in relation to foreign private individuals. Instead, we believe that the general offence of bribery that we have outlined in Parts 5 and 6 will be sufficient.

Identifying legal and equitable duties

7.8 A problem that arises in the application of our general offence to foreign public officials is being able to identify the legal and/or equitable duties to which they are subject. This is because the constitutional arrangements of certain jurisdictions are highly complex and may be based on custom rather than clearly worded and accessible provisions. In order to identify a breach of duty, it might be necessary to adduce expert evidence. We believe that this would have the potential to delay cases and distract attention from the central issues. At worst, defendants might be able to avoid liability despite clearly having conferred an advantage in order to induce the official to provide or retain business.

7.9 We do not believe that cases relating to foreign private individuals will encounter this problem. Private natural persons and companies are much more likely to have their duties clearly defined in laws and regulations rather than by custom or 'understandings'. Corporations are likely to be subject to trade rules and the duties that are imposed are likely to be much more accessible than are those that apply to foreign public officials.

Co-operation and obtaining evidence

7.10 One of the major problems highlighted to us by the Serious Fraud Office in relation to the investigations of bribery of foreign persons is the availability of evidence and documentation. Yet, such evidence would be essential in order to demonstrate that a breach of a legal or equitable duty had taken place.

---

[2] For details of this offence, see paras 7.19 to 7.21 below.

7.11   In prosecutions for bribery of foreign public officials, the co-operation of other national authorities cannot be taken for granted. This is particularly so if those who are being requested to provide evidence are themselves in some way implicated in the alleged bribery. Yet, without evidence of a breach of a legal or equitable duty, even if it were clear that P conferred an advantage in order to gain or retain business, P would be able to escape liability.

7.12   In relation to foreign private individuals and corporations, the problem is much less likely to materialise. First, because (as we noted above) it is less likely that prosecutors in England and Wales will need specific evidence from R's country of origin. In addition, even if they do, the authorities in the foreign jurisdiction are much more likely to co-operate with that request because they are less likely to have a conflict of interests.

Other means of prosecuting bribery of foreign private individuals

7.13   There is another reason for singling out bribery of foreign public officials. The international community (through the OECD Convention) has decided to focus on this class of individuals as particularly vulnerable to bribery. For this reason, it has been decided that this area requires that those who seek to bribe foreign public officials should be prosecuted for bribery.[3]

7.14   Although resort to the law of bribery will be one option in cases of bribery involving foreign private individuals and companies, we doubt whether it will be the first port of call for most prosecutors in England and Wales. This is because the focus of authorities, such as the Office of Fair Trading, tends to be based on competition law. As we observe in Appendix D, where bribery of private individuals occurs outside the jurisdiction it will usually also amount to a competition law offence. We believe that the competition law regime, which permits the prosecution of private individuals,[4] will usually be the most appropriate means of addressing such cases.

CONSTRUCTING A DISCRETE OFFENCE OF BRIBING A FOREIGN PUBLIC OFFICIAL

The TI (UK) Bill

7.15   In 2007 Lord Chidgey introduced a Bill on corruption ('the TI (UK) Bill').[5] Clause 3 provides for an offence of bribery of foreign public officials. P commits the offence if he or she gives or procures an advantage for any person with the intention of influencing that person or another person to exercise a function improperly in that or the other person's capacity as a foreign public official. Clause 7 provides that:

(1)   "exercising a function" includes exercising or failing to exercise any duty or power irrespective of whether the function is or is not within the competence of the person exercising it;

---

[3]   The OECD Convention, Art 1.

[4]   The cartel offence contained within the Enterprise Act 2002. See Appendix D below.

[5]   HL 18. The Bill was originally drafted by Transparency International UK.

(2) "improperly" means in breach of any duty, whether express or implied, including any duty to act in good faith or impartially.

7.16 Accordingly, under the TI (UK) Bill, the prosecution must prove that P intended to influence a person to act in breach of a duty under the law of the territory of the foreign official. The prosecution will need to be able to identify the duties imposed on R by the law of the foreign territory.

Building on the TI (UK) Bill

7.17 The OECD Convention makes it clear that the mischief that an offence of bribery of a foreign public official is meant to combat is the offering or conferring of undue advantages in order to obtain or retain business in cases where the advantages are designed to influence the way the official acts in his or her official capacity.

7.18 For P to commit the offence of bribery of a foreign public official in the TI (UK) Bill, P must have intended to influence a person to exercise a function improperly. This captures the essence of the conduct that the OECD Convention wishes to see proscribed. It does, however, remain the case that the prosecution would have to prove that P intended the foreign official to breach a duty under the law of his or her country.

7.19 Rather than requiring the prosecution to have to prove that P intended the foreign official to breach a duty, we believe that the prosecution should have to prove that P offered to or conferred on a foreign public official an advantage:

(1) in order to

(a) obtain business;

(b) retain business;

(c) obtain or retain a business advantage; and

(2) did so

(a) intending to influence the foreign public official in respect of any act or omission by the official in his or her official capacity; or

(b) realising that there was a serious risk that the advantage would influence the foreign public official in respect of any act or omission by the official in his or her official capacity.

7.20 At the same time, it ought to be open to P to submit that the advantage offered or conferred was "legitimate" in the sense that the foreign public official was legally entitled to accept it. We believe that to place the legal burden of proving that it was 'legitimate' on P would raise issues of compatibility with the presumption of innocence articulated in Article 6(2) of the European Convention on Human Rights and Fundamental Freedoms. However, we see no reason why P should not bear an evidential burden.

7.21   In order to comply with the OECD Convention,[6] in determining whether the evidential burden has been discharged, a court should disregard evidence relating to:

    (1)   the fact that the benefit may be customary, or perceived to be customary, in that situation; and

    (2)   any official tolerance of the benefit.

7.22   The rationale underlying the OECD Convention is clear. Those who seek to influence foreign public officials cannot be heard to claim that 'everyone accepts these advantages'. On the other hand, P could discharge the evidential burden by adducing evidence such as written rules and regulations.

Bribes through intermediaries

7.23   Article 1 of the OECD Convention mandates the coverage of cases where P offers, promises or gives an undue advantage to a foreign public official directly or through an intermediary. According to the OECD, bribes are rarely given directly to foreign public officials but are usually transferred through intermediaries, including consultants, suppliers, sub-contractors and joint venture partners. Accordingly, the non-coverage of bribery of foreign public officials if the bribe is effected through an intermediary would represent a large loophole.

7.24   In cases where P seeks to effect the bribe through the intermediary ('X'), the conduct that constitutes the conferral of an advantage is perpetrated by X. In such cases, it will usually be the case that X also has the requisite fault element for the offence. If this is the case, X will be guilty of bribery as a principal offender and P is an accessory to and guilty of the offence committed by X. P assists or encourages X to commit the offence of bribery. In Part 10 we set out and explain the current law governing P's liability for assisting and encouraging criminal conduct together with recent recommendations that we have recently made for reform of the law for assisting and encouraging the commission of crime.

7.25   However, as we highlighted in Part 5, accessorial liability will not criminalise a pure trade in influence:

Example 7A

P (a British national) is trying to set up a new business in a foreign jurisdiction. In order to do so he needs a licence from X (a public official) for which he does not qualify. P pays R (X's wife) a considerable amount of money for her to convince her husband to act improperly and grant the licence. X is unaware that R has been paid this money.

---

[6]   See para 7 of the Commentaries on the Convention on Combating Bribery of Foreign Public Officials in International Business Transactions.

7.26 In this example, P is not encouraging R to commit bribery because R is not committing bribery: the use of influence without the conferral of an advantage will not satisfy bribery's conduct element. However, P is conferring an advantage and through this conferral he or she is attempting to obtain a business opportunity unfairly. Therefore, we believe that he or she should be guilty of bribery.

7.27 In order to catch a pure trade in influence in Part 5, we extended the definition of 'improper conduct' to include the use of influence to induce a breach of a legal or equitable duty. We believe that this same method should be employed for the specific offence that we are provisionally proposing in this Part. Therefore, P would commit bribery if he or she confers an advantage on a foreign public official in order to gain or retain a business opportunity, or if P confers an advantage on a third party intending that he or she should use his or her *influence* over a foreign public official in order to gain or retain a business opportunity for P.

Bribes that benefit third parties

7.28 Article 1 of the OECD Convention also mandates the coverage of cases where a bribe is offered, promised or given to a foreign public official "for that party or a third party". The significance of this is that a foreign public official may want to obtain advantages for a third party, for example, a political party, charity, spouse, friend or business partner.

7.29 It would be a significant obstacle to the effective implementation of the OECD Convention if P were able to avoid criminal liability by conferring the advantage directly on a third party rather than giving it to the foreign public official to transmit to the third party. Accordingly, it is essential that the offence that we are proposing should cover cases where P, with the requisite state of mind, confers the advantage directly on a third party.

Facilitation payments

7.30 Some, but by no means all, jurisdictions that have a discrete offence of bribery of a foreign public official provide for defences in relation to facilitation payments.[7] These are payments made to public officials, both domestic and foreign, where the value of the payment is "small"[8] or of a "minor nature"[9] and the payment is made in relation to "a routine governmental action".[10]

---

[7] Eg, Australia, New Zealand and the United States of America.

[8] New Zealand Crimes Act 1961, s 105C(3)(b).

[9] Australia Criminal Code Act 1995, s 70.4(1)(a).

[10] New Zealand Crimes Act 1961, s 105C(3)(a) and Australia Criminal Code Act 1995, s 70.4(1)(b).

7.31 In Appendix F, we consider in detail the issue of facilitation payments. We conclude that facilitation payments made to domestic public officials that involve or, if accepted, would involve R in breaching a legal or equitable duty should be prohibited.[11] By contrast, we are provisionally proposing that facilitation payments that do not or would not involve R in breaching a legal or equitable duty should not be prohibited.

7.32 The offence of bribing a foreign public official that we are provisionally proposing requires that P gives or offers to give an advantage in order to obtain or retain business or business advantages. In our view, advantages that are given or offered in order to secure or retain business or business advantages are not generally intended merely to secure routine government action. Indeed, we note that other jurisdictions that do have a facilitation payments defence in relation to bribery of foreign public officials appear to recognise that facilitation payments and payments made in order to obtain or retain business are mutually exclusive.

7.33 Thus, in the United States of America, facilitation payments to "expedite or to secure the performance of a routine governmental action" are permitted but only if the payments are not used to encourage a foreign public official to award new business or to continue existing business.[12] In New Zealand, a routine government action is defined so as not to include any decision about whether to award new business, whether to continue existing business with any particular person or body or the terms of any new or existing business.[13]

7.34 The reason why some jurisdictions have provided for a specific facilitation payments defence may stem from paragraph 9 of the Commentaries on the OECD Convention. At first blush, it might be thought to be saying that a payment can at one and the same time be both a facilitation payment and a payment made in order to obtain or retain business. However, we believe that the better view is that Article 9 is making the opposite point, namely that small facilitation payments do not constitute payments to obtain or retain business. The converse point is that payments made to obtain or retain business do not constitute facilitation payments. In other words, at least for the purposes of the OECD Convention, paragraph 9 is clarifying that the two types of payment are mutually exclusive.

---

[11] Subject to two defences that we detail in Part 8: see paras 8.7 to 8.32 below.

[12] 15 U.S.C.$$ 78dd-1(b), 78dd-2(b), 78dd-3(b).

[13] For another provision to similar effect, see the Australia Criminal Code Act 1995, s 70.4(2)(c) and (d).

7.35 Accordingly, we are not provisionally proposing that there should be any facilitation payments defence to the offence of bribery of a foreign public official.[14] For the purposes of our policy, it is not necessary to define what is a facilitation payment. If the advantage is conferred in order to obtain or retain business, P will fall within the discrete offence. If not, P's act will fall for consideration within the general offence that we are proposing.

Provisional proposal

7.36 **We provisionally propose that it should be an offence if:**

(1) **in order to**

(a) **obtain business;**

(b) **retain business; or**

(c) **obtain or retain a business advantage,**

(2) **the payer gives, offers or agrees to give an advantage to or for any person, being an advantage to which the recipient or intended recipient is not legitimately due, and**

(3) **the payer does so:**

(a) **intending to influence that person or another person in respect of any act or omission by that person or another person in his or her capacity as a foreign public official; or**

(b) **realising that there is a serious risk that the advantage will influence that person or another person in respect of any act or omission by that person or another person in his or her capacity as a foreign public official;**

(c) **intending to influence a third party to use their influence over another person in respect of any act or omission by that person or another person in his or her capacity as a foreign public official.**

7.37 **We provisionally propose that for the purposes of determining whether an advantage is "legitimately due" no account should be taken of:**

(1) **the fact that the advantage may be customary, or perceived to be customary, in the circumstances;**

(2) **any official tolerance of the advantage.**

---

[14] However, we are provisionally proposing that there should be two defences to the offence of bribery of a foreign public official. Since these defences are not peculiar to the offence of bribery of a foreign public official, we set them out in Part 8 which deals with general defences.

USING THE DISCRETE OFFENCE TO CATCH THE RECIPIENT

7.38 The offence that we are provisionally proposing will only apply to P. We have chosen, in line with the OECD Convention, to focus on P because we believe that it will be very rare that foreign public officials can be brought to trial before an English court. Further, by focusing on the supply side of bribery and effectively policing our own nationals, the new law is intended to reduce the prevalence of bribery more generally.

7.39 However, in certain circumstances we may wish to target R as well as P. For example, if a foreign public official accepted a bribe inside England and Wales it may well be that they are tried before our courts. In this scenario, if our provisional proposals were adopted, R could be prosecuted under the general bribery offence. The prosecution would, therefore, have to demonstrate that R acted in breach of a legal or equitable duty.

7.40 The difficulty of identifying the legal and equitable duties of a foreign public official was the main concern that led to our provisional proposal to create a separate offence for P. This difficulty is equally compelling when one considers whether the offence should also extend to the foreign public official who receives the advantage from P. In this vein, we note that at least two other signatories of the OECD Convention have chosen to go beyond the minimum requirements of the Convention to provide for the liability of R in this situation.[15]

Question for consultees

7.41 **We ask consultees to consider whether our provisionally proposed offence of bribing a foreign public official should be extended to inculpate the foreign public official who accepts a bribe**.

CONCLUSION

7.42 Although two bribery offences are being provisionally proposed, as far as possible they have been designed to criminalise broadly the same kind of wrongdoing. For both, the nexus between the conferral of an advantage and an improper act underpins the offence. It is simply that when prosecuting the bribery of a foreign public official, we believe that the prosecution should have two alternative approaches: the general offence and the discrete offence.

---

[15] See, France Art 435-1 and Art 435-2; South Africa The Prevention and Combating of Corruption Activities Act 2004, s4.

PART 8
DEFENCES, BARRIERS TO PROSECUTION AND ANCILLARY MATTERS

INTRODUCTION

8.1 This Part is split into three sections. The first section asks what specific defences, if any, should be applicable to the new offences. The second section explores whether prosecution under the new offences should be conditional on the consent of a Law Officer. The final section covers some ancillary matters, for example, whether the offences should remain triable either way and whether the common law offence of bribery should be abolished.

DEFENCES

Defences rejected in Law Com No 248[1]

8.2 In our previous report on corruption we analysed a variety of potential defences.[2] These included:

> (1) disclosure: where R is excused from accepting an advantage where he or she has fully disclosed its receipt to those who have interests or duties that might be affected;

> (2) no obligation to account: where R is excused from accepting an advantage in the situation where he or she would not be under a civil law duty to account for its receipt;

> (3) normal practice: where P and/or R could both potentially be excused their part in an otherwise corrupt transaction if it was deemed to be 'normal practice' within the area in which they are operating;

> (4) small value: where P and/or R could both potentially be excused their part in an otherwise corrupt transaction if the advantage was considered to be of small value;

> (5) entrapment: where P and/or R could both potentially be excused from liability (despite either offering or soliciting a bribe) on the basis that they only completed the offence in order to expose the other party as someone who is willing either to accept or offer bribes; and

> (6) public interest: where P and/or R could both potentially be excused from liability on the basis that they were acting in the public interest (for example, through investigative reporting).

---

[1] Legislating the Criminal Code: Corruption (1998).

[2] Above, paras 5.135 to 5.152.

We concluded that none of these defences should be incorporated into a draft Corruption Bill. It is a conclusion that has not (to our knowledge) attracted any serious adverse comment and it is one that we maintain.

Defences recommended in Law Com No 248

8.3 In our previous report we recommended that there should be two defences. First, that the agent's principal consented to what was done and secondly, that the advantage represented proper remuneration or reimbursement.

PRINCIPAL'S CONSENT

8.4 The Commission considered that if an agent's principal knew all the relevant facts and consented to what was done by the agent or the payer, or both, that conduct ought not in principle to be caught by a corruption offence. The Commission stated that to hold agents guilty of corruption in such circumstances would be "unduly harsh".

PROPER REMUNERATION OR REIMBURSEMENT

8.5 The Commission also considered that proper remuneration of an agent or reimbursement of expenditure incurred by an agent in the performance of his or her functions as an agent should be excluded from the definition of "corruptly" conferring an advantage.

Departing from the recommendations in Law Com No 248

8.6 In Part 4, we have already set out many of the criticisms that have led us to jettison these defences. Moreover, in our main provisional proposals, we have departed from a previous approach in which bribery was defined very widely and then defences had to be employed to remove permissible or even beneficial conduct from the scope of the offence. Under our main provisional proposals, we believe that such conduct should not come within the scope of the offence at all, because 'improper' (formerly, 'corrupt') conduct must involve a breach of duty.[3]

The defences that we are now proposing

8.7 Nonetheless, we believe that there is a good case for the inclusion of two defences within the new structure of bribery offences. These defences, whilst special to the proposed bribery offences, will have a strong family resemblance to defences with which the courts are already very familiar. The defences are designed to apply with equal measure both to the general bribery offence set out in Parts 5 and 6, and to the specific offence relating to the bribery of a foreign public official set out in Part 7. They should also be extended in their application to any inchoate offence (such as attempt or conspiracy) that relates to a bribery offence.

---

[3] In relation to the proposed separate offence of bribing a foreign public official, the defences of principal's consent and proper remuneration will simply have no relevance.

8.8 The first defence relates to bribes paid by P in an emergency. The second relates to bribes paid by P where he or she reasonably believed that the conferral of the advantage was legally required (alternatively, legally required *or* legally permissible). Neither of these defences would apply to R. We will deal with each of them in turn.

The emergency defence

8.9 At present, being general defences, the common law defences of duress by threats and duress of circumstances apply to offences of bribery at common law and to offences under the Prevention of Corruption Acts. Our provisional proposal is that, on a charge of bribery, there should be a defence that constitutes a very limited extension of these defences, to include emergencies that do not necessarily involve a threat of death or serious bodily injury.

8.10 In the past, TRACE[4] have recommended that there should be an exception to any general prohibition on facilitation payments where the payment is to deal with a medical or security emergency. Consistent with our proposals for a simplified more general offence of bribery, we believe that the application of such a defence should extend beyond facilitation payments to cover all cases that fall within our proposed bribery offences. Although payments made, or other advantages conferred, to deal with emergencies will normally be facilitative in nature, it would be undesirable to have to establish this as a matter of law in order for the defence to succeed.

8.11 We propose that the defence of 'emergency payment' (or of advantage conferred in an emergency) should be available when the person making the payment – or conferring the advantage - reasonably believes that doing so is the only realistic way of avoiding an imminent danger of physical harm to themselves or to another:

Example 8A

P is on holiday abroad with her children. One of her children falls sick and a doctor says that the child may become too ill to fly home unless treated in hospital. The doctor says that the hospital will only treat non-nationals if payments are made to all those involved in the treatment. P agrees to make the payments in order to secure the treatment for her child.

8.12 It may be asked why such a defence is necessary, when the already existing general defences of duress and duress of circumstances apply to the offence of bribery. As indicated above, the answer is that the defence we are proposing would apply whenever there is an imminent threat of physical harm, and would not be restricted – as the defences of duress are restricted – to imminent threats of death or of *serious* injury.[5]

---

[4] www.fundworksinvestments.com/fn_filelibrary//File/co_gsri_high_cost_small_bribes.pdf, at p 10.

[5] See *Howe* [1987] AC 417.

8.13 The general defences of duress apply to offences across the board, from minor traffic violations to manslaughter. That in part explains the narrowness of their scope, including the requirement that the duress take the form of a threat of death or of serious harm. However, it would be unduly harsh on defendants to make a defence to bribery hinge on whether, as in Example 8A, P's child was in imminent danger of serious harm. An imminent danger of physical harm of any kind should be sufficient to trigger the application of the defence.[6] We believe that will be sufficient to cover the kinds of medical and security emergencies that TRACE had in mind.

Provisional proposal

8.14 **We provisionally propose that the payer should have a defence to a charge of bribery (or to an inchoate offence relating to a principal offence of bribery) if, in the circumstances that the payer reasonably believed to exist, it was reasonable to confer an advantage in order to avert what the payer reasonably believed to be an imminent danger of physical harm to him or herself or to another.**

Reasonable belief in lawfulness of conduct

8.15 Our provisional view is that it should also be a defence for someone to show that an advantage was conferred in the reasonable belief that conferring it was a legal requirement. We are provisionally proposing that this defence should apply to any bribery offence and to any inchoate offence relating to bribery.

8.16 This defence would not, as such, be a *permission* to make payments in some circumstances. Nor would it make any concession to the (in our view, mistaken) view that the application of the law of bribery should be adapted to fit the political, moral or cultural environment in which individuals and companies sometimes have to operate internationally. Instead, the defence is a tightly drawn *excuse* for those who had good grounds for thinking that they were actually complying with the law.

---

[6] There are precedents for 'emergency' defences specially tailored to fit particular defences. An analogy here, albeit not an exact one, is with the defence in the Criminal Damage Act 1971, s 5(2)(b), by virtue of which there is a lawful excuse for damaging property if it was done in the belief that the damage is necessary to protect other property in immediate need of protection and the means adopted were reasonable in all the circumstances.

8.17 According to an old adage, 'ignorance of the law is no excuse'; but that adage is not a wholly accurate statement of the law of England and Wales.[7] Moreover, in so far as it does have an application, the strength of the case for applying it without exception in all regulatory contexts becomes weaker by the year, as the number of contexts in which the conduct of individuals and companies falls to be regulated (often in highly complex ways) relentlessly increases.[8] That is in part the explanation for the making of our provisional proposal.

8.18 Alongside our provisional proposal, we are asking consultees whether the defence should be broadened to include instances in which P reasonably believes that conferring an advantage is legally *permitted*.

THE GENERAL BRIBERY OFFENCE

8.19 The provisionally proposed defence would apply if P conferred – or agreed to or attempted to confer - an advantage on R in order to induce R to do an act that amounts to a breach of a legal or equitable duty in circumstances where P believed the payment was legally required.

8.20 However, for P to be able successfully to plead the defence, his or her belief that the payment was legally required would have to be reasonable. In deciding whether it was reasonable, a jury would take into account all the circumstances. For example, a large company may be expected to know or to find out which payments must be made by law and which payments are being asked for illegally. However, individual citizens, perhaps visiting somewhere for the first time, are not in the same position:

Example 8B

P is a student organising a 'backpacking' tour overseas. P writes to officials in a country he wishes to visit to ask if there is any paperwork that he must complete before arrival. He is sent some forms to sign and return, and is told that an 'administration charge' for processing the forms will be levied when he reaches the border crossing. When he consults a British government website, he learns that in the country in question payments 'may' be requested, but he thinks this might refer to undocumented requests for 'cash-in-hand'. He signs and returns the forms, agreeing to pay the charge. In fact, the forms are not official documents and are printed and issued by the officials for the sole purpose of securing the payment at the border.

---

[7] See Andrew Ashworth, "Testing Fidelity to Legal Values: Official Involvement and Criminal Justice", in Stephen Shute and A P Simester (eds), *Criminal Law Theory: Doctrines of the General Part* (Oxford, 2002); Andrew Ashworth, "Excusable Mistake of Law" [1974] *Criminal Law Review* 652.

[8] Andrew Ashworth, "Testing Fidelity to Legal Values: Official Involvement and Criminal Justice", in Stephen Shute and A P Simester (eds), *Criminal Law Theory: Doctrines of the General Part* (Oxford, 2002).

> **Example 8C**
>
> P is the managing director of a small company seeking to secure a valuable contract in the UK. She meets the officials who award contracts. P is given some forms to sign and is told that an 'administration charge' for processing the forms will be levied. Although the size of the fee raises P's suspicions, P is not particularly suspicious because the fee is specifically referred to in the documents. P makes the payment as quickly as possible so as to ensure she stays one step ahead of her competitors. In fact, the forms are not official documents and are printed and issued by the officials for the sole purpose of securing the payment.

In these examples, although P's conduct does not come within the specific offence of bribery of a foreign public official, it has the potential to fall within the general offence.[9] This is because P possesses the fault element in that he or she is aware in each case that there is a serious risk that the payment will be the primary reason for the officials' action.[10] It would be for the prosecution to demonstrate beyond reasonable doubt that P satisfies all elements of the offence.

8.21 In relation to the defence, the burden would be on the prosecution to disprove its application. However, we believe that if P wishes to rely on this defence, he or she should have to satisfy an evidential burden.

8.22 Accordingly, on a charge of bribery, it should be a defence if P conferred an advantage – or agreed or attempted to confer an advantage – in the reasonable belief that to do so was legally required.

THE SPECIFIC OFFENCE OF BRIBING A FOREIGN PUBLIC OFFICIAL

8.23 The same defence would apply to the specific offence of bribing a foreign public official. Suppose that, in Example 8C, P is seeking to secure a valuable contract in another jurisdiction, meets the foreign officials who award contracts within that jurisdiction and then events unfold in the same way. It will be clear that P has conferred an advantage upon R in order to secure a business opportunity. As a result, P would come within the specific offence.

8.24 If P wishes to rely on the defence, he or she will have to satisfy the evidential burden. In the variation of Example 8B under discussion, this is likely to require the company to demonstrate through documentary evidence why it believed that the payment was legally required.

---

[9] In Example 8B, although R is a foreign public official, P is not conferring the advantage in relation to the creation or retention of business. In Example 8C, R is not a foreign public official.

[10] The language of 'serious risk' is not entirely apposite in this particular context, in that it suggests that P already knows that the payment may be improper. However, that is more a matter of infelicity of language than of legal principle. The issue, in point of fault, is whether P realised that it was realistic to suppose that R would treat the payment as the primary reason for acting.

A belief that it is legally permissible to confer an advantage

8.25 We are asking consultees whether the defence of reasonable belief that an advantage conferred is lawful should extend beyond advantages it is believed are legally required, to advantages it is believed are legally permitted.

8.26 This extension is meant to account for the fact that, in law as in morality, justified conduct normally includes conduct that is permitted as well as conduct that is required. The argument is, thus, that if P reasonably believes that his or her conduct is *legally* permissible (and not just tolerated less formally), P believes that his or her conduct is as justified in law as the person who believes that his or her conduct is legally required.

8.27 Further, there may in practice be examples where P reasonably believes that it is legally permissible to confer an advantage, although he or she need not confer it. A illustrative variation on Example 8B might be where P is told that, for an extra charge payable immediately, he can be given a pass that will free him from charges that would ordinarily be levied to enter certain historic sites in the country in question.[11] In such a case, P may reasonably believe that it is legally permissible to make this payment, but clearly does not believe that he or she is required to make it.

8.28 This example may seem to mount a compelling case for extending the 'reasonable belief in the lawfulness of conduct' defence to instances in which P reasonably believes that a payment is legally permissible. However, there are concerns about extending it that far.

8.29 Very many instances of bribes are instances in which the advantage to be conferred is one that P understands may, for example, speed up an administrative process, but where the advantage has not actually been required by the recipient. In such instances, there may be a fine line between P's belief that an advantage is lawfully (permissibly) conferred and a belief that it is in a broader moral, social or political sense acceptable to confer it. We would not want the fineness of this line to undermine our commitment to the view that bribery should not be tolerated simply because some people turn a blind eye to (or even welcome) it. Yet, this might happen if, for example, a jury was unable to appreciate the difference between a belief in the legal permissibility and a belief in the social or political permissibility of bribery. It is much easier to maintain a clear line between what is believed to be legal and what is merely believed to be tolerated if the focus – in relation to what is believed to be legal – is on what is thought to be legally *required*.

---

[11] One must assume that, although P has no way of knowing this, entry to the sites is in fact free of charge in any event.

8.30   The requirement that P bear the evidential burden when showing that there was reason to think that the payment was legally permissible, and the requirement that P's decision should be reasonable, ought to provide adequate safeguards against abuse of this defence. An absence of documentary evidence to back the claim that there were such grounds will usually tell against P (although it may not be fatal to the defence).

Provisional proposal

8.31   **We provisionally propose that the payer should have a defence to bribery (or to an inchoate offence relating to a principal offence of bribery) if he or she conferred an advantage in the reasonable belief that to do so was legally required. The evidential burden in relation to holding the reasonable belief should be on the payer.**

Question for consultees

8.32   **We ask whether the defence should extend to cases where the payer conferred an advantage in the reasonable belief that to do so was legally permissible.**

CONSENT TO PROSECUTION

Introduction

8.33   Under the current law, as with various other offences, certain bribery offences require the consent of the Attorney General ('the AG') before a prosecution can be instituted.[12] However, the requirements are not uniform. Consent is required for prosecutions under the 1889 Act[13] and the 1906 Act,[14] but consent is not required for prosecutions brought for bribery at common law.

8.34   The question for consultees is therefore whether consent should be required for the bribery offences that we are provisionally proposing. We will be proposing a rationalisation of the law, confining the need to obtain consent to a narrow range of cases.

---

[12]   For a list of offences that presently require the consent of the Attorney General or the Director of Public Prosecutions see: Consent to Prosecution (1998) Law Com No 255, appendix A.

[13]   Section 4. The section, as originally enacted, had also allowed the consent to come from the alternative source of the Solicitor General. However, the Law Officers Act 1997 s3(2) deleted the reference to the Solicitor General.

[14]   Section 2(1). The section, as originally enacted, also allowed the consent of the Solicitor General. However, the Law Officers Act 1997 s3(2) deleted the reference to the Solicitor General.

Justification for requiring consent under the current law

8.35　When the Prevention of Corruption Acts were enacted, a requirement of consent was justified as a protection against abuse by private prosecutors, such as blackmailers threatening to bring private prosecutions unless money was paid:[15]

> The original reasons for introducing the requirement of the Attorney General's consent were to avoid bribery, collusion, blackmail and other improper practices which frequently surrounded the private prosecution.[16]

8.36　The justification was that although it was relatively straightforward to bring a private prosecution for bribery, it was very difficult to disprove allegations of corruption.[17] It was therefore believed that the AG should review cases to 'weed out' those seeking to abuse the system.

8.37　Although this was the principal justification for requiring consent, the Home Office have since set out several other justifications. These include:

(1)　securing consistency of practice in bringing prosecutions, for example, where it is not possible to define the offence very precisely so that the law goes wider than the mischief aimed at or is open to a variety of interpretations;

(2)　preventing abuse or bringing the law into disrepute, for example, with the kind of offence which might otherwise result in vexatious private prosecutions or the institution of proceedings in trivial cases;

(3)　enabling account to be taken of mitigating factors, which may vary from case to case and so will not be susceptible to statutory definition;

(4)　providing some central control over the use of the criminal law when it has to intrude into areas which are particularly sensitive or controversial, such as race relations or censorship; and

(5)　ensuring that decisions on prosecutions take account of important considerations of public policy or of a political or international nature, such as may arise, for instance, in relation to official secrets or hijacking.[18]

---

[15]　Legislating the Criminal Code: Corruption (1997) Law Commission Consultation Paper No. 145, para 10.5.

[16]　P Fennell and P A Thomas 'Corruption in England and Wales: An Historical Analysis' (1983) 11 *International Journal of Sociology and Law* 167, 173.

[17]　Legislating the Criminal Code: Corruption (1997) Law Commission Consultation Paper No 145, para 10.7.

[18]　Home Office Memorandum on the control of prosecutions by the Attorney General and the Director of Public Prosecutions (April 1972), attached to the Report of the Departmental Committee on section 2 of the Official Secrets Act 1911 (1972) Cmnd 5104: see Legislating the Criminal Code: Corruption (1997) Law Commission Consultation Paper No. 145, paras 10.8 to 10.10.

8.38   The Home Office Memorandum, which focused primarily on the Official Secrets Act 1911, concluded that in these instances it was essential for there to be consent prior to prosecution.

Consent of the Director of Public Prosecutions ('the DPP') rather than that of the Attorney General ('the AG')

8.39   One of the main reasons why it might be beneficial to shift the requirement of consent from the AG to the DPP is one of practicality. If the DPP could give consent, by virtue of section 1(7) of the Prosecution of Offences Act 1985 any Crown Prosecutor could give consent. This would prevent a 'bottleneck' within the system and also free the AG from having to review every case, however trivial. It would also avoid the current duplication of effort whereby the DPP has to prepare a statement of relevant facts for the AG to consider before the latter makes a decision.[19]

8.40   Despite the practical utility of this suggestion, it was the Home Office's opinion, at the time they issued the Memorandum referred to in paragraphs 8.37 and 8.38 above, that the AG should still review certain issues. It was felt that, although most of the relevant considerations were within the expertise of the DPP, the AG would still have to assess issue (5) and often issue (4), referred to in paragraph 8.37 above.[20]

The Law Commission's previous position

Law Commission Consultation Paper No 145[21]

8.41   In its 1997 consultation paper, the Commission highlighted the inconsistency of the current law and offered three options for consultees:

(1)   require the consent of the AG for the new offences of bribery it was proposing;

(2)   require the consent of the DPP for the new offences; or

(3)   remove the requirement of consent altogether.

8.42   In theory, all three options remain, although there is now a fourth option:

(4)   the consent of either the AG or of the DPP should be required for a limited range of bribery cases.

8.43   This fourth option is particularly important given that we are proposing that there should be two offences of bribery, one of which has an exclusively extra-territorial focus (bribery of a foreign public official).

---

[19]   Above, para 10.6.

[20]   Above, para 10.9.

[21]   Legislating the Criminal Code: Corruption (1997) Law Commission Consultation Paper No 145.

8.44   In practice, we believe that option (1) is likely to prove unattractive both to the majority of consultees and to Government.[22] The realistic choices are between options (2) to (4).

8.45   We will be provisionally proposing that the DPP's consent be required for prosecution of the general offence of bribery (option (3)) but that – subject to any future changes to the AG's role in giving consent to prosecutions in general[23] – the AG's consent be required for any prosecution involving an extra-territorial dimension. However, before explaining these provisional proposals, we will complete the history of previous attempts to resolve the question.

Law Commission Consultation Paper No 149[24]

8.46   In between the publications of the CP and the report on corruption, the Law Commission issued a consultation paper aimed at rationalising the law generally as it relates to consent to prosecution. Inevitably, this more general paper influenced the Commission's recommendations in relation to corruption and the Commission made several references to it in the previous report.

8.47   In the consultation paper on consent to prosecution, the Commission proposed that, on account of the administrative delays brought about by the requirement of consent, and the fettering of the right to bring a private prosecution, consent to prosecution should be required only in a limited range of instances. The Commission proposed that consent should only be required for offences:

    (1)   which directly affect freedom of expression;

    (2)   which may involve national security or have some international element; or

    (3)   in respect of which it is particularly likely, given the availability of civil proceedings in respect of the same conduct, that the public interest would not require a prosecution.[25]

The conclusion in Law Com No 248

8.48   In the corruption report, the Commission concluded that the new offences did not fall into any of the categories listed above and so should not require the consent of either the AG or the DPP.[26]

---

[22]   See the discussion at paras 8.60 and 8.61 below.

[23]   See the discussion at paras 8.72 to 8.75 below.

[24]   Consent to Prosecution (1997) Law Commission Consultation Paper No 149.

[25]   Above, para 7.5.

[26]   Legislating the Criminal Code: Corruption (1998) Law Com No 248, para 7.21.

Other reasons for the Commission's recommendation in Law Com No 248

8.49 Although some respondents to the report maintained that consent should be required due to the sensitivity of prosecutions for corruption, the majority of consultees supported the Commission in its view that consent should not be required.[27]

8.50 The Commission's view was bolstered by the lack of reported abuses in relation to the current common law offence.[28] The common law bribery offence does not require consent to prosecute. Accordingly, it was argued that if there were a real danger of unwarranted and malicious private prosecutions they would already be occurring under the existing law.

8.51 The Commission explained the lack of abuse by reference to the range of procedural restraints already in place to regulate private prosecutions.[29] Examples of these restraints include magistrates refusing to issue a summons, the limited availability of legal aid and the DPP's power to take over a private prosecution and then terminate it.[30]

The Government's response to Law Com No 248

8.52 In its response,[31] the Government rejected the Law Commission's recommendation for the removal of the requirement for consent. It did so for two principal reasons.

8.53 First, the Government believed that the Law Commission had not provided sufficiently compelling reasons for removing the requirement.[32]

8.54 Secondly, the Government believed that bribery and corruption fell within one of general categories the Law Commission regarded as justifying a requirement of consent.[33] However, they came to this view on the basis of the categories identified by the Law Commission in its report on consent to prosecution,[34] which was published in 1998 after the report on corruption. In its report on consent to prosecution, the Commission had changed its policy in some respects from that set out in the CP, and added a further category that would justify the requirement of consent:

---

[27]   Above, para 7.22.

[28]   Above, para 7.24.

[29]   Above, para 7.25.

[30]   Prosecution of Offences Act 1985, s 23.

[31]   Raising Standards and Upholding Integrity: the Prevention of Corruption (2000).

[32]   Above, para 5.3.

[33]   Above, para 5.2.

[34]   Consent to Prosecution (1998) Law Com No 255.

> ... prosecutions for those offences which create a high risk that the right of private prosecution will be abused and the institution of proceedings will cause irreparable harm.[35]

8.55 It was the Government's view that corruption would fall within this category.[36] So, the Government's rejection of the Commission's recommendation in relation to bribery did *not* result from a rejection of the Commission's previous conclusion in the CP on corruption, namely that bribery and corruption did not fall within one of the categories requiring consent to prosecution identified in CP No 149. The Government was basing its view instead on the categories identified in the Commission's consent to prosecution report.

8.56 Although the Government relies on the consent to prosecution report in justifying the view that the consent of the AG should be required in bribery cases, in the consent to prosecution report the Commission distinguished the different categories in which consent should be required. It did so by reference to *whose* consent should be required. Where national security or international considerations were involved, the Commission's view was that the consent should come from the AG. However, if consent were required merely in order to prevent abuse (the category relied upon by the Government), consent need only come from the DPP.[37]

Joint Committee's response to the Government's position

8.57 The Joint Committee was set up to evaluate the Government's draft Corruption Bill (modelled on the Law Commission's recommendations, but including the Government's rejection of the Commission's recommendation in relation to consent to prosecute).[38] The Committee agreed with the Government that consent should be required. They did so because they believed that the danger of "frivolous and vexatious"[39] private prosecutions was a real one, providing the example of a private prosecution brought during an election year or other sensitive time when it could "distort the political process".[40]

8.58 However, unlike the Government, the Joint Committee concluded that consent should come from the DPP and not the AG.[41] They did so for two principal reasons. First, they said they did not see any practical need for consent to come from the AG rather than the DPP. Secondly, they commented that the involvement of the AG (as a politician) risked creating the appearance of bias.

---

[35] Above, para 6.52. The Commission also removed one of the categories provisionally proposed in the CP, the one referring to cases that are adequately catered for within the civil law.

[36] Raising Standards and Upholding Integrity: the Prevention of Corruption (2000), para 5.2.

[37] Consent to Prosecution (1998) Law Com No 255, para 7.13.

[38] Joint Committee on the Draft Corruption Bill (2002-03) HL 157, HC 705.

[39] Above, para 137.

[40] Above.

[41] Above, para 138.

The Government's response to the Joint Committee

8.59 In their formal response to the Joint Committee report,[42] the Government concurred with the Joint Committee's recommendation that the consent of the DPP should be sufficient.[43]

The Government's response to their latest consultation on bribery

8.60 In early 2007 the Government published their response to their latest round of consultation on bribery.[44] Although the consultation did not specifically ask for comments on the issue of consent to prosecution, some of the Government's consultees raised the issue in their submissions and so the Government discussed the issue briefly at the end of their response.

8.61 In their paper the Government reaffirmed their position that consent should be required and that consent should come from the DPP. However, in the light of the increasing role played by the Serious Fraud Office ('SFO') in foreign bribery cases, they also stated they would extend this to the Director of the SFO.[45]

Comments from other parties

The OECD

8.62 In the OECD's 2005 phase 2 report,[46] the OECD considered whether the current (and future) requirement of consent might affect the UK's adherence to the OECD convention. Their first concern was that the criteria upon which the AG makes a decision could be inconsistent with those allowed by the OECD Convention (Article 5).[47] However, they were reassured by the AG that the Convention would always be taken into account in order to avoid inconsistency.

8.63 Their second concern was simply that the requirement of consent created an unnecessary barrier to prosecution.[48] In their discussion, the OECD examiners make repeated references to the Law Commission's project on corruption and its previous recommendation that the consent requirement should be removed. Like the Law Commission, they highlighted the fact that the common law bribery offence had operated satisfactorily for many years without a requirement of consent.

---

[42] The Government reply to the Report from the Joint Committee on the draft Corruption Bill Session 2002-03 HL Paper 157, HC 705 (2003) Cm 6086.

[43] Above, para (21).

[44] Consultation on Bribery: Reform of the Prevention of Corruption Acts and SFO powers in Cases of Bribery of Foreign Officials: Summary of responses and next steps (2007).

[45] Above, para 97.

[46] Available at http://www.oecd.org/searchResult/0,3400,en_2649_34859_1_1_1_1_1,00.html

[47] Above, paras 168 to 171.

[48] Above, paras 174 to 177.

8.64   The OECD examiners therefore recommended that, in relation to any future reformed offence, the UK should consider the appropriateness of the requirement of consent.[49]

8.65   In their response to the OECD examiners, the Government went further than they had previously gone in justifying the requirement of consent. Referring to the Law Commission's report on consent to prosecution, the Government repeated its previously stated justification in relation to the third category, namely where the potential for abuse justifies the requirement of consent. However, the Government also argued that the second category could apply, namely the one involving national security and international considerations. However, if these categories were to be applied as the Commission set out in its consent to prosecution report, the consent should come from the AG and not from the DPP.[50]

Comments in relation to the SFO's terminated inquiry into BAE

8.66   In December 2006 the SFO terminated a major part of its corruption investigation into BAE Industries.[51] That decision has attracted considerable media attention. Some of this attention has focused on the perceived role of the AG in terminating the investigation. For example, Transparency International have recommended the removal of the consent to prosecution requirement,[52] commenting that the problems caused by it have been brought into "sharp relief by the recent SFO decision".[53]

8.67   However, in response to these concerns it is important to recognise two points. First, the investigation was still some way from the stage where prosecution would have been contemplated and so it represents a different situation to the one under discussion in this Part. Secondly, the then AG has made it perfectly clear that although he agreed with the decision to terminate the investigation, the decision itself was an internal one made by the SFO.[54]

---

[49]   Above, para 177.

[50]   Consents to Prosecution (1998) Law Com No 255, para 7.13.

[51]   That involving the Al Yamamah contracts with Saudi Arabia.

[52]   Transparency International, Corruption Bill – Background note (2007).

[53]   Above, para 2.1.

[54]   Interview transcript: Lord Goldsmith, *The Financial Times* 31 January 2007.

Our provisional conclusion in relation to the general offence of bribery.

8.68   We now believe that the long-established Government view that it is the DPP's consent (or now, where appropriate, the consent of the Director of the SFO) to prosecution for bribery that should be required is the right one.[55] This is because the way in which we are proposing to define the general offence of bribery makes it particularly important that the choice of charge, as between bribery and other possible offences, is made both consistently over time and in a way that best reflects the public interest.

8.69   Accordingly, the mere fact that, as the OECD observes,[56] the absence of a consent requirement in common law bribery has given rise to no difficulties is in itself not a sufficiently convincing basis for dispensing with a consent requirement for the new general offence.

8.70   It follows that the DPP's consent (or now, where appropriate, the consent of the Director of the SFO) should also be required when an inchoate offence - such as attempt - is charged in relation to the general offence of bribery.

8.71   We now turn our attention to the role of the AG in giving consent to prosecution.

The Government's consultation on the role of the AG

8.72   On 3 July 2007, the Prime Minister announced to MPs that:

> The role of the Attorney General which combines legal and ministerial functions needs to change. And while we consult on reform, the Attorney General has decided, except if the law or national security requires it, not to make key prosecution decisions in individual cases.[57]

8.73   In its ensuing press release indicating the start of a consultation exercise on the issue, the AG's Office set out one option for reform in the following terms:

> The requirement for the Attorney General's consent to the bringing of certain criminal prosecutions could be removed entirely, or transferred to the Director of Public Prosecutions.[58]

---

[55]   See, in particular, the first justification given for a requirement of consent, in para 8.37 above, from the 1972 Home Office Memorandum to the Franks Committee on control of prosecutions: see Legislating the Criminal Code: Corruption (1997) Law Commission Consultation Paper No 145, para 10.9.

[56]   See para 8.63 above.

[57]   See, further, the press release issued by the Attorney General's office, 'Consultation Paper on the Role of the Attorney General Published' (26 July 2007).

[58]   Attorney General's office, 'Consultation Paper on the Role of the Attorney General Published' (26 July 2007), p 2.

8.74 Obviously, it would be wrong for us to allow our proposals to be shaped by predictions about the precise outcome of any consultation process. However, it seems unlikely that the role of the AG in giving consent to prosecutions for certain types of crime is likely to be increased as an outcome of the consultation exercise. A reduction in – or even elimination of – that role in the bribery context would clearly be consistent both with the Commission's previous report on corruption, with the Joint Committee's view and with the Government's most recently expressed view.[59] This is one of the reasons for rejecting option (1) above,[60] namely the option involving a requirement of AG's consent in all bribery cases.

8.75 Nonetheless, consideration of impending legislative changes has led us to the view that the consent of the AG should be required in some bribery cases. We will now consider these impending changes.

A fourth option: confining the requirement of consent to cases with an extra-territorial element

8.76 A further option (option (4) above[61]) would be to limit the requirement of consent to those cases that involve an extra-territorial element. The requirement would obviously apply to the offence of bribing a foreign public official, but would extend to any case of bribery with an extra-territorial element. Such a requirement would be consistent with the Commission's previously expressed view that in cases involving an extra-territorial element, consent should be required.[62]

8.77 When considering this option we must bear in mind the concerns already expressed by the OECD in relation to the current law's requirement of consent, a requirement that applies to both domestic and foreign bribery. In the OECD's view, isolating the requirement of consent to those cases which have an extra-territorial element has the potential to send a negative message: that the UK does not take foreign bribery as seriously as domestic bribery. However, this option was mentioned as an attractive possibility to us during meetings that we have had with several stakeholders.

8.78 Moreover, it will be important to ensure that any requirement of consent does not vary arbitrarily depending on whether, for example, an improper advantage had actually been conferred by P on R or whether P had merely promised to confer such an advantage on R. In that respect, we believe that we should ensure that our proposals are consistent with the approach that the Government intends to take to the new inchoate offences of assisting or encouraging crime in the Serious Crime Act 2007 ('the 2007 Act').[63] That means taking the view that the AG's consent should be required in some cases.

---

[59] See paras 8.41 to 8.61 above.

[60] See para 8.44 above.

[61] See para 8.42 above.

[62] See para 8.45 above.

[63] Serious Crime Act 2007, s 53.

8.79 In broad terms, section 53 of the 2007 Act requires that the AG's consent be obtained respecting any prosecution for assisting or encouraging crime, in circumstances where there is an extra-territorial dimension to the case (as defined in schedule 4 to the 2007 Act). Section 53 will apply to instances in which it is alleged that someone has assisted or encouraged bribery. It would be right to ensure that the same approach is taken to prosecutions for the completed offence of bribery, where the offence involves an extra-territorial element. This is so, not least because it is quite possible that someone may be charged, in a case involving an extra-territorial element, both with the completed offence of bribery and, in the alternative, with assisting and encouraging bribery.

8.80 Should the role of the AG in giving consent to prosecutions be removed, following the outcome of the Government's consultation referred to above,[64] it is likely that it will fall to the DPP or to the Director of the SFO (as appropriate) to give any required consent. We ask consultees to bear this in mind when considering whether – and if so by whom - consent to prosecution should be required in bribery cases involving an extra-territorial element.

Provisional proposals

8.81 **We provisionally propose that the consent of the DPP (or the Director of the Serious Fraud Office, as appropriate) should be required for any prosecution for the general offence of bribery or for any inchoate offence relating to a principal offence of bribery, unless the offence involves an extra-territorial element.**

8.82 **We provisionally propose that there should be a requirement of consent by the Attorney General to any prosecution for an offence of bribery or for any inchoate offence relating to the bribery offence, if the offence involves an extra-territorial element.**

8.83 This second proposal is made on the understanding that – depending on the outcome of the Government's current consultation exercise – it may be the DPP and the Director of the SFO from whom all such consents will have to be obtained in future.

Question for consultees

8.84 **We ask consultees to consider whether a requirement of consent to prosecutions for bribery should be dispensed with altogether.**

ANCILLARY MATTERS

Indictment

8.85 **We provisionally propose that both bribery offences should be triable either way.**

---

[64] See paras 8.72 to 8.75 above.

Abolition of the current law

8.86   One of the central aims of this project is to create a rational and consolidated Bill that is able to replace the current Prevention of Corruption Acts. However, we are mindful that Transparency International have recommended that the common law bribery offence should not be abolished until a new Act has 'bedded in' (some time after its enactment). It is noted that this was the approach taken by Parliament in relation to the common law offence of conspiracy to defraud when enacting the Fraud Act 2006.

8.87   However, on balance, in the interests of certainty and clarity, we believe that the common law offence of bribery should be abolished.

Provisional proposals

8.88   **We provisionally propose that the Prevention of Corruption Acts 1889 to 1916 should be repealed.**

8.89   **We provisionally propose that the common law offence of bribery should be abolished.**

PART 9
CORPORATE LIABILITY

INTRODUCTION

9.1 The potential liability of legal persons for bribery has attracted considerable attention since the publication our previous report. To a large extent, this attention may simply reflect an increasing concern that the criminal liability of organisations is an area of law in need of a general review. However, the possible liability of organisations for bribery has also become a focus for several international Conventions and initiatives ('the Conventions').[1]

9.2 The Law Commission has already committed itself to review the law generally as it relates to corporate (organisational) criminality and has undertaken the preliminary stages of the project. In broad terms, we agree with the Government that reform of corporate liability for bribery would be best achieved through this wider review.[2] However, a specific concern with corporate liability in this project is warranted because the current law may not adequately meet our international commitments in relation to bribery.

9.3 We will therefore approach the issue of corporate liability for bribery in a broadly similar way to the way in which we approached our recommendations in relation to corporate killing.[3] On the one hand, we will try to identify areas of law and policy best left to a time when we are able to review corporate criminality in the round. On the other hand, we will address particular issues encountered in relation to bribery that are raised by our international commitments.

9.4 In order to focus our investigation, four forms of corporate liability can be distinguished:

   (1)   type 1: liability of companies where they commit the offence directly;

   (2)   type 2: individual liability of high-ranking members of the company for an offence committed directly by the company;

   (3)   type 3: liability of companies where they have failed adequately to supervise their workforce;

   (4)   type 4: individual liability of company directors for a company's failure adequately to supervise its workforce.

---

[1]   These include, the Council of Europe's Criminal Law Convention, the 2nd Protocol of the EU Convention on the protection of the European Communities' financial interests, the EU's Council framework decision 2003/568/JHA, the United Nation's Convention against Corruption and the OECD Convention on combating corruption of foreign public officials in international business transactions (OECD Convention). For our general review of the Conventions, see Appendix A below.

[2]   Consultation on Bribery: Reform of the Prevention of Corruption Acts and SFO powers in Cases of Bribery of Foreign Officials: Summary of responses and next steps (2007) para 127.

[3]   See Legislating the Criminal Code: Involuntary Manslaughter (1996) Law Com No 237, Part VIII.

Whilst English law has a long-standing jurisprudence in relation to the first area, the other three areas represent relatively new ground. Each of the four will be discussed in turn.

9.5 Following that discussion, we will then contribute to the recent debate concerning the supervision of foreign subsidiaries. We will then deal with two supplementary issues, including sanctions.

TYPE 1 – CORPORATE LIABILITY FOR COMMITTING THE OFFENCE DIRECTLY

9.6 We must consider the circumstances under which it would be reasonable to conclude that a corporation was responsible for bribery under our general offence (whether as recipient or as payer), and under our specific offence (as payer). It is, of course, a long established legal principle that criminal liability should attach to legal persons under certain circumstances.[4]

The Conventions' requirements

9.7 Type 1 liability can be considered a minimum requirement, so far as corporations are concerned. It is a requirement of the majority of the bribery Conventions that the UK has ratified. Those requiring this type of corporate liability include:

(1) Article 26 of the United Nations Convention against Corruption;[5]

(2) Article 2 of the OECD Convention (in relation to the bribing of foreign officials);[6]

(3) Article 18(1) of the Council of Europe's Criminal Law Convention on Corruption;[7]

(4) Article 3(1) of the Second Protocol of the Convention on the Protection of the European Communities' Financial Interests; and

(5) Article 5(1) of the European Council's framework decision 2003/568/JHA.

---

[4] For general discussion, see Celia Wells, *Corporations and Criminal Responsibility* (2nd ed 2001).

[5] Ratified by the UK 9 February 2006.

[6] Ratified by the UK 8 December 1998, in force from 15 February 1999.

[7] Ratified by the UK 9 December 2003, in force from 1 April 2004. The UK's reservations relate to general issues that are not of particular significance in the discussion of corporate liability. For discussion, see Appendix A below.

9.8   Although it may be unclear to what extent the Conventions require contracting states to use the *criminal* law,[8] with certain Conventions leaving the decision open to the individual states,[9] the UK has long recognised the potential criminal liability of legal persons.[10] Certain of the Conventions only require the criminalisation of a particular species of bribery. For example, the OECD Convention only requires states to legislate against legal persons who bribe foreign public officials. However, when viewed collectively, the Conventions require the UK to provide for the liability of legal persons in the context of both active and passive bribery.

9.9   The exact substance and form of that legislation is left as a matter for each Member State's discretion.[11] This is particularly true of (1) and (2) in para 9.7 above, where the requirements are stated in very general terms. (3), (4) and (5), almost identical in their construction,[12] provide extra detail. For example, Article 5(1) of the European Council's framework decision states:

> 5(1) Each Member State shall take the necessary measures to ensure that legal persons can be held liable for offences [of active and passive bribery] committed for their benefit by any person, acting either individually or as part of an organ of the legal person, who has a leading position within the legal person, based on:
>
> (a)   a power of representation of the legal person;
>
> (b)   an authority to take decisions on behalf of the legal person; or
>
> (c)   an authority to exercise control within the legal person.

The current law

9.10   We will now examine the current law in England and Wales[13] as it relates to this form of corporate liability. The question is whether our law adequately fulfils our international obligations.

---

8   For example, Article 5(1) of the European Council's framework decision 2003/568/JHA. See, the discussion of Art 5(2) in the recent Report from the Commission to the Council COM(2007) 328 final, pp 122 to 123.

9   For example, the UN Convention, Art 26(2) and Council of Europe Convention, Arts 18 and 19.

10   The OECD Convention opens the possibility of non-criminal regulations and sanctions for bribery (Art 3(2)). However, this is only where the state does not attach criminal liability to legal persons generally.

11   The OECD refer to this as 'functional equivalence'.

12   Although only (5) extends to both active and passive bribery.

13   To avoid wearisome repetition, we will refer simply to English law and the English courts.

9.11 The Prevention of Corruption Acts do not contain specific references to legal persons. This is hardly surprising when one considers how long ago they were enacted. However, in the light of the Interpretation Act 1978,[14] English courts are now required to interpret 'person' to include both incorporated and unincorporated bodies.[15] Therefore, although it is unlikely to have been in the minds of the original drafters, the current laws of bribery do extend liability to legal persons on the same terms as natural persons.

9.12 Like natural persons, corporations must be shown to have satisfied the various elements of the offence before they can be convicted. In relation to the conduct element of the offence this is relatively straightforward. The prosecution would have to demonstrate that an agent of the corporation, acting on behalf of the corporation, did the relevant act (offered or received a bribe). There is no requirement for this agent to hold any particular rank within the corporation.

9.13 The law becomes more complicated when we turn to the fault element of the offence. In order to be convicted under the corruption statutes, it must be demonstrated that the defendant acted 'corruptly'.[16] Unlike the conduct element, the prevailing authority in relation to the fault element dictates that the necessary fault must be located in a 'directing mind' of the corporation (the identification doctrine).[17] Only a directing mind, usually a managing director or board member, is considered as having sufficient authority to represent the mind of the corporation. This requirement represents the most substantial bar to corporate prosecutions.[18]

Satisfying the Conventions

9.14 It is generally accepted that the UK has in the main adequately met the requirements of the Conventions in this area. For example, reflecting upon the exact terms of Article 5(1) of the European Council's framework decision,[19] English law criminalises a legal person where a senior figure with authority 'to exercise control' (5(1)(c)) possesses the necessary fault.

9.15 However, although there is general acceptance that UK law complies for the most part with the expected standards, there are areas of uncertainty. An example concerns natural persons whose position within the company makes it right to say that they represent the company for the purpose of imposing liability on the company itself.

---

[14] Schedule 1 (applying to all legislation enacted after 1889 – para 4(1)(a) of sch 2.

[15] Thus, to the extent that the current law covers unincorporated bodies as well as corporations, it goes beyond the requirements of the Conventions that only require action in relation to legal persons.

[16] Although our provisional proposals would remove the term 'corruptly', they would still include a fault element (see Part 6).

[17] *Tesco Supermarkets Ltd v Nattrass* [1972] AC 153.

[18] Eg, in *Tesco Supermarkets Ltd v Nattrass*, it was held that a store manager did not represent a controlling or directing mind within Tesco. For application to corruption, see *Andrews-Weatherfoil Ltd* [1972] 1 WLR 118.

[19] See para 9.9 above.

9.16   Article 3(1) of the Second Protocol,[20] identifies someone who occupies a 'leading position' in a corporation (the directing mind) in three separate ways: "a power of representation of the legal person, or an authority to take decisions on behalf of the legal person, or an authority to exercise control within the legal person."[21] The UK bases its claim to compliance on the common law's acceptance of the third type: where the natural person is able to 'exercise control'. The problem is that in the Explanatory Report to the Second Protocol,[22] it is stated that:

> ... in order to implement the Second Protocol, Member States will have to insert all three elements in their domestic legislation as alternatives on which the leading position may be based.[23]

The clear implication is that, as the English courts rely solely on the third category, the UK is non-compliant in this respect. The question is whether, in order to achieve compliance the UK would, for example, have to extend the identification doctrine[24] to encompass fault possessed by a 'senior manager' (as well as by a director or board member), as has recently been done with respect to the liability of corporations for manslaughter.[25]

9.17   Although this statement in the Explanatory Report is a cause for concern, it is a concern that should not be overstated. First, the statement does not have an equivalent in any of the other Conventions or their commentaries. This includes those Conventions that have used almost identical language to that contained within Article 3(1). Secondly, in the European Commission's Report into the implementation of the Second Protocol,[26] the European Commission did not draw attention to the UK as a party in breach of Article 3(1). This is despite drawing attention to two other Member States who had not provided for corporate liability and drawing attention to the UK's possible non-compliance in other areas.[27] Finally, it is also worth noting that the European Commission did not recommend a follow up investigation into the UK's laws.

---

[20]   Like Article 5(1) of the Council Framework Decision cited above: see para 9.9.

[21]   Explanatory Report on the Second Protocol to the Convention on the protection of the European Communities' financial interests, OJC 091, 31 March 1999, para 3.2.

[22]   Explanatory Report on the Second Protocol to the Convention on the protection of the European Communities' financial interests, OJC 091, 31 March 1999.

[23]   Above, para 3.2.

[24]   See *Tesco Supermarkets Ltd v Nattrass* [1972] AC 153.

[25]   Corporate Manslaughter and Corporate Homicide Act 2007.

[26]   Report by the Commission COM (2004) 709 final.

[27]   Above, 3.2.

Reforming the law

9.18 We recognise that the current law governing corporate liability has encountered severe criticism. The OECD, for example, in both their Phase 2 Report[28] and their recent Follow up Report on the Implementation of the Phase 2 Recommendations,[29] criticise the current law. The OECD recommends that it should be expanded beyond the identification doctrine, because that doctrine limits corporate liability for bribery to instances in which a director or equivalent possessed the fault element.[30] However, whilst the OECD offer recommendations to improve the law, at the same time the OECD recognises that the UK is compliant with the OECD Convention.[31]

9.19 The OECD's criticisms can in fact be understood as criticisms that can be made of the current principles of corporate liability as they apply across the board, and not just in the context of bribery. Therefore, bearing in mind that it is acknowledged that the UK is compliant with its international obligations, we believe that these issues should be deferred to our wider review of corporate criminality.

Provisional proposal

9.20 **We provisionally propose that consideration of the law relating to the direct liability of legal persons for offences of bribery should be deferred until the Law Commission's wider review of this area.**

TYPE 2 – INDIVIDUAL LIABILITY OF HIGH-RANKING EMPLOYEES WITHIN A CORPORATION THAT HAS COMMITTED BRIBERY

9.21 This second area refers to a form of liability that is capable of 'piercing the corporate veil' in order to punish an individual ('Z') within a corporation who has contributed to the offence committed by the legal person. For example:

Example 9A

Z is the managing director of X Ltd. Z consents to P (an employee of X Ltd) paying several bribes on behalf of the company.

In this example, as long as P possesses the requisite fault element, he or she will be guilty of bribery. Further, as Z is a directing mind of X Ltd, it is likely that X Ltd would be guilty of the bribery offence (type 1 liability). In the current discussion, we are considering whether (alongside the corporation) Z should also be personally liable by virtue of his or her contribution to P's offence.

---

[28] (2005) paras 195 to 206.

[29] (2007) p 21.

[30] See para 9.13 above.

[31] The OECD point out in a recent publication that just two parties are non-compliant with Art 2 of the OECD Convention (which deals with corporate liability): Luxembourg and the Slovak Republic. See OECD, Mid-term Study of Phase 2 Reports (2006), para 125.

9.22 In broad terms, it might be argued that if the employee (P) is liable in such circumstances, then Z should be liable as well. As we will see, there are different bases on which Z (and others) could be made individually liable for the offence committed by P or by X Ltd. For reasons explained below, we do not have a provisional view about which basis is the right one to recommend and this is something on which we would welcome consultees' views.

The Conventions' requirements

9.23 The particular provision under discussion is not one that is required by any of the Conventions.

Reforming the law: two possibilities

9.24 The individual liability in these circumstances of high-ranking employees such as Z can come about in one of two ways. Z may be guilty of bribery in virtue of being found complicit in the offence committed by P or by X Ltd, having (putting it broadly) intentionally aided, abetted, counselled or procured the offence. Such liability is not in fact confined to high-ranking employees, because complicity is a general doctrine of liability. Anyone who intentionally aided, abetted, counselled or procured the offence – including very low-level employees – could be complicit in an offence committed by P or by X Ltd. Further, Z – and indeed any other employee – may be guilty of the inchoate offence of inciting bribery, an offence to be replaced by a wider inchoate offence of assisting or encouraging crime (in this case, bribery) under Part 2 of the 2007 Act.[32]

9.25 It is worth noting that, in limited circumstances, someone – such as a high-ranking employee – who is under a duty to take positive steps to prevent wrongdoing by his or her company or by lower ranking employees, may become complicit in a crime committed by them (or be found inchoately to have assisted or encouraged its commission) through a knowing omission to take such steps.[33] In this context, for example, suppose that an employee drew to the attention of a company director that he or she (the employee) was intending to bribe another person and the director remained silent and ignored the information. This could amount to encouragement of the employee to commit the offence, and form grounds for making the individual director guilty of bribery or of the inchoate offence of inciting (assisting or encouraging) bribery.[34]

9.26 This first possible route to liability would require no legislative change as a result of this project.

---

[32] For further discussion, see Part 10 below.

[33] See *Tuck v Robson* [1970] 1 All ER 1171, and the discussion in Smith and Hogan, 'Criminal Law (11th ed, 2005), pp 177 to 78. In *Gaunt* [2003] EWCA Crim 3925, [2004] 2 Cr App R (s) 37, the defendant was sentenced on the basis that he had encouraged his staff to racially abuse another employee by omitting to take any action to stop them. However, as a sentencing case, it is perhaps of limited value as a precedent.

[34] In such an example, in virtue of the director's knowledge of what the employee was going to do, the company itself would also be liable for bribery.

9.27   However, in some limited contexts, statute provides for a slightly wider basis on which the individual liability of high-ranking employees in particular may be imposed for a substantive offence committed by their company. This is liability based on their individual 'consent or connivance' respecting the commission of the offence by the company. This is a species of liability that has only been recognised in England in relatively few instances. It is a basis for liability slightly wider than that provided for by the doctrine of complicity.

9.28   First, in theory it is possible for someone to 'connive' at the commission of an offence (to know it may occur but to do nothing to prevent its commission) without providing actual assistance or encouragement. Secondly, connivance may occur through reckless conduct (knowing that there is a risk of offending but doing nothing) whereas, speaking in very broad terms, complicity requires intention or knowledge as to the offending behaviour.

9.29   Examples of a 'consent or connivance' basis for liability can be found in section 18(1) of the Theft Act 1968 and in section 18 of the Terrorism Act 2006.[35] It has also recently been included in the Fraud Act 2006,[36] an Act that contains offences that overlap considerably with bribery.[37] Section 12 of the Fraud Act provides:

(1)   Subsection (2) applies if an offence under this Act is committed by a body corporate.

(2)   If the offence is proved to have been committed with the consent or connivance of –

(a)   a director, manager, secretary or other similar officer of the body corporate, or

(b)   a person who was purporting to act in any such capacity, he (as well as the body corporate) is guilty of the offence and liable to be proceeded against and punished accordingly.

9.30   The question for consultees is whether such a basis for individual liability for bribery should be created to cover the following kind of example:

Example 9B

Z (a director of X Ltd) deliberately ignores documents that he knows to be evidence that P, a manager of X Ltd, is about to bribe an employee of R Ltd. P does commit the bribery offence.

---

[35]   Eg, the Theft Act 1968, s 18(1) states that "where an offence committed by a body corporate under [section 17] of this Act is proved to have been committed with the consent or connivance of any director, manager, secretary or other similar officer of the body corporate, or any person who was purporting to act in any such capacity, he as well as the body corporate shall be guilty of that offence, and shall be liable to be proceeded against and punished accordingly".

[36]   Section 12.

[37]   See Appendix E below.

Consent and connivance: similar clauses used in other jurisdictions

9.31   It is worthy of note that the recently enacted Corruption (Jersey) Law 2006[38] has incorporated this form of liability into the law of bribery in Jersey.[39] Including the central terms 'consent or connivance', these laws have gone further than their English equivalents by also allowing Z to be liable where he or she has been negligent. However, we believe in the current context that this expands the scope of the offence too widely.

Relationship between the different modes of liability

9.32   As indicated above, under the 2007 Act it will become a specific inchoate offence for anyone to assist or encourage the commission of an offence (whether or not that offence is actually committed), either through a positive act or through an omission in breach of a duty to act.[40] To be guilty of this offence, in this context, someone would have to (a) engage in acts capable of encouraging or assisting bribery, (b) intend or believe that the company (or an employee) would commit the conduct element of bribery, and (c) intend that or be reckless whether the company (or an employee) would commit bribery with the relevant fault element.

9.33   One important difference between the doctrine of complicity and the new offence of assisting and encouraging crime relates to (c) above. Whereas, to be complicit in the crime itself, someone must intend or know that the perpetrator will act with the fault element of the offence,[41] to be liable for the offence or assisting or encouraging crime, someone need only be reckless whether the perpetrator will act with that fault element, the same fault element required for 'connivance' in the commission of a crime. Accordingly, the 'consent and connivance' doctrine casts its net more widely in this respect that the doctrine of complicity. It does not cast it wider in this respect than the inchoate offence of assisting and encouraging crime, although – like complicity – it does impose liability for the full offence.

9.34   Perhaps the key difference between, on the one hand, the 'consent and connivance' doctrine, and, on the other hand, complicity and assisting and encouraging, is the need with the latter to show that the person in question - whether by omission in breach of duty or otherwise – actually influenced the perpetrator in committing the offence (whether through help or encouragement). Such influence may be hard to prove beyond reasonable doubt where one is concerned with the complex structure of many corporate decision-making procedures. No such influence need be shown when the question is simply whether the high-ranking employee or director 'connived' at the actions of his or her company in committing the offence.

9.35   The key differences between the modes of liability are thus that:

---

[38]   Section 10.

[39]   The Jersey law follows reform in Guernsey a few years earlier: The Prevention of Corruption (Bailiwick of Guernsey) Law 2003, s 6.

[40]   Serious Crime Act 2007, ss 44 and 45.

[41]   See the discussion in our recent report Participating in Crime (2007) Law Com No 305, Part 1, paras 1.5 to 1.11. If our recommendations in this area are accepted, this form of liability will remain narrow, so far as the fault element is concerned, in order to ensure comparability of culpability with the principal offender: see paras 3.68 to 3.117.

(i)   Like complicity, the consent and connivance doctrine involves liability for the offence itself, and hence such liability cannot arise unless the offence has been committed by the company. Liability for assisting and encouraging crime involves free-standing inchoate liability, and hence does not require the principal offence to have been committed.

(ii)   The consent and connivance doctrine is restricted in its application to high-ranking members of an organisation whereas, by virtue of the doctrines of complicity and of assisting and encouraging, criminal liability can attach to any person.

(iii)   'Connivance' provides a wider basis for imposing individual liability than complicity. Connivance at the culpable actions of the corporate perpetrator may be reckless on the part of a high-ranking member of an organisation, as well as intentional or knowing. Complicity requires intention or knowledge that the perpetrator will act with the fault element.

(iv)   It is possible to connive at offending without assisting or encouraging it, making it easier to prove the former as opposed to the latter. Accordingly, it is also easier to prove connivance at offending as opposed to complicity in offending.

(v)   The consent and connivance doctrine makes high-ranking members of an organisation liable only for the offence committed by the company, not for an offence committed by individual employees. Complicity and assisting or encouraging crime cover both possibilities, although the latter imposes liability only for a separate inchoate offence.

9.36   At present, we do not have a firm view on whether these different factors indicate that there is a right approach to individual liability respecting bribery committed by a company. The right approach may be to leave the matter to the law governing complicity and assisting or encouraging crime, and consider the consent and connivance doctrine as part of a future review of corporate liability (although it should be noted that this was not the approach taken by the Fraud Act 2006),[42] Alternatively, the right approach may be to extend liability to instances in which there has been consent and connivance by a high-ranking member of a company to a bribery offence committed by the company itself.

---

[42]   See para 9.29 above.

Question for consultees:

9.37 **Should the individual liability of a high-ranking employee be specifically provided for, on a 'consent or connivance' basis, or left to be governed by the inchoate offences of assisting or encouraging crime (provided for in the Serious Crime Act 2007) and the doctrine of complicity?**

TYPE 3 – CORPORATE LIABILITY FOR FAILING ADEQUATELY TO SUPERVISE

9.38 We must now consider whether legal persons should be under a duty to supervise those under their control to ensure that those individuals do not commit bribery. For example:

Example 9C

P is a an employee of X Ltd. P is under a lot of pressure from X Ltd to secure a contract with R. P bribes R in order to secure the contract.

In this example, P has committed bribery in the course of his or her employment. If P was a directing mind within the corporation, or if he or she had acted with the consent of a directing mind within the corporation, then the corporation will be guilty of the offence directly. However, a question arises whether an offence is required to make X Ltd liable for 'failing adequately to supervise' P and failing to prevent him or her from committing the bribery offence. The question is an important one because such liability is sometimes required by international Convention.

The Conventions' requirements

9.39 This is a relatively specialised form of liability and is only required by three of the Conventions so far mentioned. In each of them it is contained in a section following the general provision on corporate liability already discussed (type 1). Those Conventions requiring corporate liability for failure adequately to supervise include:

 (1) Article 3(2) of the Second Protocol of the Convention on the Protection of the European Communities' Financial Interests;

 (2) Article 18(2) of the Council of Europe's Criminal Law Convention on Corruption; and

 (3) Article 5(2) of the European Council's framework decision 2003/568/JHA.

9.40 Article 3(2) of the Second Protocol was the first to articulate this form of liability. The other two provisions then drew explicitly upon its content. Each of the provisions requires:

Apart from the cases already provided for in paragraph 1,[43] each [party] can be held liable where the lack of supervision or control by a [natural] person referred to in paragraph 1 has made possible the commission of [a bribery offence] for the benefit of that legal person by a [natural] person under its authority.[44]

The current law

9.41 English criminal law does not recognise the liability of a legal person where it has failed to prevent its workforce committing bribery unless it can be shown to have been complicit in the offence. There is currently no criminal liability for failure to supervise, as such.

9.42 In order to prove that it satisfies the relevant Conventions, the UK has sought to rely on the existence of two separate civil law actions.[45]

9.43 The first is under the Proceeds of Crime Act 2002, which allows recovery or confiscation of profits illegally obtained. The second is the tort of negligence. For liability under the law of negligence to be established, it must be demonstrated that the legal person owed another individual a duty of care, that it was in breach of that duty through negligence and that the breach led to the individual suffering compensable loss. If these requirements are satisfied, the legal person will be obliged to compensate that individual in order to restore him or her to the position that he or she was in before incurring the loss caused by the negligent breach of duty.

Satisfying the Conventions

9.44 When reviewing the compliance of the current law with the Conventions, two problems have emerged. The first is whether parties are obliged to enact a *criminal* law to meet their obligations. The second is whether, even if the civil law could be sufficient in principle, current civil law provisions are adequate. We will deal with each of these in turn.

Do the Conventions require a criminal law?

9.45 The Conventions clearly require parties to take action against legal persons who fail to supervise their workforce adequately. The prevailing belief is that all three Conventions leave it to the discretion of each Party whether to employ the criminal law.

---

[43] Paragraph 1 of the relevant Article in each Convention deals with a legal person's direct liability for bribery (discussed above, paras 9.6 to 9.20).

[44] This quotation represents the common language used within the three provisions. The squared brackets represent the only differences, save that Art 5(2) goes beyond the other two provisions by including passive as well as active bribery.

[45] We base this observation upon the Government's responses to questions concerning compliance from both international review bodies (for example, see Report from the Commission to the Council COM(2007) 328 final, p 123) and Parliament (for example, see Hansard 1 May 2007, Col WA196).

9.46   The first piece of evidence in support of this contention comes from the text of the Conventions themselves. They do not mention the creation of a 'criminal offence'; instead, they simply require Parties to make legal persons 'liable'. Further, when sanctions are discussed in later Articles, there is again no mention of 'criminal' sanctions. This second omission is particularly notable when it is contrasted with the discussion of sanctions for legal persons who commit the offence directly. Where the offence is committed directly, criminal sanctions are explicitly mentioned.[46]

9.47   In the explanatory report of the Second Protocol, it is said that sanctions for the supervisory offence "may be criminal sanctions, administrative and civil law measures are possible as well".[47] This seems to imply that Parties are free under Article 3(2) to choose whether or not to create a *criminal* offence. Indeed, this seems to have been the impression of the Council of Europe when they employed the same language as Article 3(2) in Article 18(2) of the Criminal Law Convention on Corruption. In their explanatory report,[48] they say:

> A similar provision also exists in the Second Protocol of the European Union Convention on the Protection of the financial interest of the European Communities. At paragraph 1, it does not impose an obligation to establish criminal liability in such cases but some form of liability to be decided by the Contracting Party itself.[49]

The impression here is very clearly that civil or administrative liability would be sufficient.

9.48   Compliance with the Criminal Law Convention is monitored by GRECO.[50] Based upon analysis similar to that set out above, GRECO have concluded that the UK's implementation of Article 18(2), which relies on the civil law, is sufficient.[51]

PROBLEM CASE

9.49   The reason for this slightly extended discussion is that this is a matter that has been thrown into some doubt by a recent report by the European Commission.[52] The report reviews the compliance of Member States with the Council Framework Decision, Article 5(2) of which is almost identical to both Article 3(2) of the Second Protocol and Article 18(2) of the Criminal Law Convention. In reference to Article 5(2) the European Commission commented that:

---

[46]   See for example, the Council Framework Decision, Art 6(1).

[47]   Explanatory Report on the Second Protocol to the Convention on the protection of the European Communities' financial interests, OJ C 091, 31/03/1999 para 4.3.

[48]   Explanatory Report on the Criminal Law Convention on Corruption (2000). Available at http://Conventions.coe.int/Treaty/en/Reports/Html/173.htm

[49]   Above, para 87.

[50]   Group of States against Corruption.

[51]   GRECO, Second Evaluation Round: Evaluation Report on the United Kingdom (2004) 2E, para 105.

[52]   Report from the Commission to the Council COM(2007) 328 final.

> ... the liability is a criminal liability, which must be matched by a criminal sanction and that such a criminal sanction may be supplemented by other measures which are administrative or civil in nature.[53]

9.50 As the UK bases its compliance upon the civil law and not the criminal law, the European Commission concludes:

> [The] UK does not meet the requirements of Article 5.2.[54]

9.51 Clearly, the conclusions of the European Commission in this area may have an effect on the future interpretation of Article 5(2). It is our opinion that the Commission has incorrectly interpreted the provision.

9.52 The basis for this contention has already, to a large extent, been set out above.[55] The settled interpretation of both Articles 3(2) of the Second Protocol and Article 18(2) of the Criminal Law Convention is that parties have a discretion whether or not to employ the criminal law. If the European Council had intended to modify this position it could easily have done so by inserting the word 'criminal' into the provision. The Council did not insert such a term. Instead, they adopted almost exactly the language of the two previous Conventions.[56]

If a criminal law is not required, is the current law sufficient?

9.53 Although English law has come under criticism from the European Commission for failing to provide a criminal offence, it seems to have otherwise been assumed that the current law is sufficient. Bearing in mind the Convention requirements, we would like to sound a note of caution.

9.54 The tort of negligence and the Proceeds of Crime Act are of very general application. They were certainly not designed specifically to deal with corporations that fail to prevent their employees committing bribery offences. Without this focus, it may well be that they leave unwelcome gaps in liability.

9.55 For example, where a corporation is involved in bribery, it will often be the case that the only other party to whom it in theory owes a duty of care is the other party to the bribery offence. This individual is in all probability barred from bringing a civil action for damages. Therefore, the corporation will remain free from liability. Further, any loss suffered as a result of bribery will be purely economic loss, and there is no duty of care in negligence law to avoid economic loss.

---

[53] Above, p 123.

[54] Above.

[55] See paras 9.45 to 9.48 above.

[56] The only difference of note is that the offence is extended to include passive corruption.

9.56   Other civil wrongs may be involved in bribery cases. For example, it may be that an employee who takes a bribe commits the tort of wrongful interference with an employer's economic interests. By offering a bribe that is then accepted in exchange for some action, the person making the offer is also implicated in the tort because they have procured the interference without justification.[57] There is, of course, also the possibility that the company employing the person making the bribe could be held vicariously liable for any loss incurred by the other party as a result of the bribe having been taken. That possibility might provide some incentive to supervise employees properly. However, in such cases, there will still be problems of proving loss, and of overcoming allegations of contributory negligence.

9.57   Whether or not there are civil wrongs involved, it may be questioned whether it is sufficient to use the civil law to address the involvement of individuals in bribery committed by companies. The aim of the law of tort is to put the parties back in the position they were in before the loss resulting from the commission of the tort was incurred. This does not seem to reflect the ambition of the Conventions. These seem at least to imply that there must be the possibility of imposing liability irrespective of whether the bribery has caused loss giving rise to a claim for compensation.

Reforming the law

9.58   In the following section we will set out three options for consultees: the creation of a new criminal offence, the creation of a new civil or administrative offence or the deferring of the problem until the wider review. We do not agree with the European Commission that a new criminal law is *essential* and so we are not at present proposing, as opposed to setting out the option of, the creation of criminal liability for companies for failing to supervise their workforce.

Option 1: New criminal offence of failing adequately to supervise

9.59   This option would involve the creation of a new offence that would criminalise legal persons for failing adequately to supervise their employees where that failure results in a bribery offence for the benefit of the legal person being committed. It is an option that has been employed in other jurisdictions, including Denmark[58] and Slovenia.[59] If consultees agree with the European Commission that Article 5(2) of the Council Framework Decision requires the creation of a criminal offence, then this is the only acceptable course of action in order to comply with UK commitments. However, even if consultees doubt the European Commission's interpretation, this option might still be preferred if consultees do not think that the current civil law provisions are adequate and believe that a criminal offence is more appropriate.

---

[57] See also *Clerk and Lindsell on Tort* (19th ed 2006) para 25-88 and following.

[58] The Criminal Code, s 306.

[59] Criminality of Legal Entities Act, s 4(4).

9.60   It is inappropriate to set out a potential new offence in any great detail at this stage of our review. However, any new offence is likely to be closely modelled on the Conventions' provisions themselves. Therefore, a legal person would become liable for the new offence if a 'controlling or directing mind' within the corporation was personally negligent in their duty to supervise and bribery benefiting the legal person was made possible as a result.[60] Consideration would also have to be given to whether, in deciding if there had been a culpable failure to supervise, it should be possible to aggregate the fault of 'controlling or directing minds' together with the fault of lower-level managers. The aggregation of fault on the part of different individuals within a company is now a possibility under the Corporate Manslaughter and Corporate Homicide Act 2007, for the purpose of deciding whether a company has been sufficiently negligent to be convicted of corporate manslaughter or corporate homicide.

9.61   In that regard, we note the increasingly important role, in limiting the reach of liability, played by internal corporate compliance systems in other jurisdictions.[61] A defence modelled in these terms, focusing on whether the particular company had a robust system for preventing bribery taking place, might perform a dual role. First, it may encourage corporations that do not currently have such a system, or do not have an adequate system, to put a new one in place. Secondly, it might provide a useful level of certainty for corporations trying to avoid liability. It is arguable that these advantages would not accrue if the fact that a company had such a system was only a matter of sentence mitigation.[62]

9.62   It should be noted that this option would only extend to the supervision of natural persons. The separate discussion of whether and to what extent parent companies should be responsible for supervising their subsidiaries is dealt with below.[63]

Option 2: New civil or administrative provision addressing a failing to supervise

9.63   The acceptance of this option is predicated upon two points. First, it presupposes a rejection of the European Commission's interpretation of Article 5(2) of the Council's Framework Decision. Secondly, it assumes a belief that the current law does not adequately satisfy the requirement of the Conventions.

9.64   If this option were eventually preferred, the Law Commission would make a general recommendation referring it for further study. However, this form of liability sits outside the scope of our review under our current terms of reference, and so no concrete proposals can be made within this project.

---

[60]   Where the bribery offence is done in the course of employment.

[61]   Eg, that contained in Italian Decree No 231/2001.

[62]   We note that under US federal law the possession of such a system is indeed a matter of sentence mitigation. However, the far more structured nature of sentencing in the US means that some of the advantages just referred to may be gained by reliance on sentence mitigation in a way that they might not be in the UK. See the US Sentencing Guidelines, CS2.

[63]   See paras 9.89 to 9.103 below.

Option 3: Defer the issue until our wider review of corporate criminality

9.65 This option also requires the rejection of the European Commission's interpretation. Beyond this however, it is an option that recognises that the current UK law has not attracted a great amount of criticism. On this basis, consultees may believe that this is an area of reform best deferred until a general review.

Questions for consultees

9.66 **Should a new criminal offence be created to penalise legal persons where their negligent supervision allows bribery to take place, assuming that it is a defence to such an offence to show that, notwithstanding the commission of a bribery offence, an adequate system was in place to prevent offending?**

9.67 **Should negligent supervision by a legal person that allows bribery to take place be the subject of special civil or administrative remedies or sanctions?**

9.68 **Should the whole issue of negligent supervision by a legal person be left to a more general review of the liability of legal persons and, in particular, their liability for failing to supervise their employees adequately?**

TYPE 4 – LIABILITY OF INDIVIDUALS WHO FAIL ADEQUATELY TO SUPERVISE

9.69 In the previous section, we discussed the circumstances in which a legal person should be liable for failing to supervise, thereby allowing bribery to take place. In this section we go to the next stage of liability, as we did in relation to direct corporate liability in type 2 above[64] and ask whether a high-level member of that corporation should be made personally liable for failing to supervise (whether alongside the corporation or alone). Let us again reflect on Example 9C:

Example 9C

P is an employee of X Ltd. P is under a lot of pressure from X Ltd to secure a contract with R. P bribes R in order to secure the contract.

In this example, if a 'directing mind' within X Ltd had the relevant fault element for bribery, X Ltd would be held directly liable. As we have already pointed out, it would additionally be possible (a) to create a new law under which a high-ranking employee ('Z') who has consented to or connived at the offence is individually liable for that offence,[65] and (b) to create a new law providing that if the 'directing mind' did not have the relevant fault, but was negligent in failing to supervise P, X Ltd would be liable for an offence of failure to supervise.

---

[64] See paras 9.21 to 9.37 above.

[65] See paras 9.27 to 9.37 above.

146

9.70   The question now is whether a high-ranking member of the corporation (Z) who has contributed to the corporate supervisory offence should be individually liable for inadequate failure to supervise. At first sight, it may well appear that even to ask this question goes too far in terms of contemplating criminal liability for a culpable failure on the part of individuals. However, the question has been generated by what appear to be the requirements of the Conventions.

The Conventions' requirements

9.71   There is only one relevant provision for this type of liability. This is Article 6 of the Convention on the fight against corruption involving officials of the European Communities or officials of Member States of the European Union.[66]

9.72   Drawing much of its content from a previous Convention which dealt with fraud,[67] Article 6 provides that:

> Each Member State shall take the necessary measures to allow heads of businesses or any [natural] persons having power to take decisions or exercise control within a business to be declared criminally liable in accordance with the principles defined by its national law in cases of corruption, [set out in another Article], by a person under their authority acting on behalf of the business.

9.73   One of the most striking elements of the provision, especially when one considers much of the discussion above, is that Article 6 very clearly requires Parties to provide for *criminal* liability. Beyond this, it is important to recognise that Article 6 is part of a Convention designed to tackle the bribing of public officials. Therefore, although Parties are free to go beyond that which is required by the Convention, Article 6 itself only requires states to make Z liable where his or her lack of supervision leads to those under his or her control *actively* bribing *public officials*.

The current law

9.74   At present, the criminal law does not recognise any form of direct individual criminal liability for those within a corporation who fail to supervise employees who are acting within their authority. Therefore, to the extent that the UK might claim to be in compliance with the Convention, it may do so by placing reliance on the doctrine of secondary liability and inchoate offences. We will briefly re-state the relevance of this body of law.

9.75   Secondary liability provides for the individual liability of Z for the principal offence if Z was engaged in 'aiding, abetting, counselling or procuring'[68] P in committing the offence. In addition, Z can be inchoately liable for encouraging the offence committed by P. The 2007 Act extends such liability to assisting as well as encouraging.

---

[66]   OJ C 195, 25/06/1997. Ratified by the UK on 11 October 1999. Entered into force in 2005.

[67]   Convention on the Protection of the European Communities' financial interests, OJ C 316, 27/11/1995, Art 3.

[68]   The language of the Accessories and Abettors Act 1861, s 8, and the Magistrates' Courts Act 1980, s 44. See paras 9.24 to 9.26 above.

9.76　The law of secondary liability (in this context) is independent of corporate liability. Z's potential liability for P's offence, or for assisting or encouraging P's criminal offence, is in no way reliant on X Ltd having committed an offence or on P's offence being done in the course of his or her employment. If Z is found guilty by virtue of the doctrine of complicity, he or she, as sell as P, will be labelled and punished not for failing to supervise but for the full bribery offence.

9.77　To be secondarily liable for P's offence in Example 9C, Z's lack of supervision would have to have assisted or encouraged P to commit the offence. As Z is entitled to exercise control and is under a duty to supervise P, the law has the potential to recognise liability for omissions in these circumstances,[69] although the common law is reluctant to impose liability for omissions.[70]

9.78　The other difficulty, for present purposes, is that for Z to be liable for assisting or encouraging P, he or she will have to have foreseen that P will commit the offence.[71] As a result, negligent or reckless supervision by Z, which is unaccompanied by this foresight, will leave Z beyond the reach of the complicity doctrine. There is, however, still the possibility that in some limited circumstances P may in future be found guilty under the 2007 Act of assisting or encouraging an offence of bribery, such was the nature of the inadequacy of the inadequate supervision.

9.79　We have already set out the arguments for and against reliance on the doctrine of complicity and the offences of assisting or encouraging crime to deter inadequacy of supervision, in this kind of context, without reliance on further doctrines such as 'consent and connivance'.[72] We regard it as an open question whether reliance on the doctrine of complicity and on inchoate offences of assisting or encouraging crime will be enough to satisfy our Convention obligations.

9.80　It would be right to add that it is just possible that a culpable failure to supervise employees may give rise to civil liability in negligence, a possibility that might encourage companies to ensure that adequate supervision arrangements are in place.[73] However, this possibility is very remote. There is no general duty to avoid causing purely economic loss, and even if there were such a duty, it is unlikely that there will be someone suffering such a loss who falls within the scope of the duty of care.

---

[69]　See, eg, *Tuck v Robson* [1970] 1 WLR 741, where a publican was held to have encouraged after hours drinking because he failed to exercise his control over those in the pub to stop them drinking.

[70]　See, Participating in Crime (2007) Law Com No. 305, para 2.25.

[71]　This claim can not be made with any certainty because the case law in this area is often contradictory. See Participating in Crime (2007) Law Com No. 305, Appendix B, paras B.67 to B.152.

[72]　See paras 9.32 to 9.36 above.

[73]　See paras 9.43, 9.55 and 9.56 above.

Reforming the law

9.81   In this section we will offer three options for consultees, each one progressively narrower in its approach. The creation of a new and general mode of liability of failing to supervise, the creation of a new mode of liability tailored to go no further than the requirements of Article 6 and, finally, the option to defer until our wider review.

Option 1: New mode of criminal liability for failing adequately to supervise

9.82   We have already discussed the creation of this mode of liability, where high-ranking employees contribute to direct corporate liability for bribery.[74] In the present context, liability would be imposed on Z where, by 'consent or connivance', he or she contributes to the corporation's negligent supervision of those under its authority.

9.83   When we commented on the recent bribery legislation in Jersey and Guernsey, we drew attention to the fact that a recent law allowed liability where Z's contribution came in the form of negligence.[75] We chose not to follow a similar approach in relation to direct liability. Our provisional view is that a similar approach is warranted here. High-ranking employees should not be individually liable for a company's inadequate failure to supervise its employees, on the basis of no more than their own negligence.

Option 2: New mode of criminal liability in line with Article 6

9.84   This is an option that might be preferred by those who believe the current law is insufficient, but who do not want to go beyond the requirements of the Convention. It would involve the creation of a new mode of liability along the same lines as discussed in option 1. However, liability would be limited in two ways. First, it would only apply where P has committed active bribery. Secondly, it would only apply where P has bribed a public official.

Option 3: Defer the issue until our wider review of corporate criminality

9.85   This option assumes that the current law can be regarded as adequate, at least in the shorter term, to deal with this form of liability. It recognises that the current law has not come under any sustained criticism and regards it as appropriate to deal with any new form of liability as part of a general review.

Questions for consultees

9.86   **If a legal person commits an offence of negligent supervision, and the offence is proved to have been committed with the consent or connivance of:**

   (1)   a director, manager, company secretary or other similar officer of the body corporate; or

   (2)   a person who was purporting to act in any such capacity,

---

[74]   See paras 9.21 to 9.37 above.

[75]   See para 9.31 above.

should individual criminal liability also be imposed on that person?

9.87 **If a legal person commits an offence of negligent supervision, and the offence is proved to have been committed with the consent or connivance of:**

> **(1)   a director, manager, company secretary or other similar officer of the body corporate; or**

> **(2)   a person who was purporting to act in any such capacity,**

should individual criminal liability also be imposed on that person, *but only* if the bribery offence committed by an employee of the legal person acting on behalf of the business related to a foreign public official?

9.88 **Whether or not an offence is created making it possible to convict a legal person of a negligent supervision offence, should the extension of individual liability for inadequate supervision to high-ranking members of a legal person be a matter left for a broader review of corporate criminal liability?**

STRUCTURE OF LIABILITY IF NEW OFFENCES ARE ALL CREATED

Type 1: Existing criminal offence

A legal person commits the bribery offence directly.

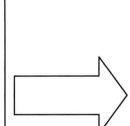

Type 2: New mode of liability

High-ranking employee who consented to or connived at the offence can be liable *alongside* the corporation.

Type 3: Additional criminal offence

A legal person fails to adequately supervise a natural person under their authority (who commits bribery).

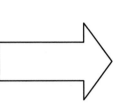

Type 4: New mode of liability

High-ranking employee who consented to or connived at the offence can be liable *alongside* the corporation.

CORPORATE LIABILITY FOR THE ACTIONS OF A SUBSIDIARY COMPANY

9.89 The question in this section is whether, and to what extent, UK registered corporations should be liable for bribery offences committed by their foreign registered subsidiaries or contractual partners. Critics of the current law claim that this is one of the, "principal ways in which foreign bribes are paid".[76] As a result, there has been pressure to extend the criminal law to address this situation.

The existing law

9.90 Under well-established principles, the directors of a subsidiary must act in ways that they believe are in the best interests of the subsidiary.[77] So, the directors of a parent company may not have the kind of control over the activities of a subsidiary that would justify imposing liability on the former for the actions of the latter. Accordingly, there is no general doctrine of 'group' liability of a kind found, for example, in German company law.[78]

9.91 This has important implications for the reach of the criminal law. For example, considering the relationship between a parent company and its foreign-owned subsidiary, the House of Lords has said that the parent company can only be regarded as having 'control' of documents possessed by the (South African) subsidiary if the subsidiary was completely subservient to the will of the parent company, and effectively its alter ego.[79]

9.92 A fundamental difficulty is that the doctrine of complicity requires that a principal offence be committed. A foreign subsidiary company which does an act of bribery outside England and Wales commits no principal offence known to English law. Accordingly, the parent company, even if a British company, cannot be convicted as a secondary party even if it assisted or encouraged the foreign subsidiary company to do an act of bribery. However, once the relevant provisions of the 2007 Act are implemented, it will be possible to convict the parent company of an inchoate offence of assisting or encouraging bribery.

Reforming the law

9.93 The Corruption Bill drafted by Transparency International (the TI Bill) includes a clause that would require UK holding companies to take all 'reasonable' steps to prevent this type of conduct. Alongside this requirement, the TI Bill also includes a corresponding offence of failing to act reasonably to prevent bribery. In this section we will consider whether a new offence along these lines would be beneficial.

9.94 The essence of the offence (as set out in the TI (UK) Bill) is as follows:

---

[76] Transparency International, *Corruption Bill – background note* (2007) p 9.

[77] *Charterbridge Corp v Lloyds Bank* [1970] Ch 62, 74.

[78] See Gower and Davies, *Principles of Modern Company Law* (7th ed 2003) pp 202 to 204.

[79] *Lonrho Ltd v Shell Petroleum Ltd* [1980] 1 WLR 627.

A holding company incorporated in the United Kingdom shall take all such steps as are reasonably open to it to secure any of its subsidiary companies incorporated outside the United Kingdom neither does nor omits to do something outside the United Kingdom which, if done or omitted to be done in the United Kingdom, would constitute an offence [of bribery] ...[80]

A company which fails to comply [with this provision] commits an offence.[81]

9.95 An offence of this type could be seen as broadly analogous to any new offence regarding the corporate supervision of employees. However, as will become clear in the discussion below, the supervision of foreign subsidiaries creates some unique problems.

Arguments against the new offence

9.96 Unlike the corporate supervision of employees, none of the Conventions that the UK has ratified require the creation of this type of offence.

9.97 Apart from an often-cited contention that it would represent an unacceptable widening of corporate liability, several other arguments have been advanced which cast doubt on the utility of this type of offence.

9.98 The first area of criticism focuses on the practical enforcement of the law. Through informal meetings with the SFO (who would be responsible for enforcing this type of new offence) we have gained the impression that, although they recognise this potential loophole in the law, they doubt whether the creation of a new offence would be of much benefit in practice. The Government too, in their recent reply to consultees,[82] agrees with an earlier statement by the Joint Committee that such a new offence would not be desirable.

9.99 The Government points out that acts of bribery by foreign subsidiaries are already likely to be covered by that country's own domestic law. In this vein, it ought to be much easier for that country to be responsible for enforcing its own laws, rather than relying on UK authorities to provide indirect enforcement of them extra-jurisdictionally. Even where a foreign country might be at fault for not enforcing its bribery laws,[83] it is still unlikely that the UK authorities would have the resources and the access to evidence in order to allow them to mount an effective investigation and prosecution.

---

[80] Corruption Bill 2007, HL 18, cl 11(1).

[81] Above, cl 12(1).

[82] Consultation on Bribery: Reform of the Prevention of Corruption Acts and SFO powers in Cases of Bribery of Foreign Officials: Summary of responses and next steps (2007) paras 124 to 125.

[83] For discussion of some of the potential problems in this regard, see J Gobert and M Punch, *Rethinking Corporate Crime* (2003) pp 146 to 150 and 160 to 162.

9.100 The Government also contends that the law of complicity, incitement and conspiracy provides enough by way of deterrence and a basis for retribution, in this context.[84] We discuss the issue in Part 11. We conclude that, with some amendments to the law, corporations who assist or encourage bribery, or conspire to commit it, can be caught even if the actions in question relate to the activities of a foreign subsidiary.

Arguments in favour of the new offence

9.101 Those who support the creation of the new offence believe that although the law may cause some practical difficulties, it is nevertheless justified in that it catches corporations wilfully turning a blind eye to the corrupt practices of their foreign subsidiaries (connivance). It must be remembered that, under the existing law, a corporation can be complicit in an offence only if it foresees that that offence *will* happen and, only then, if a principal offence known to English law has been committed. Moreover, as we have seen,[85] turning a blind eye to an activity is not necessarily to assist or to encourage that activity, in a way that would bring such conduct within the scope of the existing law (including the provisions of the 2007 Act). The creation of a new offence would mean that companies could no longer deliberately ignore possible (as well as known) corruption in their subsidiaries.

9.102 Even so, we believe that most of the justification for the creation of a new offence falls away, if the offences of conspiracy and assisting or encouraging under the 2007 Act, along with the doctrine of complicity, can be utilised effectively in this area (in ways discussed in Part 11). In any event, we believe that, to the extent that it might be useful, any new offence relating to foreign subsidiaries should be for the consideration of a general review of corporate liability.

Provisional proposal

9.103 **We provisionally propose that a new offence of inadequate supervision of foreign subsidiary companies should not be created. It is an issue that should be deferred until our wider review of corporate liability.**

SUPPLEMENTARY ISSUES

Sanctions

9.104 Although the UK has been criticised for focusing exclusively on monetary sanctions for corporate defendants,[86] our sanctions regime does not fall short of the requirements of any of the Conventions. We believe that this is an area of corporate liability where significant work can be done in the future. However, such work is in no sense exclusive to the law of bribery. We therefore believe that a review of corporate sanctions should be deferred until our wider review of corporate liability.

---

[84] See the discussion in J Gobert and M Punch, *Rethinking Corporate Crime* (2003) pp 153 to 156.

[85] See paras 9.24 and following.

[86] For example, the OECD Phase 2 Report (2005) paras 204 to 206.

Provisional proposal

9.105 **We provisionally propose to defer the issue of corporate sanctions to our wider review of corporate liability.**

Duty not to exclude individual liability for assisting and encouraging

9.106 This final point is one of clarification. Within the majority of the Conventions there are provisions that require parties enacting corporate legislation to do so in a way that does not compromise the potential liability of natural persons. Referring back to Example 9C, this means that, however we deal with X Ltd or Z, it should remain possible to convict P under the standard bribery rules.

9.107 An example of this provision is Article 5(3) of the Council Framework Decision, which states:

> Liability for a legal person... shall not exclude criminal proceedings against natural persons who are involved as perpetrators, instigators or accessories in an offence [of bribery].

9.108 We believe that our provisional proposals will not affect the criminal liability of natural persons for bribery.

PART 10
ASSISTING AND ENCOURAGING BRIBERY

INTRODUCTION

10.1 A person ('X'), although not him or herself committing an offence ('a principal offence'), may assist, encourage or conspire with another person ('P')[1] to do so. The mere fact that X assists, encourages or conspires with P to commit a principal offence does not mean that P will go on to commit it. Under the current law, there are different rules governing X's criminal liability depending on whether or not P commits the principal offence. In addition, the *nature* of X's criminal liability depends on whether or not P commits the principal offence. X's liability may be either secondary or inchoate.

Secondary liability

10.2 If P does commit the principal offence, X, if he or she has assisted or encouraged P with the requisite state of mind, is guilty not merely of assisting or encouraging P to commit the principal offence but is guilty of the principal offence itself. In such cases, commentators refer to X as a secondary party or an accessory to the principal offence. By contrast, P is referred to as the principal offender.

10.3 The term principal offender denotes that it is P who has perpetrated the conduct proscribed by the principal offence. It does not denote that P is necessarily more culpable than X. In some cases, X is as culpable as P, if not more so. For example, P, a middle-ranking employee of a company, may bribe R on the orders of senior manager, X. The law recognises that X's culpability may be commensurate with or exceed P's culpability by stipulating that X may be punished as if he or she was the principal offender.[2]

10.4 The area of the law that governs whether or not a person is guilty of an offence as an accessory is the law of complicity and the liability of the accessory is often referred to as secondary liability. Secondary liability is a derivative form of liability. X's liability derives from and is dependent on the commission or attempted commission of a principal offence. Although there are exceptions, the general principle is that if no principal offence has been committed, X cannot be secondarily liable.

---

[1] As has already been explained, the principal offence of bribery can be committed by either P or R. However, where it is not essential to specify that we are referring to R rather than P, we will simply refer to P in order to avoid wearisome repetition.

[2] Accessories and Abettors Act 1861, s 8.

10.5   Principal offences are generally defined by reference to P. The definition of a principal offence will stipulate what it is that P must do, in what circumstances, with what consequences and with what state of mind. The rules that govern P's liability for a particular offence are unique to that offence.   By contrast, the doctrine of secondary liability applies to all offences. Being a doctrine of general application, its rules are the same regardless of the offence that is assisted or encouraged. If the rules were different depending on the nature of the principal offence, the doctrine of secondary liability would cease to be one of general application. Accordingly, the rules that govern whether X is guilty of robbery by assisting or encouraging P to commit the offence are no different from those that govern whether X is guilty of the common law offence of bribery by assisting or encouraging P to commit that offence.

Inchoate liability

10.6   If a principal offence is not committed or attempted, X cannot be secondarily liable. Yet, it might be thought that X ought not to escape all criminal liability if he or she, with the requisite state of mind, has assisted, encouraged or conspired with P to commit a principal offence. The common law of England and Wales responded by developing three inchoate offences, namely conspiracy, incitement and attempt.[3] Conspiracy is where X and P agree to commit an offence. X and P commit the offence as soon as they conclude the agreement, regardless of whether any steps are taken to execute the agreement.[4] Incitement is where X encourages P to commit an offence. X is liable as soon as the encouragement comes to P's attention, irrespective of whether P acts on it. Attempt is where a person tries to commit an offence but fails to do so.

10.7   They are inchoate offences in that they serve to criminalise and punish conduct that enhances the prospect of harm occurring even if the harm does not in fact materialise. They are free-standing offences but they always relate to a principal offence. Accordingly, they are always charged in relation to a principal offence, for example attempted rape, incitement to rob and conspiracy to murder.

10.8   Importantly, as with secondary liability, the principles that govern X's liability for the inchoate offences of conspiracy, incitement and attempt do not depend on the nature of the principal offence. The rules that determine whether X is guilty of inciting P to commit robbery are the same as those that determine whether X is guilty of inciting P to commit the common law offence of bribery.

---

[3]   Attempt is now a statutory offence by virtue of the Criminal Attempts Act 1981. Conspiracy is also now a statutory offence by virtue of the Criminal Law Act 1977. However, conspiracy as a common law offence has not been completely abolished. Conspiracy to defraud, conspiracy to corrupt public morals and conspiracy to outrage public decency remain common law offences. Incitement is still a common law offence although Parliament has enacted many specific statutory offences of incitement.

[4]   Being an inchoate offence, it might be thought that conspiracy would be charged only if the principal offence is not subsequently committed. However, in practice, conspiracy is frequently charged even when the principal offence is committed. By contrast, incitement is rarely charged when the principal offence is committed.

THE UNITED KINGDOM'S INTERNATIONAL OBLIGATIONS IN RELATION TO ASSISTING, ENCOURAGING AND CONSPIRING TO COMMIT BRIBERY

10.9 The international Conventions on bribery and corruption that the United Kingdom has ratified all contain provisions on complicity or participation in offences of bribery. They require each Party to make it a criminal offence to participate in offences of bribery, either generally[5] or in relation to particular offences of bribery, for example bribery of foreign public officials.[6] The language employed in the Conventions varies ranging from "aiding and abetting", "instigating", "inciting" to "authorising".

THE CURRENT DOMESTIC LAW

Inchoate liability

10.10 The following examples illustrate the major defect of the current law:

Example 10A

X encourages P to bribe R who holds a public office. P decides not to do so.

Example 10B

X, in return for payment, provides P with some documentation that X believes P will use in order to bribe Y. Before P can do so, Y dies.

The common law distinguishes between encouragement and assistance. At common law, if X encourages P to commit a principal offence that is not subsequently committed, X may nevertheless be convicted of incitement to commit the principal offence. By contrast, at common law if X assists P to commit an offence that is not subsequently committed, X incurs no criminal liability. Accordingly, in Example 10A, X is guilty of inciting P to commit the common law offence of bribery whereas, in Example 10B, X has not committed an offence.

10.11 It is true that Parliament has enacted a number of offences that criminalise particular instances of inchoate assistance. However, it has not done so in the context of bribery and corruption. It remains the case, therefore, that if X assists P to commit an offence of bribery that P does not subsequently commit, X incurs no criminal liability unless there was an agreement between them to commit the offence. If so, they can both be convicted of conspiracy (to bribe).

10.12 The majority of the international Conventions that the United Kingdom has ratified do not expressly address whether there ought to be criminal liability for assisting an act of bribery that is not subsequently committed. An exception is the OECD Convention. Paragraph 11 of the Commentaries on the OECD Convention provides:

---

[5] Eg, United Nations Convention against Corruption, Art 27(1); Criminal Law Convention on Corruption, Art 15.

[6] Eg, the OECD Convention, Art 1(2).

The offences set out in [Article 1(2)] are understood in terms of their normal content in national legal systems. Accordingly, if authorisation, incitement, or one of the other listed acts, which does not lead to further action, is not itself punishable under a Party's legal system, then the Party would not be required to make it punishable with respect to bribery of a foreign public official.[7]

Accordingly, the fact that under the current law there is no criminal liability for assisting the commission of an offence of bribery that is not subsequently committed is not a violation of the OECD Convention.

Secondary liability

10.13 The law relating to secondary liability is complex and difficult.[8] At the risk of oversimplification, X is guilty of a principal offence that has been committed with his or her assistance or encouragement if:

(1) the offence is committed by P in the course of a joint criminal venture[9] to which X and P are parties and X intended that the offence should be committed or foresaw that it might be committed;

(2) although not a party with P to a joint venture, X foresees that P will commit the principal offence.

RECOMMENDATIONS FOR REFORM OF THE CURRENT LAW

Inchoate liability

Offences

10.14 In 2006 the Law Commission published a report on inchoate liability for assisting and encouraging crime ('the 2006 report').[10] The Commission said that the common law offence of incitement should be abolished and that the gap in the common law relating to inchoate assisting should be eliminated. We recommended that there should be two core statutory inchoate offences:

(1) doing an act capable of assisting or encouraging the commission of a principal offence *intending* that the offence should be committed. ('the clause 1 inchoate offence'),

(2) doing an act capable of assisting or encouraging the commission of a principal offence believing:

---

[7] Commentaries on the Convention on Combating Bribery of Foreign Public Officials in International Business Transactions ('the Commentaries on the OECD Convention').

[8] A detailed account of the current law can be found in Participating in Crime (2007) Law Com No 305, Appendix B.

[9] A joint criminal venture is where X and P and R share an intention to commit a principal offence. Such cases pose particular problems if P in the course of a venture commits an offence that X did not agree to. For example, X and P agree to burgle the premises of V. In the course of the burglary, P murders V. The issue is whether X should be convicted of the 'collateral' offence of murder. The problem is unlikely to arise in the context of bribery.

[10] Inchoate Liability for Assisting and Encouraging Crime (2006) Law Com No 300.

(a)   that the act will assist or encourage the commission of the principal offence; and

(b)   that the principal offence will be committed. ('the clause 2 inchoate offence')

Defences

10.15   The Commission recommended that there should be two defences:

(1)   acting for the purpose of preventing the commission of an offence or to prevent or limit the occurrence of harm;

(2)   acting reasonably in all the circumstances.

10.16   The former would have been a defence to both the clause 1 offence and the clause 2 offence while the latter would only have been a defence to the clause 2 offence. In other words, the Commission was recommending that the defence of acting reasonably in all the circumstances should not be available if it was X's intention that a principal offence should be committed. By contrast, the Commission was recommending that the defence of crime prevention or prevention of harm should be available even if it was X's intention that a principal offence should be committed provided that X was seeking to prevent greater harm.

Infinite inchoate liability

10.17   The paradigm case of assisting or encouraging crime is where X assists or encourages P to commit an offence, for example bribery. In such a case, the conduct that assists or encourages is only one step removed from the prospective principal offence. However, that will not always be the case:

Example 10C

Y encourages X to assist P to bribe R.

Example 10D

Y assists X to assist P to bribe R.

In each example, Y's conduct is two steps removed from the commission of a principal offence that P for a variety of reasons may never commit. If Y can be held criminally liable for conduct that is two steps removed from the prospective principal offence, logically there is no reason why Y should not be held criminally liable if his or her conduct is ten steps removed.

10.18   This leads to the problem of infinite inchoate liability: it can result in an over-extension of the criminal law. It allows Y, because of potentially harmful consequences that may flow if P does commit the principal offence, to be convicted on the basis of conduct that is very remote from the prospective principal offence. Accordingly, the argument is that the further removed and, therefore, the more remote Y's conduct is from the prospective principal offence, the more cautious the law should be before making Y criminally liable.

10.19   The recommendations in the 2006 report make a distinction between the clause 1 and the clause 2 offence:

Example 10E

Y encourages X to assist P to bribe R. Y is very keen that X should do so because Y stands to benefit should P bribe R.

Example 10F

In return for payment, Y provides material to X. Y believes that X will give the material to P so that P can bribe R. However, having been paid, Y is indifferent as to what X does with the material.

In Example 10E, Y has done an act intending to encourage X to commit the clause 1 or clause 2 offence. By contrast, in Example 10F, Y has done an act believing, but not intending, that X will commit the clause 1 or clause 2 offence.

10.20   The 2006 report recommended that, in Example 10E, Y should stand to be convicted of the clause 1 offence. This is because, in encouraging X, Y intended that X should commit either the clause 1 or the clause 2 offence by assisting P to bribe R. The fact that Y's act is more than one step removed from the prospective principal offence ought not to be a bar to criminal liability given Y's highly culpable state of mind. The same would be true even if Y's conduct was ten steps removed from the principal offence.

10.21   By contrast, in Example 10F, Y would not stand to be convicted of the clause 2 offence. It might be thought that his conduct is immoral. However, this has to be set against the danger of over-extending the scope of the criminal law where Y's conduct is removed from a principal offence that might never be committed. It has to be remembered that, in Example 10F, if Y were to be held criminally liable where his or her conduct is only two steps removed from the principal offence, logically he or she should also be liable where it was ten steps removed. This is acceptable where Y intends that X should assist or encourage P to bribe R but not where Y merely believes that X will assist or encourage P to bribe R.

Secondary liability

10.22 In 2007, the Law Commission published a report on secondary liability for assisting and encouraging crime ('the 2007 report').[11] The main recommendation was that the scope of secondary liability should be narrowed in cases where X and P are not parties to a joint criminal venture. Under the current law, in such cases X can be convicted of the principal offence even if he or she did not intend that it should be committed. It suffices if X believed that it would (or even simply might) be committed. By contrast, under the recommendations in the 2007 report, X would be guilty of a principal offence committed with his or her assistance or encouragement only if X *intended* that the offence should be committed.

10.23 In the absence of such an intention, X would not necessarily escape all criminal liability. Provided that X believed that his or her conduct would assist or encourage the commission of the principal offence and that the principal offence would be committed, X could be convicted of the clause 2 inchoate offence that was recommended in the 2006 report.[12]

10.24 The 2007 report, like the 2006 report, recommended that there should be a defence of acting in order to prevent the commission of crime or in order to prevent or limit harm. However, unlike the 2006 report, it did not recommend a defence of acting reasonably. This was logical because the 2007 report was recommending that secondary liability should be confined to cases where X intended that a principal offence should be committed. It will be recalled that the 2006 report did not recommend that there should be a defence of acting reasonably to the clause 1 offence.[13]

The impact of implementing the recommendations

10.25 The following example illustrates how the recommendations in both the 2006 report and the 2007 report, if implemented, would impact in cases where X and P are not parties to a joint criminal venture to commit an offence of bribery:

> **Example 10G**
>
> In exchange for payment, X provides P with material that X believes P will use to bribe R. Having been paid, X is indifferent as to whether P does bribe R.

Under the current law, should P use the material to bribe R, X is an accessory to and guilty of the bribery offence that P commits. It suffices that X foresaw that P would use the material to bribe R even though X did not intend that P should bribe R. By contrast, should P not commit the offence, under the current law, X is not criminally liable because X's conduct consisted of assistance rather than encouragement.

---

[11] Participating in Crime (2007) Law Com No 305.

[12] See para 10.14(2) above.

[13] See para 10.16 above.

10.26   Under the recommendations in the 2006 and 2007 reports, X would be guilty of the clause 2 inchoate offence irrespective of whether P bribed R. If P did bribe R, X would be guilty of the clause 2 inchoate offence of assisting bribery rather than P's substantive offence of bribery because it was not X's intention that P should bribe R. If P did not bribe R, X would nevertheless be convicted of the clause 2 offence because:

    (1)   the clause 2 offence covers assistance as well as encouragement, and

    (2)   although X did not intend P to bribe R, X rendered his assistance to P believing that P would bribe R.

10.27   In cases where X and P are parties to a joint criminal venture, the Commission's recommendations would not, in the context of bribery, alter the existing law in the event that the principal offence is committed:

Example 10H

X and P agree that they will bribe R. Pursuant to the agreement, X provides P with material to enable P to bribe R.

Should P bribe R, under the current law and under the Commission's recommendations, X is and would be guilty of the principal offence. Should P decide not to bribe R, both X and P are and would continue to be guilty of conspiracy (to bribe). In addition, under the Commission's recommendations, P would be guilty of the clause 1 inchoate offence.

The Government's response to the Law Commission's recommendations

Inchoate liability

10.28   In Part 2 of the 2007 Act, the Government has taken forward the recommendations made in the 2006 report.

OFFENCES

10.29   Sections 44 and 45 make provision for two inchoate offences of assisting or encouraging the commission of a principal offence. The offences are broadly consistent with the clause 1 offence and the clause 2 offence recommended in the 2006 report.

10.30   In one respect, however, the 2007 Act does depart from the recommendations in the 2006 report:

Example 10J

P, a self-employed businessman, approaches X and says that he needs some money to pay to R, a public official. X gives P the money believing that P probably wants the money to pay off a debt owing to R. However, X realises that there is a real possibility that P wants the money so that he can offer it to R in return for R ensuring that a contract is awarded to P rather than V. In the event, P does use the money to pay off a debt that he owes to R.

In the 2006 report, the Commission recommended that X should be liable if he or she believed that were P to perpetrate the conduct element of the principal offence (in Example 10J, the payment of the money) P *would* do so with the fault required to be convicted of the principal offence. This strict test reflected the fact that what is at issue is X's liability for assisting or encouraging a principal offence that might or might not be committed. In Example 10J, X does not satisfy that test.

10.31 However, section 47(5) of the 2007 Act provides that it suffices that X was *reckless* as to whether the conduct element of the principal offence would be perpetrated with the fault element required for conviction of the principal offence. In Example 10J, X satisfies that test because he realised that there was a possibility that P would give R the money in order to secure the grant of the contract.

DEFENCES

10.32 In the 2007 Act there is no discrete defence of acting for the purpose of preventing the commission of an offence or to prevent or limit the occurrence of harm. Instead, section 50 provides for a defence of acting reasonably:

(1) A person is not guilty of an offence if he proves:

(a) that he knew certain circumstances existed; and

(b) that it was reasonable for him to act in those circumstances.

(2) A person is not guilty of an offence if he proves:

(a) that he believed certain circumstances to exist;

(b) that his belief was reasonable; and

(c) that it was reasonable for him to act as he did in the circumstances as he believed them to be.

(3) Factors to be considered in determining whether it was reasonable for a person to act as he did include:

(a) The seriousness of the anticipated offence … ;

(b) any purpose for which he claims to have been acting;

(c) any authority by which he claims to have been acting.

It would be a defence not only to the offence in the 2007 Act which is the equivalent of the clause 2 offence in the 2006 report but also to the offence which is the equivalent of the clause 1 offence.

10.33 The defence covers but is not confined to cases where X acts in order to prevent the commission of crime:

Example 10K

X is an undercover police officer who has infiltrated a company, P Ltd, that is suspected of being involved in bribery. X is aware that the company wishes to bribe R, a public official. P asks X to find out what sort of advantage is most likely to appeal to R. In order to retain his credibility, X does so.

Example 10L

X works as a typist for P. P tells X to type a letter addressed to R who is employed by the local authority. The letter contains an offer of a substantial sum of money if R ensures that P's firm is awarded a contract by the local authority. X is very uncomfortable in typing the letter but is frightened that she will be dismissed if she fails to comply. She has no employment rights in the event of being dismissed.

In each example, the burden would be on X to prove on a balance of probabilities that he or she had acted reasonably in all the circumstances. It would be a matter for the jury to decide whether X had discharged the burden.

INFINITE INCHOATE LIABILITY

10.34   The 2007 Act contains provisions which implement the recommendations in the 2006 report.

Secondary liability

10.35   The Government is currently considering the recommendations made in the 2007 report.

PART 11
BRIBERY COMMITTED OUTSIDE ENGLAND AND WALES

INTRODUCTION

11.1 In this Part, we consider the circumstances in which English law should recognise as an offence ('an extra-territorial bribery offence') an act committed outside England and Wales which, if committed in England and Wales, would be an offence of bribery. We have stated the issue in this way because in the past there has been a tendency in cases where there has been an extra-territorial element to confuse two issues:

   (1)   determining whether conduct committed outside England and Wales constitutes an extra-territorial offence known to English law;

   (2)   determining whether a court in England and Wales has jurisdiction to try a person for an extra-territorial offence.[1]

11.2 In addition, we consider the circumstances in which it ought to be possible to convict a person of an extra-territorial bribery offence by virtue of his or her participation in the offence as an accessory.

11.3 Finally, we consider the circumstances in which it should be an inchoate offence:

   (1)   to agree, encourage or assist in England and Wales to commit an extra-territorial bribery offence;

   (2)   to agree, encourage or assist outside England and Wales to commit an offence of bribery in England and Wales; and

   (3)   to agree, encourage or assist outside England and Wales to commit an offence of bribery outside England and Wales.

The underlying principles

11.4 The common law of England and Wales evolved over centuries when relatively few offences were committed across national boundaries. However, the last fifty years have witnessed the phenomenon of globalisation. Criminal organisations have adeptly exploited the opportunities that globalisation has brought. Thus, although most serious crimes are usually still local in their commission and effect, involving a perpetrator and victim in the same country, a small but significant number transcend national boundaries. This is particularly true of bribery offences.

---

[1]   In order to avoid repetition, instead of referring to "courts of England and Wales" we will refer to "English courts".

11.5   At common law, the general principle is that conduct which would constitute an offence if committed in England and Wales is not an offence under English law if perpetrated outside England and Wales.[2] This is so even if it is a British citizen who perpetrates the conduct. Conversely, conduct committed in England and Wales that is an offence if committed by a British national or a body incorporated under English law is also an offence if committed by a foreign citizen or body incorporated under a foreign law. The function of the criminal law is to deter and punish the commission of offences in England and Wales. In order to do so effectively, English courts have jurisdiction to try all natural and legal persons whose conduct in England and Wales constitutes an offence. By contrast, conduct perpetrated outside England and Wales, however heinous, has traditionally been thought less likely to impact detrimentally on society in England and Wales.

11.6   Parliament is supreme and, when enacting an offence, can stipulate that it can be committed by conduct occurring outside England and Wales.[3] However, when construing a statutory offence, the courts start from a "strong presumption" that Parliament did not intend to enact an extra-territorial offence.[4] For the presumption to be displaced, there has to be clear words. When originally enacted, neither the 1889 Act nor the 1906 Act contained clear words indicating that Parliament was intending to enact extra-territorial offences.

THE UNITED KINGDOM'S OBLIGATIONS UNDER INTERNATIONAL CONVENTIONS

11.7   Most of the international Conventions on bribery and corruption that the United Kingdom has ratified contain Articles on 'jurisdiction'.[5] These Articles require Parties to take measures to establish jurisdiction over offences of bribery that are committed outside their territory.

11.8   However, the measures that have to be taken are limited in scope. For example, Article 17 of the Criminal Law Convention on Corruption requires each Party to adopt such measures as are necessary to establish jurisdiction over an offence of bribery committed outside its territory if:

    (1)   the payer is one of its nationals or one of its public officials or a member of one of its domestic public assemblies; or

    (2)   the recipient is:

            (a)   one of its public officials or members of its domestic public assemblies; or

---

[2]   For the purposes of this paper, the common law exceptions to the general rule are not important.

[3]   Equally, it can extend the scope of an existing common law offence to conduct occurring outside England and Wales.

[4]   *Treacy* [1971] AC 537, 551 by Lord Reid; *Air India v Wiggins* [1980] 1 WLR 815.

[5]   Eg, Art 4 of the OECD Convention, Art 17 of the Criminal Law Convention on Corruption. Art 7 of the Council of the European Union's Framework Decision of 22 July 2003 on combating corruption in the private sector and Art 42 of the United Nations Convention against Corruption.

(b)   one of its nationals who is:

(i)   an official of an international organisation,

(ii)   a member of an international parliamentary assembly; or

(iii)   a judge or official of any international court.

However, each Party is entitled to derogate from (1) and (2).   The United Kingdom has made a declaration under Article 17(2) that it reserves the right to apply the jurisdictional rule in (1) only where the offender is a national of the United Kingdom. In addition, the United Kingdom has reserved the right not to apply the jurisdictional rule laid down in (2) at all.

11.9   Under the various international Conventions that it has ratified, the only legal obligation that the United Kingdom has in relation to 'jurisdiction' is to take measures to criminalise extra-territorial acts of bribery that are committed by natural persons who are its nationals. In relation to principal offenders, this obligation has been satisfied by the enactment of section 109 of the Anti-Terrorism, Crime and Security Act 2001[6] and section 69 of the Criminal Justice (Scotland) Act 2003.

11.10   It is important to acknowledge and emphasise that as a result of the enactment of section 109, the current law goes beyond the minimum obligations imposed on the United Kingdom by virtue of the Conventions to which it is a signatory. This is because section 109 applies not only to natural persons who are British nationals but also to legal persons incorporated under the law of any part of the United Kingdom.

THE CURRENT DOMESTIC LAW

Principal offenders

Section 109 of the Anti-Terrorism, Crime and Security Act 2001

11.11   We noted above that neither the 1889 Act nor the 1906 Act created extra-territorial offences. Section 109 of the Anti-Terrorism, Crime and Security Act 2001 ('the 2001 Act') altered the position. It did so by providing that an act, which if done in the United Kingdom would constitute a corruption offence, constitutes a corruption offence if done outside the United Kingdom provided it is done:

(1)   by a national of the United Kingdom; or

(2)   by a body incorporated under the law of any part of the United Kingdom

There is no requirement that the act must also constitute an offence under the law of the foreign territory.

---

[6]   See para 11.11 below.

11.12　Importantly, 'corruption offence' means not only the common law offence of bribery and the offences under section 1 of the 1889 Act but also the first two offences under the 1906 Act. The inclusion of offences under the 1906 Act means that, unlike some other jurisdictions, it is an offence under English law (for a British national or company) to bribe a private agent outside England and Wales.[7]

11.13　On the other hand, the categories of natural and legal persons to which section 109 applies are restricted. Further, section 109 does not apply to acts done in Scotland or Northern Ireland.

NATURAL PERSONS

11.14　Section 109(4) defines a "national of the United Kingdom". It does so in a way that ensures that the majority of natural persons who live in the Crown Dependencies[8] and Overseas Territories[9] fall within the definition.

11.15　However, a foreign national does not commit an offence known to English law if he or she commits an act of bribery outside the United Kingdom, even if he or she is domiciled or is ordinarily resident in England and Wales.

LEGAL PERSONS

11.16　Section 109 permits a legal person incorporated under any part of the law of England and Wales ('a British company') to be convicted of an extra-territorial bribery offence. It follows that if P, a person employed by a British company, perpetrates an act of bribery in Moscow, the company commits an offence of bribery known to English law provided:

(1)　P is a person who "represents the directing mind and will of the company"; or

(2)　P has committed the act of bribery with the knowledge or under the direction of a person who "represents the directing mind and will of the company".

Whether or not P is a British national is irrelevant in determining the criminal liability of the British company.[10]

11.17　However, for a company to commit an offence of bribery by virtue of an act of one of its employees, it must be a British company:

---

[7]　In some countries an act of bribery committed outside the jurisdiction is only an offence if the recipient is a *public* official.

[8]　There are three United Kingdom Crown Dependencies: the Isle of Man, Jersey and the Bailiwick of Guernsey, which includes the islands of Sark and Alderney.

[9]　There are 14 Overseas Territories. They include Gibraltar, Bermuda, the Cayman Islands and the British Virgin Islands. They vary considerably in size and commercial importance. The OECD Working Group on Bribery in International Business Transactions which conducted an on-site visit of the United Kingdom in July 2004 expressed concern about the low priority given to implementation of the OECD Convention by the Overseas Territories.

[10]　It is, of course, critical in determining P's personal liability.

> **Example 11A**
>
> P is a British citizen who is employed in Moscow by a Spanish company, X Ltd. The parent company of X Ltd is a British company, Y Ltd. A director of X Ltd orders P to bribe R in Moscow. P does so.

P, being a British citizen, has committed an offence of bribery known to English law. However, X Ltd, being a Spanish company, has committed no offence known to English law. The fact that X Ltd is a subsidiary of a British parent company is irrelevant.[11]

11.18 Section 109 only applies to bodies that are incorporated under any part of the law of "the United Kingdom". "The United Kingdom" means Great Britain and Northern Ireland.[12] Crown Dependencies and Overseas Territories are not part of Great Britain. It would seem to follow that section 109 does not apply to companies that are incorporated in the Crown Dependencies and Overseas Territories.

11.19 Section 109 is restricted to bodies that are incorporated. The requirement that a body must be incorporated means that unincorporated bodies such as most types of partnerships, unincorporated foundations and associations and many trusts fall outside the ambit of section 109. On the other hand, individual natural persons such as trustees and partners who make up the unincorporated bodies may still be prosecuted.

SCOTLAND AND NORTHERN IRELAND

11.20 Section 109 applies to acts done outside the United Kingdom. Scotland is part of the United Kingdom. Accordingly, if P, a British citizen residing in Carlisle, bribes R in Dumfries, P commits no offence known to English law.[13]

Accessories

11.21 In Part 10, we explained that a person, X, who assists, encourages or conspires with another person, P, to commit a principal offence can be an accessory to and guilty of the offence should P commit it. In such cases, it is P alone who perpetrates the conduct proscribed by the principal offence. Were X to perpetrate even part of the proscribed conduct, he or she would be convicted of the offence as a principal offender rather than as an accessory.

11.22 In the light of section 109 of the 2001 Act, it might be thought that, provided X is a British national or British company, X can be convicted of an extra-territorial substantive offence of bribery even if P is a foreign national or company. However, this would be to ignore the derivative nature of secondary liability:

---

[11] In the example, Y Ltd, although a British company, has likewise committed no offence known to English law. P is not its employee.

[12] Interpretation Act 1978, s 5 and sch 1.

[13] Both the 1889 and the 1906 Acts apply to Scotland and Northern Ireland. However, even if an offence-creating provision does apply to other parts of the United Kingdom, the general rule is that any offences committed wholly in Scotland or Northern Ireland are offences under Scots or Northern Ireland law alone.

> **Example 11B**
>
> X is a British national working in Khartoum. In Khartoum, and in return for payment, he provides P, a Sudanese citizen, with material knowing that P intends to use it to bribe R, a British businessman, in Khartoum. P does so.

P, being a foreign national, has committed no offence known to English law. Since X's liability derives from and is dependent on the commission of a principal offence, X has not committed any offence known to English law.[14]

> **Example 11C**
>
> X Ltd, a British company, is the parent company of P Ltd, a foreign subsidiary. P Ltd conducts business in Bolivia. The directors of P Ltd, all of whom are Bolivian nationals, travel to London to request the directors of X Ltd to provide material that will enable the directors of P Ltd to return to Bolivia to bribe the directors of R Ltd, a Bolivian company. The directors of X Ltd provide the material knowing it will be used to bribe the directors to R Ltd. The directors of P Ltd return to Bolivia and bribe the directors of R Ltd.

P Ltd, being a foreign company, has committed no substantive offence known to English law. Accordingly, neither have the directors of X Ltd. This is so even though the assistance was rendered in London

11.23   Example 11C illustrates that, for the purposes of determining whether or not an "offence" of bribery has been committed in or outside England and Wales, X's conduct, since it does not constitute any element of the conduct proscribed by the offence, is irrelevant. Although the material was provided in London, the proscribed conduct constituting the bribery was committed in Bolivia.

11.24   In examples 11B and 11C, it is not merely a question of an English court lacking jurisdiction to try X for a substantive offence that has been committed outside England and Wales. Rather, P has not committed any substantive offence known to English law. It follows that X, even if a British citizen or a British company and even if perpetrating the act of assistance in England and Wales, cannot be convicted of bribery because the liability of an accessory is dependent on a principal offence having been committed.

---

[14]   *Johnson* (1805) 6 East 583; *Jameson* [1896] 2 QB 425.

Inchoate offences

Introduction

11.25   The inchoate offences of conspiracy, incitement and attempt pose particular problems.[15] Frequently, the intention is to bring about the commission of the principal offence in a territory other than the territory where the agreement, attempt or incitement ('the inchoate act') takes place. In broad terms, there are three situations:

(1)   the inchoate act takes place in England and Wales but is directed to the commission of a principal offence outside England and Wales;

(2)   the inchoate act takes place outside England and Wales but is directed to the commission of a principal offence in England and Wales;

(3)   the inchoate act takes place outside England and Wales and is directed to the commission of a principal offence outside England and Wales.

We will consider each in turn. However, before doing so, we consider when and where each inchoate offence is committed.

CONSPIRACY

11.26   Conspiracy consists of an agreement to commit a principal offence known to English law. X and P commit the offence as soon as they agree to commit the principal offence and the conspiracy is committed in the territory where the agreement is concluded.

INCITEMENT

11.27   Incitement consists of encouraging another person to commit a principal offence known to English law. The offence of incitement is only committed when the encouragement is communicated to the other person. Accordingly, at common law the incitement takes place in the territory where the communication is received. The offence is complete as soon as the encouragement is communicated.

ATTEMPT

11.28   Attempt is committed where a person unsuccessfully tries to commit a principal offence known to English law. The offence is committed when the person does an act which is more than merely preparatory to the commission of the principal offence. The offence is committed in the territory where the more than merely preparatory act is perpetrated.

---

[15] As explained in Part 10, under the current law there is no inchoate offence of facilitation or assisting the commission of an offence – see Part 10, paras 10.10 to 10.12 above, and for our recommendations see Part 10, paras 10.28 to 10.34 above.

Inchoate acts occurring in England and Wales directed to the commission of a principal offence of bribery outside England and Wales

COMMON LAW

11.29   The common law adopted a restrictive approach to inchoate acts occurring in England and Wales that were directed to the commission of principal offences outside England and Wales. The general principle that emerged was that conspiracy, incitement and attempt to commit an offence outside England and Wales were not offences known to English law unless the principal offence, if committed, would be an offence known to English law and triable in England and Wales.[16]

11.30   The following example illustrates the general principle:

> **Example 11D**
>
> In London, X, a British national, urges P, a Russian national who is resident in London, to bribe R in Moscow. Instead, P reports X to the British authorities.

At common law, X has not committed an offence of incitement (to commit bribery) because, were P to bribe R in Moscow, P, being a Russian national, would not commit an offence known to English law.[17] By contrast, if P were a British national, X would be guilty of an offence of incitement to commit bribery. Further, X would be guilty regardless of whether he or she was a British national.

11.31   The common law rule was re-stated in statutory form by sections 1(1) and (4) of the Criminal Law Act 1977 ('the 1977 Act') in relation to statutory conspiracies and by sections 1(1) and (4) of the Criminal Attempts Act 1981 ('the 1981 Act') in relation to attempts. The common law rule in relation to incitement has not been re-stated in statutory form.

STATUTORY MODIFICATION OF THE COMMON LAW RULE

Conspiracy – Section 1A of the Criminal Law Act 1977[18]

11.32   In relation to conspiracy, the common law rule has been superseded by section 1A of the Criminal Law Act 1977. Section 1A makes it an offence to agree to pursue a course of conduct involving the doing of an act or the occurrence of an event in a country or territory outside the United Kingdom if:

        (1)   the conduct would amount to an offence in that country or territory;

        (2)   the conduct, if committed in England and Wales, would amount to an offence under English law; or

        (3)   the party to be tried, or his or her agent:

[16]   *Board of Trade v Owen* [1957] AC 602.

[17]   By contrast, were X in London to incite P in London to murder R in Moscow, X would be guilty under Offences against the Person Act 1861, s 4 of inciting P to commit murder irrespective of whether P was a British citizen – *Abu Hamza* [2006] EWCA Crim 2918, [2007] 2 WLR 226.

(a) did anything in England and Wales in relation to the agreement before its formation; or assemblies; or

(b) became a party in England and Wales; or

(c) did or omitted to do anything in England and Wales in pursuance of the agreement.

Section 1A(11) specifically provides that any act done by means of a message, however communicated, is to be treated for the purposes of (3)(a), (b) and (c) as done in England and Wales if the message is sent or received in England and Wales.

11.33 Section 1A is far broader in scope than the common law rule which was restated in sections 1(1) and (4) of the 1977 Act. Under the latter, it is an offence known to English law for X and P, both nationals of the United Kingdom, to conspire in London to bribe R in Moscow. Section 1A goes further by making it an offence known to English law for X and P, both foreign nationals residing outside England and Wales, to agree in London to bribe R in Moscow. The fact that they are foreign nationals who reside outside England and Wales is irrelevant because, had they agreed in London to bribe R in London, they would have committed an offence known to English law had they proceeded to bribe R.[19]

11.34 Further, section 1A extends to the situation where X and P, both foreign nationals, agree in Madrid to bribe R in Moscow provided that either X or P:

(1) does something in England and Wales in relation to the agreement before its formation; or

(2) does something in England and Wales pursuant to the agreement.

11.35 The law in relation to conspiracy to commit an offence of bribery should be contrasted with the law relating to criminal liability for a substantive offence of bribery. If X, a foreign national and resident in London, without entering into a conspiracy with P in London to bribe R in Moscow, simply bribes R in Moscow, X commits no offence known to English law. Section 109 of the 2001 Act applies only to British nationals.

---

[18] Section 1A was inserted by Criminal Justice (Terrorism and Conspiracy) Act 1998.

[19] However, there is an important limitation on the scope of s1A. It does not apply to those acting on behalf of, or holding office under, the Crown – s 1A(14).

Inchoate acts occurring outside England and Wales directed to the commission of a principal offence of bribery in England and Wales

COMMON LAW

11.36 In *DPP v Doot*[20] the House of Lords held that a conspiracy formed abroad to commit an offence in England and Wales was an offence known to English law and triable in England and Wales provided an "overt act" in pursuance of the conspiracy had taken place within the jurisdiction.

11.37 In *Somchai Liangsinpraseret v United States*[21] the Privy Council dispensed with the need for any "overt act" within the jurisdiction.[22] Having noted that inchoate offences were developed with the principal objective of frustrating the commission of a contemplated crime by enabling the authorities to arrest offenders before the commission of the crime, Lord Griffiths observed:

> If the inchoate crime is aimed at England with the consequent injury to English society, why should the English courts not accept jurisdiction to try it if the authorities can lay hands on the offenders, either because they come within the jurisdiction or through extradition procedures? ... . Crime is now established on an international scale and the common law must face this new reality. Their Lordships can find nothing in precedent, comity or good sense that should inhibit the common law from regarding as justiciable in England inchoate crimes committed abroad which are intended to result in the commission of offences in England.[23]

Accordingly, if X and P agree in Paris to bribe R in London, at common law they commit an offence under English law which is triable in England and Wales. This is so regardless of whether either X or P is a British national or resides in the United Kingdom.

11.38 In *DPP v Stonehouse*[24] X faked his death in Miami so that his wife in England, who was not a party to the fraud, could claim on life insurance policies. The House of Lords held that the attempt to obtain property by deception in England and Wales was an offence known to English law even though no act that was more than merely preparatory to the commission of the completed offence had taken place in England and Wales.

[20] [1973] AC 807.

[21] [1991] 1 AC 225.

[22] This is true of both common law and statutory conspiracies – *Sansom* [1991] 2 QB 130.

[23] [1991] AC 225, 251.

[24] [1978] AC 55.

11.39 Although there is no *direct* appellate authority which confirms that the principles that apply to conspiracy and attempt also apply to incitement,[25] there is nothing to suggest that in *Liangsiriprasert v United States* Lord Griffiths intended his observations to be confined to conspiracy. Accordingly, if X in New York sends a letter to P in Chicago urging P to bribe R in London, X has committed an offence known to English law which is triable in an English court. Whether either X or P is a British national is irrelevant.

11.40 Subject to one qualification, the common law has not been re-stated in statutory form. The qualification relates to conspiracies, incitements and attempts to commit what are known as Group A offences.[26] However, the common law offence of bribery and the offences under the 1899 and 1906 Acts are not Group A offences.

Inchoate acts occurring outside England and Wales directed to the commission of a principal offence of bribery outside England and Wales

11.41 At common law, it is not an offence known to English law to do an inchoate act outside England and Wales directed to the commission of a principal offence outside England and Wales. Accordingly, if X and P agree in Paris to bribe R in Athens, neither X nor P commits an offence known to English law.[27] This is so even if X and P are both British nationals. However should either X or P, each being British nationals, actually bribe R in Athens, then each could be prosecuted in England and Wales.[28]

11.42 Likewise, if X in Paris sends a letter to P in Rome urging P to bribe R in Athens, X does not commit an offence triable in England and Wales. This is so even if X and P are both British. However should P actually bribe R in Athens, then, being British nationals, both could be prosecuted in England and Wales.[29]

---

[25] The choice of the word "direct" is deliberate. In *Goldman* [2001] EWCA Crim 1684, [2001] *Criminal Law Review* 822 G was charged with *attempting* to incite B in Holland to distribute indecent photos of children in England and Wales. In *R (O) v Coventry Magistrates' Court* [2004] EWHC 905, [2004] *Criminal Law Review* 948 O was charged with inciting B in Texas to distribute in England and Wales indecent photographs of children. A sought to challenge the decision to commit him to the Crown Court for trial. The issue was not raised. In *Tompkins* [2006] EWCA Crim 2132, for the purposes of an interlocutory appeal by the prosecution, the accused conceded that inciting a person outside England and Wales to commit an offence inside England and Wales was an offence known to English law.

[26] See the Criminal Justice Act 1993, Pt 1, s 1 for the list of "Group A offences".

[27] Unless either P or X, or the agent of either, did anything in England and Wales relating to the agreement prior to its formation or did or omitted to do anything in England and Wales in pursuance of the agreement – see para 11.32 above.

[28] Assuming it is P who bribes R in Athens, he or she would be liable as the principal offender and X would be liable as an accessory.

[29] Assuming it is P who bribes R in Athens, he or she would be liable as the principal offender and X as an accessory.

MAJOR DEFECTS OF THE CURRENT LAW

11.43 The mere fact that the United Kingdom currently complies with its international obligations in relation to extra-territorial acts of bribery does not mean that the current domestic law is satisfactory. In particular, under the current law:

(1) a natural person who is a foreign national cannot commit an extra-territorial offence of bribery, either as a principal offender or an accessory, even if he or she is domiciled or ordinarily resident in England and Wales;

(2) a company that is incorporated under the law of a Crown Dependency or Overseas Territory cannot commit an extra-territorial offence of bribery under English law;

(3) a natural person who assists or encourages a foreign national or a foreign company to commit an extra-territorial act of bribery cannot be convicted of either a substantive offence of bribery or of an inchoate offence of assisting or encouraging bribery, even if he or she is a British national and his or her act of assistance or encouragement occurs in England and Wales;

(4) a British company that assists or encourages a foreign national, who is not employed by that company, to commit an extra-territorial act of bribery cannot be convicted of either a substantive offence of bribery or of an inchoate offence of assisting or encouraging bribery, even if the act of assistance or encouragement occurs in England and Wales; and

(5) a British company that assists or encourages a foreign company, including a foreign subsidiary company, to commit an extra-territorial act of bribery cannot be convicted of either a substantive offence of bribery or of an inchoate offence of inciting or assisting bribery, even if the act of assistance or encouragement occurs in England and Wales.

PREVIOUS PROPOSALS FOR REFORM

The Law Commission's previous report on corruption

11.44 In its earlier report on corruption,[30] the Law Commission confined itself to recommending that the new offences of bribery that it was recommending should be Group A offences for the purposes of the Criminal Justice Act 1993.[31]

---

[30] Legislating the Criminal Code: Corruption (1998) Law Com No 248.

[31] Above, Part 9 para 15.

The Report of the Joint Committee on the Draft Corruption Bill

11.45   In its Report on the Draft Corruption Bill,[32] the Joint Committee referred to evidence that it had received in connection with acts of bribery committed outside England and Wales by foreign subsidiaries of companies incorporated in the United Kingdom. Without giving any reasons, the Joint Committee said that it was not persuaded that:

> UK companies should be made *explicitly* liable for the actions of non-resident subsidiaries and agents because the individuals – in many cases nationals of the countries concerned – will be subject to national law in that jurisdiction.[33]

The TI (UK) Corruption Bill[34]

11.46   Clause 13 of the Bill deals with corruption committed outside the United Kingdom. Like section 109 of the 2001 Act, the clause is restricted to acts or omissions outside the United Kingdom by nationals of the United Kingdom or by bodies incorporated under the law of any part of the United Kingdom. In addition, clause 11(1) would make it an offence for a British company to fail to take all reasonable steps to ensure that its foreign subsidiary companies do not commit acts outside the UK which would constitute an offence of bribery if done in the UK.[35]

PROPOSALS FOR REFORM

Natural persons

11.47   Under the current law, a natural person who perpetrates an extra-territorial act of bribery commits an offence known to English law only if he or she is a British national. Some other jurisdictions have adopted a more expansive approach, at least where the recipient is a foreign public official.

11.48   In New Zealand, section 105D of the Crimes Act 1961 provides that a natural person who perpetrates an extra-territorial act of bribery of a foreign public official commits an offence under New Zealand law if he or she is a New Zealand citizen or is ordinarily resident in New Zealand.

11.49   In Australia, section 70.5 of the Criminal Code Act 1995 provides that a natural person can by conduct occurring wholly outside Australia commit the offence of bribery of a foreign public official as defined in section 70.2 provided he or she at the time of committing the offence was a citizen or resident of Australia.

11.50   In English law there is a recent precedent for criminalising conduct occurring wholly outside England and Wales on the basis of residency in the UK. Section 7 of the Sex Offenders Act 1997 makes it an offence, providing certain conditions are satisfied, for any person who is a British citizen or resident in the UK to perpetrate a sexual act against a child outside the UK.

---

[32]   Session 2002-03, HL Paper 157, HC 705.

[33]   Above, para 78 (emphasis added).

[34]   (2007) HL 18.

[35]   See Part 9, paras 9.93 to 9.95.

11.51   London is of enormous global importance in the world of finance, business and trade. In recent years, this has resulted in a very considerable influx of foreign nationals who, partly because of London's strategic importance, now reside and conduct global business in and from London. In 1991, Lord Griffiths emphasised the need for the common law to respond to new realities. Compared to 1991, the number of foreign nationals residing in London and conducting global business has increased greatly.

11.52   Like Lord Griffiths, we believe that the law should reflect new realities. The law is in danger of becoming anachronistic if it continues to base criminal liability for extra-territorial offences of bribery on nationality alone. Further, if a foreign national who is resident in England and Wales commits an extra-territorial act of bribery, we do not believe that the country of which he is a national will necessarily have any desire to seek his or her extradition with a view to prosecution. For example, if P, a foreign national of country x but resident and conducting business in London, commits an act of bribery in country y, country x, if it believes that its own interests are not threatened, may have very little incentive to seek P's extradition.

11.53   If this is so, it means that British business people who reside and conduct their business in England and Wales are much more vulnerable to prosecution for extra-territorial acts of bribery than their foreign counterparts who are also living and conducting business in London. We do not believe that this is either fair or acceptable.

Provisional proposal

11.54   **We provisionally propose that an act, which if done in England and Wales, would constitute a bribery offence, should constitute a bribery offence if done outside the United Kingdom provided that it is done:**

(1)   **by a national of the United Kingdom;[36] or**

(2)   **by a natural person who is resident in the United Kingdom.**

Legal persons

11.55   We are not proposing that criminal liability for extra-territorial acts of bribery should extend to bodies that are incorporated under the law of a territory outside the United Kingdom, its Crown Dependencies or its Overseas Territories.

11.56   However, the OECD has on occasions referred to the fact that bodies that are incorporated in Crown Dependencies and Overseas Territories cannot commit extra-territorial offences known to English law.

---

[36]   We are not proposing that there should be any change to the current definition of "national of the United Kingdom".

11.57　**We invite consultees to comment on whether an act, which if done in England and Wales, would constitute a bribery offence, should constitute a bribery offence if done outside the United Kingdom by a body incorporated under the law of a Crown Dependency or an Overseas Territory.**

Accessories

The recommendations made in our 2007 report

11.58　In our report Participating in Crime, we made recommendations for determining the criminal liability of an accessory (X) where a principal offender (P) does an act outside England and Wales which, if done in England and Wales would constitute the commission of an offence. Accordingly, we are now making proposals in relation to bribery that are consistent with those recommendations (which would apply to all substantive offences).

Provisional proposals

11.59　**We provisionally propose that if the payer or recipient, with X's assistance or encouragement, commits an offence of bribery in England and Wales, X also commits an offence of bribery under English law irrespective of:**

　　　(1)　where the assistance or encouragement was rendered; and

　　　(2)　the payer's or the recipient's citizenship, nationality or place of residence.

This proposal does no more than re-state the common law.

11.60　**We provisionally propose that if the payer or the recipient, with X's assistance or encouragement, perpetrates an act of bribery outside England and Wales, X commits an offence of bribery under English law if:**

　　　(1)　X's assistance or encouragement takes place wholly or partly within England and Wales; and

　　　(2)　The payer's or the recipient's act of bribery:

　　　　　(a)　constitutes an offence of bribery under English law; or

　　　　　(b)　would have constituted an offence of bribery under English law had the payer or the recipient satisfied a condition relating to citizenship, nationality or residence.

11.61　Taken in conjunction with our provisional proposal at paragraph 11.54 above, it would mean that if X provides assistance in London to P, a Spanish national resident in London, which P then uses to bribe R in Milan, both X and P would be committing an offence of bribery under English law.

11.62　In addition, X would be committing an offence of bribery under English law even if P was not resident in London because in bribing R in Milan, P would have committed an offence under English law had he or she been a British national or resident in London.

11.63   A previous example illustrates how our proposal would operate in relation to legal persons:

> **Example 11E**
>
> X Ltd, a British company, is the parent company of P Ltd, a foreign subsidiary. P Ltd conducts business in Bolivia. The directors of P Ltd travel to London to request the directors of X Ltd to provide material that will enable the directors of P Ltd to return to Bolivia to bribe the directors of R Ltd, a Bolivian company. The directors of X Ltd provide the material knowing it will be used to bribe the directors to R Ltd. The directors of P Ltd return to Bolivia and bribe the directors of R Ltd.

Under the current law, P Ltd, being a foreign company, has committed no substantive offence known to English law. Accordingly, neither have the directors of X Ltd nor X Ltd itself. If our proposal were implemented, they would do so.

11.64   **We provisionally propose that if the payer or the recipient, with X's assistance or encouragement, does an act of bribery outside England and Wales, X commits an offence of bribery known to English law if:**

   (1)   X's assistance or encouragement takes place wholly outside England and Wales; and

   (2)   irrespective of whether the payer or the recipient committed an offence known to English law, X would have committed an offence known to English law had he or she done the act of bribery in the place where the payer or the recipient did it.

11.65   The following examples illustrate how this proposal, if implemented with our other proposals, would operate:

> **Example 11F**
>
> X is a British national working in Munich. He assists P, a Norwegian national resident in Paris, to bribe R.

> **Example 11G**
>
> X is a Spanish national resident in London. He flies to Stockholm and assists P, a Japanese national resident in Tokyo to bribe R.

> **Example 11H**
>
> X is the director of a British company, Y Ltd. He flies to Moscow and assists P, a director of a foreign subsidiary company, Z Ltd, to bribe a public official R.

In all three examples, under the current law X has not committed an offence known to English law because no principal offence under English law has been committed by P. If our proposals were implemented, in each example X would commit an offence under English law and, in the last example, so would Y Ltd.

11.66   We emphasise that the provisional proposals that we are making are not peculiar to offences of bribery. They follow on from the recommendations that we made in the 2007 report for reform of secondary liability.

Inchoate liability

The recommendations made in our 2006 report

11.67   In Part 10, we said that in our report Inchoate Liability for Assisting and Encouraging Crime,[37] we recommended that there should be two statutory inchoate offences:

(1)   doing an act capable of assisting or encouraging the commission of a principal offence *intending* that the offence should be committed. ('the clause 1 inchoate offence');

(2)   doing an act capable of assisting or encouraging the commission of a principal offence believing:

(a)   that the act will assist or encourage the commission of the principal offence; and

(b)   that the principal offence will be committed. ('the clause 2 inchoate offence")

The principal offence could be bribery. Both the clause 1 and the clause 2 offence could be committed even if the substantive offence of bribery was not subsequently committed.

11.68   We also made recommendations for determining X's liability in cases where:

(1)   X's act of assistance or encouragement occurred outside England and Wales but he or she anticipated that the principal offence would take place wholly or partly in England and Wales; and

(2)   X's act of assistance or encouragement occurred wholly or partly in England and Wales but he or she did not anticipate that the principal offence would be committed in England and Wales.

These recommendations have been carried forward by the Government in the 2007 Act. We are now making proposals in relation to bribery that are consistent with those recommendations.

Principal offence anticipated to take place wholly or partly in England and Wales

11.69   We believe that it should be an offence triable in England and Wales to commit an inchoate offence abroad intending that it should lead to the commission of a principal offence within the jurisdiction:

---

[37]   (2006) Law Com No 300.

> **Example 11J**
>
> In Munich and in return for payment, X, a German citizen, provides P, an Italian citizen, with material in the belief that P will use it to bribe R in London. In the event, R dies before P can bribe him.

In our view, it ought to be possible for an English court to convict X of the clause 2 offence.

Provisional proposals

11.70　**We provisionally propose that if X does an act capable of assisting or encouraging the payer or the recipient to commit an act of bribery knowing or believing that the act will or might be committed in England and Wales, he or she commits an inchoate offence of assisting or encouraging crime, irrespective of:**

　　　(1)　where the assistance or encouragement was rendered; and

　　　(2)　X's citizenship, nationality or place of residence.

11.71　**We provisionally propose that if the payer and the recipient conspire to commit an act of bribery in England and Wales, each commits an offence of conspiracy to commit bribery irrespective of:**

　　　(1)　where the conspiracy was formed; and

　　　(2)　the payer's or the recipient's citizenship, nationality or place of residence.

Principal offence not anticipated to take place wholly or partly in England and Wales

P'S ACT CONNECTED TO ENGLAND AND WALES

11.72　We noted above that section 1A of the Criminal Law Act 1977 provides that an agreement to pursue a course of conduct involving the doing of an act or the occurrence of an event in a country or territory outside England and Wales constitutes an offence known to English law to agree to pursue a course of conduct outside the United Kingdom if:

　　　(1)　the conduct would amount to an offence in that country or territory;

　　　(2)　the conduct, if committed in England and Wales, would amount to an offence under English law; or

　　　(3)　the party to be tried, or his or her agent:

　　　　　(a)　did anything in England and Wales in relation to the agreement before its formation; or

　　　　　(b)　became a party to the agreement in England and Wales; or

　　　　　(c)　did or omitted to do anything in England and Wales in pursuance of the agreement.

11.73 The section requires that the conduct that is the object of the conspiracy must be an offence under the law of England and Wales and also under the law of the foreign territory. The requirement of double criminality, together with the requirement that there has to be some act of X within or connected to England and Wales, certainly justifies making conspiracy to commit an offence outside England and Wales an offence under English law. However, we believe that the requirement of double criminality is too onerous to be justified.

Provisional proposals

11.74 **We provisionally propose that X can commit offences of assisting and encouraging in relation to a bribery offence if:**

(1) **X does an act wholly or partly within England and Wales capable of encouraging or assisting the payer or the recipient to commit an act of bribery;**

(2) **X knows or believes that the act of bribery will or might be perpetrated in a territory outside England and Wales; and**

(3) **if committed in that territory, the payer's or the recipient's act of bribery:**

(a) **would constitute an offence in that territory; or**

(b) **would constitute an offence under English law triable in England and Wales.**

11.75 **We provisionally propose that if the payer and the recipient conspire in England and Wales to commit an act of bribery in a place outside England and Wales, each commits an offence of conspiracy to commit bribery if the act of bribery:**

(a) **would constitute an offence in that territory; or**

(b) **would constitute an offence under English law triable in England and Wales.**

P'S ACT NOT CONNECTED TO ENGLAND AND WALES

11.76 Under the current law, X commits no offence known to English law if he or she outside England and Wales assists or encourages P to commit an act of bribery knowing or believing that the act, if done, will be done outside England and Wales. We believe that, subject to one exception, this position should remain the law. The exception is where X, were he or she to commit the act of bribery in the foreign territory, could be tried in England and Wales for an offence of bribery:

Example 11K

X, a British national working in Nigeria, encourages P, a Nigerian national, to bribe R, a Nigerian public official. In the event, P decides not to bribe R.

Under the proposal that we are making, X would commit a clause 1 or a clause 2 offence.

Provisional proposals

11.77   **We provisionally propose that X can commit offences of assisting and encouraging in relation to a bribery offence if:**

  (1)   X does an act wholly outside England and Wales capable of encouraging or assisting the payer or the recipient to commit an act of bribery;

  (2)   X knows or believes that the act of bribery, if committed, will or might be perpetrated in a territory outside England and Wales; and

  (3)   the act of bribery, if it were committed by X in that territory, would constitute an offence of bribery under English law triable in England and Wales.

11.78   **We provisionally propose that if the payer and the recipient conspire outside England and Wales to commit an act of bribery in a territory outside England and Wales, each commits an offence of conspiracy to commit bribery if the act of bribery if committed in that territory would constitute an offence under English law triable in England and Wales.**

11.79   Again, we emphasise that the provisional proposals that we are making are not peculiar to offences of bribery. They follow on from the recommendations that we made in the 2006 report for reform of inchoate liability for assisting and encouraging crime.

PART 12
LIST OF PROVISIONAL PROPOSALS AND QUESTIONS

REFORMING BRIBERY

12.1 We provisionally propose that in the domestic context the law of bribery should not draw a distinction between bribery in the public sector and bribery in the private sector.

[paragraph 1.17]

A MODEL FOR BRIBERY

12.2 We provisionally propose that the acceptance of an advantage in breach of a duty not to accept the advantage should not, without more, constitute a bribery offence.

[paragraph 4.63]

12.3 We provisionally propose that the making or acceptance of a payment to influence the recipient in the performance of his or her duties should not, without more, constitute a bribery offence.

[paragraph 4.114]

12.4 We provisionally propose that the conduct element of bribery should exist where an advantage is conferred, promised, received or solicited in connection with an improper act performed or promised by or solicited from the recipient.

[paragraph 4.143]

12.5 We invite comment on whether there should be a separate offence of accepting an advantage in breach of a duty not to accept it.

[paragraph 4.64]

THE CONDUCT ELEMENT OF THE GENERAL BRIBERY OFFENCE

12.6 We provisionally propose that the scope of improper conduct:

(1) should not be extended to cases of non-justiciable moral duties; and

(2) should not be restricted so as to exclude cases where breach of a legal duty is considered morally justifiable.

[paragraph 5.16]

12.7 We provisionally propose that, for the purposes of the definition of bribery offences, an improper act:

(1) must be a breach of a legal or equitable duty; and

(2)   must involve betrayal of a relation of trust, or breach of a duty to act impartially or in the best interests of another.

[paragraph 5.50]

12.8   We provisionally propose that:

    (1)   a person should be regarded as conferring an advantage if:

        (a)   he or she does something or omits to do something which he or she has the right to do, and

        (b)   the act or omission is done or made in consequence of another's request (express or implied) or with the result (direct or indirect) that another benefits; and

    (2)   a person should be regarded as obtaining an advantage if:

        (a)   another does something or omits to do something which he or she has the right to do, and

        (b)   the act or omission is done or made in consequence of the first person's request (express or implied) or with the result (direct or indirect) that the first person benefits.

[paragraph 5.60]

12.9   We provisionally propose that an advantage should not have to be 'undue' in order to come within the scope of the bribery offence that we are provisionally proposing.

[paragraph 5.64]

12.10   We provisionally propose that the recipient should be regarded as satisfying the conduct element of bribery if he or she:

    (1)   acts improperly (in breach of a legal or equitable duty that involves betrayal of a relation of trust or breach of a duty to act impartially or in the best interests of another); or

    (2)   represents a willingness to or agrees to act improperly.

[paragraph 5.71]

12.11   We provisionally propose that the recipient should be regarded as satisfying the conduct element of bribery if he or she:

    (1)   acts improperly (in breach of a legal or equitable duty that involves betrayal of a relation of trust or breach of a duty to act impartially or in the best interests of another);

    (2)   represents a willingness to or agrees to act improperly;

    (3)   uses his or her influence to induce a third party to act improperly; or

(4)   represents a willingness to or agrees to induce a third party to act improperly.

[paragraph 5.89]

12.12   We provisionally propose that, provided that the improper conduct requirement is satisfied, the recipient should be regarded as satisfying the conduct element of bribery even where the advantage has not been conferred and there has been no agreement regarding its conferral.

[paragraph 5.95]

12.13   We provisionally propose that it should be immaterial to the recipient's liability whether the advantage is conferred on the recipient or on a third party.

[paragraph 5.98]

12.14   We provisionally propose that, for the purposes of establishing the liability of either the payer or the recipient, the recipient's status (for example, being an agent) should be immaterial except in so far as it is relevant to whether the recipient is acting in breach of a legal or equitable duty.

[paragraph 5.101]

12.15   We provisionally propose that the payer should be regarded as satisfying the conduct element of bribery if he or she:

(1)   confers an advantage on the recipient; or

(2)   represents a willingness to confer an advantage on the recipient.

[paragraph 5.107]

12.16   We provisionally propose that the payer should be regarded as satisfying the conduct element of bribery even where the improper act has not been completed and there has been no agreement concerning its completion.

[paragraph 5.120]

12.17   As a way of narrowing the scope of 'improper conduct', is the limitation to cases involving a breach of a relation of trust, a breach of a duty of impartiality or a breach of a duty to act in the best interests of another the best that can be devised, or can it be simplified?

[paragraph 5.52]

THE FAULT ELEMENT OF THE NEW BRIBERY OFFENCE

The fault required of the recipient

12.18   We provisionally propose that for the recipient to be convicted of bribery as a principal offender, the advantage conferred must be the primary reason for the recipient doing the improper act.

[paragraph 6.19]

12.19   We provisionally propose that if the recipient knowingly accepts or states that he or she will accept an advantage from the payer:

   (1)   realising that if the payer confers the advantage the payer will do so with the intention to influence the recipient to act improperly; but

   (2)   the advantage is not the primary reason for the recipient doing the improper act

the recipient should be guilty of bribery not as a principal offender but as an accessory to the offence of bribery committed by the payer as a principal offender.

[paragraph 6.20]

12.20   We provisionally propose that it should be immaterial whether or not the recipient knew or believed that his or her act constituted a breach of a legal or equitable duty involving betrayal of a relation of trust or breach of a duty to act impartially or in the best interests of another.

[paragraph 6.30]

12.21   We provisionally propose that, provided the payer's conferral of the advantage is the primary reason for the recipient doing an improper act, it should be immaterial if the improper act done by the recipient differs from the improper act that was intended or agreed.

[paragraph 6.36]

12.22   We provisionally propose that in cases where the improper act of the recipient precedes the conferral of the advantage by the payer, it should be a necessary and sufficient condition of liability that the primary reason for the recipient doing the improper act was that the payer should confer an advantage on the recipient or another person.

[paragraph 6.46]

12.23   We provisionally propose that if the recipient does an improper act:

   (1)   intending that the payer should confer an advantage on the recipient or another person;

   (2)   knowing or believing that, if the payer confers the advantage, the payer will do so intending it as a reward for the improper act; but

   (3)   the primary reason for the recipient doing the improper act is not that the payer should confer an advantage on the recipient or another person

the recipient should be guilty of bribery not as principal offender but as an accessory to the offence of bribery that the payer commits as a principal offender.

[paragraph 6.47]

12.24   We provisionally propose that, in cases where the primary reason for the recipient representing a willingness to do an improper act is that the payer should confer an advantage on the recipient or another person, the recipient, if he or she is to be convicted of bribery as a principal offender, must intend to do the improper act if the payer agrees to confer the advantage.

[paragraph 6.58]

12.25   We ask consultees whether the fact that the recipient knows or believes that the payer has conferred the advantage without intending it to influence the recipient to do any improper act should preclude the recipient being convicted of bribery, even if the advantage was the primary reason for the recipient doing the improper act.

[paragraph 6.27]

The fault required of the payer

12.26   We provisionally propose that the payer should satisfy the fault element of bribery if, by conferring an advantage, he or she either:

(1)   intends that the advantage should be the primary reason for the recipient doing an improper act; or

(2)   foresees a serious risk that the advantage will create the primary reason for the recipient to act improperly.

[paragraph 6.83]

12.27   We provisionally propose that the payer should satisfy the fault element of bribery if he or she confers an advantage on the recipient:

(1)   knowing or believing that the primary reason for the recipient doing an improper act was to secure an advantage from the payer; and

(2)   intending to reward that improper act.

[paragraph 6.94]

12.28   We provisionally propose that the payer should satisfy the fault element of bribery if, by representing a willingness to confer an advantage, he or she either:

(1)   intends that the prospective advantage should be the primary reason for the recipient to do an improper act; or

(2)   foresees a serious risk that the representation will create the primary reason for the recipient to do an improper act.

[paragraph 6.101]

DISCRETE OFFENCE OF BRIBING A FOREIGN PUBLIC OFFICIAL

12.29   We provisionally propose that there should be a discrete offence of bribery of foreign public officials.

[paragraph 7.6]

12.30   We provisionally propose that it should be an offence if:

(1)   in order to

(a)   obtain business;

(b)   retain business; or

(c)   obtain or retain a business advantage,

(2)   the payer gives, offers or agrees to give an advantage to or for any person, being an advantage to which the recipient or intended recipient is not legitimately due, and

(3)   P does so:

(a)   intending to influence that person or another person in respect of any act or omission by that person or another person in his or her capacity as a foreign public official; or

(b)   realising that there is a serious risk that the advantage will influence that person or another person in respect of any act or omission by that person or another person in his or her capacity as a foreign public official;

(c)   intending to influence a third party to use their influence over another person in respect of any act or omission by that person or another person in his or her capacity as a foreign public official.

[paragraph 7.36]

12.31   We provisionally propose that for the purposes of determining whether an advantage is "legitimately due" no account should be taken of:

(1)   the fact that the advantage may be customary, or perceived to be customary, in the circumstances;

(2)   any official tolerance of the advantage.

[paragraph 7.37]

12.32   We ask consultees to consider whether our provisionally proposed offence of bribing a foreign public official should be extended to inculpate the foreign public official who accepts a bribe.

[paragraph 7.41]

DEFENCES, BARRIERS TO PROSECUTION AND ANCILLARY MATTERS

Defences

12.33 We provisionally propose that the payer should have a defence to a charge of bribery (or to an inchoate offence relating to a principal offence of bribery) if, in the circumstances that the payer reasonably believed to exist, it was reasonable to confer an advantage in order to avert what the payer reasonably believed to be an imminent danger of physical harm to him or herself or another.

[paragraph 8.14]

12.34 We provisionally propose that the payer should have a defence to a charge of bribery (or to an inchoate offence relating to a principal offence of bribery) if he or she conferred an advantage in the reasonable belief that it was legally required. The evidential burden in relation to holding the reasonable belief should be on the payer.

[paragraph 8.31]

12.35 We ask whether the defence should extend to cases where the payer conferred an advantage in the reasonable belief that to do so was legally permissible.

[paragraph 8.32]

Consent to prosecution

12.36 We provisionally propose that the consent of the Director of Public Prosecutions (or the Director of the Serious Fraud Office) should be required for any prosecution for the general offence of bribery or for any inchoate offence relating to a principal offence of bribery, unless the offence involves an extra-territorial element.

[paragraph 8.81]

12.37 We provisionally propose that there should be a requirement of consent by the Attorney General to any prosecution for an offence of bribery, or for any inchoate offence relating to the principal offence, if the offence involves an extra-territorial element.

[paragraph 8.82]

12.38 We ask consultees to consider whether a requirement of consent to prosecutions for bribery should be dispensed with altogether.

[paragraph 8.84]

Ancillary matters

12.39 We provisionally propose that both bribery offences should be triable either way.

[paragraph 8.85]

12.40   We provisionally propose that the Prevention of Corruption Acts 1889 to 1916 should be repealed.

[paragraph 8.88]

12.41   We provisionally propose that the common law offence of bribery should be abolished.

[paragraph 8.89]

CORPORATE LIABILITY

12.42   We provisionally propose that consideration of the law relating to the direct liability of legal persons for offences of bribery should be deferred until the Law Commission's wider review of this area.

[paragraph 9.20]

12.43   We provisionally propose that a new offence of inadequate supervision of foreign subsidiary companies should not be created. It is an issue that should be deferred until our wider review of corporate liability.

[paragraph 9.103]

12.44   We provisionally propose to defer the issue of corporate sanctions to our wider review of corporate liability.

[paragraph 9.105]

12.45   Should the individual liability of a high-ranking employee be specifically provided for, on a 'consent or connivance' basis, or left to be governed by the offences of assisting or encouraging crime (provided for) in the Serious Crime Act 2007 and the doctrine of complicity?

[paragraph 9.37]

12.46   Should a new criminal offence be created to penalise legal persons where their negligent supervision allows bribery to take place, assuming that it is a defence to such an offence to show that, notwithstanding the commission of a bribery offence, an adequate system was in place to prevent offending?

[paragraph 9.66]

12.47   Should negligent supervision by a legal person that allows bribery to take place be the subject of special civil or administrative remedies or sanctions?

[paragraph 9.67]

12.48   Should the whole issue of negligent supervision by a legal person be left to a more general review of the liability of legal persons and, in particular, their liability for failing to supervise their employees adequately?

[paragraph 9.68]

12.49   If a legal person commits an offence of negligent supervision, and the offence is proved to have been committed with the consent or connivance of:

   (1)   a director, manager, company secretary or other similar officer of the body corporate; or

   (2)   a person who was purporting to act in any such capacity,

   should individual criminal liability also be imposed on that person?

[paragraph 9.86]

12.50   If a legal person commits an offence of negligent supervision, and the offence is proved to have been committed with the consent or connivance of:

   (1)   a director, manager, company secretary or other similar officer of the body corporate; or

   (2)   a person who was purporting to act in any such capacity,

   should individual criminal liability also be imposed on that person, *but only* if the bribery offence committed by an employee of the legal person acting on behalf of the business related to a foreign public official?

[paragraph 9.87]

12.51   Whether or not an offence is created making it possible to convict a legal person of a negligent supervision offence, should the extension of individual liability for inadequate supervision to high-ranking members of a legal person be a matter left for a broader review of corporate criminal liability?

[paragraph 9.88]

BRIBERY COMMITTED OUTSIDE ENGLAND AND WALES

Principal offenders

12.52   We provisionally propose that an act, which if done in England and Wales, would constitute a bribery offence, should constitute a bribery offence if done outside the United Kingdom provided that it is done:

   (1)   by a national of the United Kingdom; or

   (2)   by a natural person who is resident in the United Kingdom.

[paragraph 11.54]

12.53   We invite consultees to comment on whether an act, which if done in England and Wales, would constitute a bribery offence, should constitute a bribery offence if done outside the United Kingdom by a body incorporated under the law of a Crown Dependency or an Overseas Territory.

[paragraph 11.57]

Accessories

12.54   We provisionally propose that if the payer or the recipient, with X's assistance or encouragement, commits an offence of bribery in England and Wales, X also commits an offence of bribery under English law irrespective of:

(1)   where the assistance or encouragement was rendered; and

(2)   the payer's or the recipient's citizenship, nationality or place of residence.

[paragraph 11.59]

12.55   We provisionally propose that if the payer or the recipient, with X's assistance or encouragement, perpetrates an act of bribery outside England and Wales, X commits an offence of bribery under English law if:

(1)   X's assistance or encouragement takes place wholly or partly within England and Wales; and

(2)   The payer's or the recipient's act of bribery:

(a)   constitutes an offence of bribery under English law; or

(b)   would have constituted an offence of bribery under English law had the payer or the recipient satisfied a condition relating to citizenship, nationality or residence.

[paragraph 11.60]

12.56   We provisionally propose that if the payer or the recipient, with X's assistance or encouragement, does an act of bribery outside England and Wales, X commits an offence of bribery known to English law if:

(1)   X's assistance or encouragement takes place wholly outside England and Wales; and

(2)   irrespective of whether the payer or the recipient has committed an offence known to English law, X would have committed an offence known to English law had he or she done the act of bribery in the place where the payer or the recipient did it.

[paragraph 11.64]

Inchoate liability

12.57   We provisionally propose that if X does an act capable of assisting or encouraging the payer or the recipient to commit an act of bribery knowing or believing that the act will or might be committed in England and Wales, he or she commits an inchoate offence of assisting or encouraging crime, irrespective of:

(1)   where the assistance or encouragement was rendered; and

(2)   X's citizenship, nationality or place of residence.

[paragraph 11.70]

12.58 We provisionally propose that if the payer and the recipient conspire to commit an act of bribery in England and Wales, each commits an offence of conspiracy to commit bribery irrespective of:

(1) where the conspiracy was formed; and

(2) the payer's or the recipient's citizenship, nationality or place of residence.

[paragraph 11.71]

12.59 We provisionally propose that X can commit offences of assisting and encouraging in relation to a bribery offence if:

(1) X does an act wholly or partly within England and Wales capable of encouraging or assisting the payer or the recipient to commit an act of bribery;

(2) X knows or believes that the act of bribery will or might be perpetrated in a territory outside England and Wales; and

(3) if committed in that territory, the payer or the recipient's act of bribery:

(a) would constitute an offence in that territory; or

(b) would constitute an offence under English law triable in England and Wales.

[paragraph 11.74]

12.60 We provisionally propose that if the payer and the recipient conspire in England and Wales to commit an act of bribery in a place outside England and Wales, each commits an offence of conspiracy to commit bribery if the act of bribery:

(a) would constitute an offence in that territory; or

(b) would constitute an offence under English law triable in England and Wales.

[paragraph 11.75]

12.61 We provisionally propose that X can commit offences of assisting and encouraging in relation to a bribery offence if:

(1) X does an act wholly outside England and Wales capable of encouraging or assisting the payer or the recipient to commit an act of bribery;

(2) X knows or believes that the act of bribery, if committed, will or might be perpetrated in a territory outside England and Wales; and

(3) the act of bribery, were it committed by X in that territory, would constitute bribery under English law triable in England and Wales.

[paragraph 11.77]

12.62 We provisionally propose that if the payer and the recipient conspire outside England and Wales to commit an act of bribery in a territory outside England and Wales, each commits an offence of conspiracy to commit bribery if the act of bribery if committed in that territory would constitute an offence under English law triable in England and Wales.

[paragraph 11.78]

APPENDIX A
INTERNATIONAL AND EUROPEAN
DOCUMENTS ON CORRUPTION AND BRIBERY

INTRODUCTION

A.1 In this Appendix we are going to provide an overview of the most important international conventions and other materials that relate to bribery. In each case we will identify those provisions that are binding on the UK.

COUNCIL OF EUROPE

Summary of relevant documents

(1) Twenty Guiding Principles (Resolution (97) 24): broadly stated principles including pledge to ensure co-ordinated criminalisation of national and international corruption.

(2) Group of states against Corruption (GRECO) established by Resolution (99)5: monitors observance of the Guiding Principles; monitors implementation of international instruments.

(3) Recommendation (2000) 10 on codes of conduct for public officials.

(4) Recommendation (2003) 4 on common rules against corruption in the funding of political parties and electoral campaigns

(5) Criminal Law Convention on Corruption: active and passive bribery involving defined category of persons; extends to both public and private sector; trading in influence; money laundering and account offences; corporate liability; mandatory obligations; note UK reservation.

(6) Additional Protocol to the Criminal Law Convention on Corruption: extends Convention's application to active and passive bribery involving domestic and foreign arbitrators and jurors.

(7) Civil Law Convention on Corruption; provides for effective remedies for persons who have suffered damage as a result of acts of corruption.

Documents (5) and (6) are of particular relevance and involve binding obligations on the UK. They will therefore provide our focus.

Overview

A.2   In 1994 it was decided that corruption posed a serious threat to fundamental values and so a Multidisciplinary Group on Corruption (GMC) was established in 1995, a programme of action introduced in 1996 and in 1997 the Committee of Ministers adopted the 20 Guiding Principles for the Fight Against Corruption.[1] These broadly stated aspirations included a reference to the "co-ordinated criminalisation of national and international corruption".[2] A Criminal Law Convention on Corruption was therefore opened for signature on 27 January 1999 and entered into force on 1 July 2002.[3] The Group of states Against Corruption (GRECO), which was established in 1999,[4] monitors its implementation. This was followed by an additional Protocol, which entered into force on 1 February 2005. The Civil Law Convention on Corruption entered into force on 1 November 2003.

Criminal Law Convention on Corruption[5]

Background

A.3   The Convention has two principal aims: first to harmonise the definition and criminalisation of corruption offences; and secondly to facilitate effective means of international co-operation in the investigation and prosecution of these offences.[6] As detailed below it applies to public and private sectors.

UK status

A.4   The United Kingdom signed the Convention on 27 January 1999 and ratified it on 9 December 2003. On ratification, the UK made a reservation to the Convention.[7] The Convention came into force in the UK on 1 April 2004.

Convention requirements

ACTIVE AND PASSIVE BRIBERY

A.5   The Convention distinguishes between "active bribery" (promising, offering or giving the undue advantage) and "passive bribery" (requesting, receiving or accepting the promise, offer or gift of an undue advantage).[8]

---

[1]   The Guiding Principles can be located at:
       http://www.coe.int/t/dg1/greco/documents/Resolution(97)24_EN.pdf.

[2]   Principle 2.

[3]   It is open to adoption by non-European countries.

[4]   Resolution (99)5. UK aceded in 18 September 1999. See:
       http://www.coe.int/t/dg1/greco/general/members_en.asp.

[5]   This can be located at:
       http://conventions.coe.int/Treaty/Commun/QueVoulezVous.asp?NT=173&CM
       =8&CL=ENG.

       The Explanatory Notes can be located at:
       http://www.conventions.coe.int/Treaty/EN/Reports/Html/173.htm.

[6]   Explanatory Notes to Convention, para 21. Explanatory Notes to Additional Protocol to the Convention, para 1.

[7]   For further detail, see below.

A.6   Active bribery is defined as:

> intentionally[9] promising, offering or giving, directly or indirectly, any undue[10] advantage to a *defined category of persons*, for himself or herself or for a third party, for him or her to act or refrain from acting in the exercise of his or her functions.[11]

A.7   Passive bribery is defined as:

> the intentional request or receipt by a *defined category of persons*, directly or indirectly, of any undue advantage, for himself or herself or for a third party, or the acceptance of an offer or a promise of such an advantage, to act or refrain from acting in the exercise of his or her functions.

SCOPE

A.8   The Convention requires that the state parties criminalise[12] both active and passive bribery of the following categories of individuals:

(1)   domestic public officials;[13]

(2)   foreign public officials;[14]

(3)   members of any domestic public assembly exercising legislative or administrative powers;[15]

---

8   "… the two types of bribery are, in general, two sides of the same phenomenon …" – Explanatory Notes to Convention, para 32.

9   "Intent must relate to a future result … . It is … immaterial whether the public official actually acted or refrained from acting as intended" – Explanatory Notes to Convention, para 34.

10   This refers to something that the recipient is not lawfully entitled to accept or receive. It excludes, for example, minimum gifts or socially acceptable gifts: Explanatory Notes to Convention, para 38.

11   "What is important is that the offender (or any other person) is placed in a better position…and that he is not entitled to the benefit": Explanatory Notes to Convention, para 37. It was not considered necessary to refer to a breach of duty, the decisive element not being whether the person actually had any discretion to act as requested but whether the bribe was offered, given or promised in order to obtain something: Explanatory Notes to Convention, para 39.

12   "Adopt such legislative and other measures as may be necessary to establish as criminal offences under its domestic law … ."

13   Articles 1 and 2. Public official is defined at article 1(a). It states that it is to be understood by reference to the definition of "official", "public officer", "mayor", "minister" or "judge" in the national law of the state in which the person in question performs that function and as applied in its criminal law. The aim is to "ensure that public administrations function … in a transparent, fair and impartial manner and in pursuance of public interests, and to protect the confidence of citizens" – Explanatory Notes to Convention, para 32.

14   Article 5. The legal interest here is described as two-fold: first to ensure transparency and fairness of decision-making and secondly the protection of fair competition for businesses: Explanatory Notes to Convention, para 48. The requirements here go beyond both the EU Convention and the OECD Convention: Explanatory Notes to Convention, para 49.

(4)   members of any foreign public assembly exercising legislative or administrative powers;[16]

(5)   any persons who direct or work for, in any capacity, private sector entities. Active and passive bribery in the private sector must be committed intentionally "in the course of business". Instead of referring to a breach of 'function', the term 'duty' is used. This is referred to as 'private sector bribery';[17]

(6)   officials of international organisations;[18]

(7)   members of international parliamentary assemblies;[19]

(8)   judges and officials of international courts.[20]

There are some notable differences between the provisions on public and private sector bribery. For example, there is an additional requirement of a breach of duty for private sector corruption.[21]

---

[15] Article 4.

[16] Article 6.

[17] Articles 7 and 8. Extension of the scope of the offence to the private sector is justified for many reasons: to maintain trust, confidence and loyalty for a good social and economic relations, to ensure respect for fair competition and also to ensure that with the transfer of public functions to the private sector, such functions are exercised in the public interest: Explanatory Notes to Convention, para 52. Three differences are cited between public and private bribery: first, 'private bribery' is restricted to the business sector (NGOs for example are excluded), secondly, the scope of the recipient persons for 'private bribery' is different, thirdly, a breach of duty is required for 'private bribery'.

[18] Article 9. The article defines such an individual as "any official or other contracted employee, within the meaning of the staff regulations, of any public international or supranational organisation or body of which the party is a member, and any person, whether seconded or not, carrying out functions corresponding to those performed by such officials or agents."

[19] Article 10.

[20] Article 11. This applies to any holders of judicial office or officials of any international court whose jurisdiction is accepted by the party.

[21] See Explanatory Notes to Convention, para 55 and n 17 above.

TRADING IN INFLUENCE

A.9 The Convention also requires those states party to the Convention to criminalise[22] both active and passive 'trading in influence'.[23] This refers to the person ("influence peddler") who has a real or supposed influence on the persons specified above (excluding those working in the private sector),[24] and who trades this influence in exchange for an undue advantage from someone seeking this influence. This targets "background corruption" and "corrupt trilateral relationships".[25] Unlike bribery, the defendant is not required to "act or refrain from acting".

MONEY LAUNDERING OF PROCEEDS AND ACCOUNT OFFENCES

A.10 The Convention also requires those states party to the Convention to criminalise[26] the laundering of proceeds derived from the offences outlined above.[27]

A.11 Further, criminal or administrative law sanctions must be adopted to criminalise those who intentionally commit, conceal or disguise the offences outlined above by creating or using an accounting document containing false or incomplete information or unlawfully omit to make a record of payment.[28]

PARTICIPATION

A.12 The Convention also requires that aiding or abetting the criminal offences outlined above must be a criminal offence under the state's domestic law.[29]

CORPORATE LIABILITY

A.13 Under the Convention the state must also criminalise corporate liability to ensure legal persons can be held liable for the criminal offences of active bribery, trading in influence and money laundering.[30]

---

[22] "Adopt such legislative and other measures as may be necessary to establish as criminal offences under its domestic law ... ."

[23] Article 12. Explanatory Notes to Convention, para 66 note that "what is important to note is the outsider position of the influence peddler: he cannot take decisions himself, but misuses his real or alleged influence on other persons."

[24] Article 12 extends to those who assert or confirm that they are able to exert an improper influence over the decision-making of any person referred to in articles 2, 4 to 6 and 9 to 11.

[25] Explanatory Notes to Convention, paras 64 and 65.

[26] "Adopt such legislative and other measures as may be necessary to establish as criminal offences under its domestic law ... ."

[27] Article 13. It was felt that there were such close links between corruption and money laundering that the latter should be criminalised by the Convention: Explanatory Notes to Convention, para 69.

[28] Article 14.

[29] Article 15.

[30] Article 18.

MEMBER STATES' OBLIGATIONS

A.14   Regarding each offence, the Convention obliges each party to the Convention to "adopt such legislative and other measures as may be necessary to establish as criminal offences under its domestic law".

A.15   Jurisdiction must be established over the criminal offences outlined above where:

(1)   the offence is committed wholly or partly in the state's territory (territoriality principle);

(2)   the offender is one of its nationals, its public officials or a member of one of its domestic public assemblies (nationality principle); or

(3)   the offence involves one of its public officials or a member of one of its domestic public assemblies, an international organisation, international parliamentary assembly or international court who is also one of its nationals (protective and nationality principle).

A.16   Effective, proportionate and dissuasive sanctions and measures must be provided. Further, measures must be adopted to enable confiscation or otherwise deprivation of the instrumentalites and proceeds of the criminal offences outlined above.[31]

A.17   State parties must ensure that there are specialised and independent persons or entities to deal with the "fight against corruption".[32] There are also provisions to allow for effective international co-operation.[33]

UK reservation to the Convention

A.18   Pursuant to article 37 of the Convention, the UK entered a reservation to article 7 (active bribery in the private sector), article 12 (trading in influence) and article 17 (jurisdiction).

ARTICLE 7: ACTIVE BRIBERY IN THE PRIVATE SECTOR

A.19   The UK acknowledged that its present law did not cover the case where the undue advantage was not given directly to the agent but to a third party. It stated that "the United Kingdom accepts this aspect of the law is in need of amendment." However, it reserved the right "not to establish as a criminal offence all of the conduct referred to in article 7."

ARTICLE 12: TRADING IN INFLUENCE

A.20   Acknowledging that not all the conduct referred to in article 12 is criminal under United Kingdom law the UK reserved the right "not to establish as a criminal offence all of the conduct referred to in Article 12".

---

[31] Article 19. Regarding corporate liability criminal or non-criminal sanctions may be provided.

[32] Article 20.

[33] Chapter III.

ARTICLE 17: JURISDICTION

A.21   The UK reserved the right only to apply the jurisdictional rule regarding public officials or members of its domestic public assemblies if the individual was a UK national. It also reserved the right not to apply the jurisdictional rule relating to the involvement of one of its public officials or a member of one of its domestic public assemblies who is also one of its nationals at all.

Additional Protocol to the Criminal Law Convention[34]

Background

A.22   Following debates concerning the extension of the Convention to cover other forms of corrupt behaviour, it was agreed that an additional Protocol should be adopted to cover corruption committed by or against arbitrators and jurors.[35]

UK status

A.23   The UK signed the additional protocol on 15 May 2003, ratified it on 9 December 2003 and it came into force on 1 February 2005.

Additional Protocol's requirements

A.24   State parties are obliged to adopt measures to establish as criminal offences under its domestic law the following:

(1)   active and passive bribery of domestic arbitrators;[36]

(2)   active and passive bribery of foreign arbitrators;[37]

(3)   active and passive bribery of domestic jurors;[38]

(4)   active and passive bribery of foreign jurors.[39]

There is no requirement that the arbitrator or juror act in breach of a duty.

---

[34]   Located at: http://conventions.coe.int/treaty/en/Treaties/Html/191.htm.

[35]   Note the other behaviour raised during the discussions: illegal acquisitions of interest; insider trading; extortion by a public official; illicit enrichment; corruption of members of NGO's; corruption of sport referees; buying and selling of votes. It is stated in the Explanatory Notes that such conduct could be "assimilated to corruption".

[36]   Articles 2 and 3.

[37]   Article 4. This applies to an "arbitrator exercising his or her functions under the national law on arbitration of any other state."

[38]   Article 5.

[39]   Article 6.

Civil Law Convention on Corruption[40]

Summary

A.25   Brief reference is made to this Convention because it forms part of the Council of Europe's Programme of Action against Corruption. However, clearly as a civil law convention, it is of limited relevance to the current project.

A.26   The Convention requires contracting parties to provide "effective remedies for persons who have suffered damage as a result of acts of corruption, to enable them to defend their rights and interests, including the possibility of obtaining compensation for damage".[41] The United Kingdom signed the Convention on 6 June 2000, but has not yet ratified or brought the treaty into force. It came into force generally on 1 November 2003.

EUROPEAN UNION

Summary of relevant documents

(1)   First Protocol of the 1995 Convention on the protection of the European Communities' financial interests: active and passive corruption involving national and community officials only; necessarily confined to acts or omissions contrary to the financial interests of the European Communities.

(2)   Second Protocol of the 1995 Convention on the protection of the European Communities' financial interests: liability of legal persons for fraud, active corruption and money laundering.

(3)   Convention of 1997 on the fight against corruption involving officials of the European Communities or officials of member states of the European Union: active and passive corruption involving national and community officials without need for financial interests of European Communities to be (likely to be) damaged; criminal liability of heads of businesses.

(4)   Council Framework Decision of 2003 on combating corruption in the private sector:[42] active and passive corruption in the private sector; liability of legal persons for active and passive corruption in the private sector.

---

[40]   Located at :
http://conventions.coe.int/Treaty/Commun/QueVoulezVous.asp?NT=174&CL=ENG.

[41]   Article 1. The Convention can be located at:
http://conventions.coe.int/Treaty/en/Treaties/Html/174.htm.

[42]   2003/568/JHA. This repealed an earlier framework decision of 1998 (98/742/JHA). See article 8 of 2003 Decision.

Overview

A.27 Corruption is defined on the European Parliament website as "an abuse of power with a view to personal gain".[43] Article 29 of the EU Treaty specifically refers to combating corruption and fraud as part of its mission to provide an area of freedom, security and justice. It was recognised in the 1990's that "the principal weakness in the fight against corruption with transnational features has been the fact that the criminal law in the member states has often failed to address the issue of the corruption of foreign officials and officials employed by international organisations".[44] Further, the Council of the EU later observed that "member states attach particular importance to combating corruption in both the public and private sector, in the belief that in both those sectors it poses a threat to a law-abiding society as well as distorting competition in relation to the purchase of goods or commercial services and impeding sound economic development".[45] In 2003 the European Commission adopted a Communication on a Comprehensive EU Policy Against Corruption.[46] The four principal relevant texts are listed above and explored in more detail below.

First Protocol to the Convention on the protection of the European Communities' financial interests[47]

Background

A.28 The 1995 Convention on the protection of the European Communities' financial interests entered into force on 17 October 2002. In September 1996 the First Protocol to this Convention was signed and it also entered into force on 17 October 2002. This Protocol was also in response to point 7h of the Council's resolution of 6 December 1994, which stated that effective measures must be taken to "punish bribery involving officials of the European Communities in relation to the financial interests of the Communities".

A.29 The Protocol is premised on the fact that member states all legislate to combat fraud and corruption of national officials and that "while the specific characteristics...vary...all have common elements which make it possible to arrive at a common definition."[48]

---

[43] www.europarl.europa.eu/comparl/libe/elsj/zoom_in/28_en.htm.

[44] Explanatory Report on the Convention on the fight against corruption involving officials of the European Communities or officials of member states of the European Union.

[45] Preamble to Council Framework Decision of 22 July 2003 on combating corruption in the private sector (2003/568/JHA).

[46] http://europa.eu.int/eur-lex/en/com/cnc/2003/com2003_0317en01.pdf.

[47] Located at: http://eur-lex.europa.eu/smartapi/cgi/sga_doc?smartapi!celexapi!prod!CELEXnumdoc&lg=EN&numdoc=41996A1023(01)&model=guichett.

[48] Explanatory Report to the Protocol, para 1. See: http://eur-lex.europa.eu/LexUriServ/LexUriServ.do?uri=CELEX:51998XG0115:EN:HTML.

UK status

A.30 The United Kingdom's date of notification for both the Convention and First Protocol was 11 October 1999 and both texts are currently binding on the UK.[49] There was no change made to existing legislation by the UK.[50] However, criticism has been made regarding the absence of an explicit reference to whether community officials are within the scope of the relevant domestic bribery offences.[51]

Protocol's requirements

ACTIVE AND PASSIVE CORRUPTION

A.31 The Protocol makes a distinction between "active corruption" (promising or giving any advantage to an official) and "passive corruption" (an official requesting, receiving or accepting any advantage).[52] Intention is a necessary component of both.[53]

A.32 Active corruption is defined as:

> "the deliberate action of whosoever[54] promises or gives, directly or indirectly through an intermediary,[55] an advantage of any kind whatsoever to an official or for himself or for a third party for him to act or refrain from acting[56] in accordance with his duty or in the exercise of his functions in breach of his official duties in a way which damages or is likely to damage the European Communities' financial interests.[57]

A.33 Passive corruption is defined as:

---

[49] See: http://ec.europa.eu/dgs/olaf/mission/legal/annex709final_en.pdf.

[50] See: http://ec.europa.eu/dgs/olaf/mission/legal/annex709final_en.pdf at p 37. At p 38 this report notes that section 108(3) of the Anti-terrorism, Crime and Security Act 2001 and the common law are considered to cover the relevant ground although criticism is made regarding the absence of an explicit reference to whether community officials are within the scope of the relevant bribery offences. At p 40 the report states that "there remains a considerable risk that the courts will deny that the offence of passive corruption can be committed by Community Officials."

[51] See n 50 above. See: http://ec.europa.eu/dgs/olaf/mission/legal/annex709final_en.pdf at pp 37 to 40.

[52] Described by the Explanatory Reports as "corollary" to one another, albeit "distinct and autonomous" at para 3.

[53] Article 2 and 3 refer to "deliberate action." The Explanatory Report to the Protocol state that "intent is a necessary component" (para 2.1).

[54] This person may be a private individual or person exercising a public function: Explanatory Report to the Protocol, para 3.1.

[55] The fault element of the intermediary is irrelevant. The Explanatory Report to the Protocol state that one identifies the criminal nature of the official's conduct "irrespective of the good or bad faith of the intermediary involved" (para 2.2).

[56] There must first be the request or acceptance and then the act or refraining from acting. "A benefit received after the act but without a prior request or acceptance therefore does not generate criminal liability under the Protocol" : Explanatory Report to the Protocol (para 2.5).

[57] Article 3.

the deliberate action of an official, who, directly or indirectly through an intermediary, requests or receives advantages of any kind whatsoever, for himself or for a third party, or accepts a promise of such an advantage, to act or refrain from acting in accordance with his duty or in the exercise of his functions in breach of his official duties in a way which damages or is likely to damage the European Communities' financial interests.[58]

SCOPE

A.34   The provisions are confined in scope to 'officials'. This term refers to both national officials (including officials of another member state)[59] and community officials.[60] The Explanatory Notes state that "the official's duties or functions are the target of the practices to which the Protocol applies".[61]

ADVANTAGE

A.35   The Explanatory Report accompanying the Protocol observes the breadth of the term "advantages of any kind whatsoever". This is said to embrace not only material objects such as money, goods and services but also indirect interests such as settlement of the corrupted person's debts and work on property belonging to that person.[62]

ASSIMILATION

A.36   Article 4 provides for "assimilation". This "commits the member states to similarly apply the definitions of corruption to both national and European officials".[63]

MEMBER STATES' OBLIGATIONS

A.37   The states party to the Convention are obliged to take necessary measures to ensure that such conduct is made a criminal offence.[64] This obligation is expanded upon in the Explanatory Report:

---

[58]   Article 2.

[59]   As defined in article 1. It "shall be understood in reference to the definition of 'official' or 'public officer' in the national law of the member state in which the person in question performs that function for the purposes of application of the criminal law of that member state … ."

[60]   As defined in article 1. It refers to officials or other contracted employees of the EC, any person seconded to the EC or any public or private body who carries out functions equivalent to those performed by EC officials/servants.

[61]   Paragraph 2.6.

[62]   Paragraph 2.4.

[63]   A Posadas, "Combating Corruption Under International Law", (2000) 10 *Duke Journal of Comparative and International Law*, 345, 398.

[64]   Articles 2(2) and 3(2). Article 4 addresses the issue of assimilation: the measures must apply similarly in cases involving national and community officials but if there is any special legislation concerning acts of omissions for which Government Ministers are responsible by reason of their special political position such a rule does not apply provided that the members of the Commission of the EC are covered by the criminal legislation implementing articles 2 and 3 of the Protocol.

It is therefore up to the member states to see whether their current criminal law does indeed cover all the relevant categories of persons and forms of conduct and, if not, to enact measures establishing one or more offences corresponding to them. They may do so either by establishing one offence of a general nature or by establishing several specific offences.

A.38   The offences must be punishable by "effective, proportionate and dissuasive criminal penalties"[65] Jurisdiction must be established when the offences occur wholly or partly in the member state's territory (territoriality principle), the offender is one of its nationals or officials (active personality principle), the offence is committed against a national or community official (passive personality principle) or the offender is a community official working for an EC community.[66]

Second Protocol to the 1995 Convention on the protection of the European Communities' financial interests [67]

Second Protocol's requirements

A.39   This provides at article 3 for the liability of legal persons for fraud, active corruption and money laundering:

> when committed for their benefit by any person, acting either individually or as part of an organ of the legal person, who has a leading position within the legal person, based on a power of representation of the legal person, or an authority to take decisions on behalf of the legal person, or an authority to exercise control within the legal person.

A.40   It further requires liability be imposed for involvement as "accessories or instigators in such fraud, active corruption or money laundering or the attempted commission of such fraud".[68]

A.41   Measures must also be taken where it is the "lack of supervision or control"[69] that has made possible the commission of a fraud or an act of active corruption or money laundering for the benefit of that legal person by a person under its authority.

A.42   Sanctions can be criminal and non-criminal.[70]

---

[65]   Article 5. This may include penalties involving deprivation of liberty which can give rise to extradition.

[66]   For precise detail on what is required, see Article 6.

[67]   Located at: http://eur-lex.europa.eu/smartapi/cgi/sga_doc?smartapi!celexapi!prod!CELEXnumdoc&lg=EN&numdoc=41997A0719(02)&model=guichett.

[68]   Article 3(1).

[69]   Article 3(2).

[70]   Article 4.

Convention on the fight against corruption involving officials of the European Communities or officials of member states of the European Union[71]

Background

A.43 The Protocols examined above were necessarily limited in scope by the requirement that there must be acts or omissions that damaged (or were likely to damage) the EC's financial interests. Substantially modelled on the provisions and definitions of this earlier protocol,[72] this Convention also aims to criminalise corruption involving officials of the EC or of member states, but without this restrictive requirement. It was signed on 26 May 1997 and entered into force on 28 September 2005.

UK status

A.44 The UK signed this Convention on 25 June 1997 and ratified it on 11 October 1999.

Convention requirements

ACTIVE AND PASSIVE BRIBERY

A.45 As with the Protocol, this Convention applies to national officials (including officials of another member state) and community officials. It provides for the offences of active and passive corruption using the same wording as the Protocol (see above), omitting only the final clause "in a way which damages or is likely to damage the European Communities' financial interests".

ASSIMILATION

A.46 Further, the principle of assimilation is also applied requiring member states to apply to Community Officials the "same descriptions of corruption offences as apply to individuals occupying similar posts within their own institutions".[73]

MEMBER STATES' OBLIGATIONS

A.47 As with the Protocol the corrupt conduct must be made a criminal offence[74] and "effective, proportionate and dissuasive criminal penalties" must be provided[75] and jurisdiction established.[76] Provisions are made for international co-operation.[77]

---

[71] Located at: http://eur-lex.europa.eu/LexUriServ/LexUriServ.do?uri=CELEX:41997A0625(01):EN:HTML.

[72] Explanatory Report on the Convention. See: http://www.legaltext.ee/text/en/T70106.htm.

[73] Article 4. See Explanatory Report on the Convention, para 4.

[74] Articles 2(2) and 3(2).

[75] Article 5.

[76] Article 7.

[77] For example, article 8 (extradition and prosecution) and article 9 (co-operation).

CRIMINAL LIABILITY OF HEADS OF BUSINESSES.

A.48　The following is a notable additional provision that is not found in the First Protocol. Pursuant to article 6, member states must provide for criminal liability of heads of businesses (or any persons having power to take decisions or exercise control within a business) in cases of active corruption by a person under their authority acting on behalf of the business.[78] This is drawn from article 3 of the 1995 Convention on the protection of the European Communities' financial interests. It aims to ensure that those persons exercising legal or effective power within a business are responsible when a person under their authority is actively corrupt.[79] It should be noted that the Second Protocol to the 1995 Convention does provide for the liability of legal persons.

The European Council's framework decision 2003/568/JHA[80]

Background

A.49　The aim of this decision, as stated in its preamble, is to:

> ensure that both active and passive corruption in the private sector are criminal offences in all member states, that legal persons may also be held responsible for such offences, and that these offences incur effective, proportionate and dissuasive penalties.

---

[78]　Article 6.

[79]　Explanatory Report on the Convention, para 6.1. Criminal liability extends to heads of businesses who have failed to exercise a duty of supervision or control.

[80]　Located at: http://eur-lex.europa.eu/LexUriServ/LexUriServ.do?uri=CELEX:32003F0568:EN:HTML.

UK status

A.50   Council decisions are binding on those to whom they are addressed as to the result to be achieved but leave to national authorities the choice of forms and methods. This Decision is addressed to all member states. In accordance with article 11 of the Decision, it came into force on the date of its publication, 31 July 2003. The UK considers that the mandatory requirements of the Decision are met by existing UK law.[81] The main provision criminalising active and passive corruption (see below) is considered to be met by section 1(1) of the Prevention of Corruption Act 1906. The provision criminalising instigation, aiding and abetting such conduct is considered to be covered by section 8 of the Accessories and Abettors Act 1961. The requirements concerning legal persons are considered to be met by the Interpretation Act 1978.[82] However, the Commission of the European Communities recently produced a report to the Council detailing a factual evaluation of the implementation measures taken by the relevant member states.[83] It concluded that the UK had successively implemented certain articles but had only partly transposed others.[84]

Decision's requirements

ACTIVE AND PASSIVE CORRUPTION

A.51   The Decision makes the distinction between "active corruption" (promising, offering or giving an undue advantage of any kind) and "passive corruption" (requesting, receiving or accepting an undue advantage of any kind).

A.52   Active corruption is defined as promising, offering or giving, directly or through an intermediary, to a person who in any capacity directs or works for a private-sector entity an undue advantage of any kind, for that person or for a third party, in order that that person should perform or refrain from performing any act, in breach of that person's duties.[85]

A.53   Passive corruption is defined as directly or through an intermediary, requesting or receiving an undue advantage of any kind, or accepting the promise of such an advantage, for oneself or for a third party, while in any capacity directing or working for a private-sector entity, in order to perform or refrain from performing any act, in breach of one's duties.[86]

A.54   Both active and passive corruption offences are expressly stated to apply:

[81]   See the House of Lords debates dated 1 May 2007, col WA194-WA196 for a detailed response to the question of "what statutory measures or common law provisions allow the United Kingdom to fulfil the obligations under European Union Council framework decision 2003/568/JHA of 22 July 2003 on combating corruption in the private sector". Found at: http://www.publications.parliament.uk/pa/ld200607/ldhansrd/text/70501w0001.htm#070501 37000024.

[82]   Which (in its schedule 1) provides that unless the contrary is stated, the word "person" in a statute is to be construed as including a "body of persons, corporate or incorporate".

[83]   Report from the Commission to the Council based on article 9 of the Council Framework Decision 2003/568/JHA of 22 July 2003 on combating corruption in the private sector, COM (2007) 328 final, 18 June 2007. Includes Annex to report.

[84]   Further detail of this report is provided at paras A.63 to A.68.

[85]   Article 2.

[86]   Article 2.

(1)   only to intentional conduct;[87]

(2)   only to conduct carried out in the course of business activities;[88]

(3)   to business activities within profit and non-profit entities; and[89]

(4)   to those who instigate, aid and abet such conduct.[90]

A.55   Any member state may declare that it will limit the scope of active and passive corruption "to such conduct which involves, or could involve, a distortion of competition in relation to the purchase of goods or commercial services".[91]

A.56   Breach of duty is defined as:

> understood in accordance with national law....[It] should cover as a minimum any disloyal behaviour constituting a breach of a statutory duty, or, as the case may be, a breach of professional regulations or instructions, which apply within the business of a person who in any capacity directs or works for a private sector entity.[92]

LIABILITY OF LEGAL PERSONS

A.57   There is a specific provision establishing the liability of a legal person if an offence of active or passive corruption (or instigating, aiding and abetting the said offence) has been committed for its benefit by a person who has a leading position within the legal person.[93] Three bases are stated: first, a power of representation of the legal person; secondly an authority to take decisions on behalf of the legal person; or thirdly an authority to exercise control within the legal person. The legal person may also be held liable if the corrupt conduct was made possible due to a lack of supervision or control. The penalties applicable to the legal person are stated at article 6.[94]

A.58   This provision is very similar to article 3 of the Second Protocol to the 1995 Convention protecting the EC's financial interests.

---

[87] Article 2(1).

[88] Article 2(1).

[89] Article 2(2).

[90] Article 3.

[91] Article 2(3).

[92] Article 1.

[93] Article 5.

[94] "Shall include criminal or non-criminal fines and may include other penalties such as: (a) exclusion from entitlement to public benefits or aid; (b) temporary or permanent disqualification from the practice of commercial activities; (c) placing under judicial supervision; or (d) a judicial winding-up order."

PENALTIES AND SANCTIONS

A.59 Member states are required to "take the necessary measures" to ensure that active and passive corruption constitute criminal offences.[95]

A.60 "Effective, proportionate and dissuasive criminal penalties" must be imposed.[96] Active and passive corruption must be punishable by a penalty of a maximum of at least one to three years' imprisonment.[97]

A.61 Further, if a natural person who occupies a " leading position in a company within the business concerned" is convicted of active or passive corruption that person may "be temporarily prohibited from carrying on this particular or comparable business activity in a similar position or capacity" if there is reason to believe that there is "a clear risk of abuse of position or of office by active or passive corruption".[98]

JURISDICTION

A.62 Jurisdiction must be established where the offences have occurred wholly or partly on the state's territory (territoriality principle), by one of its nationals (nationality principle) or for the benefit of a legal person whose head office is in the territory of that member state.[99]

Commission report evaluating implementation of the Decision

A.63 As noted above, this report,[100] which was published in June 2007, provides a factual evaluation of the implementation of the Decision in the various member states, including the UK.[101]

A.64 Regarding article 1, it states that the legal definition of 'legal person' is fully transposed by the UK but that there is insufficient information to determine if the definition of 'breach of duty' has been transposed. It states that articles 2, 3 and 7(1) are fully transposed. However, it considers that articles 4, 5 and 6 are only partially transposed.[102]

---

[95] Article 2.

[96] Article 4(1).

[97] Article 4(2).

[98] Article 4(3).

[99] Article 7.

[100] Report from the Commission to the Council based on art 9 of the Council Framework Decision 2003/568/JHA of 22 July 2003 on combating corruption in the private sector, COM (2007) 328 final, 18 June 2007. Includes Annex to report.

[101] A useful table summarising the extent of transposition by 20 member states is provided at pp 10 and 11 of the report.

[102] See Table at p 10.

A.65   Further detail is provided in the Annex to the report. Regarding article 1 and the legal definition of 'legal person', the report makes reference to schedule 1 of the Interpretation Act 1978.[103] Article 2 is transposed by means of section 1 of the Prevention of Corruption Act 1906.[104] Article 3 is transposed via the Accessories and Abettors Act 1861.[105] It notes that article 7 is considered fully transposed taking into account general principles of English criminal law, section 109 of the Anti-Terrorism Crime and Security Act and the UK declaration.[106]

A.66   Articles 4, 5 and 6 are considered only partially transposed. Regarding article 4, the summary table concludes that the UK has met the requirements of sub-paragraph (1) (regarding articles 2 and 3) and also of sub-paragraph (2).[107] However, regarding article 4(3) the report concludes that there is insufficient information to assess whether the UK has met the requirements for it has failed to provide enough details on the Company Directors Disqualification Act 1986 which the UK states is the relevant legislation.[108]

A.67   Regarding article 5, the relevant legislation cited is the Interpretation Act 1978, the civil law of negligence and the Proceeds of Crime Act 2002.[109] Article 5 requires that the liability of legal persons be established. The summary table details that the UK has met the requirements of articles 5(1) and 5(3). However, regarding article 5(2) it only partly meets the requirements.[110] Article 5(2) requires the liability of the legal person to be established where it is lack of supervision or control that has made possible the commission of the relevant offence. The UK relied on the civil law of negligence and the Proceeds of Crime Act 2002, but the Commission concluded that "administrative or civil sanctions alone are not sufficient."[111]

A.68   Regarding article 6, the relevant legislation cited is the Interpretation Act 1978 and the Prevention of Corruption Act 1906.[112] It is article 6(2) that the Commission considers the UK has not fully transposed.[113] This conclusion was based on the fact that the UK had not properly implemented article 5(2).[114]

[103] Annex to report, pp 15 and 18.

[104] Above, p 75.

[105] Above, p 85. The report concludes that there is insufficient information regarding the situation of Scotland.

[106] Above, p 150.

[107] Above, pp 88 to 90 and p 110.

[108] Above, pp 88 to 90 and p 110.

[109] Above, pp 110 and 112.

[110] Above, pp 113 and 114.

[111] Above, p 123.

[112] Above, p 127.

[113] Above, p 129.

[114] Above, p 139. See discussion above.

UNITED NATIONS

Summary of relevant texts

(1) Convention Against Transnational Organised Crime which came into force in 2003. This covers public sector bribery only and also provides for offences of concealment of property and money laundering. For our purposes, it is now largely superceded by the Convention Against Corruption.

(2) Convention against Corruption: public and private sector active and passive bribery; domestic and foreign bribery; embezzlement, misappropriation, money laundering and obstruction of justice; liability of legal persons; inchoate offences and secondary liability; longer statute of limitations; trading in influence; criminal and civil sanctions; note some articles are discretionary.

Overview

A.69   The UN considers that:

> corruption causes reduced investment or even disinvestment, with many long-term effects, including social polarisation, lack of respect for human rights, undemocratic practices and diversion of funds intended for development and essential services.[115]

A.70   In November 2000, the UN adopted the Convention against Transnational Organised Crime, which entered into force on 29 September 2003.[116]

A.71   In December 2000 a special committee was established by the General Assembly with a view to drafting an effective international instrument against corruption. On 31 October 2003, the General Assembly adopted[117] the United Nations Convention against Corruption[118] and it entered into force on 14 December 2005. A Conference of state Parties was established to monitor its implementation and they have conducted two sessions, in 2006[119] and in 2007.

The United Nations Convention against Corruption[120]

Background

A.72   The purposes of the Convention are described as three-fold:

---

[115] Legislative Guide to Implementation of UN Convention against Corruption, page iv. Found at: http://www.unodc.org/pdf/corruption/CoC_LegislativeGuide.pdf.

[116] Three Protocols have also been adopted on trafficking persons, smuggling migrants and illicit trafficking and manufacturing arms.

[117] Resolution 58/4.

[118] Also known as the Merida Convention.

[119] The resolutions made can be found at: www.unodc.org/unodc/caccosp_2006_resolutions_1.html?print=yes The only substantive one relevant here is resolution 1/7 which furthers consideration of bribery of officials of public international organisations.

[120] Located at: http://www.unodc.org/unodc/crime_convention_corruption.html .For legislative Guide see http://www.unodc.org/unodc/crime_convention_corruption_guide.html.

(1) to promote and strengthen measures to prevent and combat corruption more efficiently and effectively;

(2) to promote, facilitate and support international cooperation and technical assistance in the prevention of and fight against corruption, including in asset recovery; and

(3) to promote integrity, accountability and proper management of public affairs and public property.

A.73 The Convention is divided into eight parts. These include preventive measures (chapter II of the Convention); criminalisation (chapter III); international co-operation (chapter IV); and asset recovery (chapter V). Chapter III will be the focus for this Appendix.

A.74 The Convention is described as "unique as compared to other Conventions" by Transparency International "not only in its global coverage but also in the extensiveness and detail of its provisions."

UK status

A.75 The United Kingdom signed the Convention on 9 December 2003 and ratified it on 9 February 2006.

Convention requirements

PREVENTIVE MEASURES

A.76 At chapter II, the Convention details various preventive measures including preventive anti-corruption policies and practices, preventive anti-corruption body or bodies, systems with the public sector to ensure positions are obtained and retained fairly, codes of conduct for public officials, appropriate systems of public procurement and management of public finances and transparency in public reporting.

CRIMINALISATION AND LAW ENFORCEMENT

A.77 For the purposes of our Consultation Paper, chapter III on criminalisation and law enforcement is more pertinent. These articles can be divided into two groups: those that are mandatory and those that are discretionary.

Bribery involving national and foreign public officials and officials of public international organisations

A.78 The Convention defines bribery at article 15, but limits its scope to national public officials,[121] foreign public officials[122] and officials of public international organisations.[123] It is defined as the intentional[124] promise, offering or giving to a public official, or alternatively the solicitation or acceptance by a public official, "directly or indirectly, of an undue advantage, for the official himself or herself or another person or entity, in order that the official act or refrain from acting in the exercise of his or her official duties".[125]

A.79 Regarding foreign public officials and officials of public international organisations[126] there is an additional requirement that if a promise, offer or gift is made to the foreign public official or the official of public international organisations that this is done "in order to obtain or retain business or other undue advantage in relation to the conduct of international business".

A.80 The Convention obliges state parties to "adopt such legislative and other measures as may be necessary to establish" such conduct as criminal offences.[127]

A.81 In the Legislative Guide, the distinction is made between 'active' (promising, offering or giving) and 'passive' (solicitation or acceptance) bribery. It states that such a distinction allows more effective prosecution of corruption and "introduces a stronger dissuasive effect".[128]

---

[121] Defined in article 2: (i) any person holding a legislative, executive, administrative or judicial office of a state party, whether appointed or elected, whether permanent or temporary, whether paid or unpaid, irrespective of that person's seniority; (ii) any other person who performs a public function, including for a public agency or public enterprise, or provides a public service, as defined in the domestic law of the state party and as applied in the pertinent area of law of that state party; (iii) any other person defined as a "public official" in the domestic law of a state party. However, for the purpose of some specific measures contained in chapter II of this Convention, "public official" may mean any person who performs a public function or provides a public service as defined in the domestic law of the state party and as applied in the pertinent area of law of that state party.

[122] Defined in article 2: any person holding a legislative, executive, administrative or judicial office of a foreign country, whether appointed or elected; and any person exercising a public function for a foreign country, including for a public agency or public enterprise.

[123] Defined in article 2: an international civil servant or any person who is authorised by such an organisation to act on behalf of that organisation.

[124] Article 28 states that "Knowledge, intent or purpose required as an element of an offence established in accordance with this Convention may be inferred from objective factual circumstances."

[125] Para 183.

[126] Article 16.

[127] Articles 15 and 16.

[128] Para 192.

Embezzlement, misappropriation or other diversion of property by a public official, money laundering and obstruction of justice

A.82   State parties must also adopt measures to criminalise embezzlement, misappropriation or other diversion of property by a public official,[129] the laundering of proceeds of crime,[130] and the obstruction of justice regarding proceedings relating to the offences listed in the Convention.[131] The Legislative Guide considers these provisions "an innovation" for they criminalise activity beyond the scope of the basic corruption offences.

Liability of legal persons

A.83   The liability of legal persons is specifically addressed.[132] There must be measures establishing the liability (criminal, civil or administrative) of such persons for participation in the offences established in accordance with the Convention and effective, proportionate and dissuasive criminal or non-criminal sanctions imposed.

Inchoate offences and secondary liability

A.84   It must be a criminal offence to participate in any capacity as an accomplice, assistant or instigator in an offence established in accordance with the Convention.[133]

Sanctions

A.85   Sanctions must be provided for in accordance with articles 30 and 31. In accordance with article 35, states must also ensure that entities and persons who have suffered damage as a result of an act of corruption have the right to compensation in damages. "Appropriate measures" must be taken to ensure witnesses, experts and victims are protected.[134] A longer statute of limitations must be adopted where appropriate pursuant to article 29.[135]

Trading in influence

A.86   State parties must consider adopting measures to criminalise trading in influence. This is defined as the intentional:

---

[129] Article 17.

[130] Article 23.

[131] Article 25.

[132] Article 26.

[133] Article 27.

[134] Article 32.

[135] Criticisms largely focus on the fact that certain provisions are optional. Criticisms are also made regarding the lack of a robust enforcement mechanism. See P Webb, "The UN Convention Against Corruption: Global Achievement or Missed Opportunity" (2005) 8 Journal of International Economic Law 191.

promise, offering or giving to a public official or any other person, directly or indirectly, of an undue advantage in order that the public official or the person abuse his or her real or supposed influence with a view to obtaining from an administration or public authority of the state party an undue advantage for the original instigator of the act or for any other person; or the solicitation or acceptance by a public official or any other person, directly or indirectly, of an undue advantage for himself or herself or for another person in order that the public official or the person abuse his or her real or supposed influence with a view to obtaining from an administration or public authority of the state party an undue advantage.

Further provisions

A.87   Further provisions that the state parties must consider adopting are measures to criminalise:[136]

(1)   passive and active bribery in the private sector.[137] This provision uses the definition detailed in article 15 with the added requirement that it must be committed in the "course of economic, financial or commercial activities" by someone who directs or works in any capacity for a private sector entity. It also uses the particular term 'breach of duties';

(2)   intentional abuse of functions by a public official for the purpose of obtaining an undue advantage;[138]

(3)   intentional illicit enrichment by a public official;[139]

(4)   embezzlement of property in the private sector;[140]

(5)   the concealment or continued retention of property knowing that it is the result of one of the Convention offences;[141] and

(6)   the attempt or preparation of an offence established in accordance with the Convention.[142]

INTERNATIONAL CO-OPERATION

A.88   Chapter IV provides for measures to ensure international co-operation is efficient and effective.

---

[136] "Adopt such legislative and other measures as may be necessary to establish (such conduct) as criminal offences … ."

[137] Article 21.

[138] Article 19.

[139] Article 20.

[140] Article 22.

[141] Article24.

[142] Article 27.

ANTI-CORRUPTION UNIT (ACU) / GLOBAL PROGRAMME AGAINST CORRUPTION
(GPAC)

A.89   These measures provide practical assistance and aim to aid implementation of
the Convention.[143]

ORGANISATION FOR ECONOMIC CO-OPERATION AND DEVELOPMENT (OECD)

OECD Convention

Background

A.90   The OECD Convention on Combating Bribery of Foreign Public Officials in
International Business Transactions entered into force on 15 February 1999.[144]
All 36 participating countries have introduced legislation in an attempt to
implement the Convention.[145] There is a continuing monitoring process, in which
the OECD Working Group on Bribery checks both the introduction of
implementing legislation and its effective enforcement. Monitoring has reached
phase 2, and the report on the United Kingdom was approved on 17th March
2005.

Convention requirements

A.91   The Convention obliges participating states to introduce domestic legislation that
makes it a criminal offence to bribe foreign public officials in international
business transactions. The basic obligation under the Convention is as follows:

> 1. Each party shall take such measures as may be necessary to
> establish that it is a criminal offence under its law for any person
> intentionally to offer, promise or give any undue pecuniary or other
> advantage, whether directly or through intermediaries, to a foreign
> public official, for that official or for a third party, in order that the
> official act or refrain from acting in relation to the performance of
> official duties, in order to obtain or retain business or other improper
> advantage in the conduct of international business.
>
> 2. Each party shall take any measures necessary to establish that
> complicity in, including incitement, aiding and abetting, or
> authorisation of an act of bribery of a foreign public official shall be a
> criminal offence. Attempt and conspiracy to bribe a foreign public
> official shall be criminal offences to the same extent as attempt and
> conspiracy to bribe a public official of that party.

A.92   The OECD considers the distinguishing feature of this Convention to be that it
"deals with foreign bribery, i.e., it sanctions the natural or legal person that bribes
a foreign public official in the context of international business transactions."[146]

---

[143] See UNODC website: http://www.unodc.org/unodc/en/corruption.html.

[144] See
http://www.oecd.org/document/12/0,2340,en_2649_34859_2057484_1_1_1_1,00.html.

[145] See http://www.oecd.org/dataoecd/50/33/1827022.pdf.

[146] See OECD website at: http://www.oecd.org/dataoecd/43/8/34107314.pdf.

A.93   It should be noted that the substantive offence only covers active bribery, that is, the person giving the bribe. The foreign public official will usually be outside the jurisdiction and impossible to prosecute, though theoretically he or she could be liable for complicity.

UK status

A.94   The United Kingdom statute passed to implement the Convention is part 12 of the Anti-Terrorism, Crime and Security Act 2001, which came into force on 14 February 2002. This reads:

> 108. Bribery and corruption: foreign officers etc.
>
> (1) For the purposes of any common law offence of bribery it is immaterial if the functions of the person who receives or is offered a reward have no connection with the United Kingdom and are carried out in a country or territory outside the United Kingdom.
>
> (2) In section 1 of the Prevention of Corruption Act 1906 (c 34) (corrupt transactions with agents) insert this subsection after subsection (3):
>
> (4) For the purposes of this Act it is immaterial if:
>
> (a) the principal's affairs or business have no connection with the United Kingdom and are conducted in a country or territory outside the United Kingdom;
>
> (b) his agent's functions have no connection with the United Kingdom and are carried out in a country or territory outside the United Kingdom.
>
> (3) In section 7 of the Public Bodies Corrupt Practices Act 1889 (c 69) (interpretation relating to corruption in office) in the definition of "public body" for "but does not include any public body as above defined existing elsewhere than in the United Kingdom" substitute "and includes any body which exists in a country or territory outside the United Kingdom and is equivalent to any body described above".
>
> (4) In section 4(2) of the Prevention of Corruption Act 1916 (c 64) (in the 1889 and 1916 Acts public body includes local and public authorities of all descriptions) after "descriptions" insert "(including authorities existing in a country or territory outside the United Kingdom)".
>
> 109. Bribery and corruption committed outside the UK
>
> (1) This section applies if:
>
> (a) a national of the United Kingdom or a body incorporated under the law of any part of the United Kingdom does anything in a country or territory outside the United Kingdom; and

(b) the act would, if done in the United Kingdom, constitute a corruption offence (as defined below).

(2) In such a case:

(a) the act constitutes the offence concerned; and

(b) proceedings for the offence may be taken in the United Kingdom.

(3) These are corruption offences:

(a) any common law offence of bribery;

(b) the offences under section 1 of the Public Bodies Corrupt Practices Act 1889 (c 69) (corruption in office);

(c) the first two offences under section 1 of the Prevention of Corruption Act 1906 (c 34) (bribes obtained by or given to agents).

(4) A national of the United Kingdom is an individual who is:

(a) a British citizen, a [British overseas territories citizen], a British National (Overseas) or a British Overseas citizen;

(b) a person who under the British Nationality Act 1981 (c 61) is a British subject; or

(c) a British protected person within the meaning of that Act.

110. Presumption of corruption not to apply

Section 2 of the Prevention of Corruption Act 1916 (c 64) (presumption of corruption in certain cases) is not to apply in relation to anything which would not be an offence apart from section 108 or section 109.

A.95   In brief, the existing law of bribery is extended to cases where the person bribed is a foreign official, or the act was committed abroad, except that in these cases there is no presumption of corruption under the 1916 Act. It is not made explicit whether the two extensions can be compounded, so as to include a bribe to a foreign official which itself takes place abroad; that is, whether the definition of "corruption offence" in section 109 includes the offences as extended by section 108. Both as a matter of drafting and as a matter of purposive interpretation, it seems overwhelmingly probable that the double extension is intended.

Monitoring reports on UK

A.96   The UK legislation, as amended by the 2001 Act, was considered in phase 1 of the monitoring by the OECD.[147] The following possible problems were identified.

---

[147] Report released 3 March 2003, http://www.oecd.org/dataoecd/12/50/2498215.pdf.

(1) The definition of the offence in the 1906 Act in terms of principal and agent seems to imply a defence of principal's consent, though this is not made explicit and it is uncertain whether such a defence in fact exists in English law. The Convention calls for foreign bribery to be an offence, without any defence of principal's consent.

(2) It is not clear that all foreign public officials, as covered by the Convention, are in fact caught by the 2001 Act, as this contains no separate definition of these persons.

(3) It is not explicit on the face of the statute that either the domestic law of bribery or the 2001 Act extension covers offers made through intermediaries, or bribes consisting of payments to third parties, though the Government assured the working party that they do.

(4) The OECD express some apprehension that the existence of Parliamentary privilege may mean that bribes to members of foreign legislatures will not be covered. This must depend on whether any immunity enjoyed by MPs is a personal and procedural exemption, or a genuine exception to the scope of the offence.

A.97 Phase 2 of the monitoring[148] gave brief consideration to the draft Bill introduced following our 1998 Report. The following points are mentioned.

(1) The use of the principal and agent test may make the scope of the offence narrower than required by the Convention. However, the report notes that the defence of principal's consent will not apply to public officials, including foreign public officials.

(2) The report queries the requirement that the payer must believe that the favour will be "primarily" in return for the bribe; again some cases within the Convention's definition may slip the net.

(3) The report prefers a more detailed list of foreign public officials, in keeping with the definition in the Convention.

A.98 The report disclaims any intention to influence the domestic law of bribery, so the Working Group would be satisfied if foreign bribery became a separate offence, provided that that offence fulfilled their requirements.

OTHER INTERNATIONAL INSTRUMENTS

A.99 The following international instruments are not directly relevant because they relate to other territories and are not binding on the UK. However, they are included here for two reasons. First, to ensure that the Appendix covers all international texts on bribery/corruption and so is fully comprehensive. Secondly, the definitions and terms used may be of use in considering how to approach criminalising bribery under our domestic law.

---

[148] March 2005, http://www.oecd.org/dataoecd/62/32/34559062.pdf.

(1)   African Union Convention on Preventing and Combating Corruption.[149] Article 4 defines various acts of corruption. This includes the solicitation or acceptance by a public official or third party, or the offering or granting to a public official or a third party, "directly or indirectly, of any goods of monetary value, or other benefit, such as a gift, favour, promise or advantage for himself or herself or for another person or entity, in exchange for any act or omission in the performance of his or her public functions." It also provides for an offence of bribery in the private sector in similar terms except that it uses the term "undue advantage".[150] This article also provides for offences covering trading in influence in the private or public sector,[151] illicit enrichment, the diversion of public funds and participation in any of the offences.

(2)   Southern African Development Protocol against Corruption.[152] This defines corruption as "any act referred to in article 3" (which is closely modelled on the AU Convention) and "includes bribery or any other behaviour in relation to persons entrusted with responsibilities in the public and private sectors which violates their duties as public officials, private employees, independent agents or other relationships of that kind and aimed at obtaining undue advantage of any kind for themselves or others."[153]

---

[149] Located at: http://www.africa-union.org/Official_documents/Treaties_%20Conventions_%20Protocols/Convention%20on%20Combating%20Corruption.pdf.

[150] "The offering or giving, promising, solicitation or acceptance, directly or indirectly, of any undue advantage to or by any person who directs or works for, in any capacity, a private sector entity, for himself or herself or for anyone else, for him or her to act, or refrain from acting, in breach of his or her duties."

[151] "The offering, giving, solicitation or acceptance directly or indirectly, or promising of any undue advantage to or by any person who asserts or confirms that he or she is able to exert any improper influence over the decision making of any person performing functions in the public or private sector in consideration thereof, whether the undue advantage is for himself or herself or for anyone else, as well as the request, receipt or the acceptance of the offer or the promise of such an advantage, in consideration of that influence, whether or not the influence is exerted or whether or not the supposed influence leads to the intended result."

[152] Located at: http://www.sadc.int/english/documents/legal/protocols/corruption.php.

[153] Article 1.

(3)   ECOWAS Protocol on the Fight Against Corruption.[154] Inter-American Convention against Corruption.[155] Acts of corruption are defined at article VI. This includes solicitation or acceptance by, or the offering or granting to, a government official or a person who performs public functions "directly or indirectly who performs public functions, of any article of monetary value, or other benefit, such as a gift, favour, promise or advantage for himself or for another person or entity, in exchange for any act or omission in the performance of his public functions." It also refers to illicit enrichment, fraudulent use or concealment of the proceeds of corrupt acts and participation in corruption.

(4)   ADB-OECD Action Plan for Asia-Pacific.[156] There is no definition provided of bribery or corruption and the Plan consists of non-binding principles.

THE WORK OF OTHER BODIES

Commonwealth Secretariat

Background

A.100   In April 2006,[157] the Commonwealth Secretary-General described the Commonwealth's role in the fight against corruption as:

galvanising its members to fight corruption at large, in pushing forward its own initiatives, in providing technical assistance in the form of training or legislative drafting, and in implementing UNCAC in particular.

---

[154] Summary information available at: http://www.transparency.org/global_priorities/international_conventions/regional_coverage/list/ecowas_protocol.

[155] Located at: http://www.oas.org/juridico/english/Treaties/b-58.html.

[156] Located at: http://www1.oecd.org/daf/ASIAcom/pdf/ap_english.pdf.

[157] See transcript located at: http://www.thecommonwealth.org/shared_asp_files/gfsr.asp?NodeID=150500&attributename=file.

Commonwealth Expert Group on Good Governance and the Elimination of Corruption, 'Fighting Corruption: Promoting Good Governance'[158] and the Framework for Commonwealth Principles on Promoting Good Governance and Combating Corruption[159]

A.101   In 2000 the Commonwealth published an anti-corruption plan, which was formulated by a Commonwealth Expert Group on Good Governance. The heads of Government in Durban had endorsed this report in 1999. Its main findings are reflected in its Framework for Commonwealth Principles on Promoting Good Governance and Combating Corruption. This defines corruption at paragraph 4 as "the abuse of all offices of trust for private gain".[160] It distinguishes between 'grand corruption', 'widespread systematic corruption' and 'petty corruption'. At paragraph 22 it addresses the criminal law. It states that "both active and passive corruption should be made criminal offences, comprehensively covering the holders of all offices of trust". It also details that the law should criminalise money laundering of the proceeds and provide for the seizure and forfeiture of the proceeds of corruption.

Commonwealth Heads of Government Meeting, Malta 2005, Final Communique[161]

A.102   At paragraph 47 the heads "reiterated their commitment to root out, both at national and international levels, systemic corruption, including extortion and bribery, which undermine good governance, respect for human rights and economic development." Comprehensive preventative measures, including institutionalising transparency, accountability and good governance, combined with effective enforcement, were described as "the most effective means to combat corruption." The United Nations Convention Against Corruption was considered of paramount importance.

International Chamber of Commerce[162]

Overview

A.103   The ICC has established an Anti-Corruption Commission. It defines corruption as:

---

[158] Located at:
http://publications.thecommonwealth.org/publications/html/DynaLink/cat_id/19/pub_id/111/pub_details.asp.

[159] Located at:
http://www.thecommonwealth.org/shared_asp_files/uploadedfiles/%7BC628DA6C-4D83-4C5B-B6E8-FBA05F1188C6%7D_framework1.pdf.

[160] Compare to the definition put forward by the FCO: "Bribery can be defined broadly as the receiving or offering/giving of any benefit (in cash or in kind) by or to any public servant or office holder or to a director or employee of a private company in order to induce that person to give improper assistance in breach of their duty to the government or company which has employed or appointed them.

[161] Located at: http://www.thecommonwealth.org/shared_asp_files/uploadedfiles/BADFECEF-7663-4BEA-97FB-735D6E029944_CHOGM2005FINALCOMMUNIQUE.pdf.

[162] www.iccwbo.org/policy/anticorruption/id13018/index.html.

the abuse of entrusted power for private financial or non-financial gain. It diverts resources from their proper use, distorts competition and creates gross inefficiencies in both the public and private sectors. Corruption can occur in form of bribery, bribe solicitation or extortion

A.104   Bribery is defined as:

an offer or the receipt of any gift, loan, fee, reward or other advantage to or from any person as an inducement to do something which is dishonest or illegal.

A.105   Bribe solicitation is defined as:

the act of asking or enticing another to commit bribery.

The ICC considers this of paramount importance: "without effective action to address the "demand side" of corruption, the fight against corruption cannot be won."

A.106   In 2003 it published a comparative study of anti-bribery laws from various jurisdictions and in 2005 it produced the ICC Rules of Conduct and Recommendations for Combating Extortion and Bribery.[163] On 24 April 2007, it held a special forum rallying businesses to engage in the fight against corruption.

Multilateral Development Banks

Overview

A.107   On September 17 2006 the Heads of various Banks (including the IMF, World Bank and European Investment Bank Group) agreed a Framework for combating fraud and corruption.[164] One of the joint actions decided upon was an agreement on standardised definitions of fraudulent and corrupt practices for investigating such practices in activities financed by them. This built on the work of the Joint International Financial Institution Anti-Corruption Task Force ("IFI Task Force") which was established in February 2006 by these leaders.[165] The IFI Task Force defined corrupt practices as:

the offering, giving, receiving, or soliciting, directly or indirectly, anything of value to influence improperly the actions of another party.

It further stated that "each of the member institutions will determine implementation within its relevant policies and procedures, and consistent with international conventions".

---

[163] www.iccwbo.org/uploadedFiles/ICC/policy/anticorruption/Statements/ ICC_Rules_of_Conduct_and_Recommendations%20_2005%20Revision.pdf.

[164] Located at: http://www.ebrd.com/about/integrity/task.pdf.

[165] Also located at: http://www.ebrd.com/about/integrity/task.pdf.

APPENDIX B
COMPARATIVE LAW

B.1 This Appendix sets out some overseas approaches to the bribery of public officials, foreign and domestic, and private individuals. The Appendix should be read in conjunction with Professor Stuart Green's paper on the approach in the United States of America.

FRANCE

Public officials

B.2 The Criminal Code provides two offences that make it an offence to bribe a public official.

B.3 Article 432-11 of the Criminal Code makes it an offence for a public official[1] to directly or indirectly request or accept promises, donations, gifts or advantages, without the right to do so. In addition to this there must be an intention on the part of the public official to carry out or abstain from carrying out an act relating to his or her office or an intention to obtain "any distinction, employment, contract or any other favourable decision".

B.4 The corresponding offence is contained in Article 433-1 of the Criminal Code. This Article makes it an offence for a person to, directly or indirectly, offer or promise donations, gifts or advantages to a public official without the right to do so. In addition to this there must be an intention on the part of the person that the official carry out or abstain from carrying out an act relating to his or her office or an intention that the official obtains "any distinction, employment, contract or any other favourable decision".

B.5 The maximum penalty for these offences for natural persons is ten years' imprisonment and/or a fine of 150 thousand Euros. The maximum penalty for legal persons is up to five times the maximum fine for natural persons. Further under Article 433-25 of the Criminal Code, a legal person can be subject to any of the following for a period of up to five years:

    (1)   a ban on performing the activity in connection with which the offence was committed, either directly or indirectly;

    (2)   judicial supervision;

    (3)   closure of the office within which the offence was committed;

    (4)   exclusion from public procurements;

    (5)   a ban on appealing for public funds;

    (6)   a ban on issuing cheques;

---

[1] Defined by the section to include persons holding public authority or discharging a public service mission, or persons holding a public electoral mandate.

(7)   a ban on the use of payment cards;

(8)   confiscation; or

(9)   display of the court's ruling.

B.6   Both natural and legal persons may also be subject to the confiscation of the "instrument that was used or intended to be used to commit the offence, or of the proceeds of the offence".[2]

Foreign public officials

B.7   Articles 435-1 and 435-2 of the Criminal Code provide offences of bribing foreign public officials. Article 435-1 prohibits a foreign public official[3] from directly or indirectly requesting or accepting offers or promises of gifts to carry out, or abstain from carrying out, an act of his or her duty, mission or mandate or facilitated by his or her duty without the right to do so.

B.8   Article 435-2 carries the corresponding offence. The Article makes it an offence for a person to propose, without right, gifts, presents or advantages of any kind to a foreign public official. In addition the person must intend that the foreign public official will carry out, or abstain from carrying out, an act of his or her duty, mission or mandate or facilitated by his or her duty.

Private persons

B.9   Article 445-2 of the Criminal Code provides an offence of private corruption. The Article applies to a person:

(1)   not vested with public authority or discharging a public service mission; and

(2)   who is performing in the course of professional or social duties, a function of management or performing work for an individual or corporate entity or any organism.

B.10   Such a person is guilty of an offence if, without any right to do so to, he or she directly or indirectly, requests, accepts or promises, donations, gifts or any advantages, to carry out or abstain from carrying out an act relating to his or her duties. In addition this act or omission must infringe his or her legal, contractual or professional obligations. Article 445-1 also makes it an offence for a person to propose a bribery agreement or consent to the bribery.

B.11   The maximum penalty for these offences for natural persons is five years' imprisonment and a fine of up to 75,000. For legal persons the maximum penalty is a fine of up to five times the amount for individuals and/or one of the measures set out in paragraph B.5 above. Both natural and legal persons can also be subjected to confiscation of property.

---

[2]   Act No 2000-595 of 20 June 2000, s 3.

[3]   Defined by the article as "a European civil servant, a Member State's civil servant or a member of the European Commission, Parliament, European Court of Justice [or] European Court of Auditors".

Jurisdiction

B.12   The above laws apply to French nationals who commit bribery offences overseas, if the country within which the offence was committed also criminalises bribery.[4] However, such proceedings can only be instituted by the Public Prosecutors Office and must be preceded by a complaint by the victim of the offence or a legal successor or be preceded by an accusation made formally by the overseas authority.

B.13   The above laws also apply to a French national or foreign citizen who commits an offence of bribery abroad against a French victim.[5]

GERMANY

Public officials

B.14   There are two types of corruption offence concerning public officials, namely: accepting and granting a benefit; and accepting and granting a bribe.

Benefits

B.15   Section 331(1) of the Criminal Code contains the offence of accepting a benefit. The section provides that it is an offence for a public official[6] to demand, allow himself or herself to be promised or accept a benefit for himself or herself or another for the discharge of a duty.[7]   Section 331(3) provides a defence if R allows himself or herself to be promised or accepts a benefit, which he or she did not demand, and the public authority authorises the acceptance.

B.16   Section 333(1) of the Criminal Code contains the offence of granting a benefit. The section provides that it is an offence for a person to offer, promise or grant a benefit to a public official,[8] for him or her or another, for the discharge of a duty.[9] Section 333(3) provides a defence if the public authority authorises the public official's acceptance of the benefit.

---

[4]   Criminal Code, Article 113-6.

[5]   Criminal Code, Article 113-7.

[6]   Including a person with "special public service obligations".

[7]   Article 331(2) provides a similar offence in relation to judges and arbitrators.

[8]   Including a person with specific public service obligations and a solider in the armed forces.

[9]   Article 332(2) provides a similar offence in relation to judges and arbitrators.

Bribes

B.17   Section 332(1) of the Criminal Code contains the offence of a public official accepting a bribe. The section provides that it is an offence for a public official[10] to demand, allow himself or herself to be promised or accept a bribe, for himself or herself or another, in return for him or her performing an official act that would violate his or her official duties.[11] An attempt to commit this offence is also punishable under this section. Section 332(3) also provides that a public official will be guilty of an offence under subsection (1) if he or she accepts a bribe for a future act if he or she has either:

(1)   shown a willingness to violate his or her duties by the act; or

(2)   shown a willingness to be influenced by the bribe in the exercise of his or her discretion.

B.18   Section 334(1) of the Criminal Code contains the offence of granting a bribe to a public official. The section provides it is an offence for a person to promise or grant a bribe to a public official,[12] for himself or herself or another, in return for the official performing an official act that would violate his or her official duties.[13] Section 334(3) provides that P will guilty of an offence under subsection (1) if he or she promises a bribe for a future act if he or she attempts to induce the official to:

(1)   violate his or her duties by the act; or

(2)   be influenced by the bribe in the exercise of his or her discretion.

Penalties

B.19   The maximum penalty for these offences is imprisonment for not more than 10 years. The court can also issue a forfeiture order.

Jurisdiction

B.20   The provisions on public bribery apply to activities outside Germany if a German national commits them or they involve a public official who is employed by Germany or the EU. The German criminal law generally also applies to offences committed overseas if they are committed by a German national; or are committed jointly by co-defendants acting in Germany; or the effects of the offence are to the detriment of a German national (legal or natural persons).

---

[10]   Including a person with "special public service obligations".

[11]   Article 333(2) provides a similar offence in relation to judges and arbitrators.

[12]   Including a person with specific public service obligations and a solider in the armed forces.

[13]   Article 334(2) provides a similar offence in relation to judges and arbitrators.

Foreign public officials

B.21   Germany implemented the Act on Combating Bribery of Foreign Public Officials in International Business Transactions 1998 to implement the OECD convention of the same name. Section 1 of the Act extends the reach of Section 334 of the Criminal Code to foreign public officials.[14]

B.22   Section 2 of the Act also makes it an offence to bribe a foreign Member of Parliament. The section prohibits anyone offering, promising or granting a Member of a foreign Parliament an advantage.[15] The advantage must be for that Member or for a third party in order to obtain or retain for him or herself or a third party business or an unfair advantage in international business transactions. Further the business or unfair advantage in international business must be in return for the Members committing an act or omission in the future in connection with his or her mandate or functions. The maximum penalty for this offence is five years' imprisonment or a fine.

Jurisdiction

B.23   Section 3 of the Act provides the above sections apply to offences committed abroad by a German national.

Private persons

B.24   In Germany the focus of the criminal law on private bribery is the protection of free competition. Bribery in business transactions is set out in section 299 of the Criminal Code. Section 299 applies to both acts committed in the domestic markets and foreign markets.

B.25   Section 299(1) concerns passive bribery. An employee or agent of a business will be guilty of passive bribery if he or she demands, allows himself or herself to be promised, or accepts a benefit[16] for himself or herself or another in a business transaction[17] for the giving of a business preference to another unfairly. Under this section that it is not necessary that there be a breach of duty between the employer and employee or principal and agent.

---

[14]   Including: a judge of a foreign state; a judge at an international court; a public official of a foreign state; a person entrusted to exercise a public function with or for an authority of a foreign state, for a public enterprise with headquarters abroad, or other public functions for a foreign state; a public official and other member of the staff of an international organisation and a person entrusted with carrying out its functions; a soldier of a foreign state; and a soldier who is entrusted to exercise functions of an international organisation.

[15]   Including: a member of a legislative body of a foreign state; or a Member of a parliamentary assembly of an international organisation.

[16]   "Benefit" under these sections is widely interpreted and is not restricted to cash payments. This therefore can include modest gifts, hospitality or charitable donations.

[17]   Defined as the competitive purchase of goods or commercial services

B.26　Section 229(2) concerns active bribery. A person will be guilty of active bribery if, for competitive purposes, he or she offers, promises or grants and employee or agent of a business a benefit[18] for that employee or a third party in a business transaction. In addition the benefit must be consideration for the employee providing the person or another with a preference unfairly.　Also under this section, as above, it is not necessary that there be a breach of duty between the employer and employee or principal and agent.

B.27　Under section 299, only natural persons can be charged with bribery and therefore, both business owners and employers cannot be charged with the crime. However, both "employee" and "agent" are given a broad interpretation. 'Employee' includes person bound to the instructions of the entity.　'Agent' includes any person with a special function in the commercial enterprise and covers general managers, directors, bankruptcy administrators and commercial representatives.

B.28　The maximum penalty for both of these offences is three years' imprisonment or a fine.　Further if a natural person commits the offence, the company for whom he or she works can be made subject to a forfeiture order or an administrative fine up to one million Euros.

Jurisdiction

B.29　The provisions on private bribery apply to foreign competition as well as national competition.　As stated above, the German criminal law generally also applies to offences committed overseas if they are committed by a German national or are committed jointly by co-defendants acting in Germany or the effects of the offence are to the detriment of a German national (legal or natural persons).

ITALY

Private persons

B.30　There is no specific offence of private commercial bribery in Italy.　Therefore it is not a crime to bribe an employee of a private commercial enterprise.　However, there is a wide range of other criminal offences that are used in practice to prosecute such cases.[19]

Public bribery and foreign public officials

B.31　There are various sections in the Penal Code that cover the area of public bribery.

B.32　Article 318 covers bribery "with regard to lawful acts of the office". It provides a public officer will be guilty of this type of bribery if, acting in an official capacity, he or she receives, for himself or herself or a third party compensation, in the form of money or any other object of value, not due, or accepts a promise thereof. The maximum penalty for this offence is imprisonment for between six months to three years.

---

[18]　For the definition of "benefit" see n16.

[19]　These include offences of fraud, misappropriation, crimes against competition, protecting secrets, interference with auctions and sports fraud.

B.33   Article 319 covers bribery "with regard to acts contrary to the duty of his office". It provides that a public officer will be guilty of this type of bribery if he or she receives for himself or herself or a third party, money or any other object of value or accepts a promise thereof in return for omitting or delaying an official act. The maximum penalty for this offence is between two to five years' imprisonment.

B.34   Article 320 covers bribery "of persons charged with a public service". It provides that Article 319 applies to persons charged with a public service and that Article 318 applies to persons charged with a public service when they are public employees.

B.35   Article 321 also provides that the punishments set out in relation to Articles 318 and 319 apply equally to the person "who promises the money or other object of value to a public officer or person charged with a public service".

B.36   Where a public official is offered a bribe but does not accept it, Article 322 provides separate offence. It states that the person who has unduly offered or promised money or other assets to a public officer in order to induce the officer to do an act related to his or her office, will be liable to the punishment in Article 318 (is imprisonment for between six months to three years) reduced by one-third.

B.37   Subsection 2 of Article 322 also states if the offer or promise was made in order to induce the public officer to omit or delay an act or act in breach of his or her duties, the offender shall be liable to the punishment in Article 319 (between two to five years' imprisonment) reduced by one-third.

Foreign public officials

B.38   To meet the requirements under the OECD convention on bribery of foreign public officials in business transactions, Article 322-bis[20] extends Articles 321. It therefore now includes: "persons carrying out functions or activities equivalent to those performed by public officials and persons in charge of a public service within other foreign states or public international organisations".

Penalties

B.39   As well as the imprisonment penalties set out above, the following sanctions can also be applied to natural and legal persons:

>   (1)   closing the place of business;
>
>   (2)   suspension or revocations of licences;
>
>   (3)   disqualification from committing the acts with which the offence was concerned;
>
>   (4)   prohibition from dealing with the public administration;
>
>   (5)   temporary exclusion from advertising goods and services; and
>
>   (6)   publication of the sentence.

[20]   Inserted by Law No 300 of 29 September 2000.

Jurisdiction

B.40 Italian law applies to nationals who commit offences overseas if:

    (1)   the offender is within Italian territory;

    (2)   the offence is punishable by Italian law by at least three years' imprisonment; and

    (3)   where the offence was committed to the detriment of the EC or a foreign country, at the request of the Minister of Justice and only where extradition has not been granted or requested by the country in which the offence was committed.

B.41 Italian law also applies to non-nationals provided that:

    (1)   the offence was committed within Italian territory;

    (2)   the offence was committed to the detriment of the Italian State or an Italian citizen and the offence is punishable by at least one years' imprisonment or committed to the detriment of the EC or a foreign country or alien and be punishable by at least three years' imprisonment; and

    (3)   In the case of detriment to the Italian state or a national, at the request of the minister of justice or complaint by the victim, or, in the case of the EC or foreign country or alien, on request of the minister of justice and where extradition has not been granted or requested by the country in which the offence was committed.

JAPAN

B.42 In Japan the focus of the bribery provisions is the protection of integrity and loyalty to the principal (the Government) for public bribery and the protection of duty of loyalty or trust between and employer and employee for private bribery. Fair competition is not seen as a protected legal interest of bribery.

Private bribery

B.43 There is no express law in Japan that makes private commercial bribery an offence. However, there is an offence of breach of trust in the Penal Code that is sometimes used to prosecute situations akin to private bribery. Further the Code of Commerce prohibits private bribery. Article 493 makes it an offence to give or receive a bribe[21] "in connection with one's duties" and in response to an "unlawful solicitation". The maximum penalty for receiving a bribe is five years' imprisonment with forced labour or a fine of up to five million yen and the maximum penalty for giving a bribe is three years' imprisonment and a fine of up to three million yen.

---

[21] Under the Code of Commerce, a bribe is defined as "any benefit of a pecuniary nature".

B.44   The offence in Article 493 applies to certain types of recipients, namely, promoters, directors, auditor, acting director, acting auditor, manager or any other employee entrusted to undertake certain kinds of commercial matters. However, there are no specified types of payer.

B.45   There is also a defence of "mere gift" to the Code of Commerce provisions. Therefore if P can prove the bribe was actually a gift he or she will have a defence. However, it is not a defence that P's actions were encouraged or condoned by his or her employer although in such situations P's employer can be prosecuted as a co-principal, instigator or accessory.

Public bribery

B.46   The provisions on bribery in the Japanese Penal Code apply to bribery of government employees and "persons deemed to be a public servant".[22] By using the terms of persons deemed to be a public servant, the Penal Code opens up the bribery provisions to cover:

(1)   government officials;

(2)   public entity officials;

(3)   public corporation officials;

(4)   assembly persons;

(5)   committee persons; and

(6)   other employees in public duties.[23]

B.47   A bribe is defined as not only a benefit of a pecuniary nature but also any interest that may satisfy any demand or desire, such as sexual amusement, position, employment, entrance to public university etc.

B.48   Article 197-1 makes it an offence for a public servant to accept a bribe. Such an offence is committed when a public servant or arbitrator, upon solicitation, receives, demands or bargains for a bribe in connection with his or her duties. The maximum penalty for this offence is five years' imprisonment with forced labour. However, if the public servant or arbitrator accepts a solicitation the sentence is increased to a maximum seven years' imprisonment with forced labour.

B.49   The second part to Article 197-2 extends this offence to a person who "intends to become a public servant or an arbitrator" and who "receives, demands, or bargains for a bribe on acceptance of solicitation in connection with his/her duties he/she is to perform". The maximum penalty for this offence is five years' imprisonment with forced labour and the penalty applies once the person has become a public servant or arbitrator.

---

[22]   Article 197.

[23]   Penal Code, art 7.

B.50 Article 197-2 prohibits a public servant from bribing third parties. Such an offence is committed where a public servant or arbitrator, upon solicitation, causes, demands or bargains for a bribe to be given to a third party in connection with his or her duties. The maximum penalty for this offence is five years' penal servitude.

B.51 Article 197-4 makes it an offence for a public official to cause another official to behave dishonestly. Such an offence is committed if a public officer receives, demands or promises a bribe, as a reward for arranging or having arranged, on request, to cause another public officer to perform an improper action in the course of his or her duties. The maximum penalty for this offence is imprisonment with forced labour for not more than five years.

B.52 A person who gives a bribe in the same manner as set out in Article 197-4 is also guilty of an offence.[24] The maximum penalty for this offence is fine of not more than two million and five hundred thousand yen or a maximum three years' imprisonment with forced labour.

B.53 This offence has recently been supplemented by the Law on Punishment of Elected Public Office Holders for Receiving Graft for Arrangement. This Act makes it an offence for politicians and secretaries to receive money or goods from corporations or individuals in return for pressuring other civil servants to perform political favours. The maximum sentence for this offence is dependent on who the offender is. Politicians are liable to a maximum sentence of three years' imprisonment with forced labour. For secretaries the maximum is two years.

B.54 As with the Commercial Code a defendant is often able to argue as a successful defence that the bribe was in fact a "gift in ordinary life".[25]

Jurisdiction

B.55 The above offences apply to both domestic contracts and contracts with foreign parties and international businesses.

Foreign officials

B.56 The Unfair Competition Prevention Act revised in 1998 makes it an offence to bribe a foreign public official. The Act applies to both foreign government officials and government affiliated institutions and purports to protect fair and free competition. The Act provides that a person is guilty of an offence if he or she gives, offers or promises any undue pecuniary or other advantage so that the official acts or refrains from acting in relation to his or her official duties in order to gain an improper business advantage.

B.57 The maximum penalty for this offence for natural persons is a fine of up to three million yen for and/or imprisonment for up to three years. Legal persons can be fined up to 300 million yen.

---

[24] Penal Code, art 198.

[25] See the comments of Saito in Heine, Huber and Rose, "Private Commercial Bribery: A Comparison of National and Supranational Legal Structures" (2003, ICC) p 200.

Jurisdiction

B.58   Article 1 of the Penal Code on territorial principles results in the provisions on bribery applying to any person who commits a crime in Japan irrespective of their nationality. For offences of bribery committed outside of Japan, neither Japanese nationals nor foreign nationals are guilty of offences, even if the bribe is given to a Japanese foreign official.[26] However, a Japanese public official who accepts a bribe abroad given by a Japanese or foreign national is guilty of an offence under Article 4 of the Penal Code.

AUSTRALIA

Commonwealth

Public officials

B.59   The statutory provisions in Australia apply only to bribery of public officials. Sections 141.1 and 142.1 of the Commonwealth Criminal Code make it an offence to give a bribe or corrupting benefit to a Commonwealth public official and for a Commonwealth public official to receive a bribe or corrupting benefit.[27] Under sections 141.1(1) and 142.1(1) a person is guilty of an offence of giving a bribe or corrupting benefit to a Commonwealth public official if he or dishonestly:

    (1)   provides a benefit;

    (2)   causes a benefit to be provided; or

    (3)   causes an offer of the provision of a benefit or a promise of the provision of a benefit to be made.

B.60   In addition the person must do the above with the intention of influencing a Commonwealth public official in exercise of his or her duties The maximum penalty for the bribery offence is 10 years' imprisonment. The maximum penalty for the corrupting benefit offence is 5 years' imprisonment.

B.61   Section 141.1(3) and section 142.1(3) state that a Commonwealth public official is guilty of receiving a bribe or corrupting benefit if he or she dishonestly:

    (1)   asks for a benefit for himself or herself or another;

    (2)   receives or obtains a benefit for himself or herself or another; or

    (3)   agrees to receive or obtain a benefit for himself or herself or another person.

B.62   In addition the public official must do the above with the intention that the exercise of his or her duties will be influenced or of inducing, fostering or sustaining a belief that his or her duties will be influenced. The maximum penalty for the bribery offence is 10 years' imprisonment. The maximum penalty for the corrupting benefit offence is 5 years' imprisonment.

---

[26]   See the principles set out in the Penal Code, arts 2 and 3.

[27]   A "corrupting benefit" is defined by s 140.1 as "any advantage and is not limited to property".

JURISDICTION

B.63 Section 141.1(4) in relation to bribery of commonwealth public officials and section 142.3 in relation to giving a corrupting benefit to commonwealth public officials provide that section 15.4 on extended geographical jurisdiction applies to both offences.

B.64 Section 15.4 provides that sections falling within its provisions apply:

(1) whether or not the offence is committed in Australia; and

(2) whether or not the effects of the offence were felt in Australia.

B.65 In addition section 16.1 provides that if an offence falls within section 15.4's extended geographical jurisdiction the Attorney General's consent will be required before a prosecution can take place if:

(1) the offence occurs wholly outside of Australia; and

(2) at the time the offence was committed P was neither an Australian citizen nor a body corporate incorporated by or under a law of the Commonwealth or of a State or Territory.

Foreign public officials

B.66 Under section 70.2 a person is guilty of an offence if he or she provides, causes to be provided or offers to provide or promises to provide an offer of a benefit to another person and that is not legitimately due. In addition the person must intend to influence a foreign public official[28] (who may be the other person) in the exercise of his or her in order to:

---

[28] Under the section foreign public official means:

(a) an employee or official of a foreign government body;

(b) an individual who performs work for a foreign government body under a contract;

(c) an individual who holds or performs the duties of an appointment, office or position under a law of a foreign country or of part of a foreign country;

(d) an individual who holds or performs the duties of an appointment, office or position created by custom or convention of a foreign country or of part of a foreign country;

(e) an individual who is otherwise in the service of a foreign government body (including service as a member of a military force or police force);

(f) a member of the executive, judiciary or magistracy of a foreign country or of part of a foreign country;

(g) an employee of a public international organisation;

(h) an individual who performs work for a public international organisation under a contract;

(i) an individual who holds or performs the duties of an office or position in a public international organisation;

(j) an individual who is otherwise in the service of a public international organisation;

(k) a member or officer of the legislature of a foreign country or of part of a foreign country; or

(l) an individual who:

    (i) is an authorised intermediary of a foreign public official covered by any of the above paragraphs; or

    (ii) holds himself or herself out to be the authorised intermediary of a foreign public official covered by any of the above paragraphs.

(1)   obtain or retain business; or

(2)   obtain or retain a business advantage that is not legitimately due to the recipient, or intended recipient, of the business advantage (who may be the first mentioned person).

B.67   In determining whether a benefit is not legitimately due, the court is required to disregard the following:

(1)   the fact that the benefit may be customary, or perceived to be customary, in the situation;

(2)   the value of the benefit; and

(3)   any official tolerance of the benefit.[29]

B.68   In determining if a business advantage is not legitimately due, the court is required to disregard the following:

(1)   the fact that the business advantage may be customary, or perceived to be customary, in the situation;

(2)   the value of the business advantage; and

(3)   any official tolerance of the business advantage.[30]

B.69   The maximum penalty for this offence is 10 years' imprisonment.

B.70   Under this section "benefit" is given a wide interpretation to include any advantage and this advantage is not limited to property.

B.71   Section 70.3 provides a defence where the conduct of the foreign public official that is sought by the payer is lawful in the foreign public official's country. There is also a defence for facilitation payments.

JURISDICTION

B.72   Under section 70.5(2) a person will not be guilty of an offence under section 70.2 unless:

(1)   the conduct constituting the alleged offence occurs wholly or partly in Australia or wholly or partly on board an Australian aircraft or ship; or

(2)   the conduct constituting the alleged offence occurs wholly outside Australia and the perpetrator is an Australian citizen or resident or a body corporate incorporated by or under a law of the Commonwealth or of a State or Territory.

---

[29] Section 70.2.

[30] Above.

B.73　In addition proceedings for bribery of foreign public officials must, according to section 70.5(2) not be commenced without the Attorney General's written consent if:

> (1)　the conduct constituting the alleged offence occurs wholly outside Australia; and
>
> (2)　at the time of the alleged offence, the person alleged to have committed the offence is: a resident of Australia; and not an Australian citizen.

CANADA

Public officials

B.74　Section 119(1)(a) of the Criminal Code makes it an offence for a holder of a judicial office, a Member of Parliament or of the legislature to receive a bribe. It provides an offence will be committed if the official corruptly accepts, obtains, agrees to accept, or attempts to obtain any benefit[31] for himself or herself or another person in respect of anything done or omitted to be done by him or her in his of her official capacity.

B.75　Section 119(1)(b) of the same Code makes it an offence for a person to bribe a holder of judicial office, a Member of Parliament or of the legislature. It provides an offence will be committed if a person corruptly gives or offers any benefit[32] in respect of anything done or omitted or to be done or omitted by him or her in his or her official capacity for himself or herself or another person.

B.76　Consent of the Attorney General is required before a prosecution can be initiated[33] and the maximum penalty for both offences is 14 years' imprisonment.[34]

B.77　Section 120(a) of the same Code provides a similar offence for justices, police commissioners, peace officers, public officers or officers of a juvenile court, or employees in the administration of criminal law who corruptly accept or obtain benefits.[35] In addition to obtaining or accepting the benefit the official must do this with intent:

> (1)　to interfere with the administration of justice;
>
> (2)　to procure or facilitate the commission of an offence; or
>
> (3)　to protect from detection or punishment a person who has committed or who intends to commit an offence.

---

[31]　Defined by the same section as "any money, valuable consideration, office, place or employment".

[32]　Also defined by the same section as "any money, valuable consideration, office, place or employment".

[33]　Section 119(2).

[34]　Section 119.

[35]　Defined by the same section as "any money, valuable consideration, office, place or employment".

B.78   Section 120(b) provides the corresponding offence that makes it an offence for anyone to corruptly give or offer a benefit[36] to any of the officials in the above paragraph with the same intent.

B.79   The maximum term for both offences is 14 years' imprisonment.

Foreign public officials

B.80   Section 3(1) of The Corruption of Foreign Public Officials Act 1999 makes it an offence for any person, in order to obtain or retain a business advantage, to directly or indirectly give or offer or agree to give any loan, reward, advantage or benefit of any kind in consideration for either:

      (1)   an act or omission by the foreign official[37] in the course of his or her official duties of functions; or

      (2)   inducing the official to use his or her position to influence any acts or decisions of his or her foreign state[38] or organisation.

B.81   There is a defence available if the recipient can prove that the payment was a 'facilitation payment' to expedite or secure the performance of any act of a routine nature that is part of the official's duties of functions.[39]

---

[36]   Also defined by the same section as "any money, valuable consideration, office, place or employment".

[37]   "Foreign public official" is defined by s 2 to include:

(a)   a person who holds a legislative, administrative or judicial position of a foreign state;

(b)   a person who performs public duties or functions for a foreign state, including a person employed by a board, commission, corporation or other body or authority that is established to perform a duty or function on behalf of the foreign state, or is performing such a duty or function; and

(c)   an official or agent of a public international organisation that is formed by two or more states or governments, or by two or more such public international organisations.

[38]   "Foreign state" is defined by s 2 and means a country other than Canada.

[39]   Sections 3(4) and 3(5).

NEW ZEALAND

Public officials

B.82   The Crimes Act 1961 in New Zealand applies to bribery of public officials. Bribery is defined under the Act as "any money, valuable consideration, office or employment, or any benefit, whether direct or indirect".[40] Section 105(1) makes it an offence for a public official,[41] whether in New Zealand or not, to corruptly accept, obtain, agree, offer to accept or attempt to obtain a bribe for him or herself, in respect of his or her official duties. Section 105(2) contains the corresponding offence which prohibits anyone corruptly giving, offering or agreeing to give or offer any bribe with the intent that the bribe influence the official in respect of his or her official duties. The maximum penalty for both these offences is 7 years' imprisonment.

B.83   The Crimes Act 1961 also contains similar offences in respect of bribing judicial officers,[42] ministers of the Crown,[43] members of Parliament[44] and law enforcement officers.[45]

Jurisdiction

GEOGRAPHY

B.84   Section 105(1) states that it matters not whether the public official was in New Zealand when he or she accepted the bribe. In addition the provisions of section 105 of the Act appear to fall within the general application provisions of the same Act.

B.85   Section 5(2) provides that the Crimes Act applies to all acts done or omitted in New Zealand. Section 6 states that in general, no act done or omitted outside New Zealand is an offence in New Zealand. However, if part of the act done or omitted to be done that forms part of the commission of the offence is committed in New Zealand the offence is deemed to have been committed in New Zealand by virtue of section 7. Section 8 also provides the New Zealand courts have jurisdiction where P is:

> (1)   on board any Commonwealth ship;
>
> (2)   on board any New Zealand aircraft;
>
> (3)   on board any ship or aircraft, if that person arrives in New Zealand on that ship or aircraft in the course or at the end of a journey during which the act was done or omitted;

---

[40]   Section 99.

[41]   Officials are defined by s 99 as "any person in the service of Her Majesty in right of New Zealand (whether that service is honorary or not, and whether it is within or outside New Zealand), or any member or employee of any local authority or public body, or any person employed in the Education service."

[42]   Section 101.

[43]   Section 102.

[44]   Section 103.

[45]   Section 104.

(4)   a British subject, on board any foreign ship (not being a ship to which he belongs) on the high seas, or on board any such ship within the territorial waters of any Commonwealth country; or

(5)   a New Zealand citizen or a person ordinarily resident in New Zealand, on board any aircraft provided the act was not done or omitted by a person, not being a British subject, on any ship or aircraft for the time being used as a ship or aircraft of any of the armed forces of a country that is not a Commonwealth country

unless the act or omission would not have been an offence under the law of the country of which the person charged was a national or citizen at the time of the act or omission.

PERSONS TO WHOM THE SECTION APPLIES

B.86   A public official is defined by section 99 as: any person in the service of Her Majesty (whether honorary or not, and whether within or outside New Zealand), or any member or employee of any local authority or public body, or any person employed in the Education service.

B.87   A payer who bribes a public official would appear to mean a citizen or ordinary resident of New Zealand. Ordinary resident is defined by section 4 of the Crimes Act as someone:

(1)   whose home is in New Zealand;

(2)   who is residing in New Zealand with the intention of residing therein indefinitely; or

(3)   who having resided in New Zealand with the intention of establishing his or her home therein, or with the intention of residing in New Zealand indefinitely, he or she is outside New Zealand but has an intention to return to establish his or her home therein or to reside in New Zealand indefinitely.

Foreign public officials

B.88   Section 105C of the Crimes Act 1961 sets out an offence of bribing a foreign public official. Section 105C(2) provides a person will be guilty of such an offence if he or she corruptly gives or offers or agrees to give a bribe to a person with intent to influence a foreign public official[46] in respect of any act or omission by that official in his or her official capacity (whether or not the act or omission is within the scope of the official's authority) in order to:

---

[46] "Foreign public official" foreign public official includes any of the following:

(a) a member or officer of the executive, judiciary, or legislature of a foreign country;

(b) a person who is employed by a foreign government, foreign public agency, foreign public enterprise, or public international organisation; and

(c) a person, while acting in the service of or purporting to act in the service of a foreign government, foreign public agency, foreign public enterprise, or public international organisation.

(1)   obtain or retain business; or

(2)   obtain any improper advantage in the conduct of business.

B.89   The section does not apply if the act that is alleged to constitute the offence was committed for the sole or primary purpose of ensuring or expediting the performance by a foreign public official of a routine government action; and the value of the benefit is small.[47]

B.90   Under section 106D a person cannot be prosecuted for bribing a foreign public official without the leave of the Attorney General, who before giving leave may make such inquiries as he thinks fit.

Jurisdiction

B.91   Section 105D provides that if P commits an offence against section 105C but the public official is outside New Zealand territory he or she is still guilty of an offence provided P is :

(1)   a New Zealand citizen;

(2)   ordinarily resident in New Zealand;

(3)   a body corporate incorporated in New Zealand;

(4)   a corporation sole incorporated in New Zealand.

B.92   However, section 105E provides that no offence will be committed if the act that is alleged to constitute an offence:

(1)   was done outside New Zealand; and

(2)   was not, at the time of its commission, an offence under the laws of the foreign country in which the principal office of the person, organisation, or other body for whom the foreign public official is employed or otherwise provides services, is situated.

SOUTH AFRICA

B.93   The Prevention and Combating of Corrupt Activities Act 2004 criminalises corruption in both the public and private sectors, including foreign officials. Section 3 contains a general offence of corruption which makes it an offence for any person to, directly or indirectly, accept, agree, offer, give or offer to give to any other person any gratification (whether for his or her own benefit or not) in order to act personally or by influencing another to so act, in a manner that amounts to either:

(1)   an illegal, dishonest, unauthorised, incomplete or biased exercise of any powers, duties or functions arising out of an obligation;

---

[47]   Section 105C(3).

(2)   a misuse or selling of information or material acquired in the course of the exercise of any powers, duties or functions arising out of an obligation;

(3)   the abuse of a position of authority;

(4)   a breach of trust; or

(5)   the violation of a legal duty or set of rules;

or is designed to achieve an unjustified result or that amounts to any other unauthorised or improper inducement to do or not to do anything.

B.94   Sections 4 to 9 contain similarly worded provisions in respect of the following individuals:

(1)   public officers as defined by section 1 to include any person who is a member, an officer, an employee or a servant of a public body, except judicial officers;[48]

(2)   foreign public officials as defined by section 1 to include any person holding a legislative, administrative or judicial office of a foreign state; any person performing functions for any foreign state; and officials and agents of public international organisations;[49]

(3)   agents as defined by section 1 to include any authorised representative who acts on behalf of his or her principal,[50] including any director, officer, employee or other person authorised to act on behalf of his or her principal;[51]

(4)   members of the legislative authority;[52]

(5)   judicial officers as defined by section 1 to include any judges, arbitrators, mediators, umpires, adjudicators, assessors and other presiding officers;[53] and

(6)   members of the prosecuting authority.[54]

B.95   The Act also criminalises certain corrupt acts, including:

(1)   corrupt activities relating to witnesses and evidential material;[55]

---

[48] Section 4.

[49] Section 5.

[50] Section 1 defines a "principal" to include any employer, beneficiary and representatives.

[51] Section 6.

[52] Section 7.

[53] Section 8.

[54] Section 9.

(2)   corrupt activities relating to contracts;[56]

(3)   corrupt activities relating to procuring and withdrawal of tenders;[57]

(4)   corrupt activities relating to auctions;[58]

(5)   corrupt activities relating to sporting events;[59] and

(6)   corrupt activities relating to gambling and games of chance.[60]

B.96   Section 25 provides it is not a defence to the above offences for P to claim he or she:

(1)   did not have the power, right or opportunity to perform or not perform the act in relation to which the gratification was given, accepted or offered;

(2)   accepted or agreed or offered to accept, or gave or agreed or offered to give the gratification without intending to perform or not to perform the act in relation to which the gratification was given, accepted or offered;

(3)   failed to perform or not to perform the act in relation to which the gratification was given, accepted or offered.

Foreign public officials

B.97   On the 12 June 2007 South Africa became the 37th signatory and first African country to join the OECD's Anti-Bribery Convention which outlaws the bribery of foreign public officials in international business transactions. It is thought as the above law already extends to foreign public officials, the provisions are likely to stay the same.

---

[55] Section 11.

[56] Section 12.

[57] Section 13.

[58] Section 14.

[59] Section 15.

[60] Section 16.

APPENDIX C
BRIBERY LAW IN THE UNITED STATES

C.1 In connection with the Law Commission's consideration of new bribery legislation for England and Wales, we asked Professor Stuart Green of the Louisiana State University Law Center to draft a paper on the law of bribery in the United States. His paper forms this Appendix.

INTRODUCTION

C.2 The American law of bribery (and of corruption, more generally) consists of an enormously complex collection of overlapping and interlocking statutes and regulations enacted at both the federal and state level. In this memorandum, I begin with a survey of the four major US public bribery statutes: 18 U.S.C. section 201 (bribery and gratuities), 18 U.S.C. section 666 (federal program bribery), 18 U.S.C. section 1951 (the Hobbs Act), and 15 U.S.C. section 78 (the Foreign Corrupt Practices Act). I then offer a brief discussion of the federal law of commercial bribery and of state bribery law. I conclude by addressing a number of specific issues namely:

(1) the extent to which bribery law requires the breach of a principal-agent relationship or some other legal or equitable duty;

(2) the difficulty of distinguishing bribery from legitimate campaign fundraising; and

(3) the effectiveness of these laws in preventing bribery from occurring.

SECTION 201: BRIBERY AND GRATUITIES

C.3 The most venerable federal bribery statute is 18 U.S.C. section 201, originally enacted in 1962 to consolidate several separate provisions. There are two separate offences contained in section 201. Section 201(b) covers bribery proper (punishable by up to 15 years' imprisonment, a fine of three times the value of the bribe, and disqualification from holding federal office). Section 201(c) covers the lesser offence of illegal gratuities (punishable by up to two years' imprisonment and a fine).

C.4 To prove bribery under subsection (b), the government must show that:

(1) a thing of value was offered or given to, or solicited or accepted by;

(2) a public official

(3) for an "official act"; and

(4) with corrupt intent or intent to influence (or be influenced).

(5) The term "public official," in turn, refers to Members of Congress and any

officer or employee or person acting for or on behalf of the United States, or any department, agency or branch of the Government thereof ... in any official function, under or by authority of any such department, agency, or branch of Government.

C.5   One need not be a government employee in order to be a recipient under section 201. It is enough that one occupies a position of trust with official federal responsibilities. Thus, the provision was held applicable to employees of a private non-profit corporation that administered a sub-grant from a municipality's federal block grant.[1] The statute also applies to bribes given to, or accepted by, jurors and by witnesses.[2]

C.6   The term "thing of value" has been read broadly. It refers to a wide range of things both tangible and intangible, such as offers of future employment, unsecured short-term (and subsequently repaid) loans, restaurant meals and tickets for athletic events, ostensibly valuable (but actually worthless) stock certificates, and even sexual favours.[3] There does not appear to be any applicable *de minimis* exception.

C.7   With respect to the meaning of "official act," there has been somewhat more disagreement among the courts. Some courts have construed the term broadly to refer to acts that were not within the defendant's official duties.[4] Others have read the statute narrowly to exclude acts that were not sufficiently specific and pending.[5]

C.8   "Corruptly," under the bribery provision, is deemed equivalent to a "specific intent to give or receive something of value *in exchange for* an official act."[6] It is often referred to as a quid pro quo requirement. A vague or generalised expectation of future benefits is not sufficient to make a payment a bribe.[7] There is no requirement that the bribery attempted achieve its objective. Thus, the statute has consistently been held to be violated even if the official who is bribed has no authority to take the requested action.[8]

---

[1]   *Dixson v United States* (1984) 465 US 482, 496.

[2]   18 U.S.C. § 201(b) (3) & (4).

[3]   See Stuart P Green, "What's Wrong with Bribery?," in *Defining Crimes: Essays on the Special Part of the Criminal Law* (R A Duff & Stuart P Green, eds. 2005) 143, 149.

[4]   *United States v Parker* (1998) 133 F 3d 322 (Social Security Administration employee's use of computer to fraudulently create documents was official act though outside her official duties).

[5]   *Valdes v United States* (2007) 475 F 3d 1319 (police officer's use of computer to search police database was not official act because it did not involve any matter then pending before the police department).

[6]   *United States v Sun-Diamond Growers* (1999) 526 US 398, 404 to 405 (emphasis in original).

[7]   *United States v Arthur* (1976) 544 F 2d 730, 734.

[8]   Eg, *United States v Anderson* (1974) 509 F 2d 312, 332; *United States v Evans* (1978) 572 F d 455, 480.

C.9   It is the requirement of a quid pro quo that marks the crucial difference between bribes under section 201(b) and gratuities under section 201(c). A bribe consists of something being given "in exchange for" an official act, whereas a gratuity consists of something being given as a reward "for" an official act; it does not require an intent to influence or be influenced in any way. Furthermore, in order to be a gratuity, a payment must be made in connection with a *specific* official act. A conviction cannot rest on evidence that the defendant gave something of value merely to create goodwill or ingratiate himself or herself with a government official.[9]

C.10 The difference between payments given "in exchange for" an official act and those given "for" an official act is hardly a clear one. One way to understand the difference between bribes and gratuities is in terms of timing. If the payment is given with the intent to reward an official for conduct that has already been performed or committed to, then it is a gratuity. If the payment is made in order to influence an act that has not yet been committed to, then it is a bribe.[10] Unfortunately, the courts have been reluctant to follow such a bright line rule.[11] In any event, prosecutors typically include both offences in an indictment, allowing the jury the option to return a lesser verdict, much as the charge of manslaughter can function in an indictment for murder.[12]

SECTION 666: FEDERAL PROGRAM BRIBERY

C.11 Title 18 U.S.C. section 666 was enacted in 1984 to extend the reach of federal bribery law beyond federal officials and witnesses, where federal money is involved.[13] In order to prevail under section 666, the government must prove that:

(1)   the defendant solicited or received, or offered or gave, a thing of value;

(2)   the thing of value was solicited or received, or offered or given, in order to benefit an agent of a private organisation, or of a state, local, or Indian tribal government, or any agency thereof;

(3)   the thing of value was given "in connection with any business, transaction, or series of transactions of [an] organization, or of a state, local, or Indian tribal government, or any agency" thereof, involving anything of value of $5,000 or more;

(4)   the defendant acted "corruptly"; and

(5)   the entity for which the defendant acted as an agent received more than $10,000 a year in federal assistance.

---

[9]   See *United States v Sun-Diamond Growers* (1999) 526 US 398, 404 to 405.

[10] This is the approach recommended in Charles B. Klein, "What Exactly is an Unlawful Gratuity After *United States v Sun-Diamond Growers*?" (1999) 68 *George Washington Law Review* 116.

[11] Above.

[12] J Kelly Strader, *Understanding White Collar Crime* (2d ed. 2006) p 174.

[13] See generally George D Brown, "Stealth Statute – Corruption, the Spending Power, and the Rise of 18 USC. § 666" (1998) 73 *Notre Dame Law Review* 247.

C.12   The statute carries a maximum penalty of ten years' imprisonment.

C.13   There is some confusion in the lower courts about whether section 666 should be construed as applying only to bribes or also to gratuities. The statute says that the statute is violated if the defendant "corruptly gives ... anything of value... with intent to influence or reward" an official.[14] To the extent that things must be given "corruptly," it would seem to be limited, like section 201(b), by the quid pro quo requirement of bribery. On the other hand, unlike section 201(b), the statute refers not only to "influencing" officials, but also to "rewarding" them. As a result, some courts have said that section 666 criminalises not only corrupt bribes but also corrupt gratuities (an animal that does not exist under section 201), presumably a gift given in exchange for a specific action already performed.[15] Whether this is so is an issue that the Supreme Court might eventually have to resolve.

HOBBS ACT: EXTORTION UNDER COLOUR OF OFFICIAL RIGHT

C.14   A third major federal anti-corruption statute is the Hobbs Act, 18 U.S.C. § 1951, originally enacted in 1946. The Act criminalises three distinct forms of criminal conduct:

(1)   robbery;

(2)   extortion by force, threat, or fear; and

(3)   extortion under colour of official right.

C.15   Only the third is relevant here. Extortion under colour of official right constitutes the defendant's use of his or her official position to extract something of a value from the alleged victim – understood, essentially, as the taking of a bribe. It is punishable by up to twenty years' imprisonment.

C.16   In order to prove that the defendant committed extortion under colour of official right, the prosecution must show that:

(1)   the defendant's acts affected interstate commerce;

(2)   the defendant obtained, or attempted to obtain, another person's property to which the defendant was not entitled;

(3)   the property was obtained, or would have been obtained, with the other person's consent;

(4)   the defendant acted with the required mens rea; and

(5)   the property was obtained, or would have been obtained under colour of official right.

---

[14]   18 U.S.C. § 666(a)(2).

[15]   *Eg, United States v Bonito* (1995) 57 F 3d 167, 171.

C.17   Although the requirement is not explicit on the face of the statute, the court has held that the Hobbs Act colour of official right provision does require a quid pro quo or the promise of a quid pro quo akin to that required under section 201(b).[16]

C.18   The most significant difference between sections 201 and 666 and the Hobbs Act is that the former apply only to bribery and gratuities involving federal officials and others exercising federal responsibilities or dealing with federal funds. Thus, a local mayor or state legislator who received a bribe not involving federal funds would not be liable under either statute. He or she could, however, be prosecuted under the Hobbs Act. And because local and state prosecutors are frequently reluctant, or too politically entangled, to bring charges against corrupt local and state officials under state law, federal prosecution is often the only realistic option.

C.19   Another difference between section 201 and the Hobbs Act is that section 201 applies to both recipients and payers, while the Hobbs Act applies only to recipients. Technically, the person who pays a bribe to a state or local official in contravention of the Hobbs Act is a victim of extortion. This is so even though no coercion is required on the part of the government official under the colour of official right provision. Indeed, the Court has held that bribe need not even be "induced" by the government official; the official who takes the payment is liable even when the transaction was initiated by the payer.[17]

FOREIGN CORRUPT PRACTICES ACT

C.20   A final provision that needs to be considered is the Foreign Corrupt Practices Act (FCPA), codified in various provisions of 15 U.S.C. sections 78m, 78dd, and 78ff. It was originally enacted in 1977, in the wake of post-Watergate efforts at government reform. The Act makes it a crime to bribe foreign public officials for business reasons and further mandates corporate record keeping that would reveal the bribe payments. The statute originally applied only to payments originating inside the United States, but was extended in 1998 to reach bribes originating outside the country as well.[18] Thus, US companies are now liable for the acts of foreign employees. The statute contains both civil and criminal penalties (with a maximum penalty of twenty years in prison).

C.21   The anti-bribery provisions of the Act, 15 U.S.C. sections 78dd-1, dd-2, and dd-3, make it a crime for:

    (1)   an issuer of certain public securities or for any agent of such issuer;

    (2)   to offer or give something of value to;

---

[16]   *McCormick v United States* (1991) 500 US 257. There is, however, some disagreement about whether such agreement must be explicit. Compare *McCormick v United States* (1991) 500 US 257, 273 (agreement of quid pro quo must be explicit) with *Evans v United States* (1992) 504 US 255, 257 (quid pro quo requirement met whenever the jury finds that a "public official has obtained a payment to which he was not entitled, knowing that the payment was made in return for official acts").

[17]   *Evans v United States* (1992) 504 US 255, 265.

(3)   a foreign official; and

(4)   with the intent to corruptly influence an official act or decision, induce an action in violation of a lawful duty, or secure an improper advantage, or induce any act that would assist the company in obtaining or retaining business.

C.22   The Act applies to foreign agents of US companies who are located outside the US, but it does not apply to the foreign officials who solicit or receive such bribes.[19] In other words, the statute applies exclusively to payers. In that sense, it is the converse of the Hobbs Act.

C.23   The term "corruptly" is not defined in the statute, though the legislative history states that it refers to an intent to "induce the recipient to misuse his official position ... ."[20] It goes on to state that the word "corruptly" is

> used in order to make clear that the offer, payment, promise or gift, must be intended to induce the recipient to misuse his official position in order to wrongfully direct business to the payor or his client, or to obtain preferential legislative or a favourable regulation. The word "corruptly" connotes an evil motive or purpose, an intent to wrongfully influence the recipient.[21]

C.24   A good example of how this provision has been interpreted can be seen in the Eighth Circuit's decision in *United States v. Liebo*.[22] Liebo was an executive at NAPCO, an American military contractor which agreed to be subcontractor to a West German firm that had entered into a series of contracts with the Government of Niger. Barke was an official at the Niger Embassy in Washington and the cousin of Tiemongo, a top official in the Niger Air Force who played a key role in the contract approval process. At about the time the government of Niger was considering whether to approve the third contract, Barke was married, and Liebo paid for the airline tickets for Barke's European honeymoon. At trial, Barke testified that he considered the tickets a "gift" from Liebo personally. Liebo argued that the evidence failed to show that he had acted corruptly in giving Barke the tickets. The Eighth Circuit disagreed. It held that there was sufficient evidence from which a jury could infer that Liebo had acted corruptly. Not only was there a close relationship between Barke and Tiemongo, but Liebo had, for accounting purposes, classified the purchase of the tickets as a "commission payment."[23]

---

[18]   At about the same time, the thirty industrialised nationals belonging to the Organisation for Economic Co-operation and Development (OECD) were persuaded to sign a treaty agreeing to adopt similar criminal laws. Another six non-member nations had signed by late 2006.

[19]   *United States v Blondek* (1990) 741 F Supp 116, 119 to 120.

[20]   Sen Rep No 114, 95th Cong, 1st Sess 1, reprinted in 1977 US Code Cong & Admin News 4098, 4108.

[21]   Above.

[22]   (1991) 923 F 2d 1308.

[23]   Above at 1312.

C.25 Corruptly giving a payment to a foreign official for the purpose of securing an improper advantage is the fourth and final kind of inducement prohibited by the act.[24] There is no definition of the term "improper advantage" in the statute or in the case law. The best explanation I have seen is that the term refers to advantages obtained from an official that do not relate to any governmental function. For example, if a foreign official were induced to put in a "good word" with a commercial firm in the official's country, that would constitute an "improper advantage," even though it did not involve a government act.[25] In this sense, the FCPA sweeps more broadly than section 201.

C.26 Not all payments to foreign officials by covered US firms are prohibited under the FCPA: the statute includes several significant exceptions. First, the Act expressly allows "facilitating" or "grease" payments to foreign officials to "expedite or to secure the performance of a routine governmental action" so long as the payments are not used to encourage a foreign official to award new business or to continue business with a particular party.[26] Second, the FCPA allows an affirmative defence if the defendant can show that the payment constituted a "bona fide expenditure."[27] For example, the Department of Justice has stated that it would not take action against companies that had given money to foreign officials to allow them to travel to the US to meet with US officials about employment issues or to attend seminars.[28] Third, another affirmative defence is allowed when a "payment, gift, offer or promise of anything of value" to a foreign official" is made "in accordance with the written laws and regulations" of that country.[29]

C.27 It should be clear that the FCPA does not permit a defence based on the contention that "everyone does it." Mere custom or practice within the foreign official's country cannot form the basis of an affirmative defence.[30] Rather, the defendant must show that a given payment was authorised under the country's written laws and regulations. Thus, there are in fact instances where American law would prohibit American firms and their agents from participating in certain practices overseas even though such practices are regularly allowed in the foreign nation.

---

[24] The others being influencing the official's action in the context of the individual's official capacity, inducing the foreign official to do or not to do an act in violation of the individual's lawful duty, and inducing the official to influence or affect an act or decision of his or her government.

[25] See Stuart H Deming, *The Foreign Corrupt Practices Act and the New International Norms* (Chicago: American Bar Association, 2005) p 14.

[26] 15 U.S.C. §§ 78dd-1(b), 78dd-2(b), 78dd-3(b).

[27] 15 U.S.C. §§ 78dd-1(c)(2), dd-2(c)(2), dd-3(c)(2).

[28] See US Department of Justice, Foreign Corrupt Practices Act Review: Review Procedure Release No. 04-03 (14 June 2004), available at http://www.usdoj.gov/criminal/fraud/fcpa/opinion/2004/0403.html; US Department of Justice, Foreign Corrupt Practice Act Review: Review Procedure Release No. 04-01 (6 January 2004), available at http://www.usdoj.gov/criminal/fraud/fcpa/opinion/2004/0401.html.

[29] 15 U.S.C. §§ 78dd-1(c)(1), dd-2(c)(1), dd-3(c)(1).

[30] See also Stuart H Deming, *The Foreign Corrupt Practices Act and the New International Norms* (Chicago: American Bar Association, 2005) p 18.

C.28 There is little case law interpreting the FCPA, in part because the statute was only rarely used until recently and in part because companies charged under the Act almost always plead guilty or settle with the government rather than risk the potentially ruinous consequences of going to trial.[31]   Use of the Act is now on the upswing, however.[32]   In the last four years, the federal government has prosecuted 53 cases under the Act, more than in the previous 26 years combined.[33]   Such heightened activity seems to be the result of more demanding financial disclosure requirements under the Sarbanes-Oxley Act of 2002, increased scrutiny of American firms abroad, and greater international co-operation in the war against corruption, such as cross-border evidence gathering, asset seizures, and speedier extradition.[34]

RELATIONSHIP AMONG THE VARIOUS STATUTES

C.29 Unlike the criminal law in many states, federal criminal law is not codified. Despite various attempts, Congress has never been successful in enacting a coherent and comprehensive criminal code that would use terms consistently, eliminate redundancies, and fill in gaps. As a result, there tends to be a good deal of inconsistency and overlap among the various federal public bribery laws.

C.30 It is best to think of section 201(b) as the foundational provision. It applies to a wide range of federal officials as well as federal witnesses and jurors. Subsection (c), the gratuities provision, serves as something of a backup provision, when the government lacks proof to establish a quid pro quo. Section 666 extends the scope of federal bribery law to local governments and private individuals and entities receiving federal funds. Given the expansive definition of "federal official" in the *Dixson* case,[35] it is not obvious that Section 666 is really needed. Indeed, section 666 contains jurisdictional limitations not present in section 201.

C.31 The "extortion under colour of official right" provision in the Hobbs Act traces its lineage to a body of law separate from that of section 201. The fact that it, rather than section 201, is used to prosecute state and local officials reflects the peculiar jurisdictional requirements of a two-tier federal system, concern with which, presumably, is not relevant in the U.K.

C.32 The Foreign Corrupt Practices Act addresses a completely different set of cases from that addressed by sections 201 and 666 and the Hobbs Act. It is perhaps best thought of as addressing commercial bribery in an international context.

---

[31] Sarah N Welling, Sara Sun Beale, and Pamela H Busy, *Federal Criminal Law and Related Actions: Crimes, Forfeiture, the False Claims Act and RICO* (St Paul, Minn: West Group, 1998), vol 1, p 530.

[32] John Gibeaut, "Battling Bribery Abroad" *American Bar Association Journal* (March 2007) 48.

[33] Gerard Shields, "Corruption Act Use on Rise" *Baton Rouge Advocate* (13 June 2007) at 6A.

[34] Barbara Crutchfield George and Kathleen Lacy, "Investigation of Halliburton Co/TSJ's Nigerian Business Practices: Model for Analysis of the Current Anti-Corruption Environment on Foreign Corrupt Practice Act Enforcement" (2006) 96 *Journal of Criminal Law and Criminology* 503.

COMMERCIAL BRIBERY STATUTES UNDER FEDERAL LAW

C.33   In addition to these major federal statutes concerning public bribery, there is also a range of federal provisions concerning bribery in the commercial sphere. These include statutes that make it a crime to give or receive bribes involving subcontractors, investment advisors, television quiz shows, bank employees, alcoholic beverages, labour union officials, railroad employees, and radio disc jockeys.[36]   In practice, however, federal prosecutions for commercial bribery offences are quite rare. Indeed, this is one area of corruption law where state enforcement may be more active than federal (witness a recent resurgence of prosecutions under New York State's commercial bribery law, which has been used to combat allegedly rampant Payola in the commercial radio business[37]).

STATE LAWS CONCERNING BRIBERY

C.34   So far, we have been looking at a number of ways in which bribery can be prosecuted under federal law. It should be remembered, however, that there also fifty separate state systems, each with its own set of laws that make it a crime for a bribe to be offered to or accepted by a variety of public officials, including judges, legislators, and executive officers.

C.35   The precise formulation of these laws vary significantly, as do the sentences authorised, from a maximum of up to twenty-five years in New York,[38] to as little as one year for misdemeanour bribery in California.[39]

---

[35]   See above text accompanying n 1.

[36]   See 41 U.S.C. § 51 (prohibiting payments to contractors to secure subcontracts); 18 U.S.C. § 215 (bribery of bank employees); 27 U.S.C. § 205(c) (bribery in alcoholic beverage industry); 29 U.S.C. § 186 (bribery of labour representatives); 49 U.S.C. § 11907 (bribery of railroad employees). Commercial bribery can also serve as a predicate offence under the mail fraud, wire fraud, RICO, and Travel Act statutes.

[37]   Jeff Leeds, "Spitzer Sues Radio Chain as Part of Music Inquiry" *New York Times* (9 March 2006).

[38]   New York Penal Law §200.04 (McKinney 1999) (applying to bribery scheme in which the official act involves the investigation, detention, or prosecution of person suspected of having committed the most serious grade of felonies); see also Texas Penal Code §36.02 (Vernon 2003).

[39]   California Penal Code §67.5 (West 1999) (one year maximum for misdemeanour bribery and maximum of three years for felony bribery); see also Arizona Revised Statutes § 13-2602 (2001). Another provision worth mentioning here is Model Penal Code Art 240.1. The Article is a broadly worded provision that makes a person guilty of bribery if he or she offers, confers or agrees to confer upon another, or solicits, accepts or agrees to accept from another any pecuniary benefit as consideration for the recipient's decision, opinion, recommendation, vote or other exercise or discretion: (1) as a public servant, party official or voter; or (2) in a judicial or administrative proceeding. The Model Penal Code is often used as the model for state laws, although less so for bribery and other "white collar" crimes than for offences such as theft and homicide.

C.36 Many states also have laws that make bribery a crime in the commercial context.[40] As noted, New York's commercial bribery law has been used of late in the Payola context.[41] Some of these state laws are quite broad. Consider, for example, Texas law, which makes it a felony for a fiduciary, such as an agent, employee, trustee, guardian, lawyer, physician, officer, director, partner, or manager to accept or agree to accept any benefit from another person. In addition this must be "on agreement or understanding that the benefit will influence the conduct of the fiduciary in relation to the affairs of his beneficiary."[42] Were such statutes to be applied broadly, the impact on commercial life would be profound.

THE REQUIREMENT OF A PRINCIPAL-AGENT RELATIONSHIP

C.37 In an earlier work, I argued that the breach of the agent's duty of loyalty to his or her principal is in fact the gist of what makes the taking of a bribe morally wrong.[43] Certainly, if one looks at core cases of bribery involving judges, legislators, and Executive Branch officials, the breach of the principal-agent relationship continues to be the dominant paradigm. But, looking more broadly at how bribery law has developed in the United States in recent years, one can observe a steady movement away from this traditional paradigm.

C.38 In its earliest history, bribery was restricted to cases involving payments to judges. By taking payments from litigants, such judges presumably breached their duty as agent to a principal – whether it was the government, the courts, or the system of justice. By extending the reach of bribery law to other kinds of government officials – such as legislators and members of the Executive Branch, all of whom act as agents on behalf of their constituencies – there was no fundamental break with this paradigm.

C.39 In recent years, however, adherence to the traditional paradigm seems to have eroded. Each of the major federal statutes considered above, as well as the Model Penal Code provision,[44] offer examples of this trend. Consider first section 201. Among the kinds of persons who are capable of taking a bribe or gratuity under this section are jurors and witnesses. Unlike legislators, judges, and Executive Branch officials (who are also covered by section 201), jurors and witnesses have no obvious principal to whom they owe a duty of loyalty. They are in a sense "private contractors," obliged to obey various rules of court and to be truthful or impartial, as the case may be, but essentially answerable only to themselves. It is hard to see how a principal-agent relationship would be breached in such cases.

---

[40] See *Perrin v United States* (1979) 444 US 37 44 ns 9 and 10 (listing state commercial bribery statutes).

[41] N.Y. McKinney's Penal Law § 180.

[42] Texas Penal Code 32.43.

[43] See Green n 3 above.

[44] See n 38 above.

C.40 The departure from the principal-agent paradigm is also clear in the case of bribery under section 666. Here, the only requirement is that the bribe be paid to someone who is involved in a program that receives some substantial benefit from the federal government. Many recipients of federal program bribes are employees of private companies. Although the recipient of federal funds may have certain legal duties of care to observe, there is no principal-agent relationship in the usual sense of the term.

C.41 The extent to which a principal-agent relationship is required under the Hobbs Act is also doubtful. The focus of the statute seems to be not on the local official's breach of duty to his or her principal, but rather on the wrongful use of his or her power to extract money from an innocent citizen.

C.42 As for the Foreign Corrupt Practices Act, as noted, the statute applies exclusively to payers, rather than to recipients. The US Congress presumably has no legitimate interest in criminalising breaches of duty by foreign officials to their governments. And it would be difficult in any event for US courts and prosecutors to make a determination as to when such a duty is breached. The US Government's sole interest here is that American companies and their agents remain free of entanglements in foreign corruption (or even the appearance of foreign corruption). Once again, then, in the context of the FCPA, breach of the agent-principal relationship seems to be beside the point.

C.43 As, whether there is some legal or equitable duty *other than* that arising out of the agent-to-principal relationship – such as a duty to act impartially – of which inducement to breach might be required no such duty is explicitly mentioned in the statutes. However, it nevertheless seems reasonable to infer its existence from the requirement that the defendant be influenced in an "official act." This is defined under section 201(a) as a:

> decision or action on any question, matter, cause, suit, proceeding or controversy, which may at any time be pending, or which may by law be brought before any public official, in such official's official capacity, or in such official's place of trust or profit.[45]

C.44 The fact that the statute requires that the act induced be an official one seems to suggest the existence of a job-related duty that would be breached.

---

[45] Section 201(a)(3).

C.45 The puzzling cases, I suspect, are those in which an official is offered or given payment to do something that he or she is already required by law to do. Here we can imagine two variants. The first is the case of a legislator or judge who accepts money to do what he or she is already required to do. Such an official could be said to have breached his or her duty to his or her principal. The duty owed is not a duty to make one particular decision or another, but rather a duty to act *because* such decisions are in the principal's interest.[46] The second case is that of the juror or witness who is given money in exchange for his or her agreement to testify truthfully or rule in an impartial manner. Here, the case is even more difficult because there is no obvious duty of agent to principal. Nevertheless, I believe that these cases would still constitute bribery. Once again, the witness and juror would be agreeing to do the right thing, but for the *wrong reason*. They are required to be truthful or impartial not because they are paid to do so, but because that is what their position requires. And part of being truthful or impartial, arguably, is doing so for the right reason.

THE DIFFICULTY OF DISTINGUISHING BRIBERY FROM LEGITIMATE CAMPAIGN FUNDRAISING

C.46 The American political system, unlike the United Kingdom's, is highly dependent on private fundraising. At the federal level, candidates for Congress and the Presidency raise many millions of dollars for their electoral campaigns. The same is true in state and local campaigns for governor, state legislature, mayor, city council, district attorney, sheriff, judge, and numerous other governmental offices. Because so much money is constantly flowing from private citizens to government officials, it can be difficult to distinguish illegal bribes from legitimate donations given to a candidate because of her position on issues of importance to the donor.[47]

C.47 One court has identified a number of factors that can be taken into account in making such a distinction:

> whether the contribution was reported, whether it was unusually large compared to the contributor's normal donations, whether the official threatened adverse action if the contribution was not made, and how directly the official or those soliciting for him linked the contribution to specific official action.[48]

---

[46] I make a similar argument in Green n 3 above at 162.

[47] *McCormick v United States* (1991) 500 US 257, 272; Daniel H Lowenstein, "When is a Campaign Contribution a Bribe?" in *Private and Public Corruption* (William C Heffernan and John Kleinig, eds.) (Lanham MD: Rowman and Littlefield, 2004).

[48] *United States v Biaggi* (1990) 909 F 2d 662, 695.

C.48   Notwithstanding such guidance, however, the problem of distinguishing between bribes and legitimate campaign fundraising remains. Even the requirement in section 201 that money be given "in exchange for" a specific, pending official action does not necessarily ensure that legitimate campaign contributions will be exempt from prosecution. There are plenty of cases in which a donor, before making a contribution, would seek assurances that a public official plans to support (or oppose) some legislation. And the inclusion of gratuities, which consist of nothing more than gifts intended to obtain influence with, or good will from, an office holder, poses an even more significant potential for over-breadth. At the end of the day, it seems, the only effective way to avoid the over-broad application of such statutes is through the appropriate use of prosecutorial discretion.

DIFFICULTY OF EVALUATING EFFECTIVENESS OF CURRENT BRIBERY LAWS

C.49   As indicated above, the number and breadth of American bribery laws increased steadily during the 20th century. It is difficult, however, to assess the extent to which current legislation has been effective in reducing the actual incidence of bribery. Certainly, the fact that new bribery legislation continues to be enacted does not necessarily mean that the incidence of bribery has increased, or decreased. At best, we can say that it indicates greater legislative concern with the problem.

C.50   Two prominent commentators have said flat out that "it is impossible to say whether the multiplication of laws and prosecutions is reducing it, keeping even with it, or falling behind."[49] While there are data on how many prosecutions and convictions for "bribery" there have been in the federal courts in recent years (though not on which particular forms of bribery these have involved), there do not appear to be any data on how many cases of bribery were actually committed. It would be surprising, in any event, if there were not many more cases of bribery committed than the two hundred or so that typically make it into the US federal court system in a given year.[50]

---

[49]   See John T Noonan Jr and Dan M Kahan, "Bribery" in *Encyclopedia of Crime and Justice* (2d ed. 2002) vol 1 at 109.

[50]   *Sourcebook of Criminal Justice Statistics Online* (2005) (indicating that fewer than 200 bribery cases per year were filed during the period 2001 to 2005).

C.51   In theory, the enactment of new bribery legislation should send a signal that bribery will not be tolerated. In practice, the most important factor in preventing bribery is probably diligent enforcement, particularly when directed towards high profile defendants. Indeed, the United States seems to be in a period of heightened scrutiny for bribery crimes at the moment, with several congressmen convicted, indicted, or under investigation for bribery for the first time since the "Abscam" bribery stings of the 1980-81.[51]

C.52   One area in which there has been at least a genuine discussion about the effects of legislation on the incidence of bribery is in connection with the FCPA. Some commentators and business representatives have insisted that the large sums of money spent by corporations for FCPA compliance training and audits have surely led to a reduction in foreign bribery.[52] Many companies have also reported that their efforts at compliance have cost them business, by creating a supposedly unfair disadvantage for American companies competing abroad. All of this anecdotal evidence would tend to point to a reduction in the amount of bribery by American firms abroad since the enactment of the FCPA.

C.53   Unfortunately, such indicators are at odds with the Transparency International Bribe Payers Index, the only empirical study of the effectiveness of the FCPA in discouraging the use of bribery by US corporations in international business transactions. The Bribe Payers Index ranks the 21 leading exporting countries according to the degree to which their companies are perceived to be paying bribes abroad to senior public officials.[53] According to the latest survey of 835 experts in 15 leading emerging market countries, published in 2002:

C.54   US multinational corporations, which have faced the risk of criminal prosecution since 1977 under the Foreign Corrupt Practices Act, have a high propensity to pay bribes to foreign government officials. The US score of 5.3 out of a best possible clean 10 is matched by Japanese companies and is worse than the scores for corporations from France, Spain, Germany, Singapore and the United Kingdom.[54]

C.55   In short, contrary to what American businesses say about themselves, experts outside the US say that bribery by Americans doing business abroad is still quite common.

---

[51]   See, eg, David Johnson and Jeff Zeleny, "Congressman Sought Bribes, Indictment Says" *New York Times* (5 June 2007) at A1 (Louisiana Congressman William Jefferson); "Congressman resigns after bribery plea: California Republican admits selling influence for $2.4 million" CNN com (28 November 2005), http://www.cnn.com/2005/POLITICS/ 11/28/cunningham/(California Congressman Duke Cunningham); David D Kirkpatrick, "Lawmaker Tied to Inquiries Gives Up Seat on Committee" *New York Times* (20 April 2007) at A18 (California Congressman John Doolittle).

[52]   Wesley Cragg and William Woof, "The US Foreign Corrupt Practices Act: A Study of Its Effectiveness" (2002) 107 *Business and Society Review* 98, 100.

[53]   Transparency International, http://www.transparency.org/policy_research/surveys_indices/bpi.

[54]   Quotation from page 2 of the Summary Press Release. The full report can be downloaded from the Transparency International website.

C.56   While such survey results are not likely to be encouraging to American policy makers, there is perhaps some reason for cautious optimism. As noted earlier, the FCPA was only rarely enforced until the last several years. Assuming that enforcement, rather than mere legislation, is the more important factor in determining deterrent effect, one might expect to see American companies score higher in future Bribe Payers Index surveys.

APPENDIX D
THE HARM OF BRIBERY: INDIVIDUAL OR MARKET- BASED

INTRODUCTION

D.1 The Government's 2003 Corruption Bill,[1] closely modelled on the Law Commission's draft Bill,[2] failed to progress through the Parliamentary process largely due to the criticism it received at the Committee stage.[3] The most fundamental of these criticisms related to the Law Commission's identification of the harm of bribery in terms of duty and the resulting structure of the new offence around the agent/principal model. The Joint Committee concluded that:

> by adopting only the agent/principal approach the Bill does not proceed on the right basis and that corrupt acts outside that relationship ought to be included in the Bill.[4]

D.2 To illustrate the point, the Committee provided examples of the 'corrupt acts' which fell outside the reformed offence. Most notably, these included bribery between principals (in which no agent is involved) and bribery where the agent has the consent of his or her principal (a defence under the Government's Bill). As a solution to these perceived deficiencies, the Committee made note of an alternative model advocated by their specialist advisor Professor Peter Alldridge ('the market model').[5] Professor Alldridge contends that the agent/principal model is inappropriate because it focuses on individual betrayal, whereas, in order to encompass all corrupt acts within a reformed bribery offence and to do so accurately, the offence should be focused on the harm caused to the markets.[6]

---

[1] Cm 5777.

[2] Appended to Legislating the Criminal Code: Corruption (1998) Law Com No 248.

[3] Joint Committee on the Draft Corruption Bill, Session 2002-2003 HL Paper 157, HC 705 (2003).

[4] Above, para 55.

[5] The Joint Committee eventually rejected the market model, in part because of the lack of evidence available to them concerning its effects upon the major stakeholders. However, the Committee indicates their support for the model at several points and the report includes a lengthy note by Peter Alldridge setting out the model in full (Annex 4).

[6] Peter Alldridge, "The law relating to free lunches" 23 *Company Lawyer* (2002) 264.

D.3   The central aim of this Appendix is not to defend the agent/principal model.[7] Nonetheless, although we recognise that acts of bribery can often have a profound effect on markets, we do not accept that market distortion is the offence's principal or unifying harm. Equally, when reforming the law of bribery, we do not accept that every act subjectively termed 'corrupt' should necessarily be included within our definition. In this vein, a reformed bribery offence should be structured by taking account of the surrounding legislation that already tackles certain 'corrupt' behaviour under different heads of liability, for example, through competition law.

D.4   In what follows, this argument will be expanded upon considerably. We will first set out key elements of the market model. Following this, we will provide an overview of the existing competition law regime, asking to what extent it applies to conduct commonly referred to as corrupt. We will then consider whether a reformed offence of bribery would be more appropriate or effective at dealing with this type of conduct. Finally, we will identify the harm upon which a newly reformed offence of bribery should focus.

THE MARKET MODEL

D.5   The market model constructs its proposed offence of bribery upon the premise that the main harm created by corrupt conduct is its effect upon economic markets. To support this, reference can be made to the preambles of a series of international Conventions and declarations in which bribery's negative effect upon competition features prominently.[8] On this basis, it is possible to argue that the Law Commission's original approach was too narrow and that a new direction is required.

D.6   Professor Alldridge claims that the market model involves recasting the public/private distinction in the following way:

> That distinction is between, on the one hand, distorting the operation of a legitimate market, and, on the other, operating a market in things that should never be sold.[9]

He goes on to comment that:

> The lawyer may not be able to make a rigid and defensible distinction between the public and private sector, but both the economist and the lawyer know the difference between a legitimate market and a black market.

---

[7]   In fact, our eventual conclusion is that the agent/principal model is inappropriate for the reformed offence of bribery.

[8]   Peter Alldridge, "The law relating to free lunches" 23 *Company Lawyer* (2002) 264, 267. These include the OECD convention and the Lima declaration.

[9]   Above.

D.7   The term "a black market" usually refers to transactions of a market-type that are prohibited for some legal reason, for example, food rationing during and after World War Two. Arguably, such markets, although illegal, promote economic efficiency. Such transactions might fortuitously involve bribery but do not necessarily do so. They should not be equated with bribery. By contrast, Professor Alldridge uses the term "a black market" in a special sense. He means a market which involves trading in things which in principle ought not to be bought or sold, for example, information obtained by a policeman in the course of investigating an alleged offence.

D.8   On this basis, the market model constructs two separate offences. The type 1 offence, 'distorting competition within a legitimate market' is broadly intended to cover private sector bribery and would include a fault element of intention or recklessness. By contrast, the type 2 offence of 'creating or inducing the creation of a black market' is broadly intended to tackle public sector bribery. The mental element of this offence will merely require evidence that the person being offered an inducement was aware that he or she was being so offered.

D.9   Although our position will be explored in more detail later,[10] it is important to note that we agree with Professor Alldridge that inducing someone (or accepting an inducement) to create a black market should be caught within a reformed bribery offence.[11] However, so far as the type 1 offence of distorting competition within a legitimate market is concerned, we believe that the existing competition law regime is a more appropriate vehicle through which to approach this class of 'corrupt' conduct.

COMPETITION LAW AND 'CORRUPT' CONDUCT

D.10   Generally speaking, UK competition law is referable to two statutes. The first, the Competition Act 1998, contains the main prohibitions and borrows much of its substance from Articles 81 and 82 of the EC treaty. The second, the Enterprise Act 2002, introduces new offences that target individuals within undertakings that have been directly or indirectly involved in a breach of competition law. The Enterprise Act 2002 will become relevant when we discuss penalties below.[12]

D.11   Chapter 2 of the Competition Act (equivalent to Art 82 EC), targets undertakings that abuse their dominance within a market. Such abuse is largely irrelevant to the discussion of corrupt practices. By contrast, Chapter 1 (equivalent to Art 81 EC) targets anti-competitive agreements between undertakings. It is this prohibition that will provide the focus of the following discussion.

---

[10]   See paras D.48 to D.65 below.

[11]   Although we do not agree that it should be expressed in those terms or that it should be subject to that fault element.

[12]   See paras D.32 to D.36 below.

D.12 Although the Chapter 1 prohibition is almost identical to Article 81 EC, a few minor differences are apparent.[13] With this in mind, it is important to note that the national competition authorities and the national courts have a duty to apply Article 81 alongside Chapter 1 whenever it is applicable.[14] Beyond this, they also have a duty to interpret Chapter 1 "as far as is possible" to be consistent with European jurisprudence.[15] It is for this reason that the discussion will frequently refer to the case law of the European Court of Justice ('ECJ').

To what extent does Chapter 1/Article 81 deal with 'corrupt' practices?

D.13 The type 1 bribery offence of inducing another to act anti-competitively in a legitimate market, and the Chapter 1/Article 81 prohibition of anti-competitive agreements, appear relatively similar in their construction. With this in mind, the type 1 offence must offer something beyond the competition law prohibition if it is to be a useful addition to the criminal law. It is in this section that we explore the various elements of the Chapter 1/Article 81 prohibition to see if there are any 'corrupt' practices that fall outside its reach and therefore justify the creation of the type 1 offence.

Anti-competitive agreements between undertakings

D.14 The three-fold requirement that there must be an *agreement* to act *anti-competitively* and that this agreement must be made between *undertakings*, despite sounding restrictive, has been interpreted widely by the ECJ.

UNDERTAKING

D.15 The Chapter 1/Article 81 prohibition focuses, not on individual moral agents, but on economic entities. Therefore, even if it is possible to identify the individual employee who brokered an anti-competitive agreement, so long as they were only acting in the course of their employment, it will be the company and not the individual who breaches the prohibition.[16] That is not to say that an individual is incapable of constituting an undertaking, for example, someone who is self-employed.[17] Equally, a public body that does not have an economic function will not be an undertaking. The point is that the focus of Chapter 1 and Article 81 is on the function of the entity and not its legal personality.

D.16 Despite this wide 'function-based' approach from the ECJ, the contrast with the type 1 bribery offence, which focuses on the criminal liability of individuals, is stark. Already we can identify two classes of defendant that would not fall within the scope of the competition law provisions, but might be caught by a type 1 bribery offence. These are:

---

[13] For example, to breach Art 81(1), an agreement must have an effect on interstate trade, where as to breach s2 of Ch1, it need only effect UK trade.

[14] Article 3(1) of Reg 1/2003.

[15] Competition Act 1998, s 60.

[16] Case C-22/98 [1999] ERC 1-5665, para 26.

[17] Eg, in *Wouters v Alegemene Raad van de Nederlandse Order van Advocaten*, Case C-309/99 [2002] ECR 1-1577, the ECJ held members of the Dutch bar were to be considered individual undertakings for the purpose of Art 81.

(1)   an employee who gives or receives a bribe in the course of his or her employment. Although the employer is likely to be classed as an undertaking and therefore caught by Chapter 1/Article 81, the employee will not;[18] and

(2)   a body or organisation that does not fulfil an economic activity and is therefore not an undertaking. An example would be a sporting regulator when making or amending the rules of a sport.[19]

D.17   Although employees generally (as a class of defendant not adequately dealt with by the existing competition law) will be reassessed later in our discussion,[20] the second class of defendant identified above will not. We note that the competition law regime has chosen to expressly exclude this class of defendant because the risk they pose to the markets is so minimal. With this in mind, it would be unnecessary and undesirable for the criminal law of bribery to seek to target these individuals unless a secondary harm can be identified.[21]

AGREEMENT

D.18   As with the ECJ's interpretation of 'undertaking', 'agreement' has been given an expanded definition so as to include any anti-competitive act that is not truly unilateral.[22] In this vein, for an agreement to be found to exist, there is no need to demonstrate that it would be legally enforceable, with the European Court of First Instance (CFI) going so far as to include a simple "concurrence of wills".[23]

D.19   Although this purposive interpretation may be enough to deal with completed acts of bribery where there is an agreement between the two parties, there is a clear gap where an agreement is not reached. For example, if company X agrees with company Y that, in exchange for a sum of money, company Y will no longer market their product in a certain area, the Chapter 1/Article 81 prohibition will apply. However, if company Y refuses, there will be no agreement and so the competition law provisions will not apply.[24]

---

[18]   See Advocate General Jacobs in Case C-67/96, Albany International BV v Stichting Bedrijfspensioenfonds Textielindustrie [1999] ECR 1-5751, [2000] 4 CMLR 446.

[19]   When making or amending the rules of a sporting activity it is unlikely that the regulator will affect competition. Therefore under the function-based approach the regulator will not be an undertaking. However, if the regulator carries out an economic function, the fact that they are a sporting regulator will not automatically exclude them from Art 81. For example, in a case concerning the 1990 World Cup, both FIFA and the Italian FA were held to be undertakings and therefore within the scope of Art 81.

[20]   See paras D.49 to D.53 below.

[21]   See paras D.56 to D.57 below.

[22]   Anti-competitive unilateral acts are prohibited by Chapter 2/Article 82 and are contingent on the undertaking involved being the dominant actor in the relevant market.

[23]   Case T-41/96 Bayer AG v Commission [2000] ERC 11-3383. This was latter affirmed on appeal Cases C-2 & 3/01 P.

[24]   However, if the undertakings change their competitive behaviour after the failed agreement as a result of their discussions, a court may well still find that a form of agreement (concerted practice) had come about. This is why, in this example, it is likely that company Y would have to make full disclosure in order to avoid suspicion. However, the point remains that if company Y was successful in distancing itself from a potential agreement, the competition provisions would be unable to catch company X.

D.20   The representation of a willingness to confer an advantage is sufficient to come within the conduct element of our provisionally proposed new bribery offences. As a result, drawing on the previous example, company X (and/or the individual within company X who made the agreement) will be liable for bribery. This is therefore another example where Chapter 1/Article 81 alone would leave a gap in liability.[25]

ANTI-COMPETITIVE

D.21   Chapter 1/Article 81 proscribes agreements that prevent, restrict or distort competition by their "object or effect". This definition creates a two-stage approach that casts the net of the provisions extremely wide. The first stage is to inquire whether the object of the agreement was to harm competition.[26] If it was, there is no need to demonstrate that it actually had that result.[27] If it can not be shown that this was the object of the agreement, the second stage is to examine its effect. If the effect of the agreement was to harm competition, the agreement will come within the scope of the competition provisions.

D.22   The type 1 offence also focuses on the distortion of markets and so is unlikely to extend beyond the competition law in this regard.[28]

Exemptions from the Chapter 1/Article 81 prohibition

D.23   Article 81(3) allows for the possibility of an anti-competitive agreement being exempted from the Article 81(1)/Chapter 1 prohibition.[29] The exemption will only be available in extremely limited circumstances and only where it is essential to benefit the end consumer. It is therefore unlikely that it would apply to the majority of bribery-type offences.

D.24   However, considerably wider exemptions have emerged in the form of block exemptions for certain types of agreement. Most notably, this includes a block exemption that exempts all but the most anti-competitive vertical agreements (hard-core restrictions).[30] It was created because the European Commission took the view that vertical agreements are generally regarded as promoting, or at least having a neutral effect on, competition.

---

[25]   Later, when we discuss the Enterprise Act 2002, we will see that this *apparent* gap in the law is already filled by another competition law provision.

[26]   The subjective intention of the undertakings involved is not relevant to the question of whether an agreement had as its object the distortion of competition. Rather the court will look at the form of the agreement and make an assessment based on objective reasoning. See, for example, *Memorandum of Understanding on the Supply of Oil fuels in an Emergency,* 25 October 2001, paras 39 and 40.

[27]   *GISC* Case No 1003/2/1/01 [2001] CAT 4, [2001] CompAR 62.

[28]   It is interesting to note that, under the type 1 offence, bribery that seeks to open a market and increase competition would (presumably) not be covered.

[29]   Competition Act 1998, s 10 provides that the art 81(3) and block exemptions also apply to the ch 1 prohibition.

[30]   Regulation 2790/1999 and the Competition Act 1998, s 50. A vertical agreement is an agreement between undertakings that operate at different levels in a market. For example, if there is an agreement between a supplier and a distributor.

D.25   Although Article 81(3) and the block exemptions expose new gaps in the competition law regime, they are not gaps that a reformed bribery offence could fill. This is because of Article 3(2) of Regulation 1/2003. This Article prevents member states from legislating or applying existing legislation to prevent agreements that have been explicitly exempted from Article 81 in order to maintain a level playing field for competition. As a result, this particular species of agreement must remain legal.

Exemption under the De Minimis principle

D.26   For an anti-competitive agreement to be caught by Article 81(1) it must have the potential of affecting "trade between member states". This requirement has in turn led to the creation of a de minimis rule. The de minimis rule allows undertakings that have a very low share in a market, and whose agreements do not represent hard-core restrictions,[31] to be exempted from the Article 81 prohibition. The European Commission uses a market share percentage test, with agreements between competitors exempted only if their combined market share is lower than 10%, and non-competitors 15%.[32]

D.27   The UK Competition Act appears to impose an even more restrictive threshold, with the Chapter 1 prohibition only requiring agreements to have an appreciable effect on UK trade (as opposed to inter-state trade). Although the national courts have not adopted a de minimis rule as such,[33] the term 'appreciable' has been interpreted in such a way as to become a de facto rule. In its guidelines, the Office of Fair Trading ('OFT'), again excluding more stringent restrictions, sets out a combined market share threshold of 25% before an agreement can be said to have an 'appreciable' effect on UK trade.[34]

D.28   With potentially corrupt agreements between undertakings with low market shares being exempted from the Chapter 1/Article 81 prohibition, a gap in the competition law regime is clearly exposed. Further, unlike the agreements exempted by Article 81(3) and the block exemptions, there is no restriction at a European level preventing the UK from prosecuting these cases. However, this type of rule is the natural consequence of a policy based on competition principles. Accordingly, it is unlikely that an offence of bribery based on a market model (the type 1 offence) would fill this gap.

---

[31] For example, price fixing or market sharing.

[32] Commission notice on agreements of minor importance [2001] OJ C368/13, [2002] 4 CMLR 699.

[33] Case No 1009/1/1/02 *Aberdeen Journals Ltd v Office of Fair Trading* [2003] CAT 11, paras 459 to 462.

[34] *The Chapter 1 prohibition* (OFT Guideline 401), paras 2.18 to 2.22.

TARGETING INDIVIDUALS WITH THE CRIMINAL LAW

D.29 The Chapter 1 and Article 81 prohibitions on which this Appendix has so far been concentrating on are civil law provisions. As a result, the consequence for an undertaking that is found in breach is first that their anti-competitive agreement is declared void;[35] and second, that the regulators (whether at national or EC level) may impose a fine.[36] Beyond this, third parties who have suffered a loss as a result of the anti-competitive agreement can also bring separate actions for damages.[37]

D.30 As the undertakings have acted in order to make illicit profits or unfairly reduce losses, it seems appropriate to punish them in a financial way. However, the obvious deficiency of this, as with any civil law regime, is that although fines are able to punish the undertaking, one must rely on the internal policies of the undertakings involved to punish the individuals responsible for the agreement itself. As a result, there might seem to be a need for a criminal law offence that will target the individuals, possibly along the lines of the type 1 offence.

D.31 However, although the Chapter 1/Article 81 prohibitions are civil, they are already supplemented by a series of criminal laws. Therefore, we must also take account of these offences before we can make any firm conclusions in relation to the market model.

The Enterprise Act 2002

D.32 If an employee from undertaking X makes an anti-competitive agreement with undertaking Y in the course of his or her employment, undertaking X will itself be in breach of the Chapter 1/Article 81 prohibition.[38] To supplement this prohibition and create a further deterrent to its breach, the Enterprise Act 2002 'pierces the corporate veil' and allows for the prosecution of individuals within undertaking X.

D.33 The lesser of the two principal 'offences' created by the Enterprise Act is again a civil law offence. Section 204 applies to directors who either had knowledge of the brokering of the anti-competitive agreement, or should have had knowledge.[39] Without any further fault required, if found in breach, a director is liable to be disbarred from the role of director at that or any other undertaking, for up to 15 years.

---

[35] Article 81(2) EC and Competition Act 1998, Ch1 s 2(4).

[36] Competition Act 1998, s 36(1).

[37] The Enterprise Act 2002 has made several amendments to the Competition Act, which make it easier and more desirable for third parties to bring claims for damages. Section 20, for example, makes an original court's ruling of a breach in relation to Chapter 1 or Article 81 binding on a subsequent court ruling on third party damages. This means that the third parties no longer have to go over all the original evidence in order to make their claim.

[38] Assuming the agreement does not qualify for exemption.

[39] This second limb to the section casts its net considerably wider and prevents undertakings with poor internal reporting machinery profiting from their own negligence.

D.34   The principal offence created by the Enterprise Act is a cartel offence provided by section 188. The offence imposes criminal liability on those individuals that are personally involved in the brokering of the most serious anti-competitive agreements.[40] Although it does not cover all agreements that come within the Chapter 1/Article 81 prohibition, the list provided in the statute is still relatively wide, and, in relation to the reform of bribery, it is of particular note that one of the categories expressly included is that of bid-rigging.[41] Once convicted, an individual is potentially liable for up to five years' imprisonment and an unlimited fine.[42]

D.35   Having earlier identified the liability of individual employees as a potential gap in the current competition law regime that might have been filled by a type 1 bribery offence, we are now able to reassess this point in the light of the cartel offence. The cartel offence will catch any individual within an undertaking that takes part in a hard core anti-competitive agreement. Further, as the cartel offence is criminal, it will be subject to the inchoate offences of attempt, incitement and conspiracy. As a result, a charge of attempt could be brought where company x attempts, but fails, to make an anti competitive agreement with company y. This accounts for another of the potential gaps highlighted earlier in our discussion.[43]

D.36   As a result of the cartel offence, we already have broadly the same coverage that a reformed type 1 bribery offence would hope to install. This was precisely the point made by the Government in their response to the Joint Committee's criticism of the original Corruption Bill for not catering for principal to principal bribery.[44]

International application

D.37   Alongside the OECD convention,[45] which requires signatories to provide legislation to combat the bribery of foreign public officials, there has been an appreciation of the need to adequately cater for international bribery more generally. With this in mind, we will now examine the extra-territorial reach of the Article 81 and Chapter 1 prohibitions, as well as the cartel offence.

[40] The relevant fault element is one of "dishonest" agreement. Enterprise Act 2002, s 1(1).

[41] Enterprise Act 2002, s 188(2)(f). It is also interesting to note that the Serious Fraud Office, the authority responsible for investigating and prosecuting overseas bribery, also works closely with the OFT in relation to the cartel offence.

[42] Enterprise Act 2002, s 190. It is the eventual conclusion of this part that a reformed bribery offence should be designed to work in tandem with the cartel offence. It is therefore concerning that, with the Prevention of Corruption Act 1916 setting a maximum sentence of 7 years imprisonment for those convicted of bribery, the penalties for the two offences are inconsistent.

[43] See para D.20 above.

[44] The Government Reply to the Report from the Joint Committee on the Draft Corruption Bill, Session 2002-2003 HL Paper 157, HC 705 (2003), para 6.

[45] OECD Convention on Combating Bribery of Foreign Public Officials in International Business Transactions (1997), ratified by the UK in 1998.

Article 81 EC

D.38   For an anti-competitive agreement to be caught by the Article 81 prohibition, it must be capable of affecting "trade between member states".[46] The paradigm case is where at least one of the undertakings involved is registered within one of the member states. However, it has become clear from the case law of the ECJ that European competition law can apply even when neither of the undertakings are registered within the Union or even physically based within the Union.

D.39   As a result, the main debate has focused upon whether the competition law provisions have incorporated a US style 'effects doctrine' into the EC.[47] Despite the efforts of some notable advocates of that doctrine,[48] the ECJ has so far found other methods of assuming jurisdiction without explicitly endorsing its use. Two main routes have emerged.

D.40   The first route came via the *Dyestuffs*[49] case. This case is particularly interesting because it was an appeal based on the fact that the European Commission had started applying the 'effects doctrine'. However, the ECJ chose to assume jurisdiction based, not on that doctrine, but on the basis that the undertakings involved had subsidiaries which were based within the Union. As a result, the undertakings too, as parent companies, were held to affect trade between member states.

D.41   The second route came via the *Wood Pulp*[50] case. This case concerned an anti-competitive agreement between several foreign undertakings and associations of undertakings to fix the price of wood pulp. Again, despite the Advocate General calling on the court to adopt the 'effects doctrine', the court was able to establish jurisdiction via a different route. Drawing on *Dyestuffs* (but also extending it) the court held that because the undertakings sold their product within the Union, they therefore effected trade between states. This has become known as the 'implementation doctrine'.

D.42   Although to a large extent these cases have created a de facto 'effects doctrine' within the Union, they leave open the possibility of foreign undertakings making anti-competitive agreements to boycott certain European markets. However, as such a case is yet to emerge, we will have to wait to see how the court deals with it.

---

[46]   Article 81(1).

[47]   US Foreign Trade Antitrust Amendment Act (1982), s 6(a). The extremely wide doctrine allows the court to apply competition law to any agreement that could potentially have any effect on the national markets.

[48]   Eg, AG Mayras in *Dyestuffs* case 48/69 [1972] ECR 619, and AG Darmon in *Wood Pulp* cases 114/85 [1988] ECR 5193.

[49]   *Dyestuffs* case 48/69 [1972] ECR 619.

[50]   *Wood Pulp* cases 114/85 [1988] ECR 5193.

UK Competition Act

D.43 Consistent with Article 81, the international application of the Chapter 1 prohibition is expressed in relation to 'implementation' as opposed to effect.[51] Thus, for the Chapter 1 prohibition to apply, it must be demonstrated that the particular undertaking at least sells their product or service within the UK. If this is not the case, Chapter 1 will not apply. The national courts will then ask whether Article 81 applies.

UK Enterprise Act

D.44 The Enterprise Act cartel offence will only apply to foreign undertakings if the anti-competitive agreement "has been implemented in whole or in part in the United Kingdom."[52] Unlike the Chapter 1 prohibition, there are no European equivalents to the cartel offence. As a result, if an anti-competitive agreement has an effect on other member states but not the UK, the courts will not apply the cartel offence. This makes the international application of the cartel offence considerably narrower than that of the Article 81 prohibition.

D.45 Although the jurisdictional reach of a reformed bribery offence might extend beyond that of the cartel offence, if its focus were also on anti-competitive behaviour, this would make little sense. If an anti-competitive agreement has no effect on a country's territory or market, then there is little advantage in spending money enforcing national laws to prevent it.

OECD Convention

D.46 It is important to note again that the OECD Convention only requires signatories to legislate against the bribery of foreign public officials. Therefore it has no direct application to the discussion of anti-competitive behaviour unless the public official (or office they represent) can be defined as an undertaking.

D.47 Where this is the case, although the cartel offence will apply, its jurisdictional reach may cause problems. It is for this reason that the Government chose to legislate specifically on the matter in Part 12 of the Anti-terrorism Crime and Security Act 2001.

TARGETING INDIVIDUALS WITH A REFORMED BRIBERY OFFENCE

D.48 Having provided an overview of the most important competition law provisions, we now return to the issue of bribery legislation. In this section we look back at the most problematic areas within the competition law regime that we have highlighted as potential gaps to be filled by a reformed bribery offence. We consider first whether there is a genuine need for criminal liability, and secondly, if there is, whether this is most appropriately provided by an offence of bribery.

---

[51] Competition Act 1998, s 2(3).

[52] Enterprise Act 2002, s 190(3).

Individuals within an undertaking

An employee acting in the course of their employment

D.49   As indicated above, if an employee brokers an anti-competitive agreement in the course of their employment, the undertaking that they work for will be caught by the Chapter1/Article 81 prohibition. The potential gap highlighted concerned the individual liability of the employees themselves. This was then resolved when we went on to discuss the cartel offence and the Enterprise Act.

D.50   The Law Commission's previous recommendations on corruption[53] pre-dated the Enterprise Act and cartel offence. However, despite that lack of criminal sanction for employees at that time, the Commission concluded that the bribery offence should not cover this type of defendant because the 'consent' of the principal should act as a defence. This was criticised by the Joint Committee.[54]

D.51   Part of this criticism focussed on employees who might abuse the consent-based defence. As we have already heard from early consultation, it is extremely difficult for the prosecuting authorities to disprove a consent-based defence (to prove a negative). There are also issues, highlighted by the Joint Committee,[55] in relation to those that 'unreasonably' believe that they have been given consent. However, neither of these concerns lead us automatically to the rejection of consent as a legitimate defence. It simply means that when formulating the policy, we should give particular attention to alternative possibilities, for example, a reverse burden of proof on the employee to demonstrate consent and the importation of an objective standard.

D.52   However, this line of argument assumes that employees who genuinely have the consent of their employers should not be the targets of the criminal law. With the cartel offence came the rejection of this line of argument. The problem cases involve employees who are fully informed. At worst, these could be individuals specifically employed for their expertise at operating within corrupt markets. It was decided through the cartel offence, and it is also our current position, that the consent of an equally culpable employer should not be a sufficient excuse for such an employee to avoid the criminal law.

A rogue employee acting outside the course of their employment

D.53   When this was discussed above we concluded that there was no gap in the law. As soon as the employees act outside the course of their employment they are severed from their employers and become, for the purposes of the competition law, an undertaking in their own right.[56] Despite being the sole member of the undertaking, they may also be liable for the cartel offence.

---

[53]   Legislating the Criminal Code: Corruption (1998) Law Com No 248.

[54]   Joint Committee on the Draft Corruption Bill, Session 2002-2003, HL Paper 157, HC 705 (2003), paras 30 and 31.

[55]   Above.

[56]   We are taking for granted that they are performing an economic function if they are making an anti-competitive agreement.

A new bribery offence to supplement the cartel offence

D.54 Although, as demonstrated above, in theory the cartel offence can deal with this type of defendant, a bribery offence may be found to be more effective. It is noted, for example, that the cartel offence requires the prosecuting authority to demonstrate dishonesty in the defendant. This may prove to be a major barrier to prosecution, with the lack of case law in this area going some way to support this view. However, the cartel offence is still in its infancy.

D.55 An overlapping bribery offence would be possible under the market model. However, it would also be possible under the improper conduct model that we are advocating. Therefore, this does not provide conclusive support for the market model. Further, it is our belief that an overlapping bribery offence would add very little to this area of the law and if a problem is discovered, it seems more appropriate to amend the existing legislation rather than creating a new law. In fact, with industry becoming familiar with the existing competition regime, a further criminal offence that does not appear to add anything substantial would provide unnecessary complication.

Bribery where there is little or no effect on competition

D.56 At several points in our discussion we have highlighted gaps in the competition law regime that are unlikely to be filled by a bribery offence that is also structured around the harm of anti-competitive behaviour. This is one of the main dangers where two offences share the same rationale.

D.57 The gaps have included:

(1) bribery between bodies that perform no economic function and are not therefore undertakings within the meaning of the competition law provisions;

(2) bribery conducted by UK citizens in foreign territory where there is no implementing effect in the UK;

(3) bribery between undertakings with low market shares, resulting in exemption under the de minimis principle; and

If unfair competition is the central harm around which bribery should be defined, each of these gaps is likely to fall outside of the definition. We agree that in many cases this will be the appropriate result. However, we do not believe that this would always be true.

FILLING THE GAPS WITH THE MARKET MODEL

D.58 The market model claims that the central harm in bribery is its negative effect on markets. The type 1 offence would criminalise any inducement that is intended to subvert an organised market, and the type 2 offence would criminalise any inducement to create an illegitimate or black market. However, having examined the type 1 offence alongside the existing competition law regime and particularly the cartel offence, it does not appear to offer any *new* practical benefits.

D.59 Beyond the issues of practical utility, a further question arises over the theoretical soundness of the market model. The problem lies with the basis for the distinction between a legitimate and an illegitimate market, on which the market model relies.[57] We may recall that it was Professor Alldridge's contention that:

> The lawyer may not be able to make a rigid and defensible distinction between the public and private sector, but both the economist and the lawyer know the difference between a legitimate market and a black market.[58]

Professor Alldridge goes on from this statement to introduce his paradigm of the type 1 offence, that of a "buyer on the take",[59] much like the rogue employee.

D.60 However, if we are to accept (as we must under the type 2 offence) that bribing a policeman creates a black market because he is trading in things that "should not be bought and sold",[60] the case of the employee acting improperly (whether with or without the consent of his or her employer) does not seem so very different. As with the policeman, the employee is either breaching the terms of his or her employment or acting improperly in his or her role and thereby creating a market that should not exist (involving an advantage to him or her personally).

D.61 In fact, the only situation where an anti-competitive agreement would not result in the creation of an illegitimate market would be where the agreement had been exempted from the competition law regime. Here, it is neither desirable, nor possible under the UK's European obligations, to impose a criminal offence.

D.62 It is our contention that a bribery offence will only be committed where there is evidence of improper conduct.[61] This *may* be referred to as the creation of a black market, but this description does not alter the theoretical basis. If anything, it distracts attention from the truly universal harm of bribery that lies within ones individual responsibilities.

CONCLUSION

D.63 We believe that the current competition law regime is the most appropriate vehicle by which to tackle anti-competitive agreements, even if the conduct may also be described as corrupt. If an undertaking makes an anti-competitive agreement that is not exempt, the agreement will be void, they will be subject to a fine. Further, the individuals that were directly involved with the agreement will be individually subject to possible civil and criminal law sanctions, and those that conspired, encouraged or assisted will also be liable.

---

[57] It is important to note that this distinction is of more than academic interest as different fault elements apply depending on whether a type 1 or type 2 offence is prosecuted.

[58] Peter Alldridge, "The law relating to free lunches" 23 *Company Lawyer* (2002) 264, 267.

[59] Above.

[60] Above.

[61] We are including within this statement, both the general offence we are provisionally proposing, and the specific offence of bribing a foreign public official to gain or retain business.

D.64   The only gaps that we have exposed in the competition law regime have arisen where there is also improper conduct. As a result, we have been able to manage without the distinction made between offences under the market model.

D.65   Much crime has an indirect effect on markets. Yet, in order to give this consideration due weight, we do not find it necessary to structure every offence with reference to the markets. Equally, whilst the criminal law is based on the protection of society as a whole, each individual offence tends to refer only to those directly involved. As Professor Alldridge advocates and we accept, the market-based harm caused by bribery offences should be kept in mind when drafting a reformed offence. However, it is our contention that a general offence based on improper conduct can not only protect the markets to the same extent as the bribery offence created under the market model, but it can do so more effectively.

APPENDIX E
BRIBERY AND FRAUD

THE IMPORTANCE OF CONSIDERING THE RELATIONSHIP BETWEEN THESE OFFENCES

E.1 Just as it is important to set our proposals for reform of the law of bribery alongside existing competition law offences, so it is important to understand the relationship between these proposals and the law of fraud. The issue is given added significance by the fact that the Fraud Act 2006 ('the 2006 Act') post-dates our consideration of similar issues in 1998.

E.2 The 2006 Act considerably widens the scope of fraud offences in English law. This means that the 2006 Act now covers a range of conduct that, prior to the Act coming into force, it might only have been possible to address through the law of bribery. This is significant in that, as we have indicated,[1] where another offence already covers particular kinds of conduct, we take the view that it may be less controversial if the offence of bribery is also allowed to cover that conduct. This will permit conduct that is already criminalised in one way, to be dealt with through a different criminal offence (bribery) if that is more appropriate in the circumstances.

E.3 This point has particular importance so far as 'commission payments' are concerned, payments made by P to R in relation to the sale by R of P's (financial) products to a consumer.[2] It is much clearer now than it was prior to the passing of the 2006 Act that offences under the 2006 Act, and section 2 in particular, will apply to the worst kinds of unethical selling practice in this field. That being so, we do not believe it to be a problem – and it may be a benefit – that our proposed offence of bribery will also outlaw such practices.[3]

E.4 Our previous report[4] includes a discussion about the difference between fraud and corruption. It concluded that corruption should not be viewed as a fraud offence.[5] Two principal justifications were advanced:

(1) the actions of the *bribed* agent will not necessarily prejudice the material interests of the principal: it will not necessarily lead to a loss being suffered. For example, if the agent is bribed to do that which he or she is already bound to do by the principal;[6] and

(2) there is no requirement within bribery for the principal to be identifiable. Therefore, bribery extends to include public officials who are bribed to act against the interests of the state or population at large.

---

[1] See Part 1, paras 1.30 to 1.31 above.

[2] See Appendix F below.

[3] See paras E.42 to E.48 below.

[4] Legislating the Criminal Code: Corruption (1998) Law Com No 248.

[5] Above, para 5.129.

[6] Above, para 5.129.

E.5   Beyond this, the report further contends that making bribery into an offence of 'dishonesty' would unduly restrict its operation. Again, two principal arguments are advanced:

(1)   because the fault element of bribery ('corruptly') already identifies those cases that warrant criminal sanction, a further restriction of dishonesty is unnecessary;[7] and

(2)   the *Ghosh* test of dishonesty focuses first on societal and then on individual perception of wrongdoing. The risk is that corrupt practices will go unpunished simply because they have become 'normal practice' within a society. This is particularly relevant when it comes to the extra-territorial reach of bribery law into other legal and political cultures. It will materially affect, for example, the law's attempts to distinguish between legitimate and illegitimate corporate hospitality. If it is better to have a reasonably strictly defined scope for a bribery offence, rather than a fluid one based on societal perception, then the inclusion of an element of dishonesty in the offence is probably not desirable.

E.6   Significant though the changes have been to the law of fraud since 1998, we continue to believe that the observations in relation to 'dishonesty' are sound. Nonetheless, there is still good reason to re-consider the relationship between the new law of fraud and our provisional proposals for reform of the law of bribery.

Bribery and conspiracy to defraud

E.7   The Government has not abolished the offence of conspiracy to defraud in the 2006 Act. Accordingly, that offence remains available to deal with instances in which two or more people dishonestly agree to commit fraud. Some such instances will inevitably overlap with, and to a considerable extent go beyond, an offence of bribery. The very wide scope of the offence of conspiracy to defraud was made plain by Viscount Dilhorne in the decision of the House of Lords in *Scott v Metropolitan Police Commissioner*:[8]

... it is clearly the law that an agreement by two or more by dishonesty to deprive a person of something which is his or to which he is or would be or might be entitled and an agreement by two or more by dishonesty to injure some proprietary right of his, suffices to constitute the offence of conspiracy to defraud.[9]

[7]   Above, para 5.133.

[8]   [1975] AC 819.

[9]   [1975] AC 819, 840.

E.8   There is considerable overlap between conspiracy to defraud and bribery. An example would be where a witness agrees with a claimant to give false evidence so that, when the claimant receives judgment in his or her favour, they can share the award of damages. This constitutes both bribery and conspiracy to defraud (as well as a conspiracy to pervert the course of justice). There are also instances where the offence is either bribery or a conspiracy to defraud, but not both. Suppose a claimant threatens to dismiss an employee who is to appear as a witness unless the employee gives false evidence so that the claimant can win, and so the employee reluctantly agrees to give false evidence. This is a conspiracy to defraud (and a conspiracy to pervert the course of justice) but not bribery. By way of contrast, if a defendant pays a judge to give a favourable direction to the jury, this is bribery (and a conspiracy to pervert the course of justice) but not a conspiracy to defraud.[10]

E.9   It should be noted that a conspiracy to defraud can be committed when one or more of the conspirators enters the conspiracy in England and Wales (or does something in pursuance of it in England and Wales), even when the crime is intended to take place outside England and Wales.[11] Suppose D1 and D2, both British nationals, agree in Scotland to defraud a bank in Scotland. D2 is arrested in Carlisle after crossing the border into England to collect documents needed to perpetrate the fraud. D2 can be indicted in England and Wales for conspiracy to defraud.

E.10   By way of contrast, suppose D1 and D2, both British nationals, agree in Scotland to bribe a public official in Scotland. D2 is arrested in Carlisle having crossed the border into England to withdraw the money that is to constitute the bribe. D2 cannot be indicted in England and Wales for conspiracy to commit bribery.

E.11   Of perhaps more significance to the current project are some of the new offences of fraud created by the 2006 Act. These offences will in a considerable number of instances overlap with or go beyond bribery (although they may also be narrower in scope).

The new offence of abuse of position

E.12   Section 4 of the 2006 Act creates the offence of fraud by 'abuse of position':

> (1) A person is in breach of this section if he-
>
>> (a) occupies a position in which he is expected to safeguard, or not to act against, the financial interests of another person,
>>
>> (b) dishonestly abuses that position, and
>>
>> (c) intends, by means of the abuse of that position-
>>
>>> (i) to make a gain for himself or another, or

---

[10]   In our report Fraud (2002) Law Com No 276 paras 4.5 and 4.37, we set out those forms of conduct that can only be prosecuted as a conspiracy to defraud.

[11]   Criminal Justice Act 1993, s 5(3).

> (ii) to cause loss to another or to expose another to a risk of loss.
>
> (2) A person may be regarded as having abused his position even though his conduct consisted of an omission rather than an act.

E.13 In a 'bribery-like situation' where section 4 has been charged, the person receiving the bribe would be the person abusing their position for the purposes of section 4. The person offering the bribe would be inciting the commission of the section 4 offence.

General considerations about the overlap with bribery

E.14 The creation of this new offence encompasses a good deal of, and in some respects goes beyond, the existing offence of bribery. In other respects, it has a narrower application than bribery. Here are some examples.

E.15 First, section 4(1)(c)(i) states that fraud (by abuse of position) does not require the offender to be an 'agent' who has acted contrary to the interest of his or her 'principal', unlike section 1 of the Prevention of Corruption Act 1906 ('the 1906 Act'). Under section 4 it is sufficient that the person bribed is in a position in which they are expected to safeguard, or not to act against, another's financial interests: a wider concept.[12]

E.16 In that regard, the language used in section 4 has attracted some criticism, on the grounds of its vagueness.[13] It was proposed in the Standing Committee that "expected to safeguard" be replaced by "under a fiduciary duty", for reasons of clarity and certainty. This was ultimately rejected on the basis that the proposed amendment would draw the offence too narrowly. Examples were given of possible cases that should be regarded as fraud, which it was argued fell outside the ambit of fiduciary duty. This rejection is highly significant, in that in this CP we have also rejected reliance on already existing private law concepts, such as 'principal' and agent', in part for essentially similar reasons.

E.17 Parliament has taken the view that section 4 satisfies the need to strike the right balance between the requirements of justice and certainty when defining the conduct element of a fraud offence.[14] In the closely allied field of bribery, we believe that our understanding of a duty to act in another's best interests (as well of a duty to act impartially), is capable of striking that balance correctly in a similar way. In that regard, the fact that the question whether such a duty existed is a matter for the judge is an important safeguard against unpredictability.

---

[12] We consider in paras E.23 to E.31 below whether the relationship in which someone is expected to safeguard the financial interests of 'another person' can extend to public officials acting on behalf of the state or the general public, for the purposes of section 4.

[13] Standing Committee B, cols 11 to 28 (20 June 2006). See also David Ormerod, "The Fraud Act 2006 – Criminalising Lying" [2007] *Criminal Law Review* 193.

[14] We are not concerned here with the fault element: see Part 6 above.

E.18   Secondly, bribery used to be wider than the older fraud offences in that unlike, for example, obtaining property by deception, bribery did not require someone (the principal) to have suffered a loss. It was sufficient under section 1 of the 1906 Act that the agent agreed to accept an inducement or reward for (say) showing favour or disfavour to someone in relation to the principal's affairs. Now, however, the new fraud offence created by section 4 likewise requires no actual loss to be suffered as a result of the fraud. It requires only an intention to make a gain, to cause someone a loss or to expose someone to a risk of loss. So, in exchange for money, to grant someone access to confidential financial information for which one has responsibility may contravene section 4, even though no actual loss results from this action. However, the section 4 offence is narrowly concerned with financial or proprietary loss or gain. By way of contrast, bribery can be committed when the advantage at issue is non-financial, such as excessive corporate hospitality.

E.19   Thirdly, the concept of 'abuse' of position may include conduct that R is ordinarily entitled to do, in just the way that such conduct may amount to bribery. An example might be where R accepts money from a third party to invest trust money in that third party's investment fund. In this instance, R may well have been perfectly entitled to invest the trust money in that particular fund under the rules of the trust. Nevertheless, for R to choose that particular fund simply because he or she has been paid to do so seems to be an abuse of position, and therefore fraud (as well as bribery), whether or not the trust beneficiaries suffer loss in consequence.

E.20   Where public officials are concerned, a question arises whether the section 4 offence includes cases where R accepts payment for doing what he or she is already bound to do in precisely the way R was bound to do it, whereas our provisionally proposed offence does not. It may be easier to argue that the official's action in such cases is an 'abuse of position' as that concept is defined in the 2006 Act, because the acceptance of the payment may itself be regarded as an abuse of position. By way of contrast, under our provisional proposals, the focus on improper conduct rather than on improper payment will mean that in this kind of case there must – independent of the payment - be a breach of a duty of impartiality, or of the duty to act in someone's best interests, to which the payment relates.

E.21   Having said that, in this respect the difference between the scope of the two offences is not likely to prove great in practice. We believe that most cases of so-called 'facilitation' payments will involve a straight-forward breach of the duty of impartiality, and will hence be bribery; and in cases involving non-financial reward, they will only be bribery, not the section 4 offence.

Focus on victim as 'another person'

E.22   A feature of the section 4 offence is its apparent focus upon an individual victim. Section 4(1)(a) talks about the "financial interests of *another person*". Depending on the court's interpretation, this focus upon the individual has the potential to limit the breadth of the offence. Two points stand out in that regard.

APPLICATION TO PUBLIC OFFICIALS

E.23   The first question is whether the duty to safeguard the financial interests of 'another person' can properly be interpreted so as to encompass a duty to safeguard the financial interests of the state or of the general public. Were that approach to be taken, the offence would cover public officials who abuse their position.

E.24   A reference to public officials is conspicuously absent from the Law Commission's discussion of what became the section 4 offence. In the Law Commission report, instances where 'abuse of position' might be founded on a particular kind of relationship are described as follows:

> The necessary relationship will be present between trustee and beneficiary, director and company, professional person and client, agent and principal, employee and employer, or between partners.[15]

E.25   Having said that, by virtue of section 4(3) of the Prevention of Corruption Act 1916, a person serving under a public body is an 'agent' for the purposes of the 1906 Act which prohibits corrupt behaviour on the part of agents with regard to their principals. There may have been no intention to exclude that meaning of 'agent' when the scope of the offence under section 4 of the 2006 Act came to be considered by the courts in relation to facts resembling bribery of a public official.[16]

E.26   Professor Ormerod argues that the section 4 offence is capable of including public officials.[17] Further, in the Government's response to consultation just prior to the passing of the 2006 Act, an example of a section 4 offence is given involving foreign officials.[18]

E.27   If section 4 does apply to public officials, there will be many instances in which public officials are under a 'section 4 expectation' that they will safeguard the financial interests of 'another person'.[19] These instances will extend well beyond cases in which public officials have specific responsibilities for managing funds. That would be a change from the position under the old law of fraud.

E.28   It is possible, for example, that the acceptance by officials of undisclosed corporate gifts from companies which have been awarded contracts by those officials on behalf of Government could be covered by section 4, as well as by the offence of bribery. This seems likely to depend on whether the intention to make a gain (in the form of the gift received) by awarding the contract, in itself turns the award of the contract into an abuse of position.

[15] Paragraph 7.38.

[16] In our previous report on corruption, we took the view that the agent/principal relationship extended to the relationship between public officials and public bodies.

[17] David Ormerod, "The Fraud Act 2006 – Criminalising Lying" *Criminal Law Review* (2007) 193.

[18] Fraud Law Reform: Government response to consultation, para 26. Available at www.homeoffice.gov.uk/documents/cons-fraud-law-reform/Government_response.pdf? view=Binary.

[19] A point highlighted by Professor Ormerod in "The Fraud Act 2006 – Criminalising Lying" *Criminal Law Review* (2007) 193, 209.

E.29 Having said that, there will be instances in which only bribery can be charged against a public official. Not all public officials are expected to safeguard financial interests. Further, the section 4 offence is confined to gains and losses of money or other property. So, in the example just given in paragraph E.28, if the contract was awarded and the benefit subsequently accepted was lavish hospitality rather than gifts, the conduct would not fall within section 4.

E.30 What if a gift was accepted *before* the contracts were awarded? The conduct of the public officials in question would be bribery - or possibly conspiracy to defraud – but it might not amount to the section 4 offence. This is because the contracts may not have been awarded with the intention to make a gain or cause a (or expose to a risk of) loss thereby. However, situations in which section 4 did not apply might turn out to be quite unusual. A more typical situation might be one in which the decision to favour a company that provided a gift involved failing to award the contract to other bidders. If so, then an intention to expose someone (the British Government and the public at large) to a risk of loss – through being bound by a possibly less favourable contract - could be inferred. As we said in our report on Fraud:

> In our view it should be sufficient for the new fraud offence if the defendant causes [the victim] to part with money or other property, whether or not the [victim's] overall financial position is adversely affected.[20]

E.31 Clearly, section 4 is concerned only with the abuse of a position in which there is an expectation that P will safeguard *financial* interests. So, as indicated earlier, if a judge accepts money to give a direction to a jury favourable to the defendant, bribery is committed but not the section 4 offence. This is because the judge has not abused a position in which he or she is expected to safeguard the financial interests of another person.

PRIVATE SECTOR EXAMPLES NOT CAUGHT BY SECTION 4

E.32 In some instances, the restriction in section 4 to cases where someone was under a duty to safeguard the financial interests of 'another person' may also limit the impact of the offence in the private sector.

E.33 A useful example might be one in which a football player ('R') agrees to accept a bribe from P to lose a match, in circumstances where the payment is to be made after the match has been played.

---

[20] Fraud (2002) Law Com No 276, para 7.44.

E.34   If the player is a professional at a club, he or she will have knowingly accepted an inducement in exchange for breaching an express or implied term in his or her contract with a football club.[21] In these circumstances, it is perhaps arguable that R has abused his or her position, in that there is an expectation that footballers will, by playing to the best of their ability, at least ensure that they do not 'act against' (to use the language of section 4) the financial interests of the club and its shareholders.

E.35   That argument may involve a somewhat stretched interpretation of section 4, an interpretation that the courts could reject. In any event, as we will see shortly, the footballer is much more likely to have committed an offence under section 3 of the 2006 Act.

E.36   If the player is not a professional, then section 4 has no application, even though the player has behaved immorally. It should be noted, however, that if in each case the known purpose of the agreement between P and R is to win bets made with bookmakers, then in each case P and R are guilty of a conspiracy to defraud.

The new fraud offence under section 3

E.37   Section 3 of the 2006 Act makes it an offence to fail to disclose information in certain circumstances:

> A person is in breach of this section if he-
>
> (a) dishonestly fails to disclose to another person information which he is under a legal duty to disclose and
>
> (b) intends, by failing to disclose the information-
>
>> (i) to make a gain for himself or another, or
>>
>> (ii) to cause loss to another or to expose another to a risk of loss.

E.38   This provision may cover a great deal of conduct related to bribery, as well as covering instances in which bribery may have no application.

---

[21] He or she will also have breached regulations governing professional football. See, FIFA Status and Transfer of Players Regulations art 5(1) which states that when signing for a professional club, the player is agreeing to be bound by FIFA's rules. These rules, for example art 12 which deals with the bribery of match officials, forbid all parties from receiving advantages in exchange for affecting the outcome of a match.

E.39   For example, consider the hypothetical case mentioned in paragraph E.28 above in which public officials accept gifts from companies, on the basis of which contracts are then awarded. Whether or not this conduct is covered by section 4, it is highly likely to be covered by the section 3 offence, if the gifts are retained and never declared or handed over to the relevant Government department. The public officials will in such circumstances have failed to disclose information that they are under a duty to disclose (that they have accepted corporate gifts in the course of their employment). They will also have done this intending the department – the owner of the gift in equity – to make a loss in the form of the gift itself.

E.40   The offence will also have a wide application in the private sector where bribery also applies. An example would be where R agrees to accept money offered by P if R will give financial advice on investment funds to X that favours P's investment funds. This is bribery if R is X's agent with respect to the giving of financial advice. It will also contravene section 3 if R fails to inform X of the transaction with P, intending thereby to make a gain in the form of the payment from P, because R is under a legal duty to disclose this information. If R is paid *before* he or she gives X the advice, the section 3 offence will probably still apply, because it can be inferred that R intended to expose X to a risk of loss by failing to disclose the information.

E.41   In the example in paragraph E.33 in which a professional football player accepts money to lose a match, the player may be guilty of a section 3 offence. He or she is almost certainly under a legal duty to disclose to the club his or her sources of income (other than the club itself) from playing for the club. Further, his or her failure to make disclosure is motivated by an intention to make a gain (where the payment comes after the match). If the payment is made before the match, the question will be whether an intention to expose the club to a risk of loss can be inferred from the failure to disclose the information.

The new fraud offence under section 2

E.42   Under section 2 of the 2006 Act:

(1) A person is in breach of this section if he –

(a) dishonestly makes a false representation, and

(b) intends, by making the representation –

(i) to make a gain for himself or another, or

(ii) to cause loss to another or to expose another to a risk of loss.

(2) A representation is false if –

(a) it is untrue or misleading, and

(b) the person making it knows that it is, or might be, untrue or misleading.

(3) 'Representation' means any representation as to fact or law, including a representation as to the state of mind of –

    (a) the person making the representation, or

    (b) any other person.

(4) A representation may be express or implied.

E.43   This offence may be of importance in a number of areas on which the law of bribery also impinges. As indicated above, an example is commission payments.

E.44   The kind of case that would be covered by section 2 is one in which an agent (R) decides that, for example, the nature or size of the commission being paid to him or her by a company (P) for selling their financial products is such that R will seek to sell those products to consumers even if it is not in their interests to purchase such products. In such a case, R is likely to be caught by section 2 in any case where, expressly or by implication, he or she has falsely represented that it is in the consumers interests to purchase the product but the real reason for making the sale is that R wishes to earn the commission.

E.45   In that regard, the breadth of section 2 is worth noting. R will be criminally liable under section 2 if his or her express or implied representation (section 2(4)) relates only to his or her *belief* (section 2(3)) that it is in the consumer's interests to buy the product. The representation does not have to relate to whether, in fact, it is in the consumer's interests to buy the product. Further, it is sufficient if R knows that the representation may be untrue or misleading; it is not necessary for it actually to be untrue or misleading. Finally, R will commit the offence even if the consumer is not fooled and refuses to buy the product. The offence is committed when the representation (that it is in the consumer's interests to buy the product), and not only when the consumer goes on to purchase the product.[22] Finally, it will not make a difference that R has, for example, received commission payments 'up front', and so does not intend to make a gain from any individual transaction. It is sufficient that, by recommending that the consumer buy the product, R intends to expose the consumer to the risk of loss, in that R knows it may not be in the consumer's interests to buy it (section 2(1)(b)(ii)).

E.46   For the sake of completeness, it should be noted that in this example P may also be complicit in the fraud offence committed by R, if there was a joint enterprise (between P and R) involving the commission of the offence by R, or if P intentionally encouraged or assisted R to commit it. P may also be found guilty of a conspiracy to defraud the consumers, in cases where there was an agreement to commit the offence.

---

[22] Overturning, in effect, the case of *Hensler* (1870) 11 Cox CC 570.

E.47   Under our provisional proposals, in this kind of case R (and in some cases also P) may additionally commit bribery. R will commit bribery if the commission payment is R's primary reason for recommending P's product to the consumer, and in recommending it R breaches an equitable duty involving a breach of a relation of trust or a duty to act impartially or in the best interests of the consumer. P will be guilty of bribery if, when agreeing to make the commission payment:

    (1)   P intends the payment to be the primary reason for R to sell the products over and above the best interests of the consumer; or,

    (2)   P realises that there is a serious risk that it will be R's primary reason for selling the products, over and above the best interests of the consumer, but goes ahead nonetheless to promise to make (or to make) the payment.

E.48   We do not believe that the proposed bribery offence will cover more ground, or intrude on a greater range of (unethical) market practices, than the new fraud offence already does. What the new offence will do is give prosecutors an alternative offence to fraud that can be charged when, for example, labelling considerations suggest that what has been done bears the hallmarks of bribery rather than fraud. This might be the case, for example, when no consumer has been fooled by R's false representations, and so prosecutors are reluctant to charge fraud, for fear that the jury will – in spite of the language of section 2 – fail to see how fraud has been committed when no one was actually deceived.

Extra-jurisdictional questions under the 2006 Act

E.49   The offences under the 2006 Act do have as wide an extra-jurisdictional application as does the offence of bribery. The common law offence of bribery as well as the statutory offences under the 1889 Act and the 1906 Act extends to cases in which a United Kingdom national commits an offence of bribery outside the United Kingdom. In their response to consultation on the Fraud Bill, the Government specifically ruled out extending, in accordance with the 'nationality principle', fraud's extra-territorial reach so that it matched that of the bribery offences.[23]

E.50   The Government explained that while it was appropriate to provide corruption offences with extra-territorial application, the same logic did not apply to fraud. This was because:

    (1)   fraud is considerably wider than bribery and is committed much more often (resource implications);

    (2)   the UK has ratified treaties which require the extra-territorial enforcement of bribery laws; and

---

[23]   Fraud Law Reform: Government response to consultation, para 58. Available at www.homeoffice.gov.uk/documents/cons-fraud-law-reform/Government_response.pdf ?view=Binary . See also David Ormerod, "The Fraud Act 2006 – Criminalising Lying" [2007] *Criminal Law Review* 193, 215.

(3)   the damage that can be done to the reputation of the UK by its nationals committing bribery abroad is more serious than fraud.

ARGUMENTS IN FAVOUR OF A REFORMED BRIBERY OFFENCE DISTINCT FROM FRAUD

E.51   It would in theory be possible to expand the scope and jurisdictional reach of conspiracy to defraud, and of the new fraud offences, in such a way as to make all but a limited category of bribery offences redundant. In our view, that would not be the right course.

E.52   Fraud will almost certainly continue to involve a requirement of 'dishonesty' in its definition, which we have argued is an inappropriate restriction in an offence of bribery.

E.53   Fraud is primarily concerned with wrongful conduct intended to make a financial or proprietary gain or to impose a financial or proprietary loss (or risk of loss). While such gains or losses are often at issue in bribery cases, bribery cases are by no means confined to such gains and losses. Someone can also be bribed by non-financial inducements, such as excessive hospitality or sexual favours.

E.54   To seek to account for bribery through expansion of the definition and reach of other offences, like fraud and conspiracy to defraud, may distort the application of those offences in other as yet unknown contexts. An offence designed to tackle fraud will be interpreted with that purpose in mind. The same is true of a specific bribery offence. The danger of one offence being employed to fulfil both purposes would be either that the two purposes conflict and gaps develop or that the offence is defined too broadly and provides inadequate legal certainty.

E.55   More broadly, there is a very strong argument that we should not dispense with the label of 'bribery' for certain kinds of criminal conduct, even if that conduct falls within the scope of some other offence. Such offence labels – like 'arson', 'murder', 'rape', 'burglary', and so forth – have an intrinsic moral significance that is lost when it is sought to define the offending conduct without reference to the label, or by merging the offence with another offence. Moreover, to dispense with an offence of bribery because it is thought that the conduct in question will be covered by other offences has the potential to send a message that bribery is no longer a problem or a priority.

E.56   Finally, to seek to account for bribery through expansion of the definition and reach of other offences would not do full justice to the international obligations the United Kingdom has accepted with regard to the modernisation of the law of bribery. For example, the OECD often expresses a preference for specific bribery legislation. This most often occurs in relation to competition law, but the same points are easily transferred to the discussion of fraud.

APPENDIX F
FACILITATION PAYMENTS, COMMISSION PAYMENTS AND CORPORATE HOSPITALITY

INTRODUCTION

F.1 In this Appendix we examine in further detail three areas which have already emerged in discussion. The first section addresses facilitation payments, the second discusses commission payments and the final section focuses on corporate hospitality.

F.2 In each of these areas, which are particularly controversial within the law of bribery, certain commentators have contended that specific provisions and/or defences are required. We explore in each case whether such provisions would be desirable.

F.3 It is our belief that the general offence of bribery that we are provisionally proposing is equipped to deal with each of these areas. We will set out the reasons for this belief in each case.

FACILITATION PAYMENTS

Overview

F.4 This section is divided into four parts as follows:

(1) it begins by explaining what a facilitation payment is and the problems it poses when formulating an offence of bribery;

(2) the arguments for and against allowing facilitation payments are then outlined, highlighting the approaches taken and difficulties experienced by other jurisdictions;

(3) the application of the concept of "improper conduct" to facilitation payments is considered; and

(4) our provisional proposal is stated and questions for consultees detailed.

What are facilitation payments?

F.5 It is generally accepted that a facilitation (or "speed" or "grease") payment is a payment made with the purpose of expediting or facilitating the provision of services or routine government action which an official is normally obliged to perform.

F.6 However, TRACE[1] has observed that the precise definition of facilitation payments is "often unclear and stretched to breaking point".[2] Various definitions include:

(1) "payments made to petty officials to induce them to perform their public duties where otherwise they may be disinclined to do so";[3]

(2) "small payments made to secure or expedite the performance of a routine or necessary action to which the payer of the facilitation payment has legal or other entitlement";[4]

(3) ""according to rule" corruption (as opposed to "against the rule" corruption) whereby a bribe is paid to receive preferential treatment for something that the bribe recipient is required to do by law";[5]

(4) "payments or gifts to, or favours for, government officials in exchange for preferential treatment";[6]

(5) "payments made to secure or speed up routine legal government actions, such as issuing permits or releasing goods held in customs";[7]

(6) "payments ... made to a person who is already under a duty to do something and ... designed to make him either do that duty or do it more quickly or more efficiently."[8]

The problem posed by facilitation payments

F.7 On the whole, it is agreed that facilitation payments are a form of bribery and so in principle should be prohibited. But it is also often maintained that, in practice, they are a necessary and acceptable part of business.

---

[1] An international non-profit membership organisation providing anti-bribery support to companies and their intermediaries worldwide. Members include Microsoft, Exxon Mobil, Northrop Grumman, United Parcel Service, General Electric, Honeywell, Marathon Oil, Dow Chemical, American Express and FedEx.

[2] The High Cost of Small Bribes, TRACE (2003): www.fundworksinvestments.com/fn_filelibrary//File/co_gsri_high_cost_small_bribes.pdf.

[3] Nicholls, Daniel, Polaine and Hatchard, *Corruption and Misuse of Public Office* (2006), para 2.10.

[4] Business Principles for Countering Bribery, December 2002, produced by Transparency International, Social Accountability International and a Steering Committee.

[5] Transparency International: http://www.transparency.org/news_room/faq/corruption_faq.

[6] The High Cost of Small Bribes, TRACE (2003): www.fundworksinvestments.com/fn_filelibrary//File/co_gsri_high_cost_small_bribes.pdf.

[7] BP Code of Conduct, p 49: http://www.bp.com/liveassets/bp_internet/globalbp/STAGING/global_assets/downloads/C/coc_en_full_document.pdf.

[8] Oral evidence of Mr A Berkely, barrister and arbitrator, CBI, before the Draft Corruption Bill Joint Committee, 11 June 2003: www.parliament.the-stationery-office.co.uk/pa/jt200203/jtselect/jtcorr/157/157.pdf.

F.8 Therefore, when formulating an offence of bribery, opinions vary as to whether facilitation payments should be prohibited or whether a defence or exemption should be provided.

F.9 The law of England and Wales currently prohibits facilitation payments as a form of bribery.[9] Our provisional view is that this position should not be altered.[10]

Arguments in support of exempting facilitation payments

F.10 The principal argument in favour of tolerating some facilitation payments is that they are either legally or socially permissible within certain jurisdictions. It would therefore be detrimental to UK businesses and competitive enterprise if such payments could not be made. It is important that the reality and pragmatics of business are not dismissed.

F.11 It is also said that facilitation payments are invariably minor in nature and so have minimal detrimental consequences.

F.12 A further point is that inadequate wages abroad and/or foreign custom may necessitate such payments.

F.13 Finally, it could be argued that effective elimination of facilitation payments can only be secured through staff training and joint action lobbying of local governments rather than immediate prohibition by the law.[11]

Arguments against exempting facilitation payments

A difficult distinction

F.14 One of the principal arguments against providing an exemption or defence is that it "blurs the distinction between legal and illegal payments"[12] and may open the floodgates for abuse. There will be "inherent difficulties in determining when a payment … crosses the line from defendable minor payment to an actual bribe."[13]

---

[9] The common law definition of bribery encompasses such payments and they are not treated as a distinct category in the Prevention of Corruption Acts. See Nicholls, Daniel, Polaine and Hatchard, *Corruption and Misuse of Public Office* (2006), para 2.07 following.

[10] See paras F.14 to F.26 below.

[11] This argument is less relevant to England and Wales, where the current position is that it is already prohibited.

[12] R Koch, "The Foreign Corrupt Practices Act: It's time to cut back the grease and add some guidance" (2005) 28 *Boston College International and Comparative Law Review* 380. See also the Select Committee on International Development, Fourth Report, Corruption, April 2001, para 181.

[13] M Wilder and M Ahrens, "Australia's Implementation of the OECD Convention on Combating Bribery of Foreign Public Officials in International Business Transactions Commentary" (2001) 2 *Melbourne Journal of International Law* 583. See also "Bribery and corruption – the impact on UK small and medium sized enterprises" published by the Association of Chartered Certified Accountants in 2007, which stated that only 46% of its respondents felt able to differentiate between a facilitation payment and a bribe (p 10 and fig 2).

F.15   The fact that the distinction between legal and illegal payments is hard to make "can weaken the enterprise's ability to implement its anti-bribery programme"[14]. It may also send a confusing message to employees.[15]

F.16   Commentators have observed the risk of a "slippery slope"[16] to large-scale bribery, creating a "pyramid scheme of bribery" as money is funnelled through a series of officials.[17] This destroys any meaningful distinction between "petty and grand bribery".[18]

Drafting problems

F.17   If an exemption or defence were adopted, there would be considerable difficulty in interpretation. For example, to provide an exemption or defence for "minor" payments begs the question "what is minor?". A payment of £10,000 to a foreman is a lot of money but is "very minor when compared to the financial implications of such a payment not being made, especially when the cargo involved may be worth millions of dollars."[19] Also, a series of "minor" facilitation payments may be made which are not "minor" when taken cumulatively. This ambiguity hinders effective business practice and is precisely the difficulty faced by many foreign jurisdictions that have attempted to enforce such exemptions or defences.[20] It is worth noting that none of the major international instruments allow for an exemption or defence,[21] with the exception of "small facilitation payments" in paragraph 9 of the OECD Convention. But even there, the recent Mid-Term Study of Phase 2 concludes that:

[14]   Transparency International comment at
        www.transparency.org/content/download/573/3493/file/bpcb_ti_guidance_doc_november_%202004.pdf.

[15]   The High Cost of Small Bribes, TRACE, 2003 at p 6:
        www.fundworksinvestments.com/fn_filelibrary//File/co_gsri_high_cost_small_bribes.pdf.

[16]   See n 16 above.

[17]   www.ethicalcorp.com/content.asp?ContentID=4471. The author is the president of TRACE, the Chair of the Women in International Regulatory Law ("WIRL") Symposium, vice-chair of the ABA's Committee on Anti-Corruption Initiatives and Compliance Issues, a member of the Steering Committee for Business Principles for Countering Bribery and a member of the Working Group for the United Nation's Global Compact 10th Principle.

[18]   www.transparency.org/content/download/573/3493/file/bpcb_ti_guidance_doc_november_%202004.pdf.

[19]   See M Wilder and M Ahrens, "Australia's Implementation of the OECD Convention on Combating Bribery of Foreign Public Officials in International Business Transactions" 2 *Melbourne Journal of International Law* (2001) 583.

[20]   See www.oecd.org/document/49/0,3343,en_2649_34859_1933144_1_1_1_1,00.html.

        In the United States, there is an exemption under the Foreign Corrupt Practices Act 1977 for facilitation payments made to foreign officials to secure routine governmental action, although no such exception exists in the law governing domestic bribery. Koch criticises the word "routine", which could mean either "frequently" or "commonplace" ("The Foreign Corrupt Practices Act: It's time to cut back the grease and add some guidance" (2005) 28 *Boston College International and Comparative Law Review* 389). The OECD Phase 2 Report recommended that further guidance be issued to companies attempting to implement the exemption.

The Working Group might decide to undertake a mid- to long-term analysis about whether the exception for "small facilitation payments" in Commentary 9 is too vague to implement in practice.[22]

Business hindrance

F.18   In answer to the argument that business will "lose out" to rival foreign companies that do make facilitation payments, the UK Trade and Investment Department argues that "UK companies may lose some business by taking this approach, but equally there will be those who choose to do business with UK companies precisely because we have a no-bribery reputation, and the costs and style of doing business are more transparent".[23] Two examples of companies successfully adopting a zero-tolerance approach to facilitation payments are BP[24] and Shell.[25] Research conducted by the World Bank demonstrated that in fact payment of bribes results in firms spending "more, not less, management time … negotiating regulations and fac[ing] higher, not lower, cost of capital."[26] Further, it may be more difficult then to resist subsequent demands for payment.[27]

In Australia, there is a defence under the Bribery Act for "minor" facilitation payments not involving influencing a decision to award business. The OECD Phase 2 Report details confusion over the recording requirement and over a pamphlet issued by the Attorney-General's Department (subsequently amended) indicating that it might be possible for payments involving influencing a decision to award business to fall within the defence. Further, it notes that there is no such defence in most State criminal codes.

In Canada, the OECD Phase 2 Report "notes a high level of dissatisfaction with the exception for facilitation payments on the part of corporate and criminal defence lawyers, and that it was the opinion of some lawyers that the defence creates a large area of uncertainty".

In Japan, no express exemption is made, but the METI Guidelines contain discussions on certain forms of acceptable facilitation payment. The Phase 2 Report considered parts of these "misleading and contrary to Commentary 9 on the Convention".

[21]   Ie, the Council of Europe Convention, the Inter-American Convention and the African Union Convention or the UN Convention Against Corruption.

[22]   www.oecd.org/dataoecd/19/39/36872226.pdf at para 67.

[23]   www.uktradeinvest.gov.uk/ukti/fileDownload/Bribery_Leaflet_October_2006.pdf?cid=360030.

[24]   BP's code of conduct (p 49) clearly states that it "does not permit so-called 'facilitation' or 'grease' payments to be made to government officials, even if such payments are nominal in amount": http://www.bp.com/liveassets/bp_internet/globalbp/STAGING/global_assets/downloads/C/coc_en_full_document.pdf. Within two years, BP reported that "there were no known payments made directly by BP employees" in Indonesia, effectively eliminating facilitation payments in that country.

[25]   Principle 3 of Shell's Business Principles states that "the direct or indirect offer, payment, soliciting or acceptance of bribes in any form is unacceptable. Facilitation payments are also bribes and should not be made."

[26]   "Does Grease Money Speed Up the Wheels of Commerce?" Daniel Kaufmann, World Bank Institute and Shang-Jin Wei, Development Research Group, Public Economics, World Bank.

[27]   www.transparency.org/content/download/573/3493/file/bpcb_ti_guidance_doc_november_%202004.pdf.

F.19   In addition, if a multinational company does not adopt a zero-tolerance approach to facilitation payments, this may cause problems when it has subsidiaries in various jurisdictions only some of which allow for such payments. This then necessitates different compliance programmes depending on the location of the office and also the nationality of the employees.[28]

F.20   Difficulties may also be identified in accounting obligations. A business may be required to record a facilitation payment in its accounts by one jurisdiction, but this may then formalise an illegal act which, if concealed, may amount to tax evasion in another jurisdiction.[29] It has been observed that often companies must opt between "falsifying their records in violation of their own laws or recording the payments accurately and documenting a violation of local law".[30]

Wider issues in society

F.21   Facilitation payments potentially have negative impacts on society. They may facilitate violation of local laws prohibiting such payments[31] and can delay, impede and distort the proper functioning of government. This may even go as far as encouraging governments to fix their employees' salaries in expectation of these payments.[32]

F.22   Facilitation payments can also "create a perception that governments select only certain individuals for those strategic jobs that provide opportunities to accept bribes, leading to feelings of inequity (and resentment)".[33]

F.23   There is the danger that those living or working locally may be alienated as companies are perceived to buy their way past officials[34] and the loss of a local community's confidence has been identified as a real problem.[35]

---

[28]   The High Cost of Small Bribes, TRACE, 2003 at p 8: www.fundworksinvestments.com/fn_filelibrary//File/co_gsri_high_cost_small_bribes.pdf.

[29]   www.transparency.org/content/download/573/3493/file/bpcb_ti_guidance_doc_november_%202004.pdf.

[30]   The High Cost of Small Bribes, TRACE, 2003 at p 6: www.fundworksinvestments.com/fn_filelibrary//File/co_gsri_high_cost_small_bribes.pdf.

[31]   R Koch, "The Foreign Corrupt Practices Act: It's time to cut back the grease and add some guidance" (2005) 28 *Boston College International and Comparative Law Review* 395.

[32]   Ethics Resource Center Fellows Program at http://www.ethics.org/resources/articles-organizational-ethics.asp?aid=852. See also www.transparency.org/content/download/573/3493/file/bpcb_ti_guidance_doc_november_%202004.pdf: facilitation payments can "lead public officials to rely on them as part of their income."

[33]   R Koch, "The Foreign Corrupt Practices Act: It's time to cut back the grease and add some guidance" (2005) 28 *Boston College International and Comparative Law Review* 396.

[34]   www.ethicalcorp.com/content.asp?ContentID=4471&ContTypeID=43.

[35]   The High Cost of Small Bribes, TRACE, 2003 at p 6: www.fundworksinvestments.com/fn_filelibrary//File/co_gsri_high_cost_small_bribes.pdf.

F.24   Concerns are also expressed about the impact on international security: "if you pay government officials to manage differently, you shouldn't be surprised if criminals and terrorists are doing the same".[36] The increasing intolerance of facilitation payments on an international scale is reflected in the stance taken recently by the International Development Committee in its fourth report on Corruption:

> We see no difference between bribery and facilitation payments. Our legislation should make clear facilitation payments are not acceptable and that anyone making them would be breaking the law.[37]

F.25   Finally, it is noted that criminal prosecution of facilitation payments can expose and so help to remedy the problem.[38]

Application of our provisional proposals to facilitation payments

F.26   We believe that the observations above lend strong support to the continued prohibition of facilitation payments under the law of England and Wales.

F.27   This section considers how our current proposal would apply to facilitation payments. The focus here is on the application of the concept of 'improper conduct'.[39]

How we have defined 'improper conduct'

F.28   In Part 4, we stated that the core of bribery can be reduced to the nexus between two central components: the conferral of an advantage from P and the improper act or omission by R.[40] In defining what "improper conduct" means, we favour a breach of duty model.[41] Under this model, R acts improperly when he or she acts in breach of a legal or equitable duty that involves betrayal of a relation of trust, or a breach of a duty to act impartially or in the best interests of another.

Applying the concept of improper conduct to facilitation payments

F.29   As is evident from the discussion above, a facilitation payment is normally made from P to R in order to secure or expedite conduct that R is already obliged to perform. Therefore, in acting as P desires, R is simply being paid to do something that he or she is already bound to do and so it could be argued that there has been no breach of duty. The danger that the concept of improper conduct may be under-inclusiveness, as highlighted in Part 4,[42] is therefore exemplified.

---

[36]   TRACE: www.ethicalcorp.com/content.asp?ContentID=4471&ContTypeID=43.

[37]   www.publications.parliament.uk/pa/cm200001/cmselect/cmintdev/39/3911.htm, paras 181 to 186.

[38]   "Bribery and corruption – the impact on UK small and medium sized enterprises" published by the Association of Chartered Certified Accountants in 2007, stated that its respondents' most popular anti-corruption solution by far was high profile prosecutions (see p 14 and fig 8).

[39]   For fuller discussion, see Part 5, paras 5.6 to 5.55 above.

[40]   See para 4.3 above.

[41]   See Part 4 above. The alternative was the 'influence' model.

[42]   See Part 4, paras 4.129 to 4.133 above.

F.30   However, we consider that the vast majority of facilitation payments would still be caught by our proposed new offence on the basis that such conduct breached an equitable duty, involving, in particular, breach of a duty to act impartially. Although R is not necessarily breaching a duty in relation to the outcome of his or her decision, by basing that decision upon the advantage provided by P, R would be in breach of his or her equitable duty and would therefore be acting improperly. As noted in Part 4, expressly extending breach of duty to include a duty to act impartially therefore satisfies a major part of the criticism relating to under-inclusiveness.

THE PROBLEM CASE

F.31   There may be certain instances of facilitation payments that are not caught by our provisional proposal. This would be the case if the conduct did not constitute a breach of any equitable duty. The following example illustrates this point:

Example F1

R is a state employee responsible for completing routine paperwork. P is a private individual who wants the paperwork relevant to him processed quickly. At 6 o'clock on Friday evening, R is about to leave the office. P phones R to ask if his paperwork has been completed. R explains that he is working his way through the list of names and that P is next so will be dealt with first thing on Monday morning. In order to persuade R to stay after hours to complete P's paperwork immediately, P offers to pay R a small sum of money. R accepts the money and completes the paperwork that Friday evening.

F.32   In this example, there is no breach of a legal or equitable duty. P's paperwork was the next on the list to be dealt with. None of the other entities on the list were disadvantaged by R's actions. The conferment of the advantage simply ensured that R would stay after hours to complete P's paperwork rather than completing it on Monday morning. As no duty has been breached, R's conduct is not improper and it would not be caught by the bribery offence that we have provisionally proposed.

RESOLVING THE PROBLEM CASE

F.33   There are three options available to address such cases.

Option 1

F.34   The first option is to extend the concept of a breach of duty. Our current provisional proposal confines a breach of duty to the acceptance of an advantage which induces a breach of a legal or equitable duty, involving breach of a relation of trust or a breach of a duty to act impartially or in the best interests of another. Option 1 would extend the concept of a breach of duty to the mere acceptance of an advantage (in contravention of the individual's contractual terms of employment or of an applicable code of conduct). The numerous problems with this option are identified in Part 4 at paragraphs 4.55 to 4.59.

Option 2

F.35　The second option would be to create a separate offence to deal with facilitation payment cases which involve a breach of duty by the mere acceptance of an advantage. This distinct offence would be in addition to the general bribery offence and it could be confined to public officials.

F.36　We consider this option undesirable. There will be so few cases of facilitation payments that do not constitute a breach of a duty under our proposal that it would be disproportionate to introduce a separate offence to deal with them.

Option 3

F.37　The third option is that such cases could be left outside the ambit of the bribery offence. As already stated in Part 4, this is our preferred solution and one which would still catch any serious cases of facilitation payments. For example, if the payment induces R to advance P in the queue, it is likely that a breach of a duty of impartiality would have occurred. Also, those who are not caught by our proposed offence of bribery could still be subject to internal disciplinary measures, which may be severe and which may present a better option for regulators than a criminal sanction.

COMMISSION PAYMENTS

Overview

F.38　This section is divided into four parts as follows:

(1)　it begins by explaining what a commission payment is;[43]

(2)　it then identifies the problem posed by commission payments when formulating an offence of bribery;

(3)　it then discusses how our provisional proposal for a new bribery offence would apply to commission payments;

(4)　it then considers the options available for our current project.

What are commission payments?

F.39　The following example illustrates how commission payments classically operate. This is the scenario about which consultees were concerned in their responses to the Home Office Consultation Paper.

---

[43]　This definition is drawn from the examples used in the consultees' responses (2006) to the Home Office paper – Bribery: Reform of the Prevention of Corruption Acts and SFO Powers in Cases of Bribery of Foreign Officials: a Consultation Paper (Dec 2005).

> **Example F2**
>
> There are three parties. The first party (P) provides the relevant product (such as an insurance policy) or is the financial product manufacturer (such as a fund management company).
>
> The second party (R) is the broker or other financial adviser who distributes or sells the product.
>
> The third party (V) is the customer who buys or invests in the product.
>
> When R sells P's product to V, R receives a payment ("commission") from P.
>
> It is often the case that R is paid in this way rather than by a fee paid by V, although R is effectively working for V.

Identifying the problem

F.40   As is apparent from the example above, a commission payment bears the hallmarks of a bribery offence.[44] An advantage is conferred from P to R and this advantage may influence the behaviour of R when conducting business with V. If R were to advise or sell a product to V primarily in order to receive the commission conferred by P, this risks appearing improper. R will often have a duty to act impartially when advising and selling to V, whether as an equitable duty or as a legal duty under his or her terms of employment.

F.41   The danger of corruption was highlighted by the Financial Services Authority:

> The current incentives in the advice market, where most advisers are remunerated by commission payments from the product providers, may mean that advisers act in their own interests rather than the customer's. Such behaviour by financial advisers may cause particular problems because customers are ill-equipped to discern when advisers are acting in their own interests. An adviser may therefore be inclined to recommend to a customer a product that is unsuitable where it is in the adviser's interests to do so.[45]

F.42   However, the practice of commission payments is generally well-established and accepted within certain markets, most notably the financial services sector. However, the problem associated with commission payments is not confined to the financial markets. A supplier of a product may offer a dealer in the product improved terms dependent on the volume of the product sold by the dealer (frequently called "overriders").

---

[44]   The Jersey Financial Services Commission in March 2006 issued the following advice: "Jersey businesses should exercise extreme caution when asked to structure services involving … commission payments … . Jersey businesses and their personnel may be vulnerable to prosecution for making corrupt payments … or aiding and abetting such an offence": http://www.jerseyfsc.org/pdf/guidance_notes_march_2006.pdf.

[45]   www.fsa.gov.uk/pubs/discussion/dp07_04.pdf.

F.43   Clause 5 of the Government's draft Corruption Bill[46] includes as bribery the situation where P confers an advantage (pays the commission) intending or believing that R will act or has acted (by advising or selling to V) primarily to secure an advantage (ie, to get paid). The Bill was criticised on this ground for

> ... risking criminalising behaviour which has not previously been regarded as criminal and which is commonplace in the financial sector (and possibly in other sectors) where businesses and services are structured on a commission payment basis.[47]

Application of our provisional proposals to commission payments

F.44   In determining how our provisional proposals would apply to commission payments, it is useful to refer to Example F2 above.

OVERVIEW

F.45   Where R receives the advantage, there is clearly scope for argument that R would be acting in expectation of an advantage (a commission) from P.

F.46   P, as the person conferring (or offering to confer) the advantage, may also come within the offence. By offering a commission to R, it could be inferred that P's primary intention was to encourage R to sell P's product, or that P would foresee a serious risk that the commission paid could be a primary reason for R acting.

---

[46]   www.archive2.official-documents.co.uk/document/cm57/5777/5777.pdf.

[47]   Response of the City of London Law Society, which also pointed out that R would not be doing his or her job at all but for being paid.

F.47   R's act or omission must still be *improper* (in breach of a legal or equitable duty). When advising or selling to V, it is arguable that R would be under an express or implied duty of impartiality which necessitates acting in V's best interests. The existence of such a duty is bolstered by the FSA, [48] which regulates commission payments in certain spheres of work, and the EU Market in Financial Instruments Directive.[49] However, the mere fact R sold a product to V which objectively turned out not to be in V's best interests would not in itself mean that R had breached a legal or equitable duty. R would be under a duty to exercise reasonable care to recommend a suitable product for his or her client. Provided that he or she exercised reasonable care, there would be no breach of duty even if the product turned out to be unsuitable. By contrast, R would be in breach of a duty that he or she owed to V if R honestly but carelessly recommended a product.

F.48   On this analysis, as long as R ensures that he or she acts in the best interests of his or her client and is impartial in his or her advice, the payment of a commission would not infringe the provision.[50] This accords with the approach of the FSA and EU Market in Financial Instruments Directive, which do not impose a blanket prohibition on commission payments but instead provide strict controls to ensure that R fulfils his or her duties to V, whose best interests are protected.

F.49   One could question whether it is realistic to suppose that R will be wholly impartial when there are extra "bonuses" associated with certain products. However, the financial sector appears to operate on the basis that the availability of these bonuses does not preclude R from being able to act in V's best interests.

F.50   Therefore, under our proposal, it is only when a case arises of a breach of duty, because R is acting primarily in his or her own financial interests, that the commission payment would be "improper" and a charge of bribery could be brought. However, it may still be argued that it would be more appropriate for a civil or regulatory sanction to be imposed in such a scenario.

---

[48]   The FSA Conduct of Business requirement 2.2 (htttp://fsahandbook.info/FSA/html/handbook/COB/2/2) addresses inducements and states that a firm must "conduct its business with integrity, to pay due regard to the interests of its customers and to treat them fairly". The purpose of this section is "to ensure that a firm does not conduct business under arrangements that might give rise to a conflict with its duty to its customers". The FSA also produced rules to address "soft commission payments", which, among others, require investment managers to disclose to their customers details of how commission payments have been used: www.fsa.gov.uk/pubs/cp/cp05_05.pdf.

[49]   In effect from November 2007 (www.fsa.gov.uk/Pages/About/What/International/EU/fsap/mifid/index.shtml). Article 18 requires Member States to ensure that investment firms take all reasonable steps to identify conflicts of interest between themselves or their agents, and their clients. If administrative arrangements are not sufficient to ensure with reasonable confidence that the risk of a conflict cannot be prevented, the investment firms must disclose the conflict to the client. Article 21 requires Member States to ensure that investment firms take all reasonable steps to ensure the best possible outcome for their clients.

[50]   This is supported by the comment made by the City Liaison Group that the draft Corruption Bill does not require "even breach of agent's duties to his principal".

Options for our current project

F.51   Our current provisional thinking would exclude "acceptable commission payments" from the ambit of the offence of bribery. That is to say, commission payments that do not cause R to infringe his or her duty of impartiality or his or her obligation to act in V's best interests, would not be caught. The offence of bribery would only apply to those cases where the system is exploited by P and R so that R fails to act in V's best interests.

F.52   Our options are as follows:

(1)   retain the current proposal without qualification. A commission payment will only be caught when there is a breach of a legal or equitable duty (including a duty to act impartially);

(2)   provide a specific exemption or defence to cover certain commission payments; or

(3)   wholly exclude commission payments from the ambit of the offence on the basis that it is for regulatory bodies (such as the FSA) to impose sanctions rather than the criminal law.

Providing an exemption or defence (option 2)

F.53   An exemption or defence may have the advantage of clarifying the position for the relevant sectors that utilise commission payments.

F.54   The draft Corruption Bill[51] contained a defence (applicable in all cases of bribery, not only commission payments) of the principal's consent.[52] In theory, commission payments would not be caught if V consented to the payment made by P to R. Concern was raised over whether this would be effective in practice. For example, it could prove very difficult to establish that V was apprised of the "material facts" (a phrase itself not free from complexity). This concern led consultees[53] to propose an additional exemption for which two criteria were to be met. First that the commission payment was made in accordance with prevailing market practice, and secondly that it was made in an area subject to regulatory oversight. However, "prevailing market practice" may be difficult to establish and would also present the danger that the law could ultimately condone undesirable customs. The existence of the second limb suggests that this area is more appropriate for administrative and civil regulation rather than criminal sanction. It should also be remembered that this exemption was proposed on the basis of the draft Corruption Bill's perceived inadequacy in dealing with commission payments: our current proposals may provide a more appropriate solution.

---

[51]   Drafted in 2003 and based on the Law Commission's earlier report Legislating the Criminal Code: Corruption (1998) Law Com No 248.

[52]   Clause 7.

[53]   The City Liaison Group and the Investment Management Association.

F.55   We are of the provisional view that an additional exemption would only be required if the concept of a breach of a legal or equitable duty does not draw the correct line between "acceptable" and "unacceptable" commission payments.[54]

Leaving commission payments entirely outside the ambit of bribery (option 3)

F.56   We consider this option undesirable for two main reasons. First, not all sectors that utilise commission payments are subject to supervisory regulation. This would risk leaving a gap in sanction against those deliberately abusing the commission payment system, simply because of their particular area of business.

F.57   Secondly, the criminal law may already be invoked in commission payment cases where the requirements of the Fraud Act 2006 are satisfied – namely that R made a dishonest representation with the intention of making a financial gain. This has been considered in detail in Appendix E. Therefore it may be argued that, since defendants will already be subject to criminal sanction in these circumstances, a new bribery offence would not be stretching the criminal law further than it presently applies. As we indicated in Appendix E, all that will change is that prosecutors will have a choice of charges in some instances (bribery or fraud) whereas at present they must opt for a charge of fraud. We do not regard such a change as an inappropriate extension of the criminal law, particularly when the alternative is the drafting of a special exception, of complex and uncertain scope, in circumstances when prosecutors can charge such conduct as fraud in any event. It should also be noted that requiring the consent of a law officer to prosecution for bribery acts as an extra check on inappropriate prosecutions. No such check is in place for charges of fraud.

Provisional proposal (option 1)

F.58   We provisionally propose that only commission payments that result in a breach of legal or equitable duty (involving betrayal of a relation of trust, or breach of a duty to act impartially or in the best interests of another) should be prohibited. Those commission payments that do not result in such a breach should fall outside the scope of bribery.

CORPORATE HOSPITALITY

F.59   This section examines corporate hospitality. It is divided into four parts as follows:

(1)   it begins by identifying the principal problems this issue poses when formulating an offence of bribery;

(2)   it then highlights some of the ways that various organisations have dealt with the issue of corporate hospitality;

(3)   it then turns to consider our proposed formulation and outlines the various options that could be adopted, briefly noting the advantages and disadvantages of each;[55]

---

[54]   Ie, those payments that should be subject to the criminal law and those that should not.

(4)   our provisional proposal is stated;

The problem posed

F.60   Corporate hospitality or gift-giving arguably bears some of the hallmarks of corrupt activity: an "advantage" is conferred and such conferment may be motivated by the hope of influencing a business relationship.[56] However, it is also generally considered an acceptable part of business activity.[57]

F.61   There is virtually no support for a complete prohibition on all forms of corporate hospitality. On the other hand, exempting all corporate hospitality from the ambit of bribery "would open the door to abuse: bribery would simply be dressed up as hospitality".[58] However, there is general support for prohibiting conduct that crosses the threshold from what is considered "legitimate entertainment" to "illegitimate", "unacceptable" or "improper" activity.

F.62   We must therefore consider what test and/or principles should determine when this threshold is crossed.[59] As noted recently by the Government "the problem lies in defining the point where corporate hospitality…become(s) improper".[60] As Professor G R Sullivan has put it:

> The borderline between the conferring of legitimate and illegitimate advantage are inextricably bound up with social and cultural mores and is very hard to capture within the terms of any definition.[61]

F.63   Nevertheless, corporations and individuals must be able to understand the parameters within which they may lawfully operate.[62] The borderline between what is, and what is not, acceptable must be identified and at least some guidance provided. This is particularly important considering the stigma attached to the label of "bribery".

---

[55]   This information is largely drawn from the consultees' responses (2006) to the Home Office paper – Bribery: Reform of the Prevention of Corruption Acts and SFO Powers in Cases of Bribery of Foreign Officials: a Consultation Paper (Dec 2005).

[56]   Legislating the Criminal Code: Corruption (1998) Law Com No 248, para 5.75.

[57]   "Corporate entertainment is seen as a vital marketing tool … . Both business-people and officials will want to have good business and social relations for all kinds of legitimate reasons": Simmons and Simmons, consultees' responses, February 2006. "It is regarded as an important aspect of customer/client relationships and as such may be generally beneficial rather than harmful": Council of HM Circuit Judges, consultees' responses, 2006.

[58]   Legislating the Criminal Code: Corruption (1998) Law Com No 248, paras 5.75 to 5.82.

[59]   Including the relevance, if any, of accepted practices or local custom in foreign jurisdictions, if rules regarding corporate hospitality are to have extra-territorial effect.

[60]   Consultation on Bribery: Reform of the Prevention of Corruption Acts and SFO Powers in Cases of Bribery of Foreign Officials: Summary of responses and next steps (2007) para 26.

[61]   "Proscribing corruption – some comments on the Law Commission's Report" (1998) *Criminal Law Review* 547, 552.

[62]   Research published by the Association of Chartered Certified Accountants showed that only 45% of small and medium sized enterprises felt able to differentiate between bribery and corporate hospitality.

Case studies

F.64 This section provides some examples of how different organisations approach the issue of corporate hospitality in order to draw the line between acceptable and unacceptable conduct.

The BG Group[63] Business Principles

F.65 Hospitality and appropriate gifts are offered to build relationships, but do "not expect favours in return". Strict limits on the value of hospitality are specified and all accepted gifts must be recorded.

Chartered Institute of Personnel and Development[64]

F.66 Inappropriate business gifts are prohibited. These are gifts "designed to influence the recipient in carrying out their work". Further, "corrupt" conduct is that which "goes beyond the consolidation of a business relationship". Significant factors in determining this are the value of the gift, the identity of the giver, the sector in which it is given and the timing of the transaction in relation to other business transactions.

Institute of Business Ethics[65]

F.67 Giving or accepting "excessive hospitality" is prohibited.

Securities and Investment Institute[66]

F.68 Corporate hospitality is only acceptable when proportionate to the nature of the relationship and the seniority of those involved, and is not acceptable where it can be construed as an inducement to use the services of the company.

Financial Services Authority

F.69 The FSA Code of Conduct[67] states that networking improves contact but must not give grounds for suggestions of undue influence. A gift over the value of £25 must be declared and surrendered to the Ethics Officer. Hospitality should be refused if it "could be construed by a critic to be unusual or to risk creating a sense of obligation to the host or bias in their favour". Relevant factors include the circumstances of the invitation and the cost or exclusivity of the event.

F.70 The Code is modified slightly regarding overseas visits to allow conformance with "local customs".

---

[63] Involved in building and supplying natural gas markets around the world.

[64] Involved in the management and development of people, with over 127,000 members.

[65] A London-based charity established in 1986 to encourage ethical business practices.

[66] The largest professional body for those in the securities and investment industry in the UK. Originally set up by members of the London Stock Exchange as the "Securities Institute".

[67] Revised May 2005: http://www.fsa.gov.uk/pubs/staff/code_conduct.pdf. See ch 6.

British Medical Association[68]

Guidance issued in 2006 by the General Medical Council states that doctors "must not ask for or accept any inducement, gift or hospitality which may affect or be seen to affect the way [they] prescribe for, treat or refer patients. [They] must not offer such inducements to colleagues".

The Association of the British Pharmaceutical Industry

F.71   Clause 18 of the Code of Practice[69] states that no gift, benefit in kind or pecuniary advantage may be given as an inducement to prescribe, supply, buy or sell any medicine. Promotional aids may be distributed as long as they are inexpensive and relevant to their profession or employment.

Bar Standards Board

F.72   The general principles[70] governing hospitality and gifts are that:

   a. The conduct of BSB members and Secretariat should not give rise to any suspicion of any conflict between the requirements of their post and personal interest or advantage;

   b. BSB members and Secretariat should not accept hospitality or a gift which would or might: appear to place them under any obligation to the giver; compromise their impartiality or judgement; or otherwise be improper;

   c. Taking into account the monetary value, the offer should not be repeated more frequently or regularly than would be regarded as normal;

   d. Any gift given should be proportionate and appropriate to the nature of the relationship between the BSB/member/staff member and the intended recipient, and should only be provided in an exceptional case;

   e. Any gift received should be proportionate and appropriate to the nature of the relationship between the donor and the BSB/members/staff member;

   f. If members or Secretariat staff are unsure about the propriety of accepting hospitality or a gift then it should be refused; if refusal would cause offence, it should be donated to the BSB; and

   g. The receipt of any gift by members/staff must be disclosed to the BSB.

---

[68]   http://gmc-uk.org/guidance/good_medical_practice/GMC_GMP.pdf.

[69]   www.abpi.org.uk/links/assoc/PMCPA/pmpca_code2006.pdf.

[70]   www.barstandardsboard.org.uk/assets/documents/BSB%20Policy%20on%20hospitality%20Final%2020%20Apr%2007.doc, at para 5.

F.73 There is no explicit restriction on barristers offering hospitality to solicitors, but "the "blush test" is a useful guide: barristers should not normally offer entertainment which either party would feel embarrassed to disclose to colleagues, clients or regulator".[71]

The Law Society

F.74 Section 2 of the Solicitor's Introduction and Referral Code allows solicitors to accept "normal hospitality".[72] Practice Rule 1 lays down an overriding duty to act in the client's best interests. Therefore, "if the solicitor's choice is based on what hospitality, or gift, s/he has received, rather than on the barrister's merit, then clearly the solicitor will have breached his duty to the client".[73]

Ministerial Code[74]

F.75 This states that Ministers must ensure that no conflict arises, or appears to arise, between their public duties and their private interests. Ministers should avoid accepting any gift or hospitality which might, or might reasonably appear to, compromise their judgement or place them under an improper obligation.[75]

The Recommendation of the Committee of Ministers to Member States on Codes of Conduct for Public Officials

F.76 Article 18 prohibits demanding or accepting hospitality that may influence, or appear to influence, the impartiality with which one conducts his or her duties. However, "conventional hospitality" and "minor gifts" are expressly exempted.

Trace

F.77 Trace has produced guidelines on gifts and hospitality for public officials.[76] It states that all benefits provided to foreign officials should:

  • be reasonable and customary under the circumstances;

  • not be motivated by a desire to influence the foreign official inappropriately;

  • be tasteful and commensurate with generally accepted standards for professional courtesy in the country where the company has its headquarters;

  • be provided openly and transparently;

  • be given in good faith and without expectation of reciprocity;

---

[71] www.barstandardsboard.org.uk/news/press/497.html.

[72] Undefined.

[73] www.lawsociety.org.uk/secure/file/167187/e:/teamsite-deployed/documents/templatedata/Internet%20Documents/Non-government%20proposals/Documents/response_bar_consultation_entertainment_220207.pdf.

[74] www.cabinetoffice.gov.uk/propriety_and_ethics/publications/pdf/ministerial_code_current.pdf.

[75] Clauses 7.20 to 7.24.

[76] www.traceinternational.org/winter2005.pdf. From newsletter dated 2005.

- be provided in connection with a recognised gift-giving holiday or event in the case of gifts;

- be provided in connection with a bona fide and legitimate business purpose in the case of hospitality and travel;

- not be provided to any foreign official or group of foreign officials with such regularity or frequency as to create an appearance of impropriety or undermine the purpose of this policy; and

- comply with the local laws and regulations that apply to public officials.

OECD Working Paper: 'Business Approaches to Combating Corrupt Practices'[77]

F.78 This review noted that "the public statements show little evidence of a common model for describing acceptable or unacceptable gift giving and entertainment practices".[78] It observed that "words such as appropriate, legitimate, reasonable, business-related, courtesy, token, modest and nominal were often used". The following examples were given of tests used by multinational enterprises for prohibiting unacceptable corporate hospitality:

(1) gifts or entertainment excessive in value and/or that exceed normal business customs;

(2) gifts or entertainment that are an inducement to business;

(3) gifts or entertainment that violate the law;

(4) appearance of impropriety.

Our formulation

The role of the criminal law

F.79 In broad terms, our provisional view is that criminal sanction should not be imposed unless no other sanction is appropriate or adequate. There will frequently be other means of punishing those who give or receive corporate hospitality where they should not. For example, public officials and many company employees are subject to codes of conduct which make clear what kinds of hospitality may or may not be given and accepted, and which provide for ongoing awareness training. Disciplinary sanctions follow for breaches of these codes. The offence of bribery must therefore be restricted to those cases of such serious wrongdoing that disciplinary action alone is insufficient.

---

[77] www.oecd.org/dataoecd/63/57/2638716.pdf.

[78] Page 9.

The public/private distinction

F.80 It is sometimes suggested that a wider scope for the offence of bribery is needed because stricter tests should be applied in the public sector. The Home Office has said that "there is a recognisable difference between the standards we expect as regards receiving gifts from those who clearly exercise essential public functions, as compared with those clearly in the private sector".[79] Whilst there may be some merit in this, it would be counterproductive to formulate an offence of bribery that was then so wide that it caught conduct in the private sector that could be adequately dealt with by disciplinary sanction. By contrast, conduct that appears particularly corrupt by virtue of it taking place in the public sector could be a factor relevant to sentencing. It must also be kept in mind that the standards by which public officials must abide are themselves subject to public control and scrutiny.

Summary of various solutions

F.81 This section considers the different options in attempting to draw the correct line between acceptable and unacceptable corporate hospitality.

PRIMARY MOTIVATOR

F.82 This option, which we have adopted as our provisional view, states that the provider of an advantage (P) should be liable for bribery in two situations. First, if he or she gives (or represents that he or she will give) an advantage, in exchange for, in expectation of, or as a reward for R doing an improper act, for the primary reason that it will encourage R to act improperly (whether or not it turns out to be R's primary reason for acting). Secondly if he or she foresees a serious risk that the advantage will constitute the primary reason for R doing an improper act, or realises that the advantage did constitute the primary reason for R doing an improper act.[80]

Advantages

F.83 This test targets that which appears improper: the attempt to influence the decision-making process with gifts and entertainment. It would also ensure that generally accepted "reasonable" behaviour, such as hospitality that only seeks to cement old relationships and foster new ones or that aimed to facilitate the sharing of information, would not be caught by the offence.

---

[79] Reform of the Prevention of Corruption Acts and SFO Powers in Cases of Bribery of Foreign Officials: a Consultation Paper (Dec 2005) para 46.

[80] The second limb of this proposal is very close to the model recommended in our previous report, which was taken forward by the Home Office in the draft Corruption Bill: http://www.archive2.official-documents.co.uk/document/cm57/5777/5777.pdf.

F.84　In response to the criticism that the test of primary motivation would be impossible to apply, it can be demonstrated first that the law already requires such a determination to be made in other spheres, and secondly that the courts have been able to implement this requirement. In cases involving the defence of duress, juries have successfully identified the relevant cause of certain conduct where there are various contributory motives.[81] This suggests that juries would be able successfully to identify whether the advantage conferred was the "primary" motivator. Further, in *Killick v Rendall*,[82] the Court of Appeal had to decide whether the "primary purpose" of a businessman's trip to a football match was for social or for business reasons (in order to decide if an insurance claim could be made relating to a helicopter accident that occurred on the trip). The Court was able to decide what were incidental or subsidiary purposes or motives for the trip and what was the primary reason the trip was made.

Disadvantages

F.85　Alongside the potential difficulties of proving what the primary motivator for conduct is (dealt with above), it may also be questioned whether such a test is sufficiently strict for public sector entities.[83] This may place too high a burden on the prosecution.

SUBSTANTIAL MOTIVATOR

F.86　This option would use the model outlined above but would replace the term "primarily" with "substantially", thus widening the ambit of the offence by reducing the degree to which the bribe need motivate R's conduct.[84]

Advantages[85]

F.87　A qualitative test would remain but this term would provide a lower threshold than a test of "primarily". The effect would be "to bring more borderline behaviour within the scope of the offence."[86] This may be particularly significant for maintaining strict standards in the public sector.

---

[81] For example, in *Valderrama-Vega* [1985] *Criminal Law Review* 220, the defendant was threatened with financial loss, exposure of his homosexuality and physical violence. The Court of Appeal held that the last of these gave rise to a valid defence of duress; the fact that the first two causes were also operating was immaterial.

[82] [2000] 2 All ER, applying *Seddon v Binions* [1978] 1 Lloyd's Rep 381.

[83] This was the concern apparent from the Home Office paper – Bribery: Reform of the Prevention of Corruption Acts and SFO Powers in Cases of Bribery of Foreign Officials (Dec 2005).

[84] Put forward as an option in the 2005 Home Office paper at question 6.

[85] In the consultees' responses dated 2006, this option was supported by OLAF, the Law Society, the London Criminal Courts Solicitors' Association and the Police Federation for England and Wales. It was not supported by Clifford Chance, Investment Management Association, Belfast City Council, CBI, Financial Services and Markets Legislation City Liaison Group, International Chamber of Commerce, Ministry of Defence Police, SFO.

[86] Consultation on Bribery: Reform of the Prevention of Corruption Acts and SFO Powers in Cases of Bribery of Foreign Officials: Summary of responses and next steps (2007) para 64.

F.88   A test that covers any influence more than de minimis would ease the burden on the prosecution and the courts, since it would no longer be necessary to demonstrate the main reason for the recipient's conduct.

Disadvantages

F.89   Several consultees felt that this test would broaden the scope too much,[87] particularly in the private sector. It risks criminalising acceptable corporate activity (or unacceptable activity that can be adequately dealt with by disciplinary measures).

F.90   A further danger highlighted by consultees was that the broad test could lead to an "increase in defensiveness and isolation from the business world among public servants".[88]

F.91   There is also the possibility that juries would in practice convict only those who intended the advantage to be a "primary" motivating factor.[89]

JURY TO DECIDE AS GUIDED BY LIST OF FACTORS

F.92   This option would identify certain factors relevant to the assessment of whether the alleged hospitality is "improper". These would include the value of the benefit conferred and whether the activity was open or secret. It would then be left to the jury to decide if the conduct came within the parameters of the offence.

F.93   A possible model was provided in the Law Commission consultation paper of 1997,[90] which proposed that it should not be a specific defence that

(1)   what was done was done openly;

(2)   what was done was done with the consent of the agent's principal;

(3)   the agent was under no obligation to account for the benefit in question;

(4)   what was done was normal practice in the environment in question; or

(5)   the benefit in question was of small value;

but that each of these factors should be capable of having a bearing on the issue of whether the defendant's conduct was corrupt.

Advantages

F.94   This test would be flexible, avoiding a rigid test that may be too indiscriminate, and would ensure a fair reflection of the factors relevant to an assessment of corruption. For those that support the inclusion of cultural factors, it would also be an advantage that culturally accepted norms could be taken into consideration.

[87]   The Home Office Consultation Paper of 2005 states that "case law has established [this term] covers any factor which is more than de minimis" (para 51). See also Simmons and Simmons (consultees' responses, February 2006).

[88]   Simmons and Simmons (consultees' responses, February 2006).

[89]   Above.

[90]   Legislating the Criminal Code: Corruption (1997) Law Com No 145, paras 8.40 to 8.58.

Disadvantages

F.95   Such a test would be imprecise and therefore it would be difficult to predict what conduct would be permitted. Further, "normal practice in the environment in question" may be difficult to establish and may have the effect of permitting businesses to exploit undesirable customs. In addition, it could be criticised for not expressly referring to the reason why the advantage was conferred: it is arguably this "motive" that distinguishes acceptable from unacceptable behaviour.

ORDINARY STANDARDS OF REASONABLE PEOPLE AND MARKET PRACTICE

F.96   This option would provide an exemption whereby a person will not be liable if the advantage conferred was not improper according to the ordinary standards of reasonable and honest people, having regard to any prevailing market practice in the sector concerned. Alternatively, one could provide an exemption for corporate hospitality if it is "reasonable" as genuine promotional expenditure.[91]

Advantages[92]

F.97   This would ensure the test would be sufficiently flexible so that only practices generally accepted as illegitimate would be unlawful. It would allow the law to evolve with current practice and expectations. It would also reflect the fact that what is acceptable in one sphere of work may not be acceptable in another field.[93]

Disadvantages

F.98   Such a test may be too vague to provide adequate guidance for companies as to what they are permitted to do. Again, "prevailing market practice" may be difficult to establish or prove. There is also the danger that certain practice could become lawful without any proper assessment of whether this would be desirable or not.

DISHONESTY TEST

F.99   A test of dishonesty could be used to determine if the advantage conferred constituted corruption. The leading authority is *Ghosh*,[94] which establishes a two-stage test. First, the jury must decide whether what was done was dishonest according to the ordinary standards of reasonable and honest people. Then the jury must consider whether the defendant realised that what he or she was doing was by dishonest those standards.

---

[91]   CBI consultee response (2006) para 12.

[92]   The Bar Standards Board have recently reviewed its stance on client entertainment and has advised barristers to follow the "blush test", which is akin to a test of acceptable business practice. See also the City Liaison Group consultee response (2006) paras 5 and 10.

[93]   Most notable when contrasting the public and private sectors.

[94]   [1982] QB 1053.

Advantages

F.100 A test of dishonesty would be consistent with the Fraud Act 2006, which may be appropriate given that there is a substantial overlap between conduct that is "fraudulent" and conduct that constitutes bribery.[95]

Disadvantages[96]

F.101 Dishonesty is ill-suited in this context. An advantage conferred may be illegitimate, unreasonable, disproportionate or otherwise "improper" without being dishonest. Also, such a test may make it difficult to predict what conduct will be acceptable, and may be difficult for juries to apply in practice.

SEPARATE TEST FOR PUBLIC SECTOR OFFICIALS

F.102 This option advocates a separate test for private and public sector entities, relying on internal codes for public sector officials.[97]

F.103 The provision would state that for public officials any giving or receipt of an advantage will be criminal unless:

(1)   authorised by law;[98] or

(2)   both of small value; and

(3)   in accordance with the terms and conditions of the official's employment.

(4)   (and possibly also declared).

F.104 The test for private sector entities could follow one of the other models suggested above.

---

[95] The relationship between the Fraud Act 2006 and an offence of bribery is addressed in Appendix E, and the argument is made that two distinct offences of fraud and bribery are still necessary.

[96] This proposal was rejected by the London Criminal Courts Solicitors' Association in its response (p 5). The Government response to consultees' comments concluded that case law "has at least made clear that dishonesty is not a requirement of the offence" (para 18).

[97] Set out in Bribery: Reform of the Prevention of Corruption Acts and SFO Powers in Cases of Bribery of Foreign Officials (Dec 2005) para 46.

[98] The Government has clarified in its response to consultees' comments that this requirement has the potential to allow foreign laws to be taken into account (ie, if a foreign law required a declaration to be made).

Advantages[99]

F.105 The principal advantage of this approach is that it reflects the widely held view that a stricter approach should be taken for public officials than for those in the private sector.[100] At the same time, it would not criminalise the acceptance of low level corporate hospitality or small gifts on formal occasions which are authorised by the terms of the official's employment.[101] It would also reflect the approach taken in Conventions such as the OECD, Council of Europe and the UNCAC.[102]

Disadvantages[103]

F.106 This proposal was put forward by the Home Office on the premise that the "agent-principal relationship provides a strong workable basis for the offences in the private sector" but that it is not appropriate in the public sector.[104] If the agent-principal model is abandoned, there is less need to have distinct offences applicable to the private and public sector.

F.107 The distinction between public and private sector entities is increasingly difficult to make. This is one of the main problematic areas of the current law of bribery.[105] It is also a problem in the wider law (for example, interpretation of the term "public authority" in section 6 of the Human Rights Act 1998, which has necessitated a report[106] on the issue and a Bill[107] being put before Parliament for clarification). This difficulty then risks injustice in borderline cases.[108]

---

[99] Supported by: Council of HM Circuit Judges; Investment Management Association and OLAF. The Government in its response to the consultees' comments voiced support for a distinct test for the public sector and for the test to be remodelled for the private sector based on what was reasonable by the standards of ordinary people and by prevailing practices in the sector concerned (paras 45 and 57).

[100] Commentary to *Natji* [2002] EWCA Crim 271, (2002) 1 WLR 2337, noted that "the private sector does not always appreciate that local government operates on totally different rules, which can rebound on the private sector donor … . Hospitality between private sector firms and professionals may be blithely dismissed as 'networking'. But offers of gifts or hospitality to a councillor or officer by a person who has, or is seeking a local authority contract, are presumed in law to be corruptly intended unless the donor can prove otherwise".

[101] The example given in the Home Office Consultation Paper is that of permitted advantages under the Civil Service Management Code (para 41).

[102] Chapter III.

[103] The SFO, Ministry of Defence Police, Law Society, LCCSA and ICC-UK all expressed reservations, most notably about the difficulties of distinguishing between public and private sector entities. CBI suggested that the same law should apply but with extra exemptions applicable only in the private sector.

[104] Paragraphs 39 and 46.

[105] The recent case of *Natji* [2002] EWCA Crim 271, (2002) 1 WLR 2337, in which the Court of Appeal had to deal with the interpretation of "public body" in section 7 of the Public Bodies Corrupt Practices Act 1889, shows that the courts are still struggling with this distinction.

[106] www.publications.parliament.uk/pa/jt200304/jtselect/jtrights/39/39.pdf.

[107] www.publications.parliament.uk/pa/cm200607/cmbills/043/07043.i-i.html.

[108] The Government response to consultees' comments (2007) questions whether the distinction is "actually achievable in practice".

F.108   Additionally, it is possible for the Government to provide strong disincentives against unacceptable behaviour through terms of employment in the public sphere. This is something that cannot be provided in a consistent way for the private sector, even though there may be codes of conduct. Therefore the public sector can arguably regulate itself to a stricter standard and so avoid the need for a broader or distinct offence of bribery.

Our provisional proposal

F.109   As noted above, it appears generally accepted that only corporate hospitality which crosses the threshold of "unacceptable" conduct should be unlawful. A proposed bribery offence must therefore seek to draw the line between acceptable and unacceptable conduct. Our previous report[109] concluded that corporate hospitality for purposes such as information sharing, the cementing of old relationships and the forming of new ones was acceptable. By contrast, conduct will be unacceptable in situations "where you could be expected to behave in a particular way as a result".[110] This highlights the crux of unacceptable corporate hospitality as that which aims to influence the decision-making of the recipient.[111]

F.110   This focus on influencing decision-making led to our previous report adopting the "primary motivator" test.[112] We remain of the view that this test identifies the correct threshold for acceptable corporate hospitality.

Provisional proposal

F.111   We provisionally propose that P commits an offence if he or she gives an advantage, or represents that he or she will give an advantage, in exchange for, in expectation of or as a reward for R doing an improper act:

(1)   for the primary reason that it will encourage R to act improperly, whether or not the advantage turns out to be R's primary reason for acting; or

(2)   foreseeing a serious risk that the advantage will create the primary reason for R doing an improper act, or realising that the advantage was the primary reason for R doing an improper act.[113]

---

[109] Legislating the Criminal Code: Corruption (1998) Law Com No 248.

[110] Charles Proctor, finance law partner with Tite and Lewis, UK Legal News Analysis, 2 April 2003.

[111] This analysis is supported by Professor Green in *Lying, cheating and stealing – a moral theory of white collar crime* (2006) ch 16. He considers the difference between a bribe and an acceptable gift as being the bilateral nature of a bribe: "[bribery] involves an agreement to exchange something of value in return for influence, whereas gifts, tips and campaign contributions involve no such agreement." Thus, impropriety in corporate hospitality stems from the influence exerted on the recipient by the bilateral nature of the advantage. The recipient will then act or make a decision for the wrong reasons because the decision-making process has been corrupted.

[112] It must be noted, however, that the primary motivator test recommended in our previous report focused solely on foresight. In this consultation paper, we believe that P should also be liable if he or she, whilst not foreseeing that the advantage would cause R to act improperly, nevertheless intended that it should do.

[113] "Improper act" means an act which constitutes a breach of a legal or equitable duty and which involves betrayal of a relation of trust, or breach of a duty to act impartially or in the best interests of another – see Part 5, para 5.50 above.

APPENDIX G
THE PROPOSED OFFENCES' FOUNDATIONS AND THE UNITED KINGDOM'S INTERNATIONAL OBLIGATIONS

INTRODUCTION

G.1   In this Appendix, we consider whether the offence of bribing a foreign public official (the discrete offence, set out in Part 7), as well as the more general bribery offence that we are proposing, meet our international obligations.

G.2   The two bribery offences that we are proposing have different targets, and have differences in terms of their construction. As we have explained, the general offence we propose is based on the improper conduct model. It does not require the advantage conferred itself to be undue. The discrete offence is a hybrid, drawing on different models, but maintaining a focus on the undue character of the advantage conferred.[1]

G.3   Although the two offences differ in these ways, they are both attempting to target broadly the same kind of culpable behaviour. More importantly, in spite of the slight differences between the theoretical foundations of each offence, we believe our scheme as a whole will satisfy the UK's international obligations in relation to criminalising bribery.[2]

THE GENERAL OFFENCE OF BRIBERY

G.4   It would be convenient to divide the analysis into a discussion of private sector and of public sector bribery, even though that distinction is not integral to our scheme as a whole.

---

[1]   It is a hybrid because the offence is not satisfied simply by R being induced to do *any* act or omission. Rather, R must be induced by P's conferral of an advantage to do some act or omission that either creates new business for P or aids P in retaining a business interest already secured.

[2]   For further details on the UK's international obligations, see Appendix A above.

Private sector bribery

G.5　In common with all International Conventions to which the UK is a signatory, our proposals define 'improperly' as a breach of duty.[3] Therefore, P will only commit bribery in a private sector context if he or she intends or foresees that the conferral of the advantage will induce R to breach a duty owed to a third party.[4] However, unlike our provisional proposals, many of these Conventions also make reference to P's advantage being 'undue'.[5]

G.6　Whilst satisfying the conventions, we have chosen not to include the qualifier that the advantage must be undue. We believe that all advantages conferred with the intention or foresight of inducing improper conduct (defined as the breach of a legal or equitable duty) should come within the offence. Therefore, we believe that a further qualification that the advantage should be undue is both unnecessary and undesirable.

G.7　Consider the following example:

Example G1

R is an insurance broker. R sells P's products and receives a commission payment whenever a policy is sold. However, R is also under a duty to act in the best interests of the customer (V). R sells a product to V knowing that is not in V's best interests because he (R) wants the commission.

In this example, it may be difficult to demonstrate that the advantage (commission) received by R was undue, but its conferral has clearly induced R to act improperly. Therefore, under our policy, R has committed bribery without the necessity of having to demonstrate that the payment was also undue.[6]

Public sector bribery

G.8　Under our provisional proposals, the same general bribery offence that applies to the private sector will also apply to the public sector. Therefore, as long as the advantage induces an improper act (defined as the breach of a legal or equitable duty), there is no need to demonstrate that the advantage was undue. However, unlike private sector bribery, this approach mirrors very few of the International Conventions.

---

[3]　The relevant texts are the Council of Europe Criminal Law Convention on Corruption, arts 7 and 8; the Council of the EU Framework Decision on combating corruption in the private sector, art 2; and the UN Convention against Corruption, art 21 (optional). Note that the UN Convention provision is optional and that reservations may be made to the Council of Europe Criminal Law Convention (see art 37(1)).

[4]　It is important to remember that this breach must constitute conduct other than the mere acceptance of the advantage itself.

[5]　For example, the United Nations Convention against Corruption (art 21), the Council of Europe's Criminal Law Convention against Corruption (arts 7 and 8) and the European Council's Framework decision2003/568/JHA (art 2).

[6]　Whether P has also committed bribery will depend on whether he intended or foresaw that the advantage would induce R to act and whether he reasonably believed that the payment was legally permissible (would not influence R to act improperly).

G.9   The general approach adopted by the Conventions is to define R's conduct element very widely (along the lines of the influence model) and then to qualify this with a requirement that the advantage be undue.[7] For example, Article 15 of the United Nations Convention on Corruption states:

> Each State Party shall adopt such legislative and other measures as may be necessary to establish as criminal offences, when committed intentionally:
>
> (a)   the promise, offering or giving, to a public official, directly or indirectly, of a undue advantage, for the official himself or herself or another person or entity, in order that the official act or refrain from acting in the exercise of his or her official duties;
>
> (b)   the solicitation or acceptance by a public official, directly or indirectly, of a undue advantage, for the official himself or herself or another person or entity, in order that the official act or refrain from acting in the exercise of his or her official duties.

G.10   Despite the difference in construction, we believe that our general offence will still satisfy the UN Convention. If an advantage is being unduly conferred on a public official in order to induce that official to act or refrain from acting in the exercise of his or her official duties, it is very likely that it will involve that public official breaching a duty. This is especially true if one includes, as our policy does, the duty to act impartially or in someone's best interests. Therefore, it is our belief that the conduct targeted in provisions like the one above is the same conduct targeted by our policy.

G.11   The same conclusion can be reached with respect to the Council of Europe Criminal Law Convention on Corruption. The Convention does not expressly refer to a breach of duty but criminalises the conferment of an "undue advantage" for the domestic public official "to act or refrain from acting in exercise of his or her functions".[8] However, the explanatory notes make clear that the provision's principal aim is to ensure that the public official fulfils his or her functions "in a transparent, fair and impartial manner".[9] Our notion of improper conduct, which extends to a breach of an equitable duty such as the duty to act impartially, would satisfy this objective.

---

[7]   See, for example, the United Nations Convention against Corruption (art 15) and the Council of Europe's Criminal Law Convention against Corruption (art 2).

[8]   Articles 2 and 3.

[9]   Paragraph 32.

G.12 Further, in explaining why the term 'breach of duty' was not used, the concern expressed by the drafters of the Convention was that the public official should still be liable "even if (he or she) would have acted in the same way without the bribe".[10] Again, our provisional proposals address this concern. Under the offence that we are proposing, as long as the bribe is the primary reason for doing an improper act acting, the individual who acts in breach of his or her duty to act impartially or in someone's best interests will be criminally liable even if he or she would have acted in the same way without the bribe.[11] In the context of its discussion of the term 'breach of duty', the drafters of the Convention place great emphasis on the fulfilment of the "objective"[12] of the relevant provisions and it is our view that our provisional proposals satisfy this requirement.

G.13 Having identified several problems with an approach based on 'undue' payments, we have provisionally decided to adopt the improper conduct model (defined in relation to the breach of a legal or equitable duty) to cover public sector bribery as well private sector bribery. We believe that we are still able to satisfy the relevant conventions because each approach simply represents a different way of targeting the same culpable behaviour.[13] Beyond this, we are also able to remove from this area of the law the increasingly problematic requirement of distinguishing between a private and a public entity.

Our preferred approach: any advantage (not necessarily undue) and an improper act

G.14 As we have explained, under this approach, the nexus between the conferral of an advantage and an improper act becomes essential. However, beyond this it is immaterial whether the advantage is undue.

G.15 This approach that is mirrored to a large extent by EU documents and Conventions relating to bribery. For example, Article 2 of the 1997 EU Convention[14] states:

> For the purposes of the Convention, the deliberate action of an official, who, directly or through an intermediary, requests or receives advantages of any kind whatsoever, for himself or for a third party, or accepts a promise of such an advantage to act or refrain from acting in accordance with his duty or in the exercise of his functions in breach of his official duties shall constitute passive corruption.

---

[10] Paragraph 39.

[11] The fact that R would have done the improper act in any event does not preclude the advantage being the primary reason for R doing the act.

[12] Paragraph 39.

[13] In this regard, it is interesting to note that in drafting a Corruption Bill in May 2006, Transparency International (UK) "primary concern" was compliance with the relevant international conventions and it also chose to define the term improper conduct in terms of a breach of a duty (including the duty to act impartially). See, Corruption Bill – Background Note (March 2007), p 3.

[14] The 1997 Convention on the Fight against Corruption involving Officials of the European Communities or Officials of Member States of the European Union.

G.16　It should be noted that, in common with our policy, Article 2 makes it clear that the advantage does not have to be undue. Further, explicit reference is made to breach of duty as an essential element.

G.17　The slight concern, from the point of view of consistency with our policy, is that the Article refers both to breach of duty and "acting in accordance with his duty". This appears to open up the possibility that bribery can be committed even if the improper act is not one that constitutes a breach of duty. Indeed, without the qualifier that the advantage must be undue, the Article has the potential to extend to any payment to an official to influence him or her in any way. However, it is clearly not the intention of the drafters to extend the scope the offence in this manner. For example, one would not wish the state to be held liable for bribery simply for paying the wages (conferring an advantage) of its officials (for them to act in accordance with their duty).

G.18　Despite the apparent breadth of the Article, the explanatory report makes it clear that the reference to acting in accordance with a duty is only intended to cover those bribed to 'do the right thing'.[15] In order to avoid confusion (and the type of defences employed in our previous report), we prefer to cover this category of defendant by including within the definition of 'improper' the breach of a duty to act impartially or in someone's best interests. We believe that this part of our policy ensures compliance with the Conventions. Indeed, in the explanatory report of the 1997 EU Convention, the wording of the Article is justified in reference to certain States that have chosen to apply the law of bribery where an official has breached a duty of impartiality.[16]

THE DISCRETE BRIBERY OFFENCE OF BRIBING A FOREIGN PUBLIC OFFICIAL

G.19　We have provisionally proposed that a separate offence should be created that will apply to the bribery of a foreign public official. However, the offence will still be called bribery and we are still targeting the same conduct as that which comes within the general offence. As such, the focus of the separate offence (in common with the general offence) is still centred on the nexus between the conferral of an advantage and an improper act. As we will explain below, the separate offence is simply an alternative means of achieving the same result.

G.20　As we are attempting to target the same conduct as the general offence, the obvious question is to ask why a separate offence is required at all. Indeed, the general offence that we are provisionally proposing will already apply to the bribery of foreign public officials.

---

[15]　OJC 391, 15/12/1998 P. 0001 – 0012, para 2.6.

[16]　Above.

G.21 The proposal for a separate offence is based on practical utility. As we have explained,[17] we believe that in many cases the requirement within the general bribery offence that the prosecution must demonstrate a breach of a legal or equitable duty will be far too onerous in relation to the conduct of foreign public official. As a result, we do not believe that the general offence would be sufficient to satisfy the UK's international obligations in this area.[18]

A requirement of undue payment but no requirement of improper act?

G.22 In that regard, we could have made the creation of a separate offence a basis for a very different theoretical approach, under which an undue payment is required but no improper act. By avoiding the requirement of improper conduct (in the sense of a breach of a legal or equitable duty) this approach may appear ideal in this context.

G.23 However, it is not only our intention to create a discrete offence that will avoid the problems of the general offence. We also wish the discrete offence to mirror (as far as possible) the scope of the general offence, in the interests of generating simplicity and accessibility in this area of the law.

G.24 In order justifiably to categorise conduct as bribery, we believe that a nexus must be established between the conferral of an advantage and an improper act. We recognise that in many cases where P does no more than confer an undue advantage on a public official, it is likely that he or she is also intending or foreseeing that the public official will act improperly (in breach of a legal or equitable duty) in return. However, without further qualification, we believe that a significant minority of cases will come within an 'undue payment' based offence even where this further consequence is not P's intention or foresight. This would leave the discrete offence over-inclusive.

G.25 Consider the following example:

Example G2

P Ltd is a small company attempting to set up business in a foreign jurisdiction. During the extremely long process they have been aided by a particularly helpful official (R) who has explained the various application procedures to the company directors and gone beyond the call of duty to aid them. At the end of the process, although the company knows that R is not entitled to receive advantages, P Ltd confers a small sum of money to express their gratitude.

In this example, P Ltd has conferred an undue advantage and so would commit bribery on a pure 'undue payment' model. However, given that P does not expect R to do any act in return for the payment, we do not believe P should be labelled and punished for bribery.

---

[17] See Part 7, paras 7.2 to 7.14 above.

[18] Most notably, the obligations imposed by the OECD Convention.

An undue payment as well as an improper act?

G.26   This approach would require both an improper act and an undue payment. We must consider whether the requirement that the advantage be 'undue' can be further qualified to restrict its scope to the conduct targeted in the general offence.

G.27   In order to narrow the scope of the discrete offence, the requirement that the advantage conferred by P must be undue could be qualified with the requirement that R's conduct must be improper. However, we have justified the creation of the discrete offence on the basis that the improper conduct model (defined in relation to the breach of a legal or equitable duty) will often cause practical difficulties when prosecuting the bribery of foreign public officials.

G.28   Following the terms of the OECD convention we are therefore led to an alternative approach. This is to define 'improper conduct' in the discrete offence, not as the breach of a legal or equitable duty, but as a *decision relating to the obtaining or retaining of business.*[19]

G.29   The discrete offence is therefore intended to mirror the general offence in its underlying rational and will not extend its scope. If P confers an undue advantage on a foreign public official in order to induce that official to provide or retain a business interest, we believe that it is perfectly reasonable to infer that the official will be expected to breach a legal or equitable duty. The difference will be that under the discrete offence the prosecution can proceed on the basis of this inference and proof of such a breach will not need to be demonstrated.

---

[19]   OECD Article 1, which states that:

> Each party shall take such measures as may be necessary to establish that it is a criminal offence under its law for any person intentionally to offer, promise or give any undue pecuniary or other advantage, whether directly or through intermediaries, to a foreign public official, for that official or for a third party, in order that the official act or refrain from acting in relation to the performance of official duties, in order to obtain or retain business or other improper advantage in the conduct of international business.